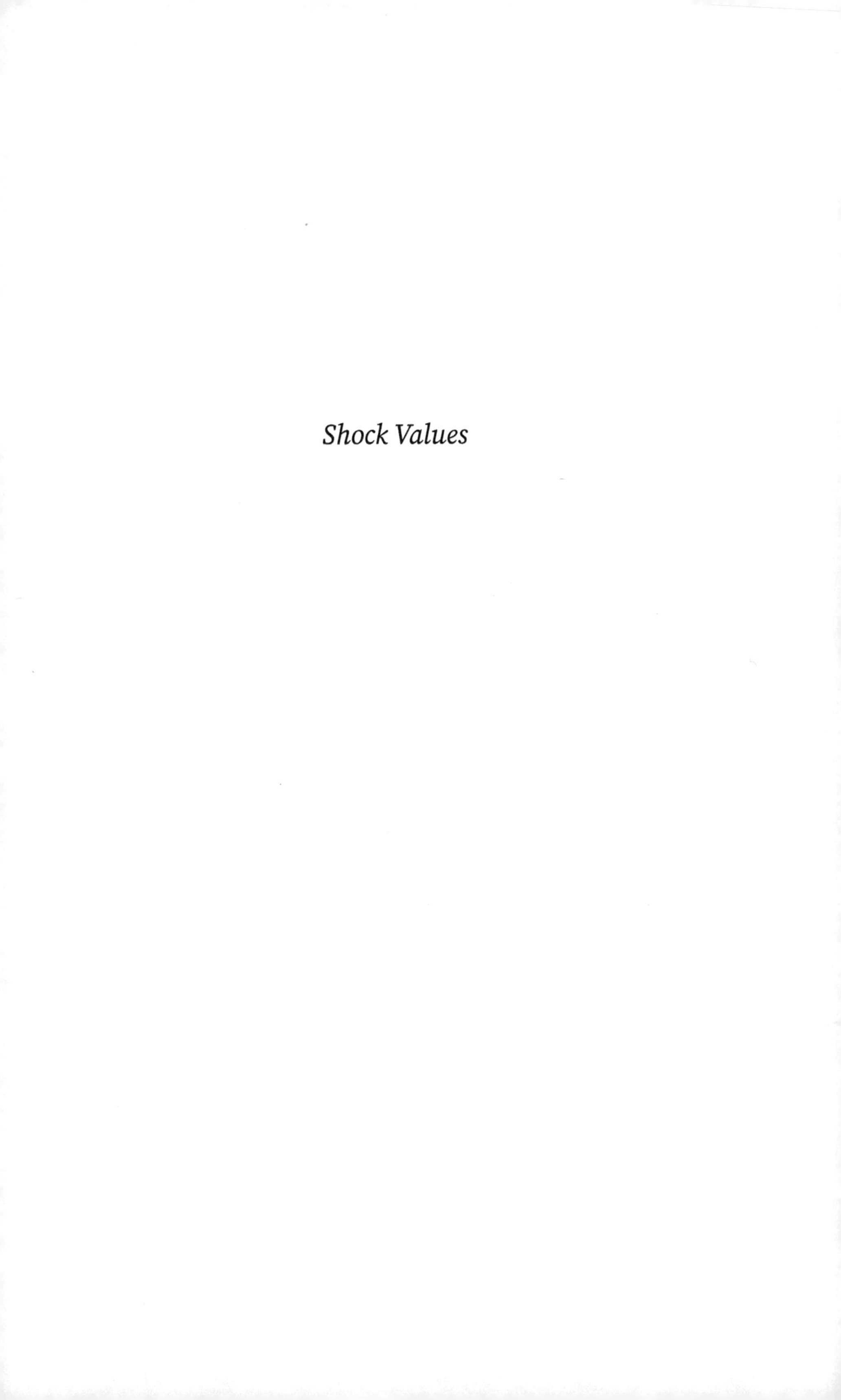

Shock Values

SHOCK VALUES

Prices and Inflation in American Democracy

CAROLA BINDER

The University of Chicago Press
CHICAGO AND LONDON

The University of Chicago Press, Chicago 60637
The University of Chicago Press, Ltd., London

Published 2024
Printed in the United States of America

33 32 31 30 29 28 27 26 25 24   1 2 3 4 5

ISBN-13: 978-0-226-83309-5 (cloth)
ISBN-13: 978-0-226-83310-1 (e-book)
DOI: https://doi.org/10.7208/chicago/9780226833101.001.0001

Library of Congress Cataloging-in-Publication Data

Names: Binder, Carola Conces, author.
Title: Shock values : prices and inflation in American democracy / Carola Binder.
Other titles: Prices and inflation in American democracy
Description: Chicago ; London : The University of Chicago Press, 2024. | Includes bibliographical references and index.
Identifiers: LCCN 2023045913 | ISBN 9780226833095 (cloth) | ISBN 9780226833101 (e-book)
Subjects: LCSH: Prices—Government policy—United States. | Price regulation—United States—History. | Monetary policy—United States—History. | Inflation (Finance)—United States—History. | Anti-inflationary policies—United States—History. | Democracy—United States. | United States—Economic conditions.
Classification: LCC HB236.U5 B54 2024 | DDC 338.5/260973—dc23/eng/20231106
LC record available at https://lccn.loc.gov/2023045913

♾ This paper meets the requirements of ANSI/NISO Z39.48-1992 (Permanence of Paper).

To Joe, Ruby, Maria, Paul, Felicity, and Louisa

CONTENTS

INTRODUCTION

Of the People, by the People, for the People, Price Control.

OFFICE OF PRICE ADMINISTRATION,
"Historical Reports on War Administration"[1]

Price Stabilization in American Democracy

In 2021, inflation in the United States exceeded 5 percent for the first time in decades. From there, it continued to climb. Like most economists, I carefully tracked this ascent, eagerly poring through the inflation reports that came out each month. I earned a PhD in economics in 2015; for my entire career, policy makers and scholars had been concerned about inflation that was too low rather than too high; almost overnight, the situation had dramatically reversed.

The United States had not experienced such high inflation since the Great Inflation of the 1970s and early 1980s. Back then, neither President Richard Nixon's price and wage controls nor President Gerald Ford's notorious red "Whip Inflation Now" buttons stopped wages and prices from spiraling upward. The Great Inflation ended only when Federal Reserve chairman Paul Volcker finally committed to, and followed through with, a program of severe monetary tightening. This so-called Volcker disinflation was a painful process involving a long recession, high interest rates, and high unemployment. But it demonstrated the power of monetary policy for stabilizing prices and pointed to a solution to the problem of recurrent inflation: delegate price stability to the central bank, and give the central bank independence in the pursuit of this goal.

Following the Volcker disinflation, the practice of raising interest rates in the face of inflation became consensus among academic economists around the world. And the academic consensus became the political reality. Central banks were granted substantial political independence to facilitate their pursuit of price stability. Many central banks announced explicit numerical targets for inflation in the 1990s and 2000s. In the United States, the Federal Reserve kept inflation low and relatively stable for years, but it waited until 2012 to explicitly announce its own 2 percent inflation target. Its preferred measure of inflation, the annual change in the Personal Consumption Expenditures (PCE) price index, averaged 2.1 percent from 1985 to 2020.

The return of inflation in 2021, in a time after central bank economists had seemingly solved the riddle of price control and produced decades of price stability, shook the economics profession hard. But the return of inflation was not only, or even primarily, an academic concern. It was, even more, a social and a political one. The impacts of inflation are widespread, and its causes are difficult to understand. Rising prices affect every member of society and can be especially devastating to families struggling to afford groceries, gas, and other necessities. Unsurprisingly, people suffering the ill effects of inflation are loath to leave it in the hands of central bankers—they want their elected officials to do *something* to slow the pace of price increases, preferably without Volcker-style rate hikes and rising unemployment.

But what can be done? In January 2022, the *Washington Post* asked a dozen economists for ideas to combat inflation.[2] One of them, Todd Tucker of the Roosevelt Institute, proposed using price controls. "The time is now," he wrote, "to begin destigmatizing greater democratic control over price levels." Tucker's characterization of price controls as "democratic" echoed the logic of his think tank's namesake, President Franklin Delano Roosevelt, whose administration implemented an extensive system of price controls and rationing during World War II. This system, Roosevelt argued, was "the only Democratic, equitable solution" for the wartime economy, as "those who can afford to pay more for a commodity should not be privileged over those who cannot."[3] Pamphlets of Roosevelt's Office of Price Administration proclaimed, "Of the People, by the People, for the People, Price Control."[4]

Tucker was not alone in calling for price controls. For example, in the *Guardian*, the economist Isabella Weber compared the inflation situation of 2021 to World War II, suggesting that "the government could target the specific prices that drive inflation instead of moving to austerity which risks a recession."[5] Price controls, which had seemed relegated to history after the Volcker disinflation, were back on the table.

It is worth emphasizing the difference between price controls and the current approach of allowing the Federal Reserve to "control" prices. The Fed's 2 percent inflation target is a target for aggregate inflation—the rate of change of an official measure of the overall price level. The Fed does not target the prices of specific goods or services. Thus, the *relative* prices of different products can vary freely depending on supply and demand conditions. Price controls, in contrast, impose restrictions on particular prices and prevent relative prices from fluctuating freely. They thus disrupt the powerful informational and coordinating role of prices in a market economy.[6] The effects of such disruption, or course, depend heavily on circumstances.

As I am writing this book, it seems unlikely that anything resembling the World War II price controls will become a serious policy contender in the United States. But that doesn't mean that the calls for price controls can be ignored. They are a symptom of deep discontent with our economic and political system and its approach to price stabilization. High inflation in 2021 and 2022 did not, by itself, cause this discontent, but it did make it more apparent. Public trust in the Federal Reserve began to decline, and calls for other forms of state intervention in prices abounded.[7] Because I am an economist who studies inflation, central banking, and economic history, I have followed these developments closely as they unfolded. And I have become convinced that understanding our current inflation environment requires much more than just economic analysis. As a society, our approach to inflation and price stabilization is closely tied to our approach to democracy. And both of these approaches have changed over time.

I wrote this book to provide an account of how price fluctuations and attempts to manage them—through price controls, monetary policy, tariff policy, and other means—have shaped American democracy since its very beginning. By *price fluctuations*, I mean movements in both aggregate and particular prices. For much of US history, especially before aggregate inflation statistics were readily available, certain prices, like land prices, crop prices, and energy prices, have been especially consequential. The book proceeds chronologically from the colonial era to the present, tracing the evolution of beliefs about price fluctuations and the role of the state in American democracy. It is not just an economic or monetary history but also a history of thought, synthesizing views from legal scholars and the courts, economists, political scientists, politicians, and the popular press. I do provide policy recommendations in the last chapter, but more than I hope to convince anyone of my recommendations, I hope to equip readers with and without formal economics training to think more deeply about what alternative approaches to price stabilization might mean, not just for the economy but for the social and political system.

The history of American democracy can be viewed through the lens of many different tensions: between liberty and security, between agriculture and industry, between Wall Street and Main Street, and between populism and liberalism, among others. As this book shows, these tensions have shaped the struggle to find a legitimate role for the state in managing and stabilizing prices. This is one of the defining struggles of American democracy, and it is a continuing struggle.

The former central banker Paul Tucker (no known relation to Todd), uses the term *legitimacy* to mean "that the public—society as a whole—accepts the authority of institutions of the state, including [independent agencies], and their right to deploy the state's powers. . . . Legitimacy grounds and comprises the capacity of an agency to pursue its mandate as part of the broader state apparatus, without relying wholly on coercive power."[8]

Tucker's reference to coercive power is crucial for understanding the debates about legitimacy as it relates to prices. In a free market, the price mechanism coordinates economic exchange without the need for coercion.[9] Interference in free markets at least implicitly relies on the coercive power of the state. The Founders were aware of this and highly skeptical of allowing coercive power to lead to tyranny. For example, the Reverend John Witherspoon, a member of the Continental Congress, argued that the price controls that state and local governments imposed during the Revolutionary War were illegitimate because they forced, or coerced, a seller to sell his wares at a price to which he did not consent.

Tucker's definition of legitimacy also makes it clear that legitimacy, insofar as it depends on public acceptance, is a dynamic and contestable concept, because public values and beliefs vary over time and across people. We can see this in the evolution of beliefs about not only price controls but also monetary policy. Changing public priorities, jurisprudence, power structures, and economic theories have shifted the feasible set of approaches to price stabilization over the decades.

Recurrent Themes in American Democracy and Price Stability

Several key themes emerge in this exploration of price stabilization in American democracy.

THE DISPARATE IMPACTS OF PRICE FLUCTUATIONS

An important theme of this book is that price fluctuations affect different interest groups in different ways. The early United States was largely a nation of farmers. For some of the Founders, like Thomas Jefferson and James Madison, the self-sufficient small farmer was the economic and social foundation of democracy. By the time of the Constitutional Convention, the Founders had already seen how fluctuations in land prices and crop prices could increase and then wipe out the prosperity of a large segment of the population. Debates about the new nation's monetary and banking institutions reflected the concern that price fluctuations could exacerbate tensions between agrarian and industrial interests.

Deflation is especially hard on farmers because they tend to be debtors. Inflation erodes the *real* (inflation-adjusted) value of debt, benefiting creditors at the expense of debtors. Deflation does just the opposite. If farmers have taken on debt to purchase land or seeds and prices subsequently fall, it will be more costly than they anticipated to pay back the debt. If the price of the particular crop that they sell falls, perhaps due to declining global demand or a bumper crop abroad, their plight will be even worse.

Throughout American history, farmers and their advocates have pushed for a variety of different policies to address the ill effects of price fluctuations. One such policy is a tariff, intended to protect farmers from low prices of foreign competitors. It is important to recognize, however, that farmers have not universally embraced tariffs. Farmers in different regions of the country grow different types of crops and have different exposure to foreign markets. Some have opposed tariffs for fear of retaliatory tariffs that would hurt their export revenue. Thus, tariff debates have had a tendency to exacerbate not only tensions between agriculture and industry but also regional tensions. They have also prompted disputes between producers and labor interests over whether wages have kept pace with tariff-induced price increases.

Farm interests have also played a large role in the development of monetary policy. Jeffersonian and Jacksonian Democrats' skepticism of paper money came partly from a fear that paper money would contribute to price fluctuations that were so harmful to farmers. For Andrew Jackson, hard money was a way to protect the common man from the dangers of price fluctuations. But years of deflation in the late nineteenth century led to a shift in this view. The

Democrats came to view gold not as the solution but as the problem. Removing the shackles of gold, some thought, would allow the government to more actively promote farm interests through monetary expansion. Farm representatives spent decades advocating for an end to the gold standard and a more activist central bank before this finally came to pass.

Even as the farming share of the population declined, a major challenge for politicians has been to reconcile farmers' demands for higher crop prices with consumers' demands for lower food prices. This has led to a recurrent tendency to blame food price inflation on (and to legitimize regulation of) profiteers, price gougers, and monopolists. Other examples of the disparate impacts of price fluctuations and their political consequences appear throughout the book.

CONTRACTING AND DUE PROCESS

The first theme is closely related to the second: contracting and due process. Because inflation has different effects on debtors and creditors, and contracts are typically written in nominal terms—that is, not inflation-adjusted terms—the evolution of contract jurisprudence has played an important role in shaping the government's response to price fluctuations. The Founders' discomfort with paper money came largely from the recognition that monetary depreciation and price inflation alter the value of debts that have been contracted and from concern that government interference with contracts was unjust.

The Founders' regard for contracts is apparent in the Constitution. The contract clause, in Article I, Section 10, prohibits the states from passing any "law impairing the obligation of contracts." This clause, and the related due process clauses of the Fifth and Fourteenth Amendment, have been central to the courts' interpretations about when, whether, and how the government can conduct monetary policy and regulate prices. The Fifth Amendment, which applies to the federal government, states that no person shall "be deprived of life, liberty, or property, without due process of law," and the Fourteenth Amendment adds, "Nor shall any State deprive any person of life, liberty, or property, without due process of law." The interpretation of these clauses has been contentious. Does a legal-tender law impair contract obligations? Does a price ceiling deprive a producer of his or her property?

In the Civil War, when government-issued legal-tender paper money called greenbacks contributed to wartime inflation, major legal cases concerning greenbacks centered on contract obligations and due process. Later, in the New Deal era and World War II, contracts and due process were again in the spotlight when President Roosevelt attempted first to reverse the deflation of the Great Depression and then to control prices during the war. These are just the most salient of many examples throughout the chapters of this book.

The concern that price fluctuations interfere with contracting has also been used as motivation for a more active state role in price stabilization. The economist Irving Fisher, one of the central characters of this book, argued that with either inflation and deflation, "incalculable injustice would be wrought. One of the parties to every contract would be swindled for the benefit of the other; and the swindle would affect the fortunes for good or ill of almost every family in the land."[10] This motivated his decades-long campaign for the central bank to adopt a price stabilization mandate, which he framed as a social justice issue.

CRISIS AND LEVIATHAN

A third theme of this book is that wars—or emergencies more broadly defined—have a tendency to legitimize a more activist role of the state in the economic system. Of course, I am not the first to point this out—notably, *Crisis and Leviathan* is the title of Robert Higgs's 1987 history of the federal government's widening authority of over economic decision-making in response to national emergencies.[11] Higgs describes a ratchet effect of government growth, in which the expanded scale and scope of government activities in a crisis fails to fully recede after the crisis.

The history of price stabilization in America provides many examples that support Higgs's thesis. Most of the major inflationary episodes in US history have been associated with wars, which require large increases in military spending.[12] To finance these expenditures, the government has often resorted to monetary policies that would not have been considered acceptable outside of wartime. For example, I have referred already to the greenbacks in the Civil War. Political and legal debates about the greenbacks, as I noted, focused on contract impairment and due process. But they also focused on the necessary and proper clause, of Article 1, Section 8, which gives Congress the power "to make all Laws which shall be necessary and proper for carrying into Execution" the enumerated powers, including the power to "declare war; and raise and support an Army and Navy."

During the Civil War, there was intense disagreement about whether the Legal Tender Acts that authorized the greenbacks were necessary or proper. After the war, the Supreme Court first ruled the acts unconstitutional, then subsequently reversed its opinion. Eventually, the 1884 case *Juilliard v. Greenman* upheld the constitutionality of the Legal Tender Acts even outside of wartime, authorizing Congress to issue greenbacks in times of peace—the ratchet effect in action.[13]

In both world wars, efforts to address wartime inflation included price controls, especially on strategically important products like coal, steel, and wheat. These wartime experiences with controls had lasting impacts on public and political beliefs about the economic role of the state, even as the controls themselves were rolled back. The imposition of price controls required major expansions of administrative agencies, also with lasting effects.

Numerous court challenges to emergency price controls have played an important role in shaping jurisprudence on economic rights and due process. Price controls, as I mentioned in the discussion of the previous theme, have prompted much debate about the interpretation of the Constitution's due process clauses. Constitutional scholars disagree about the extent to which the due process clauses limit the government's actions in time of war, and the Court's approach to this question has been inconsistent.[14] Some aspects of wartime price control legislation have been ruled unconstitutional on due process grounds, but the Court has also acknowledged that "a public exigency will justify the legislature in restricting property rights . . . to a certain extent without compensation."[15]

Price fluctuations and the governments' responses to them have also had a tendency to shift the balance of power between the branches of government and between the federal government and the states, and this is especially true during times of emergency. In particular, the president's role as commander in chief of the army and navy carries with it very broad war powers, which have at times legitimized a larger role of the executive in economic affairs and restrictions on the jurisdiction of the federal courts. During World War II and the Korean War, the War Powers Acts of 1941 and 1942 and the Defense Production Act of 1950 gave the executive branch substantial authority over domestic industry, including powers to set prices and wages.[16] Even nonwar emergencies, like the Great Depression, have expanded the role of the executive. For example, the Thomas Amendment of the Agricultural Adjustment Act of 1933 granted President Roosevelt unprecedented monetary powers to support his goal of reflating prices.

More recently, the COVID-19 pandemic has been described as a "global war," and both President Donald Trump and President Joe Biden invoked the Defense Production Act to respond to the emergency, for example to prevent price gouging on designated items.[17] The pandemic, like other wars, prompted major fiscal and monetary stimulus that contributed to rising inflation. Pandemic-related supply-chain disruptions and the Russian war against Ukraine have also contributed. Together, these global emergencies have brought inflation and the government's role in price stabilization into the spotlight.

THE POWER OF IDEAS AND THE LONG ROAD TO INFLATION TARGETING

A fourth thread of this book is the long road to inflation targeting in the United States. Typical accounts of inflation targeting begin in the late twentieth century, when central banks around the world began formally adopting inflation-targeting frameworks for monetary policy.[18] The untold history of inflation targeting is much longer, and highlights both the power of ideas and the complex interactions of economic theories, politics, and policy reform.

Because today's inflation hawks tend to be conservative, it may also surprise readers to learn that the earliest advocates of a price stabilization mandate for the Federal Reserve were progressive reformers and the farm lobby. Irving Fisher, as I mentioned, is a central character in this book. An academic, a public intellectual, and a progressive activist, Fisher spent decades pushing for the Federal Reserve to have a price stabilization mandate. (He also spent decades promoting the eugenics movement; luckily, that campaign bore less fruit.)[19] Fisher's work on price stabilization began even before the Fed existed, and he nearly convinced Congress to give the Fed a price stabilization mandate at its inception. Instead, the Federal Reserve Act of 1913 kept the United States on the gold standard. But throughout the 1920s and 1930s, he gained the ear of several congressmen who introduced bills that would have amended the Federal Reserve Act to make price stability the Fed's primary goal.

These bills were considered quite radical, because they implied a departure from the gold-standard orthodoxy, in which the dollar was to be kept convertible to a fixed weight of gold. Instead, Fisher thought that the dollar's value in terms of gold should be allowed to fluctuate in order to stabilize the dollar's purchasing power. His own work on the development of price indexes would facilitate such a task. The price stabilization bills that Fisher championed tended to gain the support of farm interests, who wanted to avoid the bouts of deflation that the gold standard sometimes produced.

Although these price stabilization bills were not enacted, Fisher's ideas and lobbying had lasting influence. During the Great Depression, Fisher collaborated with the Committee for the Nation to Rebuild Prices and Purchasing Power, a pressure group that mobilized public opinion in support of dollar depreciation. When President Roosevelt did devalue the dollar and take the United States off the gold standard, Fisher declared his ideas vindicated.[20]

From there, the road to modern inflation target was a winding one and makes an excellent case study of how economic ideas make their way into policy—and on the flip side, how other ideas do not. For example, nominal income targeting, which I discuss in the later chapters of this book, is another possible approach that central banks could have taken to stabilize prices and macroeconomic conditions.

The inflation-targeting thread of this book also highlights the difficulties in balancing technocratic discretion with democratic accountability. Under the gold standard, at least in theory, monetary policy followed a rule-based framework. Policy makers were constrained by the requirement that the dollar be convertible to a fixed weight of gold. The end of the gold standard lifted this constraint, giving monetary policy makers more discretion to pursue objectives like price stability and full employment, especially after the Treasury-Fed Accord of 1951 gave the Fed more independence from the Treasury in the pursuit of its policy goals.

This independence of unelected technocrats at the Fed sat uneasily with certain elected officials, like congressmen Wright Patman and Henry Gonzalez, who wanted to make the Fed more accountable to the public and pushed for more transparency about how the Fed would balance its price stability and employment goals. Later developments in monetary theory helped policy makers realize that greater transparency might not only make central bank independence more palatable in a democracy; it might also make monetary policy more effective. Thus, transparency is typically described as a hallmark of the inflation-targeting approach and a key legitimizer of central bank independence.[21]

Overview

The remaining chapters of this book are organized as follows: chapter 1, "The Colonies and the Revolution," discusses the colonial and Revolutionary War eras, focusing on monetary arrangements, inflation, and price controls in the colonies and new nation. To finance the war, the Continental Congress issued paper currency that, as the saying goes, became "not worth a Continental." State and local governments attempted to address the resulting inflation with price controls, which Congress debated imposing at larger scale. Postwar deflation and Shays' Rebellion demonstrated the intense political ramifications of price fluctuations, and put questions about the legitimate form, creation, and management of money and prices into the spotlight.

Chapter 2, "Financing the New Nation," covers the years from the Constitutional Convention until the election of President Andrew Jackson. These years include the eras of the First and Second Banks of the United States, which bookended the War of 1812, and the United States was on a bimetallic standard. I discuss the connections between the Founders' choices about money and banking institutions and price fluctuations in the new American democracy.

Chapter 3, "The Jacksonian Era and the Civil War," includes the Jacksonian era and the Civil War. The Jacksonian Democrats' "hard money" policies were premised on the belief that the US government had a duty to protect its people from the practical and moral dangers of price fluctuations, which they blamed on the banking system and paper money. But even after they defeated the Second Bank of the United States, booms and busts in land and crop prices continued to plague the nation and exacerbate regional tensions. During the Civil War, the greenbacks and the inflation they could produce prompted political and legal controversy and had lasting effects on the nation's monetary institutions.

Chapter 4, "The Money Question in the Postbellum Era," explains how price fluctuations and stabilization were central in postbellum politics before the founding of the Fed. The deflation that followed the Civil War, especially after the Coinage Act of 1873 effectively demonetized silver, outraged silver miners and farmers, prompting a variety of proposals for tariff adjustments, regulatory policies, antitrust policies, and monetary expansion. William Jennings Bryan nearly won the presidency on the promise to free the country, and especially its farmers, from the "cross of gold." Although he was unsuccessful and the gold standard endured, new gold discoveries reversed the deflationary trend. But the subsequent inflation led to new forms of political unrest. This is when several different proposals for price stabilization policies were published, most prominently Irving Fisher's *The Purchasing Power of Money*.[22]

Chapter 5, "The Federal Reserve Act and World War I," covers the creation and early years of the Federal Reserve System through the end of World War I. Fisher pushed, unsuccessfully, for the Fed to have a price stabilization mandate. President Woodrow Wilson, a scholar of administrative studies before he became president, relied on a set of new administrative agencies to combat wartime inflation using price controls. I discuss the challenges and successes of these controls and their effects on postwar beliefs about the role of the government in the economy.

Chapter 6, "Deflation and Stabilization," begins with the deflationary recession of 1920 to 1921 and ends with the Roaring Twenties. The deflation at the start of the decade led the farm bloc to advocate, mostly unsuccessfully, for a variety of price support policies in hopes of bringing farm product prices, which had fallen more severely after the war, back to "parity" with other prices. After the recession, as the Fed discovered new tools for influencing credit conditions and prices, Congress and Fed officials continued to debate the formal role that the Fed should play in price stabilization. Later in the decade, the Federal Reserve Banks and the Federal Reserve Board struggled with how to respond to rising stock prices.

Chapter 7, "The Great Depression and the New Deal," covers the critical period from 1929 through 1938. I highlight the parallels between the recession of 1920 to 1921 and the Great Depression, discussing how the especially sharp decline in the prices of exported farm products reopened previous policy debates about farm price supports, protectionist tariffs, and monetary policy reform. I explain how the interwar gold standard and economic thought at the time affected the political and economic response to the Depression and discuss the responses of the Court, business interests, and the public to President Roosevelt's unprecedented efforts to "reflate" the economy. This chapter also introduces the ideas and influence of the "purchasing power" school of New Deal economists.

Chapter 8, "World War II and the Office of Price Administration," discusses inflation, price controls, and monetary policy during and immediately after World War II. Price controls were administered by the Office of Price Administration (OPA), led by Leon Henderson of the purchasing power school. The OPA relied on both an enormous regulatory state and popular mobilization—what the historian Meg Jacobs calls "state building from the bottom up."[23] I describe how price controls came to be accepted, implemented, and eventually dismantled, and the legacy of the wartime experience for popular conceptions about the legitimate economic role of the state.

Chapter 9, "The Korean War and the Treasury-Fed Accord," begins with the start of the Korean War and ends with the late 1960s. Price controls were reimposed during the Korean War, but were weakened by industry lobbying and a lack of public and congressional support. With wartime inflation soaring, a dispute between the Fed and the Treasury over interest rate policy intensified, culminating in the Treasury-Fed Accord of 1951. Under Chairman William McChesney Martin, the Fed "leaned against the wind" of inflationary pressures in the 1950s, stabilizing prices but angering critics like Congressman Patman. The final part of the chapter discusses President John F. Kennedy's handling of rising steel prices and the roles of the Bretton Woods system, the Cold War, and the Great Society programs in sowing the seeds of the Great Inflation.

Chapter 10, "The Great Inflation," discusses the political pressures and policy mistakes that contributed to rising inflation in the 1960s and 1970s. Federal Reserve chairman Arthur Burns thought that relying on monetary policy to reduce inflation would be too costly and would be inconsistent with Congress's commitment to full employment. At Burns's urging, in 1971, President Richard Nixon imposed wage and price controls. Nixon also ended the convertibility of the dollar to gold. The Nixon price controls, though initially very popular, lost public support by the time of Nixon's resignation. Nixon's successors, Gerald Ford and Jimmy Carter, introduced anti-inflation campaigns of their own, both hoping to stabilize prices without resorting to either formal price controls or a monetary-policy-induced recession. But inflation continued to soar.

Chapter 11, "The Volcker Disinflation and the Greenspan Standard," describes how Federal Reserve chairman Paul Volcker's commitment to monetary restraint, at the cost of two recessions, eventually brought the Great Inflation to an end. The Volcker disinflation revealed the power of monetary policy and the importance of a credible commitment to price stability. But it also led many to question why such power should be left in the hands of unelected central bankers. This chapter discusses the debates surrounding central bank independence, accountability, and transparency that followed the Volcker disinflation and continued throughout Alan Greenspan's chairmanship. It also discusses how, even when aggregate inflation was stabilized, certain specific prices, such as for health care, energy, and housing, continued to receive special attention from policy makers and the public.

Chapter 12, "Inflation Targeting and the Great Recession," which spans roughly 2005 through 2019, discusses the debates and hesitations surrounding inflation targeting in the United States, both before and after the Great Recession, and the Fed's efforts to avoid deflation during the recession. The Fed adopted an explicit inflation target in 2012 but struggled with years of below-target inflation in the subsequent years. In the face of low inflation, the Fed faced growing pressures to reduce its focus on price stability and put more emphasis on full employment. This was a common refrain in the Fed Listens events that the Fed conducted in 2019 and 2020 as part of a review of its monetary policy framework.

Chapter 13, "The Pandemic and the Return of Inflation," discusses how the COVID-19 pandemic and responses to the pandemic affected both relative and aggregate prices. All fifty states declared active emergencies during the pandemic, and in most states, these emergency declarations activated anti-price-gouging statutes. I also discuss the fiscal and monetary policy responses to the pandemic, the Fed's adoption of an average inflation-targeting framework, and the politics surrounding the rise of inflation in 2021. The Russian invasion of Ukraine in 2022 exacerbated the inflation problem and prompted policy debates over how to respond to rising oil and gas prices. By mid-2022, the Fed had begun raising interest rates aggressively and emphasizing its commitment to restoring price stability, even if it comes at high cost.

Chapter 14, "Looking Back and Looking Ahead," reviews the earlier chapters and discusses how the recent rise in inflation is related to broader political discontent. I point to several troubling trends in American democracy, including overreliance on emergency declarations, executive actions, and the technocratic bureaucracy. I caution that recent proposals to implement price controls in response to the climate crisis and the pandemic would exacerbate these trends and heighten the sense of disconnect between public opinion and government policy. I suggest that an independent central bank committed to a single, clearly defined mandate, in particular a nominal income target, would have the best shot at promoting economic stability and reducing political unrest.

ONE

THE COLONIES AND THE REVOLUTION

That among these are life, liberty, and the pursuit of happiness. That to secure these rights, Governments are instituted among Men, deriving their just powers from the consent of the governed.

DECLARATION OF INDEPENDENCE

Mercantilism and the Wealth of Nations

In the century after Christopher Columbus's voyage to America, the quantity of metal money in Europe roughly quadrupled as gold, silver, and copper were extracted from the New World.[1] Shipments of precious metal from the Americas were prized in Western Europe, where economic thought from the fifteenth through the eighteenth centuries was dominated by mercantilism. Mercantilists believed that a nation-state could become wealthy and powerful by maintaining favorable trade balances, that is, by exporting more than it imported and accumulating the gold that was used in payment for its exports.

By accumulating gold, mercantilist nations thought that they could maintain a strong military, deter enemy attacks, and expand their territory.[2] To help build their gold hoards, mercantilist governments heavily intervened in the economy, relying on colonialism and slavery to help create a surplus of exports over imports. They also used protectionist policies, including tariffs, import quotas, and grants of monopolies, to protect domestic producers and merchants (i.e., the mercantile classes) from foreign competition. In exchange for this protection, the mercantile classes paid taxes and levies to support the army.

Mercantilist doctrines are famously critiqued in Adam Smith's *An Inquiry into the Nature and Causes of the Wealth of Nations*, first published in 1776. The essence of Smith's argument is that free trade enriches both parties of an exchange. Mercantilism erroneously views trade as a zero-sum game, because one nation can gain gold only at the expense of another. Moreover, mercantilism is based on a collusion between the mercantile classes and the government, who protected each other's interests, whereas free markets can enrich the broader population.[3]

Even before *The Wealth of Nations*, Smith's friend and fellow Scottish philosopher David Hume argued that mercantilism would fail to enrich a nation. His "quantity theory of money" argument, articulated in *Political Discourses* in 1752, was centered on prices. Hume explained that if a country increases its net exports so that more gold flows into the country, then prices in that country rise proportionally to the increase in the quantity of money, for "it is the proportion between the circulating money, and the commodities in the market, which determines the prices."[4] Higher prices make the country's exports less competitive, so its net exports decline, reversing the gold flow and the rise in prices. This process is called the price-specie-flow mechanism, and it is an equilibrating mechanism—a means by which the market restores equilibrium, or balance, to an economic system.

Hume acknowledged that gold inflows could temporarily boost economic activity, noting that "since the discovery of the mines in America, industry has encreased in all the nations of Europe." But this boost to industry, he believed, only lasted while prices gradually adjusted to the increase in the money supply. As he wrote:

> Though the high price of commodities be a necessary consequence of the encrease of gold and silver, yet it follows not immediately upon

> that encrease; but some time is required before the money circulates through the whole state, and makes its effect be felt on all ranks of people. At first, no alteration is perceived; by degrees the price rises, first of one commodity, then of another; till the whole at last reaches a just proportion with the new quantity of specie which is in the kingdom. In my opinion, it is only in this interval or intermediate situation, between the acquisition of money and rise of prices, that the encreasing quantity of gold and silver is favourable to industry.[5]

Hume and his contemporaries could observe that prices of different commodities could rise and fall at different rates, and Hume understood that prices as a "whole" eventually adjusted to the monetary increase. But they did not have data on the aggregate or overall price level like we have now. Today, economists rely on a variety of price indexes that are constructed by government agencies. In the United States, for example, the Consumer Price Index (CPI), by the Bureau of Labor Statistics, is constructed from the prices of thousands of goods from more than two hundred categories, which fall or rise at different rates in any given month.[6] Price indexes enable us to study the rate of change in the overall price level, or *inflation,* which is one of the most important macroeconomic variables, and one of the most highly monitored and discussed by policy makers and the public.

Just a few years after Hume published his *Political Discourses,* Count Gian Rinaldo Carli, an Italian professor of astronomy and navigation, constructed what is now credited as the first price index.[7] A polymath, Count Carli was also interested in economics, and he set out to study the relationship between the supplies of gold and silver from the Americas and rising prices in his own country. Carli gathered data on the prices of grain, wine, and olive oil in the late fifteenth century, just before European colonization of the Americas. These would serve as prices in the base period. He also gathered data on prices of the same commodities in a later period, 1744 to 1755. Then he computed the percentage change in each price from the base period to the later period, added those three figures together, and divided by three. That is, he took a simple, unweighted average of the three percentage changes.

Count Carli's index, though simpler in its construction than the CPI and other modern price indexes, was quite useful. He showed that prices in terms of gold or silver had risen much less than prices in terms of lire, the Italian unit of account.[8] This meant that prices had risen not because gold or silver bullion was worth less, but because the bullion content of Italian coins had declined as a result of government debasement of the coinage. In other words, to finance their spending, Italy's rulers had reduced the precious metal content of Italian coins—expanding the money supply without expanding the supply of gold and silver. In fact, Carli showed that the supply of gold and silver in Italy was actually declining, contrary to popular belief at the time.[9] For his efforts, Carli subsequently received an appointment as the president of the Council of Finance in Milan and helped to reform the coinage.

Carli's study did not contradict Hume's quantity theory of money; in fact, it supported it. The quantity theory, again, predicts that prices change proportionally with changes in the money supply. But the money supply may or may not be linked directly to the supply of gold or silver. In the Italian example, it was not. The government expanded the money supply by expanding the supply of lira-denominated coins, without expanding the supply of gold, and this increased prices in terms of lire. Currency debasement, an age-old temptation for rulers, has become nearly synonymous with inflation.[10]

Currency in the Colonies

While the intellectual dominance of mercantilism faced challenges from Hume and Smith, it also faced practical challenges from colonial subjects who were frustrated with the imperialist powers and the mercantilist policies they relied on. The British Crown was determined to maintain a trade surplus with its American colonies by keeping them agricultural and therefore reliant on British imports. Specie flowed from the colonies to Britain in payment for imports and for taxes.

British mercantilism kept silver and gold coins in short supply in the American colonies. The Crown banned the exportation of British sterling coin to the colonies and banned the colonies from minting their own coins, leaving the colonists to rely on foreign specie from Spain, Portugal, or France. Although a variety of foreign coins circulated in the colonies, the units of account were local pounds, shillings, and pence—a shilling in Philadelphia was different from a shilling in New York, for example.

Given the limited specie and restrictions on coinage, many transactions in the colonies relied on an arrangement called *book credit,* in which the buyer of goods would be debited on the seller's books in the local unit of account. To extinguish the debt, the buyer could later pay with the local medium of exchange or with mutually agreed-on goods or services—such as a week's labor fixing fences or a delivery of chickens.[11] Another alternative was payment in local commodities like corn, beef, or pork, which was known as *country pay.*

While the book credit arrangement relied on private parties' determination of value and freely given consent to exchange, the country pay arrangement involved state assignment of value. A colonial legislature would assign specific monetary values to each commodity and declare the commodities *legal tender,* that is, required to be accepted in payment of taxes and sometimes for all private debts.[12] The trouble was that the legislature overvalued certain commodities relative to others. The debtor could always choose which commodity to pay with, so would choose the most overvalued commodity.

Creditors resented being forced to accept country pay in payment of debts. The satirical poem "The Sot-Weed Factor" tells the tale of a British tobacco merchant (the sot-weed factor) who agreed to exchange his trade goods for tobacco with a Quaker merchant who later failed to deliver. The British merchant took the Quaker merchant to court and sailed away ruined:

> The Byast Court without delay,
> Adjudg'd my Debt in Country Pay.[13]

In addition to book credit and country pay, colonists used bills of credit to make payments. Colonial governments issued these paper bills, which circulated much like modern paper money. Bills of credit were backed not by specie—they could not be redeemed in gold or silver on demand—but by taxes. A tax-backed currency, as Smith described in *The Wealth of Nations,* derives its value from its liquidity and its usefulness in paying for future taxes: "A prince who should enact that a certain proportion of taxes should be paid in a paper money of a certain kind, might thereby give a certain value to this paper money, even though the time of its final discharge and redemption should depend altogether on the will of the prince."[14] Colonial governments often issued bills of credit to finance military expenditures. For example, Massachusetts was the first to issue bills of credit, in 1690, to pay soldiers in a failed military expedition against Quebec.[15] South Carolina, New York, New Jersey, Rhode Island, and North Carolina followed suit to finance military expenses during Queen Anne's War of 1702 to 1713; Georgia and Virginia did so during the Seven Years' War of 1755 to 1762.[16]

The first colony to issue bills of credit for a reason other than the financing of wartime expenditures was Pennsylvania, in 1723, the year that seventeen-year-old Benjamin Franklin arrived in Philadelphia. The paper money issue was intended as a temporary tool to relieve an economic crisis in the colony, to be removed from circulation by the end of the decade.[17] Franklin observed how the new paper money boosted trade, employment, and construction in the colony, and he became an ardent advocate of making paper money a permanent feature in the colonies.[18] In his treatise on paper currency, he explained that when money is scarce, local interest rates are high, reducing investment, and people have to resort to barter, which makes trade less efficient. Paper money can alleviate both of those problems.[19] He also explained that paper money was not inherently inflationary. True, some of the New England colonies and South Carolina had suffered inflation as their paper monies depreciated, but that could be avoided if the quantity of money did not increase more rapidly than the volume of internal trade within the colony. His pamphlet was well received by the common people of Pennsylvania, but not by the wealthy, who still feared that paper-money-induced inflation would erode the value of their wealth.[20]

In 1733, Maryland became the second colony to introduce paper money during peacetime, intending to make it a permanent feature in the colony.[21] The Maryland economy was heavily reliant on tobacco, its primary crop. In fact, before 1733, money in the colony took the form of claims on tobacco production. The Maryland government collected taxes in the form of tobacco leaves, where one hundred pounds of tobacco leaves could pay ten shillings of taxes.[22] Local sheriffs served as tax collectors, receiving a share of the collection as income. Subjects who did not grow their own tobacco had to obtain it through barter to pay their taxes, which became increasingly burdensome as the Maryland economy began to diversify away from a tobacco monoculture.

The price of tobacco on the transatlantic market was volatile and could differ from the government price of ten shillings per hundred pounds. In the 1710s and early 1720s, market prices were higher than the government price, leading to complaints that tax collectors were benefiting at the expense of taxpayers.[23] The sheriff collectors were "left to their liberty to charge either in money or tobacco, so that when tobacco rises they charge in tobacco and thereby get double the price assessed by the justices."[24] The high tobacco prices also encouraged the expansion of tobacco production. By the mid-1720s, higher supply led to declining tobacco prices. Large tobacco producers lobbied the government to raise prices by restricting the supply. This is where colonial bills of credit came in. Maryland designed a scheme to inject the paper money into the economy by paying small farmers thirty shillings of paper money in exchange for destroying three hundred pounds of tobacco. Tobacco exports did fall and prices did rise in the years following Maryland's Paper Money Act of 1733, although the increase in prices may have resulted from greater French demand for tobacco rather than small farmers' destruction of their crops.[25]

Maryland's paper money suffered rapid depreciation because it lost its usefulness for paying taxes. In principle, taxes could be paid in either paper money or tobacco after the Paper Money Act, still at a rate of ten shillings per hundred pounds. But as the market price of tobacco rose above ten shillings per hundred pounds, tax collectors found ways to refuse payment in paper money, insisting on payment in tobacco. As Marylanders became less confident that paper money could be used for future taxes, they were less willing to accept it as a medium of exchange.

More generally, the colonies' different experiences with depreciation and inflation following paper money issuance depended on the colonial governments' fiscal policy regimes. When increases in the paper money supply were accompanied by increases in anticipated tax obligations payable in paper money, maintaining a strong tax backing, inflation was avoided.[26] Thus the bills of credit depreciated dramatically in New England and the Carolinas, causing high inflation, but not in the middle colonies.[27]

The ability to issue bills of credit was a powerful form of monetary authority that the Crown viewed as a threat to the mercantilist system. With the Currency Act of 1751, the Crown prohibited the New England colonies from issuing such bills. Subsequently, the Currency Act of 1764 extended the prohibition to all American colonies, pointing to the costs of inflation imposed by the bills: "Great quantities of paper bills of credit have been created and issued in his Majesty's colonies or plantations in America. . . . Whereas such bills of credit have greatly depreciated in their value, by means whereof debts have been discharged with a much less value than was contracted for, to the great discouragement and prejudice of the trade and commerce of his Majesty's subjects, by occasioning confusion in dealings, and lessening credit in the said colonies or plantations." The Crown was voicing a common complaint about the redistributive nature of inflation. Inflation erodes the real value of debts, benefiting debtors (in this case, the colonists) at the expense of their creditors (the Crown). The wealthy of Pennsylvania, remember, had opposed Franklin's proposals about paper money for the same reason. Franklin himself returned to London in 1764 to lobby for the repeal of the Currency Act, continuing to argue that paper money was necessary so long as the Crown limited the colonies' supply of gold and silver and that, with the proper institutional arrangements, paper money need not cause inflation.[28]

The Birth and Worth of a Continental

Just a year after the Currency Act, the Stamp Act of 1765 infuriated the colonists by imposing taxes on colonial newspapers, pamphlets, cards, dice, and other papers. The Stamp Act sparked the creation of the Sons of Liberty, a secret political organization that fought for the rights of the colonists. John Adams, a member of the Sons of Liberty and later the second president of the United States, wrote, "We have always understood it to be a grand and fundamental principle of the constitution, that no freeman should be subject to any tax to which he has not given his own consent, in person or by proxy."[29]

Indeed, two years earlier, James Otis Jr., a Boston lawyer and legislator, decried that the colonists had been "disfranchised of rights, that have been always thought inherent to a British subject, namely, to be free from all taxes, but what he consents to in person, or by his representative."[30] Otis is thought to have popularized the phrase "Taxation without representation is tyranny." Delegates at the Stamp Act Congress that October echoed Otis's and Adams's resolve that "it is inseparably essential to the freedom of a people, and the undoubted right of Englishmen, that no taxes be imposed on them, but with their own consent, given personally, or by their representatives."[31]

This emphasis on consent reflects the influence of English philosopher John Locke, whose *Second Treatise* asserted that political legitimacy depends on the consent of the governed:

> For no government can have a right to obedience from a people who have not freely consented to it; which they can never be supposed to do, till either they are put in a full state of liberty to choose their government and governors, or at least till they have such standing laws, to which they have by themselves or their representatives given their free consent; and also till they are allowed their due property, which is so to be proprietors of what they have, that nobody can take away any part of it without their own consent, without which, men under any government are not in the state of freemen, but are direct slaves under the force of war.[32]

Locke firmly opposed authoritarianism and tyranny, which he defined as "the exercise of power beyond right, which nobody can have a right to. And this is making use of the power any one has in his hands, not for the good of those who are under it, but for his own private, separate advantage."[33] He argued that rebellion against tyranny could be legitimately pursued because a despotic government lacks the legitimacy to rule: "If a long train of abuses, prevarications, and artifices, all tending the same way, make the design visible to the people, and they cannot but feel what they lie under, and see whither they are going; it is not to be wondered, that they should then rise themselves, and endeavor to put the rule into such hands which may secure to them the ends for government was at first erected."[34] His influence on the colonists is clear. The Declaration of Independence repeats the "long train of abuses" phrase and gives prominence to the principle of governance by consent. Its second paragraph declares that to secure the rights of life, liberty, and the pursuit of happiness, "Governments are instituted among Men, deriving their just powers from the consent of the governed."

Governance by consent was a principle that the American Revolutionaries were willing to fight for. And to fight, the colonies needed money—which, thanks to the policies of the Crown, was in short supply. Thus, in defiance of the Currency Act, the states issued their own bills of credit to finance the Revolutionary War, and the Articles of Confederation adopted by the Second Continental Congress authorized Congress to emit bills of credit as well. The bills issued by Congress were known as Continental currency, or Continentals, and they also were not backed by silver or gold.

The phrase "not worth a Continental," still used today, refers to the massive depreciation of the Continentals. Prices rose more than two-hundred-fold from 1775 to 1781, as Congress issued eleven emissions of Continentals.[35] The later emissions, like some of the earlier colonial bills of credit, also were not sufficiently backed by expected future tax collections, contributing to their depreciation.[36] The British also issued counterfeit Continentals in 1778 and 1779, hoping to contribute to their depreciation by increasing their volume. Franklin explained: "Paper money . . . being the instrument with which we combatted our enemies, they resolved to deprive us of its use by depreciating it; and the most effectual means they could contrive was to counterfeit it."[37]

In his later years, Franklin noted that the Continental currency depreciation had allowed the government to finance the war in a relatively fair manner, through an inflation tax. Currency depreciation, he wrote, was a "Tax on Money . . . and it has fallen more equally than many other Taxes, as those People paid most, who, being richest, had most Money passing thro' their Hands."[38]

Price Controls in the Revolution

Even before the Declaration of Independence was signed, the colonists began considering how to control prices that were sure to rise during the war. The 1774 Articles of Association, for example, declared "that all manufactures of this country be sold at reasonable prices . . . venders of goods or merchandise will not take advantage of the scarcity of goods, that may be occasioned by this association, but will sell the same at rates we have been respectively accustomed to do, for twelve months last past."[39]

Price controls were not totally new in the colonies—Virginia and Massachusetts Bay, for example, had imposed price and wage controls in the seventeenth century—but eighteenth-century interest in price controls was quite limited until stoked by the exigencies of the Revolution.[40] The Continental Congress, in 1775 and 1776, recommended maximum prices for tea, coffee, salt, and sugar, but it lacked the power to enforce controls across the states.[41] Thus, most attempts to control prices in the Revolution were at the state and local level, with prices fixed and regulations enforced by local authorities.[42]

In December 1776, representatives from New Hampshire, Massachusetts, Connecticut, and Rhode Island convened in Providence, Rhode Island, to discuss how they could coordinate their controls to make them more effective. All four states subsequently enacted the policies on price and wage controls recommended by the convention, which were quite popular with their residents.[43] In Massachusetts, for example, many supporters of controls blamed "avaricious conduct" for the "exorbitant price of every necessary and convenient article of life, and increasing the price of labour."[44] But the controls were less popular among merchants, who often resorted to barter rather than complying with regulated prices.[45]

Congress debated whether to endorse the Providence price and wage controls across all the states but never agreed to recommend these or other price controls more widely. Some members of Congress, like Benjamin Rush of Pennsylvania, argued that rising prices could be remedied only by reversing the monetary expansion that caused them. The only remedies for "the excessive quantity of our money" were "1 Raising the interest of the money we borrow to 6 per cent. This like a cold bath will give an immediate Spring to our affairs—and 2 taxation. This like tapping, will diminish the Quantity of our Money, and give a proper value to what remains."[46]

Others argued against price controls on both economic and philosophical grounds. Again, their arguments reflected the influence of John Locke, who believed that it was both impractical and illegitimate for the government to regulate prices, which are determined by the laws of nature.[47] Famously, when Parliament had considered regulating the price of borrowing money by imposing an interest rate ceiling of 4 percent, Locke wrote a letter opposing the proposal:

> The first thing to be considered is, "Whether the price of the hire of money can be regulated by law?" And to that I think, generally speaking, one may say, it is manifest it cannot. For since it is impossible to make a law that shall hinder a man from giving away his money or estate to whom he pleases, it will be impossible, by any contrivance of law, to hinder men, skilled in the power they have over their own goods, and the ways of conveying them to others, to purchase money to be lent them, at what rate soever their occasions shall make it necessary for them to have it.[48]

One of the most ardent opponents of price control was Reverend John Witherspoon, a member of the Continental Congress, signer of the Declaration of Independence, and president of the College of New Jersey (now Princeton University). Witherspoon argued against price controls explicitly on grounds of consent: "We know, that in cities, in case of a fire, sometimes a house, without the consent of its owner, will be destroyed to prevent the whole from being consumed. But if you make a law that I shall be obliged to sell my grain, my cattle, or any commodity, at a certain price, you not only do what is unjust and impolitic, but with all respect be it said, you speak nonsense; for I do not sell them at all: you take them from me. You are both buyer and seller, and I am the sufferer only."[49] Witherspoon also argued that price controls were "not only unjust and unwise, but for the most part impracticable": "They are an attempt to apply authority to that which is not its proper object, and to extend it beyond its natural bounds; in both which we shall be sure to fail. . . . Accordingly we found in this country, and every other society who ever tried such measures found, that they produced an effect directly contrary to what was expected from them.

Instead of producing moderation and plenty, they uniformly produced dearness and scarcity."[50] But others argued that relief from inflation was urgently needed, and price controls could take effect more quickly than a reduction in the money supply. At a 1778 convention in New Haven, Connecticut, participants asked, "Must we be suffered to continue the exaction of such high prices to the destruction of the common cause, and of ourselves with it, merely because the reduction of the quantity of our currency may in time redress the evil; and because any other method may be complained of as an infringement of liberty?"[51]

Increasingly, the Continental Congress agreed with Witherspoon's Lockean arguments. By June 1778, Congress concluded that "limitations on the prices of commodities are not only ineffectual for the purposes proposed, but likewise productive of very evil consequences to the great detriment of the public service and grievous oppression of individuals."[52] The last regional convention on price controls, in January 1780 in Philadelphia, adjourned without coming to any agreement on new controls.

Deflation and Shays' Rebellion

The Continentals were last emitted in 1779, and by 1781, they had mostly ceased circulating.[53] After the demise of the Continental, gold and silver coins circulated as currency. Their supply was supplemented by loans from France in 1781 and 1782. After the war ended with the Treaty of Paris in 1783, the revolutionaries, though victorious, faced an economic crisis. The national and state governments owed massive war debts but had little means to repay, as the national government had no power to tax, the states could not raise enough tax revenue, and the trade deficit was large. Americans shipped precious metal to Britain to pay for British exports. Creditors, recognizing the unsustainability of the situation, began to refuse further loans, demanding payment in hard currency, which was in shorter and shorter supply.

As lending contracted and the money supply shrank, prices began to plummet. In Philadelphia, for example, wholesale prices for farm products fell to one-third of their value from 1784 to 1786.[54] Land prices also fell. The combination of falling land prices and falling farm products prices hit debtors hard. Many war veterans, who remained unpaid or underpaid for their service, had taken out loans to buy land to farm when prices were at their wartime highs, and they were facing foreclosure. As a result, there was frequent agitation for issues of paper money to reverse the price decline.

Many of the Founders resisted this call for paper money, looking back with disfavor on the Continental currency. Witherspoon critiqued the Continentals on the same grounds as price controls—as a violation of liberty and consent and an illegitimate interference of law with commerce. In these arguments, Witherspoon again echoed Locke, who defined money as "some lasting thing that men might keep without spoiling, and that by mutual consent men would take in exchange for the truly useful, but perishable supports of life." Gold and silver, according to Locke, "has its value only from the consent of men." Witherspoon wrote:

> Why will you make a law to oblige men to take money when it is offered them? Are there any who refuse it when it is good? If it is necessary to force them, does not this system produce a most ludicrous inversion of the nature of things. For two or three years we constantly saw and were informed of creditors running away from their debtors, and the debtors pursuing them in triumph, and paying them without mercy. . . . Money is itself a commodity. . . . To give, therefore, authority or nominal value by law to any money, is interposing by law, in commerce, and is precisely the same thing with laws regulating the prices of commodities, of which, in their full extent, we had sufficient experience during the war. Now nothing can be more radically unjust, or more eminently absurd, than laws of that nature.[55]

Many of the other Founding Fathers agreed with Witherspoon. George Washington, who had decried the Continental depreciation and its tendency to raise prices, wrote that paper money had a tendency "to ruin commerce, oppress the honest, and open the door to every species of fraud and injustice."[56] James Madison declared paper money unjust, "for it affects the rights of property as much as taking away equal value in land." Alexander Hamilton believed that "the stamping of paper is an operation so much easier than the laying of taxes" that a government would "indulge itself too far . . . to avoid as much as possible one less auspicious to present popularity."[57]

The state governments, which had a large degree of autonomy under the Articles of Confederation, considered the paper currency question individually. Georgia, North and South Carolina, New York, New Jersey, Pennsylvania, and Rhode Island all began issuing paper currency. The Rhode Island legislature passed a law requiring that merchants and creditors accept payments in the paper currency. In other states, paper currency measures were successfully opposed by creditors, who did not want to allow inflation to erode the value of the debts they were owed.[58]

Most notably, in Massachusetts, state lawmakers resisted demands for paper currency and relied on heavy taxes to make payments on the state debt. Many farmers who could not pay their taxes or mortgage payments lost their property and went to debtors' prison. In 1786 and 1787, the farmer and veteran Daniel Shays led four thousand men in an armed uprising against the government. Although Shays' Rebellion was crushed, it made an important impact. For many, called Federalists, it pointed to the need for a reform of the Articles of Confederation to strengthen the central government.[59] As the next chapter discusses, this federalism question, and the currency question, were among the most important issues at the Constitutional Convention of 1787.

TWO

FINANCING THE NEW NATION

> That paper money has some advantages is admitted. [B]ut that it's abuses also are inevitable and, by breaking up the measure of value, makes a lottery of all private property, cannot be denied.
>
> THOMAS JEFFERSON to Josephus B. Stuart[1]

The Constitutional Convention

The United States currently has a system of fiat currency and a central bank responsible for price stability. But this system that we are so familiar with today was not in place after the Revolution, nor was it obvious that such a system would or should be established. When the Framers of the Constitution met in Philadelphia in 1787, the choices they made concerning the monetary authorities of the federal and state governments would have profound implications for the money and banking system and, in turn, for prices in the new nation.

Price fluctuations, the Framers had already seen, affected not only the economic but also the political and social well-being of the states and the union. Shays' Rebellion and the political unrest that followed the Revolutionary War, for example, had followed declining land and crop prices that exacerbated tensions between agrarian and mercantile interests. These tensions were an important influence in the development of American democracy and were quite apparent at the Convention.

Thomas Jefferson, of Virginia, viewed agriculture and the individualism of small farmers as the foundation of democracy. Here, Jefferson was heavily influenced by Locke, for whom property rights are derived from agricultural labor, and the "great and chief end" of government is to preserve those property rights.[2] Jefferson hoped to preserve America as a society of small farmers, in opposition to the commercial capitalism of England.[3] He wrote to fellow Virginian James Madison that "our governments will remain virtuous for many centuries; as long as they are chiefly agricultural; and this will be as long as there shall be vacant lands in any part of America. When they get piled upon one another in large cities, as in Europe, they will become corrupt as in Europe."[4]

Jefferson and Madison's agrarianism went hand in hand with their republican ideals, including rejection of monarchy and aristocracy, limited governance, and protection of states' rights and individual rights. Governance, they believed, could best be conducted at a more local level. Jefferson viewed westward expansion as a way to extend republicanism, and he was instrumental developing a land policy that divided western land into plots that the government could sell.[5]

In contrast, Alexander Hamilton thought that manufacturing and commerce were crucial to the nation's prosperity, and he envisioned a strong national government that could promote those interests and "correct the prejudices, check the intemperate passions, and regulate the fluctuations of a popular assembly." He questioned the "zeal for liberty" that had become "predominant and excessive" in the states: "We appear to have had no other view than to secure ourselves from despotism. . . . But, Sir, there is another object, equally important, and which our enthusiasm rendered us little capable of regarding—I mean a principle of strength and stability in the organization of our government, and vigor in its operations."[6]

To reconcile these competing visions of American democracy, the delegates had to draft a constitution that would balance powers between the federal and state governments, and also between the branches of government, in a way that would preserve liberty and prevent tyranny while allowing for effective governance.[7] This was a challenging task when it came to the monetary powers of government. Recall that the colonial governments had emitted bills of credit, which circulated like cash in the colonies. In the Revolutionary War, the states had continued to emit bills of credit, and Congress had issued its own bills of credit, the Continentals. This issuance of paper money by both the states and by Congress was controversial because of the tendency toward overissuance to raise prices.

The delegates voted to prohibit the states from emitting bills of credit. Article I, Section 10, Clause 1 of the Constitution says that no state shall "coin Money; emit Bills of Credit; make any Thing but gold and silver Coin a Tender in Payment of Debts." This restriction was intended to strengthen the national strengthening government and to restrain the states from excessive printing of paper money. Madison noted, "In the internal administration of the States, a violation of contracts had become familiar, in the form of depreciated paper made a legal tender."[8] In other words, states had been inflating away their debts to one another through currency expansion.

The delegates debated whether Congress should have the power to emit bills of credit. Gouverneur Morris, of Pennsylvania, proposed to remove the authority for the US government to issue paper money, arguing that "if the United States had credit such bills would be unnecessary: if they had not, unjust and useless."[9] Oliver Elsworth, of Connecticut, concurred: "The mischiefs of the various experiments which had been made, were now fresh in the public mind and had excited the disgust of all the respectable part of America. . . . Paper money can in no case be necessary."[10]

Some of the Southern delegates were less staunchly averse to paper money. George Mason, of Virginia, argued against prohibition, not wanting to tie the hands of the legislature in the case of an unforeseen future emergency. John Francis Mercer, of Maryland, took the same view, adding that it would "stamp suspicion on the Government to deny it a discretion on this point. It was impolitic also to excite the opposition of all those who were friends to paper money."[11] The "friends" of paper money, remember, tended to be farmers and common people, not merchants. Madison asked whether it would "not be sufficient to prohibit making [bills of credit] a tender? This will remove the temptation to emit them with unjust views."[12]

In something of a compromise, the delegates voted to remove but not explicitly prohibit the authority of the United States to emit bills of credit. Article I, Section 8, which enumerates the powers of Congress, says nothing about bills of credit or the power to declare a legal tender, but it does list the power "to coin Money" and "regulate the Value thereof."

The First Bank, Bimetallism, and the Land Boom

The deflation and depression that followed the American Revolution came to an end in 1788, when grain and livestock prices surged, reflecting strong demand in England and southern Europe.[13] As mercantilism fell out of favor, the Americans could reap the gains of agricultural trade with those markets. More than three-fourths of Americans were engaged in agriculture, compared to just a third of the British population.[14] The high prices of farm products, which Americans exported to Europe, ushered in years of prosperity.[15]

Even with the Constitution ratified, the Founders still faced the task of designing institutions—in particular, banking institutions—to enhance prosperity. The banking system, money, and prices are closely intertwined, as banks' lending behavior helps determine the money supply. So unsurprisingly, debates about the nature of the new nation's banking system, and in particular about whether there should be a national bank, were similar to debates at the Convention about monetary powers, pitting Southern agrarians against the financial powers in the Northeast and contributing to a partisan divide that dismayed President Washington.[16]

Washington appointed Jefferson as the first secretary of state and Hamilton as the first secretary of the Treasury, despite the men's very different views. Jefferson, who remained deeply suspicious of concentrated political power, suspected that a national bank would foster despotism, and others in his Jeffersonian Republican Party, or Democratic-Republican Party, agreed. "What was it [that] drove our forefathers to this country?" asked James Jackson of Georgia. "Was it not the ecclesiastical corporations and perpetual monopolies of England and Scotland? Shall we suffer the same evils to exist in this country?"[17] Jefferson and the Democratic-Republicans preferred to allow state-chartered banks to issue money. They feared that a national bank would undermine state banks and adopt policies favoring financiers and merchants over farmers.

Hamilton and the Federalist Party envisioned a national bank with branches throughout the states that could create a uniform national currency and act as the government's fiscal agent by collecting the government's tax revenues and paying the government's bills. When Hamilton claimed that the bank would serve "the general welfare," Andrew Jackson, of Tennessee, countered: "What is the general welfare? Is it the welfare of Philadelphia, New York and Boston?"

Debates also focused on whether or not a national bank was constitutional. Madison and other Democratic-Republicans argued that a national bank was unconstitutional, because the Constitution does not grant Congress the power to establish corporations, such as a national bank. But Article 1, Section 8, which enumerates the powers of Congress, also gives Congress the power "to make all Laws which shall be necessary and proper for carrying into Execution the foregoing Powers," and Hamilton argued that a national financial institution was in fact necessary and proper to enable the government to carry out its enumerated powers to collect taxes, regulate interstate commerce, and provide for the common defense. Jefferson and Madison worried that such a loose interpretation of the necessary and proper clause would eventually allow the national government to do almost anything.

The question of interpretation of the necessary and proper clause would remain unresolved for years to come, but on the question of the bank, the Federalists prevailed; Congress chartered the First Bank of the United States in 1791. The bank's largest shareholder was the US government, but it also had many foreign shareholders, to some Americans' dismay. The bank became the largest financial institution in the nation because it was the only institution permitted to hold federal government deposits and to operate branches.[18] The First Bank also operated as a commercial bank. When the bank accepted deposits from private citizens, its banknotes, which were accepted in payment of federal taxes, entered circulation.[19]

In some respects, the First Bank was like a central bank, conducting a rudimentary version of monetary policy and affecting prices and inflation. Its banknotes were redeemable in gold on demand and were backed by substantial gold reserves, so their value was relatively stable. To tighten credit, the bank would present state banknotes that it received to the state banks for redemption in specie. This would limit the state banks' ability to make loans, shrinking the money supply and reining in inflation. To loosen credit, the bank would lend more freely and avoid bringing state banknotes for redemption, with the opposite effect.[20]

Hamilton also played a major role in designing the American coinage system. Recall that Article I, Section 8 of the Constitution gives Congress the authority to coin money and regulate its value. To exercise these authorities, Congress passed the Coinage Act of 1792, which established the national mint in Philadelphia and set up a coinage system with the dollar as the unit of account. On Hamilton's recommendation, the United States adopted a bimetallic standard, by which each dollar was assigned the value of 371.25 grains of pure silver or 24.75 grains of pure gold. This implied a ratio of 15 to 1 between the value of gold and the value of silver.

In some respects, bimetallism was similar to the earlier country pay system and to the Maryland tobacco money system. With country pay, the state assigned relative prices of different commodities used as legal tender. When the relative market prices differed from the relative assigned prices, only the overvalued commodity was used in payments. With tobacco money, the state assigned a price ratio of ten shillings per hundred pounds of tobacco for use in tax payments. Again, if the assigned ratio overvalued tobacco relative to its market price, subjects would prefer to use tobacco to pay taxes. Likewise, the assigned price ratio of silver to gold could differ from the market price ratio, to similar effect. Hamilton noted that "one consequence of overvaluing either metal in respect to the other" would be "the banishment of that which is undervalued."[21]

The phenomenon Hamilton referred to was later named Gresham's law, and it is usually summarized as "bad money drives out good." More precisely, when legal tender laws are enforced, legally overvalued currency tends to drive legally undervalued currency out of circulation.[22] Arbitrageurs send the undervalued coins abroad, where their purchasing power is greater than under the domestic administered price ratio.[23]

Hamilton, though aware of this possibility, was not too concerned. He thought that the legal ratio between gold and silver could be kept near enough to the market ratio to keep both types of coins circulating. But the French government established a ratio of 15.1 to 1, and the London market ratio was 15.4 to 1. Because silver was overvalued in the United States compared with Europe, silver coins were used in domestic transactions and gold was exported. Gold coins could not be kept in circulation domestically. Therefore, US currency consisted of paper money, silver coins, and copper coins (which had no legal tender status but could be used for small transactions). Congress criticized the Mint for its failure to circulate all of its coins and only narrowly passed legislation to permanently establish the Mint.[24]

The decade following the establishment of the First Bank and the Mint was characterized by a land boom as the bank's branches throughout the country helped finance westward expansion.[25] Wealthy speculators purchased huge tracts of land, hoping that land prices would rise in the future. Washington himself was one of the largest acquisitors of land, writing, "Lands are permanent, rising fast in value, and will be very dear when our Independancy is established, and the importance of America better known."[26]

To improve the ability of small farmers to purchase farmland in the west, the Land Act of 1800 reduced the minimum purchase amount to 320 acres and allowed people to buy land from the federal government on credit, through a series of installment payments.[27] Many farmers eagerly took up this offer, also in the hope that land prices would continue to rise. And they expected rising crop prices to make it easy to make their future installment payments. This expectation was correct: the Napoleonic Wars, which lasted from 1803 to 1815, reduced European agricultural output, leading to a larger market and higher prices for US agricultural goods.[28]

By the time the First Bank's twenty-year charter was set to expire in 1811, the political landscape had evolved substantially. The Democratic-Republicans, the original opponents of the First Bank, became the dominant party. Jefferson was elected president in 1800, succeeding the Federalist John Adams, and Hamilton died in a duel in 1804. The Democratic-Republicans also gained control of Congress and held the presidency with Madison's election in 1809. The Democratic-Republicans became less overwhelmingly agrarian and less hostile to banking in general as the party gained a business wing.[29]

Support for the bank, by 1811, was not so neatly split on party lines, on regional lines, or by agrarian versus business interests. In fact, many Southern agrarians had come to support the bank, believing that it played a necessary role in supporting the state banks and preventing them from excessively emitting paper money.[30] Debates about whether to renew the bank's charter focused largely on its constitutionality rather than its economic effects.[31] In the end, the bank's supporters narrowly lost, and the charter renewal was defeated by one vote.

The War of 1812

The timing of the First Bank's demise was inconvenient, to say the least. In the War of 1812, a British naval blockade prevented farmers and manufacturers from exporting their goods and merchants from sailing the seas. This led to an economic downturn and disrupted the government's primary source of revenue, tariffs, just when major expenditures were needed to fund the war. From the adoption of the Constitution until that point, the US government had funded its deficits by borrowing, mostly from Holland or from the First Bank, and from customs duties.[32] The new nation had no income tax, and Treasury secretary Albert Gallatin had dismantled most mechanisms for internal tax collection during Jefferson's presidency.

In 1812, with war on the horizon, Gallatin, who continued as Treasury secretary under Madison, proposed doubling tariff duties and taking out a loan of $11 million. Gallatin realized that this approach to raising funds would be insufficient, as many potential creditors in New England lacked sympathy for the war effort and were disinclined to make low-interest loans to the government.[33] As an alternative means of raising funding, Gallatin urged the House Ways and Means Committee to authorize an issue of $5 million in interest-bearing one-year Treasury notes.[34]

The proposed note issue was the subject of heated debate in Congress. Opponents argued that the notes, like the Continental currency, would quickly depreciate and that issuing them would signal impending bankruptcy. Proponents countered that the notes would address the shortage of an adequate circulating medium and that depreciation could be avoided by making the notes receivable for taxes. Congress authorized the notes on June 30, 1812, just twelve days after war was declared. Because of the reluctance to force men to accept currency against their consent, the Treasury notes were made partial legal tender—they could be used for paying public dues and taxes, but they were not required to be accepted in payment of private debt.

The first note issue was quickly sold to banks. Because the notes came in large denominations ($100 and $1,000) they did not freely circulate, but banks held them as reserves, allowing for monetary expansion. An editorial in *Niles Weekly Register* praised Gallatin's plan as "the most eligible that could possibly have been adopted, as it will mutually accommodate the Government and the people, and be advantageous to both."[35] With expenditures mounting, Congress authorized a second issue of Treasury notes in February 1813, a third in March 1814, and a fourth in December 1814, the same month that the Treaty of Ghent ended the war. The fifth and final issue, in February 1815, included smaller-denomination notes that did not bear interest and that circulated freely as a paper currency. Most state banks also began issuing more notes after they suspended specie redemption of their notes in August 1814. Notes outstanding doubled from $2.3 million in 1811 to $4.6 million in 1815.[36]

Throughout this time, Congress debated whether to reestablish a national bank. A national bank could make loans to the government and help reduce its reliance on note issuance, which many, including Gallatin's successor, Treasury secretary Alexander Dallas, saw as a national embarrassment.[37] Like other financiers, Secretary Dallas believed and hoped that a new national bank could restore currency stability and prevent inflation. President Madison, who had firmly opposed the First Bank, reluctantly agreed that a new national bank might be necessary, but he withdrew his support when the peace treaty was eminent.[38]

The Treasury notes never suffered from massive depreciation like the Continentals and some of the colonial bills of credit. But by serving as bank reserves, allowing for increased lending, they did contribute to monetary expansion and rising prices.[39] Cotton prices doubled, and imported and domestic commodity prices increased by about 70 percent and 20 percent, respectively.[40] Prices of imported commodities rose more than those of domestic commodities because of their restricted availability. This was also the case for the prices of textiles and other manufactured goods. These high prices encouraged the development of new domestic manufacturing, which had been very limited before the war. Cotton textile factories, for example, proliferated in New England, Pennsylvania, and New York.[41]

Prices, Protectionism, and the American System

After the War of 1812, increased European demand fueled continued agricultural price increases. The eruption of Indonesia's Mount Tambora in 1815, the most powerful volcanic eruption in recorded human history, led to summer snow in the Northern Hemisphere and crop failures that drove up prices. Cotton, tobacco, and wheat prices soared, to the benefit of American farmers.

But domestic manufacturers fared less well. Britain, escaping the influence of mercantilism, was eager to resume trade with America, and Americans were eager to purchase many of the manufactured goods that they had gone without during the war. A flood of lower-priced British manufactured goods threatened the viability of the new domestic manufacturing industry. Manufacturers, mostly in the North, called on Congress for protection from foreign competition-induced low prices.[42] This protection, Treasury Secretary Dallas suggested, could take the form of a tariff that would raise the price of foreign manufactured goods by imposing a tax on them. A protective tariff, Dallas thought, would also help the government raise revenue to avoid budget deficits.

Many policy makers were sympathetic to this call, recognizing the importance of domestic manufacturing for reducing reliance on foreign nations and ensuring a supply of war industry products in the interest of national defense. Even Jefferson came to this opinion: "We must now place the manufacturer by the side of the agriculturist." He wrote: "Shall we make our own comforts, or go without them, at the will of a foreign nation? He, therefore, who is now against domestic manufacture, must be either for reducing us to dependence on that foreign nation, or to be clothed in skins, and to live like wild beasts in dens and caverns. I am not one of these; experience has taught me that manufactures are as necessary to our independence as to our comfort."[43] Farmers tended to oppose the tariff, preferring to enjoy lower-priced manufactured imports. They also likely recognized that trade partners could impose retaliatory tariffs, raising the prices abroad of American farm products and hurting their revenues. But enough Southern legislators eventually came to support a temporary tariff as a means of raising revenue that the Tariff Act of 1816 was passed.

The tariff became the first pillar of what Senator Henry Clay of Kentucky called the "American System," which aimed to promote American industry while reducing reliance on foreign nations. Tariff revenue would be used to support the second pillar, government investment in roads and canals to facilitate transportation of American goods around the country. The third pillar of the American System was a national bank. The Democratic-Republican Party, still the dominant party, had become more sympathetic to the idea of a national bank, which it had once so vigorously opposed. After the First Bank lost its charter, state-chartered banks had proliferated, making loans to people who wanted to buy land. The continued proliferation of state banks and the perception that they were contributing to speculation and inflation through their note issuance helped convince the Democratic-Republicans that a national bank was necessary. If banking was here to stay, they thought, it should at least be regulated to best protect the public interest.[44]

Thus, in April 1816, President Madison signed an act establishing the Second Bank of the United States, which opened in Philadelphia the next year. Reflecting republican values and designed to encourage westward expansion, the Second Bank had twenty-five branches (compared to eight for the First Bank) spread throughout the expanding country, with limited oversight from the headquarters in Philadelphia. The Second Bank, like the First Bank, acted as the federal government's fiscal agent, holding deposits of specie from the government's budget surpluses. This allowed the Second Bank, which was also a commercial bank, to make loans to businesses and individuals, putting its banknotes into circulation, and gave it an advantage over state banks, which issued their own banknotes but were not allowed to have branches or to hold the government's deposits.[45]

But the new Second Bank was not easily able to restrain the state banks or to contribute to price stability in its early years. William

Jones, the bank's first president, was a political appointee, with little experience in banking.[46] His first major task was to convince the state banks to resume specie redemption in order to limit their note issuance, rein in speculation, and reduce inflation. The state banks refused to resume redemption until the bank finally agreed to accept the state banks' greatly depreciated notes at face value. This weakened the bank's balance sheet while allowing the state banks to continue expanding credit.[47] Jones also had trouble restraining the note issuance of the bank's southern and western branches.

Thus, in the bank's first two years, the already-booming economy continued to expand and prices continued to rise. Continued credit expansion by the state banks and some branches of the Second Bank spurred investment in real estate, stoking higher land prices. The federal government also contributed to the boom through its increased construction expenditures and the sales of large tracts of land with liberal terms of credit in the Southwest and the Northwest.[48] In these boom years, the New York Stock exchange and the first US investment banks opened.[49] Motivated by high crop prices, farmers took on debt to finance farm improvement projects so that they could expand their production. But the precarious nature of the boom was revealed when the European harvest recovered in 1817. A bumper crop that year made it much more difficult for Americans to export their farm goods abroad, and prices plummeted. At the same time, as monetary and credit expansion continued, the public lost confidence in the ability of the state banks and the Second Bank to continue to redeem notes in specie.[50] Specie was valued at a premium over the Second Bank's notes and rapidly drained from the bank's vaults.

To complicate matters further, payments to foreign lenders for the Louisiana Purchase were due in late 1818 and early 1819 and had to be made in specie. As these dates approached, the bank was compelled to reverse its expansionary policies. To acquire specie, it brought its holdings of state banknotes to the state banks for redemption in specie. The state banks, to make the specie payments, had to quickly contract their loans and notes outstanding.

This severe contraction of the money supply precipitated the Panic of 1819, a widespread economic and banking crisis marked by severe price deflation. Many debtors, including farmers and land speculators, became insolvent and went bankrupt, and many businesses failed.[51] The deflation and recession led to increasing calls for protectionism, especially from states in the Midwest and West that grew farm products like wool, hemp, corn, wheat, and flax. Farmers in those states thought that higher duties on foreign rum and brandy, for example, could boost the demand for and prices of spirits distilled from domestic grains.[52] The strongest opposition to protectionism came from Southerners, who were averse to paying higher prices for manufactured goods and feared that England might tax American cotton in retaliation.[53] Regional tensions over tariff policies, as we will see, continued to intensify in coming years.

Despite the economic crisis, the bank and the American System did secure one victory in 1819, when the Supreme Court confirmed that Congress could incorporate a national bank. The *McCulloch v. Maryland* decision, delivered by Chief Justice John Marshall, broadened the interpretation of the necessary and proper clause, as well as the scope of the federal government's authority: "Let the end be legitimate, let it be within the scope of the constitution, and all means which are appropriate, which are plainly adapted to that end, which are not prohibited, but consist with the letter and spirit of the constitution, are constitutional."[54]

Price Convergence and Biddle's Bank

Price fluctuations, including the deflation of 1819, affected regions of the country in different ways because of their different exposures to the prices of agricultural and manufactured goods that they produced and consumed. It is also important to note that prices themselves varied across the regions, so price fluctuations could be more intense in some regions than in others. For example, prices along the Eastern Seaboard fell around 50 percent from 1816 to 1820 while prices in the West barely declined.[55] Regional price differences reflected the lack of uniform currency across the nation. Before the Second Bank was established, the currency in each region consisted of the notes issued by the state banks in that region, and the exchange rates between regions could fluctuate. This meant that prices could be substantially higher in some regions than in others, depending on the note issue of their state banks.[56]

This situation gradually changed in 1823, when the bank came under the leadership of Nicholas Biddle, a Philadelphia banker and intellectual. Biddle had supported Hamilton's plans for the First Bank and had served on the Second Bank's board of directors. He was, in some respects, like a modern central banker, asserting himself "not an active partisan, not even a party man—but a man in whom the Government would confide."[57] Under Biddle's leadership, the bank began more actively buying and selling state banknotes in exchange for specie to loosen or tighten money and credit conditions.[58] The bank also managed the interregional flow of funds to ensure the availability of its notes across the country, establishing a uniform national currency. Biddle's financial savvy in these operations has been widely recognized.[59] Not only was inflation avoided; prices also converged across regions.

Although the United States had become a monetary union, regional tensions remained, and even intensified, over the issue of protectionism. An act that raised tariff rates in 1824 passed Congress with support from the North and the West, both of which desired protection from cheap British manufactured goods, and opposition from the South.[60] Antagonism between the North and South only grew with the approach of the election of 1828, a race between President John Quincy Adams, a National Republican, and Democrat Andrew Jackson.

Democrats generally favored lower tariffs, but the Democratic senator Martin Van Buren, of New York, introduced an 1828 bill that would raise tariffs even higher. Van Buren expected the bill to be defeated, hurting Adams's reelection chances. He was counting on the fact that New Englanders would not support such high rates on goods that they imported. Unexpectedly, enough New Englanders voted for the bill that it did pass, and President Adams signed it into law.[61] Although Van Buren never intended for the Tariff of 1828 to pass, part of his aim was achieved because the tariff hurt President Adams's popularity, contributing to Jackson's victory. As the next chapter discusses, protectionism and the Second Bank were critical issues during Jackson's presidency, which shook the foundations of the American System.

THREE

THE JACKSONIAN ERA AND THE CIVIL WAR

> The paper system being founded on public confidence and having of itself no intrinsic value, it is liable to great and sudden fluctuations, thereby rendering property insecure and the wages of labor unsteady and uncertain. . . . These ebbs and flows in the currency and these indiscreet extensions of credit naturally engender a spirit of speculation injurious to the habits and character of the people.
>
> ANDREW JACKSON, "Farewell Address"[1]

The Bank War and the Nullification Crisis

The period from 1828 through roughly 1850 is often called the Jacksonian era or the Age of the Common Man. During this time, franchise was extended to all adult white men, without property requirements. Much like the Jeffersonians before them, Jacksonian Democrats hoped to see the West settled by yeoman farmers and were skeptical of a strong central government that could create corporate monopolies and favored the rich.[2]

Jackson distrusted banks in general and the Second Bank in particular. He thought that the bank threatened democracy by putting too much power in the hands of a few private citizens without enough oversight from Congress and the president.[3] Thus, although the Second Bank of the United States was not a major issue in the 1828 campaign, it became one soon after. In his first annual message to Congress in 1829, Jackson referred to the 1836 expiration of the bank's charter and asserted, "Both the constitutionality and the expediency of the law creating this bank are well questioned by a large portion of our fellow citizens, and it must be admitted by all that it has failed in the great end of establishing an uniform and sound currency."[4]

In the face of Jackson's antagonism, Biddle launched a nationwide public opinion campaign, transmitting articles, pamphlets, and petitions in support of the bank around the country.[5] Biddle found support from the National Republicans, who had fractured from the Democratic-Republicans around the time of the 1824 election. Their leader, Senator Clay, convinced Biddle to seek an early recharter before the election of 1832. The bank was popular enough that Clay bet that Jackson would not veto a recharter before the election—but Clay bet wrong. On July 10, 1832, Jackson vetoed a bill that would have extended the charter by fifteen years, declaring the bank "unauthorized by the Constitution, subversive to the rights of States, and dangerous to the liberties of the people." Of course, the Supreme Court had already ruled that the bank was constitutional, but Jackson argued that "each public officer who takes an oath to support the Constitution swears that he will support it as he understands it, and not as it is understood by others."[6]

The so-called Bank War intensified after Jackson defeated Clay in the 1832 election. In 1833, Jackson, against the wishes of most of his cabinet and Congress, removed the government's deposits from the bank, redistributing the funds from the government's surplus to various state "pet banks." Explaining the deposit removal to his cabinet, Jackson argued that the bank had "gradually increased in strength from the days of its establishment. The question between it and the people is one of power. . . . The Bank has by degrees obtained almost entire dominion over the circulating medium, and with it, power to increase or diminish the price of property and to levy taxes on the people in the shape of premiums and interest to an amount only limited by the quantity of paper currency it is enabled to issue."[7]

The deposit removal spelled the beginning of the end for the Second Bank, for it ended the bank's ability to regulate the state banks' note issuance. To many in Jackson' cabinet and in Congress, it seemed like an extreme, even tyrannical, action on the part of the president, just when tensions over federal government overreach were at a peak surrounding the nullification crisis.

The nullification crisis was a dramatic episode in which tensions between state and federal authority almost led to civil war. It began when Vice President John Calhoun, a strong supporter of states' rights, penned the South Carolina Exposition and Protest, arguing that states had the right to reject unjust or unconstitutional laws, like the Tariff of 1828: "The whole system of legislation imposing duties on imports, not for revenue, but for the protection of one branch of industry, at the expense of others, is unconstitutional, unequal and oppressive; calculated to corrupt the public morals, and to destroy the liberty of the country."[8]

Recall that high tariffs were a response to Northern manufacturers' desire for protection from the low prices of their foreign competitors. Southerners tended to dislike high tariffs that raised the prices they paid for manufactured goods and wanted to avoid retaliatory tariffs on the agricultural products they exported. Congress passed a new tariff bill in 1832 with only slightly lower rates. Unsatisfied, the South Carolinians issued the Order of Nullification of the Tariffs of 1828 and 1832. Shortly after, Calhoun resigned as vice president and became a senator representing South Carolina.

President Jackson proclaimed the nullification unconstitutional.[9] In March 1833, Congress passed the Force Bill, which authorized the president to deploy the army to force South Carolina's compliance with federal tariff law. At the same time, Congress passed a compromise tariff, which scheduled a gradual reduction of tariffs back to their 1816 rates, in the hopes that civil war could be averted. The South Carolinians considered the compromise tariff a victory, and military intervention was avoided. Although the compromise tariff ended the immediate crisis, it did not settle the issue about the legitimacy of secession or how to resolve disputes between the federal government and the states. When disputes about slavery arose in the coming years, they would, of course, lead to civil war.

Hard Money and the Independent Treasury

Jackson had weakened the bank when he removed the government's deposits. But the bank had a few years remaining before its charter expired, and its notes continued to circulate as currency. Jackson and his supporters wanted to further weaken the bank and institute a system of hard money in the United States. The "hard-money men" seemed to think that by promoting the use of gold coins, rather than paper money, the government could protect people from the evils of inflation.[10] Jackson later proclaimed that it was the duty of every government, but "more especially the duty of the United States, where the Government is emphatically the Government of the people," to shield "the class of society least able to bear it" from paper money's "impositions of avarice and fraud."[11]

To promote the use of gold money, the hard-money men relied on Gresham's law. Recall that the Coinage Act of 1792 had set a ratio of 15 to 1 between the value of gold and the value of silver. This ratio overvalued silver and undervalued gold, so gold coins could not be kept in circulation; they were worth more as metal than as coins. Jackson thought that changing the ratio to 16 to 1 would allow gold coins to supplant the use of banknotes, steadying prices and further weakening the bank. An editorial in the pro-Jackson *Washington Globe* explained that Jackson hoped that "a law changing the standard value of gold" would "place our currency beyond the reach of those fluctuations which are now so much complained of."[12]

Another *Globe* editorial argued that "a gold currency alone can circumscribe, and hold in check, the issues of Bank paper" and would allow the United States, with its own gold mines, to "supply our own NATIONAL CURRENCY. . . . Less than 16 to 1 will not do this. Here then will be the battle ground between the paper men and the hard money men, and every friend to gold should understand the point, and march up to it."[13] The hard-money men won this battle when the Coinage Act of 1834 adjusted the legal ratio of gold to silver to 16 to 1, overvaluing gold relative to the markets. As intended, people preferred to use gold coins and to export silver.[14]

Jackson's victory over the bank was sealed in 1836 when the Democrat-led House of Representatives voted not to recharter the bank and to leave the federal deposits in the state banks, kicking off the period that is now called the free banking era. Jackson later contended that, had the bank not been defeated, "the Government would have passed from the hands of the many to the hands of the few. . . . The distress and sufferings inflicted on the people by the bank are some of the fruits of that system of policy which is continually striving to enlarge the authority of the Federal Government beyond the limits fixed by the Constitution."[15]

But the hard-money men did not succeed in their aim of stabilizing prices. In fact, the whole period from Jackson's veto of the charter renewal to 1836 was characterized by monetary expansion and high inflation, with wholesale commodity prices rising by around 50 percent over those four years.[16] The price of cotton, still the primary US export, rose from about ten cents per pound in 1832 to sixteen cents per pound in 1836, and land prices also began rising.[17] The rising prices resulted from monetary expansion. Without the Second Bank's regulatory influence, state banks were able to expand their note issuance and reduce their specie reserves. Banks on the western frontier could do more lending, fueling the land boom.[18] Monetary expansion also stemmed from increased inflows of silver from Mexico, an indirect result of the growing sales of opium from Great Britain to China.[19]

It is worth noting that price controls were not even considered during the inflation that followed the Bank War, so antithetical were they to the laissez-faire ideology of the Jacksonians and so negative was the memory of price controls in the American Revolution. This distaste for controls, we will see later in this chapter, also meant that they were not imposed during the Civil War. Instead, to counter inflation in land prices, Jackson issued an executive order, the Specie Circular, on July 11, 1836. The order required that payment for the purchase of public lands be made exclusively in gold or silver. This aimed to reduce note issuance by western banks and to restrain rising land prices by making it harder for speculators to raise specie to make land purchases.[20]

The Specie Circular did not immediately curb land speculation; land sales continued at a high rate in the last quarter of 1836 and the first quarter of 1837. But the Specie Circular did contribute to a flow of specie away from the New York City commercial center and to the west, as land speculators needed gold to purchase land. By March 1837, newspapers were reporting on the troubling shortage of specie in the New York banks. Bankers, merchants, and the press urged newly elected president Martin Van Buren, formerly Jackson's vice president, to repeal the Specie Circular in order to resolve the westward specie drain and allow the land boom to continue.[21]

President Van Buren's decision not to repeal the Specie Circular helped spark the Panic of 1837. When the New York banks realized that specie flows would not be reversed, they suspended the convertibility of their notes to specie, and other banks soon followed, propagating a widespread banking panic and credit contraction. Land prices began to decline as specie became more difficult to acquire. The situation was exacerbated by declining global cotton prices, which hurt American farmers and further depressed land prices.[22]

The Panic of 1837 made President Van Buren highly skeptical of the state banks, which he held to blame for the recent destructive price fluctuations, including the land boom and bust. The Treasury's connection to the banks, he argued, "stimulates a general rashness of enterprise, and aggravates the fluctuations of commerce and the currency."[23] The president believed that the Treasury's reliance on the banks for holding its deposits not only contributed to price fluctuations but also lacked constitutional legitimacy. He explained that the relationship between the Treasury and the banks was "forced on the Treasury by early necessities . . . but these causes have long since passed away. We have no emergencies that make banks necessary to aid the wants of the Treasury."[24]

Van Buren was influenced by the writings of William Gouge, who had for several years advocated an "independent Treasury" arrangement.[25] He thought that the Treasury should manage the government's funds, held exclusively in specie, independently of the banking system. Gouge was a Philadelphia journalist and Treasury employee who, as a great fan of Adam Smith, believed that prices were "much better regulated by free competition than . . . by governmental enactments."[26] In the Panic of 1837, seeing an opportunity to gain support for his idea, he quickly published *An Inquiry into the Expediency of Dispensing with Bank Agency and Bank Paper in the Fiscal Concerns of the United States* to relatively wide acclaim.[27]

When Congress debated the independent Treasury proposal, Congressman Isaac Toucey, of Connecticut, accused the banks of having caused "a great and rapid expansion of prices" and of leaving the currency "inflated, false, and hollow, ready to explode at the slightest shock." This bank-produced inflation, he argued, was "one of the greatest calamities which can befall a people, because it reaches every individual in the country. No one so humble, no one so exalted, as not to taste its bitter fruits. . . . The value of every man's property is unsettled, every contract is changed, and every human being in the land is visited with injustice, fraud, and robbery, under the forms of law."[28] Despite Toucey's advocacy, the independent Treasury proposal was blocked by conservative Democrats and by the Whigs, a new party composed of National Republicans and other bank supporters. Democrats who supported the Independent Treasury proposal, mostly based in New York, were known as Locofocos.[29]

But the proposal gained more support when, after a brief period of economic recovery, another banking panic occurred in late 1839, and state banks again suspended specie payments, kicking off the start of a long and deflationary depression that would last until 1843.[30] The independent Treasury bill passed in June 1840, and President Van Buren waited to sign it on the symbolic date of July 4.

The independent Treasury had a shaky start. When President Van Buren lost to the Whig candidate, William Henry Harrison, in the 1840 election, the Whigs repealed the independent Treasury bill and pushed for a new national bank. This push was led by Senator Henry Clay, who had been Nicholas Biddle's ally at the Second Bank. When Harrison died of pneumonia only a month into his presidency, Vice President John Tyler became president. Tyler's political views were quite different from those of Harrison and the other Whigs. A strict constructionist, he disagreed with the constitutionality of a national bank and vetoed two national bank bills, causing the Whigs to expel him from the party.[31] President Tyler's successor, Jacksonian Democrat James Polk, of Tennessee, made revival of the independent Treasury one of his top policy priorities, achieved with the passage of the Independent Treasury Act of 1846.

The Gold Rush and Westward Expansion

President Polk reinstituted the independent Treasury just as the country was entering the Mexican-American War, pursuing further territorial expansion after the annexation of Texas. Polk also signed the Walker Tariff, named for Treasury Secretary Robert Walker, reducing tariff rates. The independent Treasury and the tariff reduction limited the government's options for financing the Mexican-American War, as tariff revenues were limited and the Treasury could not resort to inflationary finance as easily as it had during the War of 1812. Instead, the war was funded mainly by borrowing. High foreign demand and prices for American agricultural exports also helped, as more specie flowed into the United States, making it easier for Americans to pay taxes in specie.[32]

With the 1848 Treaty of Guadalupe Hidalgo, which ended the Mexican-American War, Mexico ceded Alta California and other parts of its northern territory to the United States. The discovery of gold in California then catalyzed more rapid westward expansion and a California population boom but exacerbated political and sectional tensions regarding the status of slavery in new states and territories, especially when California was admitted to the Union.[33] The gold rush also led to major economic changes. Gold discoveries in California and Australia together more than quadrupled annual gold production worldwide, increasing the money supply and prices. Wholesale prices increased by around 30 percent from 1850 to 1855.[34] Moreover, the increased supply of gold reduced its commodity price, so that gold became overvalued and silver undervalued by the legal ratio of 16 to 1 established by the Coinage Act of 1834.[35] Thus, as Gresham's law set in—that is, bad money drove out good—silver coins were melted down and sold for bullion, making it difficult for businesses to obtain change. Small-denomination coins became so scarce that hordes of people bought stamps from New York City post offices just to receive small silver coins as change.[36]

Legislators debated a variety of proposals to stem the outflow of silver by reducing the silver content of silver coins worth less than one dollar. Doing so would convert them into fiduciary coins, a commodity worth less than face value. Such proposals sat uneasily with many congressmen. The congressman and future president Andrew Johnson, for example, considered proposals to lower the silver content of subsidiary coins "the merest quackery."[37]

These congressmen held the metallist view, in which money derives its value from the value of the commodity it is made of.[38] Under metallism, coinage is "only the certification of value already existing in the gold or silver."[39] Metallism supports a hard constraint on the money supply, which limits price increases but also constrains the government's ability to use monetary policy for its own purposes. In the contrasting chartalist view, which is more accepting of state issuance of fiat currency, "money is a creature of law."[40] Metallist predilections had led Congress to resist at least eleven different fiduciary coinage proposals since 1800.[41] This long run of resistance ended in 1851, when Congress approved a new three-cent coin, or trime, made of three parts silver to one part copper. The metal in the trime was worth considerably less than the trime's face value. The trime was not general legal tender but could be used to purchase postage stamps.[42] The trime held "public favor," according to the director of the Mint, and it brought partial relief in the small coin shortage.[43]

Congress continued to debate proposals to reduce the silver content of coins. Befitting his Jacksonian views, Representative Johnson was the most outspoken critic of these proposals, exclaiming that "of all the problems that have come up for solution from the time of the alchemists down to the present time, none can compare with that solved by this modern American Congress, they alone, have discovered that they can make money."[44] He claimed that the government had no legitimate authority to reduce the silver content of coins because doing so would violate natural law:

> Let us see how this thing will work in practice. Here is a dollar. Do you talk about fixing the value of that? It is an absurdity. A man has a dollar to-day, containing four hundred and twelve and a half grains of silver. He goes into market and purchases a bushel of corn, containing so much nutriment, indispensable to the existence of man. To-morrow he again goes into market, but cannot get more than half a bushel for his dollar. Now where is the power to fix the value of that dollar? Do you not see that it is with the commercial world? Do you not see that the natural laws which regulate commerce, determine the value?[45]

Against these objections, the Senate Finance Committee passed the Coinage Act of 1853, reducing the silver weight of all subsidiary silver coins by 6.91 percent and making them legal tender in all transactions up to five dollars. The silver content of the silver dollar was unchanged. In 1853, $100 of the new subsidiary coins were worth $97.09 as a commodity.[46] As intended, the new coins passed quickly into circulation and were widely used.[47]

After the Coinage Act, sectional tensions continued to build. The Kansas-Nebraska Act of 1854 created two new territories, Kansas and Nebraska, whose constituents would choose their slave or free territory status by popular sovereignty. The act repealed the Missouri Compromise of 1820, which did not permit the area that is now Nebraska to become a slave territory.[48] Amid the political turmoil that followed the repeal, antislavery Whigs formed the Republican Party in 1854, whereas proslavery Whigs joined the Democrats.

Despite growing political unrest, westward migration continued. This was encouraged by rising wheat prices, as the Crimean War, from 1853 to 1856, disrupted Russian grain exports to Europe, increasing the demand for American wheat. Another land boom began as farmers took on large debts, counting on continued high grain prices to help them make repayments.[49] At the same time, "railroad fever" swept the county in the spring of 1857 as investors began to purchase railroad bonds and stocks, expecting high railroad profitability to accompany westward expansion.[50]

But with the end of the Crimean War, Europe's reliance on American grain decreased, and so did grain and land prices. And by the summer of 1857, confidence in railroad profitability began to falter, partly due to political uncertainties surrounding the slavery question. As railroad stocks depreciated and westward immigration slowed, several railroad companies defaulted or went bankrupt, and Ohio Life Insurance and Trust Company, which was heavily exposed to the western railroads, collapsed.[51] Perceiving an increase in bank risk, investors began converting banknotes into specie. Banks struggled to maintain sufficient reserves and eventually suspended convertibility of their notes into specie, enraging merchants, politicians, and journalists.[52]

Low grain prices continued for the next two years. Western farmers and the northwestern railroad companies were hit hardest, as they earned most of their revenues from transporting western grains. The recession also hurt eastern industrialists because western farmers could no longer afford their wares. Some industrialists accused western farmers of contributing to financial distress by withholding their crops from the market as they waited for prices to rebound. "FARMERS! Sell your Grain and pay your Debts," urged a Milwaukee newspaper.[53] The impact was much milder in the South, where cotton and tobacco prices fell but then rebounded quickly.[54] The railroads in the South, which hauled cotton, fared much better than their counterparts in the Northwest. The differences in regional exposure to the price declines contributed to regional and partisan differences in the desired political response. Republicans saw the panic as proof that greater protectionism was necessary for farmers to get higher prices in domestic markets and not rely on demand from abroad. Southern Democrats remained opposed to protectionist tariffs and instead, in Jacksonian fashion, placed the blame on the imprudence of the banks.

In Democrat James Buchanan's 1857 State of the Union address, he chastised the state banks for suspending convertibility, arguing that they owed a duty to the public "to keep in their vaults a sufficient amount of gold and silver to insure the convertibility of their notes into coin at all times and under all circumstances."[55] Buchanan's Jacksonian influences were evident when he argued that the Framers of the Constitution "supposed they had protected the people against the evils of an excessive and irredeemable paper currency. . . . It is one of the highest and most responsible duties of Government to insure to the people a sound circulating medium."[56] He went on to criticize the "paper system of extravagant expansion" for "raising the nominal price of every article far beyond its real value when compared with the cost of similar articles in countries whose circulation is wisely regulated," reducing the United States' competitiveness in foreign markets.

Buchanan also echoed Jackson in his appeal to American exceptionalism, proclaiming, "No other nation has ever existed which could have endured such violent expansions and contractions of paper credits without lasting injury; yet the buoyancy of youth, the energies of our population, and the spirit which never quails before difficulties will enable us soon to recover from our present financial embarrassments."[57] The relative mildness of the panic, when compared to those in 1837 and 1819, Buchanan attributed to the independent Treasury: "Thanks to the independent treasury, the government has not suspended payments, as it was compelled to do by the failure of the banks in 1837. It will continue to discharge its liabilities to the people in gold and silver. Its disbursements in coin pass into circulation and materially assist in restoring a sound currency."[58]

Greenbacks in the Civil War

President Buchanan, tremendously unpopular for his handling of slavery and secession, chose not to run for reelection in 1860. After Abraham Lincoln's victory and before his inauguration, the Morrill Tariff of 1861 raised tariff rates substantially, in line with the Republican Party platform. At that time, the government relied on tariff revenues and on high-interest private bank loans to finance its operations, but the increased threat of Southern secession made it more difficult for the federal government to raise funding in the bond market.

When the Civil War began, Congress saw that borrowing would not be sufficient to finance the war effort. Much as in the War of 1812, Congress sought to use note issuance to meet wartime needs. In July 1861, the first issue of non-interest-bearing Treasury notes, called demand notes, were authorized in denominations of ten to fifty dollars. They could be redeemed for specie at assistant treasurers' offices in several locations. A subsequent act allowed denominations as small as five dollars and made the notes receivable in payment of all public dues. Thus, the demand notes were similar to the later notes issued in the War of 1812 in that they were partial legal tender, came in smaller denominations, and bore no interest. For a time, the notes circulated widely among the public at face value (known as *par*), and banks were willing to redeem the notes for coinage.[59]

By the start of 1862, however, with war expenditures exceeding projections and revenues falling short, the government could not obtain adequate supplies of specie to continue redeeming notes on demand. The Union suspended specie redemption, and the state banks also suspended specie redemption of their own banknotes.

Congress intensely debated a Republican proposal to authorize the issue of paper money, not backed by gold or silver, with legal tender status for public and private payments. The proposal shocked Treasury Secretary Salmon Chase and most members of Congress, who still held hard-money convictions.[60]

Secretary Chase, however, quickly came to support the legal tender proposal on grounds of necessity, urging, "The Treasury is nearly empty."[61] Supporters of the proposal argued that Article 1, Section 8 of the Constitution grants Congress the power to raise and support armies and maintain a navy. Issuing fiat currency is a power not explicitly denied to the federal government by the Constitution, as Article 1, Section 10 only prevents the states from making anything but gold or silver coin legal tender. Therefore, because legal tender paper money was necessary for supporting the army, the necessary and proper clause allowed Congress to issue it. Opponents of the proposal disagreed with this interpretation, arguing on the basis of the Tenth Amendment that Congress could assume only explicitly enumerated powers. Others argued that legal tender paper money was not in fact necessary for supporting the army, as sufficient revenue could be raised through taxes and borrowing.[62]

Opposition also centered on the immense inflation that would likely occur with paper money, as "inevitably there would follow bloated currency, high prices, extravagant speculation, enormous sudden fortunes, immense factitious wealth, and general insanity."[63] Of course, for certain interest groups, inflation caused by the issuance of paper money was a welcome prospect. Iron and steel interests thought the declining value of the dollar would encourage the sale of their exports, and railroad interests saw that inflation could erode the real value of their large outstanding debts.[64]

Appeals to necessity prevailed, and Congress passed the Legal Tender Act of 1862, permitting an emission of $150 million in Treasury notes called *greenbacks*. Shortly after, the Second and Third Legal Tender Acts of 1862 and 1863 expanded the limit for greenback emissions to $450 million. Lincoln supported the greenbacks. Still, when his cabinet discussed adding "In God We Trust"—

then engraved on US coins—to the greenbacks, Lincoln reportedly quipped, "If you are going to put a legend on the greenbacks, I would suggest that of Peter and Paul, 'Silver and gold I have none, but such as I have I give to thee.'"[65]

Lincoln's support for the greenbacks was part of his broader vision of "the privilege of creating and issuing money" as "the Government's greatest creative opportunity."[66] In fact, as early as 1832, Lincoln proclaimed himself "in favor of a national bank," as he believed that economic performance under the First and Second National Banks was superior to performance in times without a national bank.[67] As president, he continued to support some form of national banking system, arguing that "the financing of all public enterprises, the maintenance of stable government and ordered progress, and the conduct of the Treasury will become matters of practical administration. The people can and will be furnished with a currency as safe as their own government. Money will cease to be the master and become the servant of humanity. Democracy will rise superior to the money power."[68]

Lincoln's aspirations for a national banking system became more politically feasible with the secession of the heavily Democratic Southern states.[69] The National Banking Acts of 1863 and 1864 established a nationalized bank chartering system and a system of national banks to facilitate the administration of a uniform national currency. National banks could issue paper notes printed by the government in proportion to the federal government bonds they deposited with the comptroller of the currency at the Treasury. The paper notes were redeemable in gold or silver coin or greenbacks, which remained legal tender. If an issuing bank were unable to redeem notes on demand, the government could sell the bonds that the bank had deposited at the Treasury to pay off the noteholders. President Lincoln claimed that this system would "protect the people against losses in the use of paper money."[70]

In the first years of the system, national banknotes were not actively redeemed for specie but rather circulated nearly indefinitely and held by banks virtually interchangeably with specie and greenbacks.[71] This meant that an increase in national banknote issuance would have a similar impact on the money supply and inflation as an increase in greenbacks. To address concerns that excess note issuance would lead to inflation, a tax was imposed on state banks' notes, driving the state banks out of note issuance, and a ceiling was placed on the total national banknotes that could be issued. This ceiling, which remained in place until 1875, meant that note issue had to be rationed among banks in different regions, leading to complaints that insufficient allotment restricted the establishment of new banks in some regions.[72]

As the war progressed and the monetary base expanded, greenbacks declined in value relative to gold: the gold price of $20.67 per ounce that had prevailed since 1834 increased to more than $40 per ounce in 1864.[73] News about the war affected the exchange rate between greenbacks and gold dollars by changing expectations about the probability and timing of resumed specie convertibility.[74] For example, news of a Union battle victory would increase the probability of quick resumption, raising the relative value of greenbacks. War news also affected the price of Confederate graybacks, which depreciated much more severely, leading to hyperinflation in the South.[75]

Official price indexes and inflation statistics were not recorded at the time—their development, as will be discussed later, was still in progress. But Secretary Chase himself published some simple averages of prices, likely intending to show that inflation in the North was not as extreme as critics claimed.[76] Official price indexes constructed retrospectively suggest that inflation was around 20 percent to 30 percent per year from 1862 to 1864.[77] Again, the wartime inflation did not lead to a resort to comprehensive price controls, as laissez-faire ideology and the memory of ineffective controls during the Revolution were still strong.[78]

The Legal Tender Acts and wartime inflation ignited a debate about contract jurisprudence and state rights, especially in the western states like California, which did not use paper currency before the war.[79] Businesspeople in these states resisted the requirement that greenbacks be made legal tender for the repayment of debts, as creditors expecting to be repaid in gold preferred not to be repaid in depreciated paper currency.[80] Even California farmers, who sold their grain surplus to England, wanted to continue using gold currency, which had kept the exchange rate and grain prices stable for the prior decade.[81] An article in California's *Daily Alta* newspaper read: "The people desire no currency save gold. This is shown by the fact that while there is nothing in our laws to prevent the circulation of greenbacks with all the facilities allowed to gold, yet the metal is universally preferred, and no contracts, or none worthy of note, are made payable in paper, except in a few official cases where gold contracts cannot be enforced under the laws."[82]

California's Specific Contract Act of 1863 required that if a written contract specified that payment must be made in a particular commodity, the obligation could be satisfied only through delivery of that commodity. When the California Supreme Court upheld the law in 1864, Justice John Currey wrote that if a debtor "contracts to pay his debt in a particular kind of money, his obligation cannot be discharged in accordance with his stipulation by payment in a different kind of money."[83] Currey argued that the moral obligation to discharge debt in the specified commodity is especially pressing when paper money's worth relative to the commodity is difficult to estimate, as was the case with a "fluctuating medium of exchange" like greenbacks, which posed a constant "specter of inflation."[84]

Thus, the government held—to the dismay of Treasury Secretary Chase—that even if the national government made a currency legal tender, it could not require that the legal tender satisfy every contract. The California legislature recognized how its refusal to comply with the full extent of the Legal Tender Acts put it in conflict with the federal government. One legislator remarked: "I believe we shall have to do one of two things, either accept the national currency as money, and make it the basis of California, or secede from the Union. We cannot continue to live under the present state of affairs, repudiating the government's currency, its life blood, and pretending at the same time to be loyal."[85] Luckily, the end of the war reduced the government's reliance on greenbacks before the foundations of federalism could crumble.

Contraction and the Legal Tender Cases

When the Civil War ended, the major changes that it brought to the monetary system—greenbacks and national banking—remained in place. Greenbacks continued to circulate at a floating exchange rate with gold. Treasury Secretary Hugh McCulloch, who saw the greenbacks as an emergency measure justified only in wartime, sought approval from Congress to retire them from circulation. With the support of President Andrew Johnson, Secretary McCulloch proposed a bill to convert some greenbacks into interest-bearing notes redeemable in coin. This Contraction Act passed in 1866 with strong public support, and for a time, greenbacks were aggressively withdrawn, reducing the monetary base by around 20 percent from 1865 to 1867, resulting in sharp price deflation.[86] This deflation was intentional—Congress wanted to reduce the price level to its prewar levels to facilitate a return to a specie standard at prewar specie prices.

But deflation was unpopular, especially among farmers and other debtors, because deflation increased the real value of their debts. Thus, in his first inaugural address in 1869, President Ulysses S. Grant, a Republican who had served as commanding general of the Union Army, announced his intention to "return to a specie basis as soon as it can be accomplished without material detriment to the debtor class or to the country at large"—that is, without too rapid a deflation.[87] The Public Credit Act of 1869 pledged that the government would repay its debt in specie within ten years; the long time line was designed to allow a smooth and gradual decline in prices.[88]

The same year, the constitutionality of the Legal Tender Act came before the Supreme Court. In *Hepburn v. Griswold*, Chief Justice Chase (the former secretary of the Treasury) held for a 5–3 majority that the Legal Tender Act violated the Fifth Amendment's due process clause, which states that no person shall "be deprived of life, liberty, or property, without due process of law." Chase noted that "an act making mere promises to pay dollars a legal tender in payment of debts previously contracted, is not a means appropriate, plainly adapted, really calculated to carry into effect any express power vested in Congress; that such an act is inconsistent with the spirit of the Constitution; and that it is prohibited by the Constitution."[89] Notice that Chase did not argue that Congress lacked the authority to issue paper money. Rather, he ruled that the notes could not be made legal tender for *preexisting* debts.

Shortly after the *Hepburn* decision, one of the justices in the majority resigned, giving President Grant the opportunity to make two appointments, one to replace this new vacancy and another to fill an already-existing vacancy. The new justices were Republicans who supported the full legal tender provisions.[90] This shift in the balance of the Court enabled *Hepburn* to be overturned when the legal tender question was retried the next year in *Knox v. Lee* and *Parker v. Davis.*[91] Later, *Juilliard v. Greenman* would uphold the constitutionality of the Legal Tender Acts more broadly, authorizing Congress to issue greenbacks even outside of wartime.[92]

The majority in *Knox* quoted Chief Justice Marshall's famous "let the end be legitimate" language in *McCulloch v. Maryland.* To reach the conclusion that "the legal tender acts were an appropriate means for carrying into execution the legitimate powers of the government," the majority noted that "Congress was called upon to devise means for maintaining the army and navy, for securing the large supplies of money needed, and, indeed, for the preservation of the government created by the Constitution. It was at such a time and in such an emergency that the legal tender acts were passed."[93]

The Court also addressed the argument that the legal tender acts were not necessary, as some other means might accomplish the same ends. They wrote: "Admitting [that fact] to be true, what does it prove? Nothing more than that Congress had the choice of means for a legitimate end, each appropriate, and adapted to that end, though, perhaps, in different degrees. What then? Can this court say that it ought to have adopted one rather than the other?" Here again, the Court quoted Chief Justice Marshall in *McCulloch*, insisting that the Court not "tread on legislative ground" by telling Congress how to choose among alternative appropriate means to an end.[94]

Supporters of the greenback referred to it as a wartime hero, as in the following ballad, published in the *New York Tribune*:

> O, Greenback, veteran of the years!
> Thou crippled soldier of the war!
> Baptized with blood and wet with tears.
> To-day thou art without a scar.[95]

But neither public sentiment nor the Legal Tender Cases changed the fact that the Grant administration and Congress wished to return to a specie basis. As the next chapter describes, there was disagreement as to what sort of specie basis the country return to: gold, silver, or bimetallism.

FOUR

THE MONEY QUESTION IN THE POSTBELLUM ERA

> You come to us and tell us that the great cities are in favor of the gold standard; we reply that the great cities rest upon our broad and fertile prairies. Burn down your cities and leave our farms, and your cities will spring up again as if by magic; but destroy our farms and the grass will grow in the streets of every city in the country.[1]
>
> WILLIAM JENNINGS BRYAN, "Cross of Gold"

The Grange Movement and the Crime of 1873

During the Civil War, the issuance of greenbacks and their subsequent contraction resulted in a major inflation followed by deflation. These price fluctuations affected the relative positions of creditors and debtors, especially farmers. Crop prices fell not only because of monetary contraction but also because of the increased production of crops as young men returned to their farms after the war.[2]

In 1867, the postwar deflation led Minnesota farmer Oliver Hudson Kelley to found the National Grange, a fraternal organization devoted to the improvement of agricultural conditions.[3] Membership in the Grange movement exploded as deflation continued over the next decades; deflation averaged around 1.7 percent per year from 1873 to 1896.[4] Grangers lobbied Congress and state legislatures for policies to relieve farmers from their financial difficulties. As I discuss in this chapter, three types of policy approaches were proposed for dealing with the deflation: monetary policies, regulatory policies, and fiscal (tariff) policies.

Deflation was most severe in the years following the banking panic and major changes to the monetary system in 1873. Under the bimetallic standard established by Hamilton's Coinage Act of 1792, there was free coinage of both gold and silver. Free coinage meant that the US Mint would convert any specie that individuals brought to the Mint into legal tender currency.[5] After the Coinage Act of 1853, private depositors could have their silver struck only into silver dollars; free coinage of smaller denomination silver coins was not permitted. When the Coinage Act of 1873 listed the types of coins that could be minted, the silver dollar was omitted, effectively ending the free coinage of silver. This demonetized silver and put the United States on a de facto gold standard.

Many other countries, including Germany, France, Italy, Belgium, Switzerland, Denmark, Norway, Sweden, the Netherlands, and Russia had also switched to a gold standard following Britain's leadership. India and China were the only major countries on a silver standard by the end of the 1870s. This shift to an international gold standard increased worldwide demand for gold for monetary purposes.[6] At the same time, the growth of the world's gold stock slowed. Gold became scarcer relative to the growing output of goods and services, which contributed to falling prices.[7]

The Coinage Act of 1873 became known as the Crime of '73 by proponents of bimetallism, including western silver miners. Even many members of Congress had voted for the act without realizing that it would effectively demonetize silver and later criticized it. Farmers, who suffered most from the deflationary reduction in the money supply, "were particularly susceptible to propaganda representing the 'crime of '73' as the evil machinations of a cabal of eastern and foreign capitalists: Wall Street versus Main Street."[8]

Farmers and silver producers pushed for more expansionary

monetary policy to counter the Crime of '73. The platform of the newly formed Greenback-Labor Party called for currency expansion via free coinage of silver or a return to greenbacks. By 1878, Congress was nearly evenly divided between supporters and opponents of currency expansion. The Greenback-Labor Party held fourteen seats in Congress, and Democrats partially supported the Greenback movement. Although Lincoln, a Republican president, had supported the greenbacks, the Republican Party came to champion the gold standard. As a compromise, the Bland-Allison Act of 1878 allowed limited resumption of silver dollar coinage and required the government to purchase a minimum amount of silver bullion at market price each month. These minimum purchases of silver, however, were not enough to reverse the decline in silver prices or to greatly expand currency in circulation.[9]

Farmers also sought nonmonetary solutions to their problems. A particular subject of the Grangers' ire were the railroad companies, which were heavily entangled in the Panic of 1873. The panic followed a similar pattern to those of 1819 and 1837. Before the panic, land prices were rising and the railroad industry was expanding rapidly, with thirty-three thousand miles of new track laid between 1868 and 1873; speculators invested in both land and railroad stock.[10] This boom likewise ended in a bust, which had a number of causes, including financial distress in Europe. In the United States, the precipitating event was the failure of Jay Cooke & Company, an important bank that was heavily invested in the railroads. As investors began to sell of their railroad investments, many railroad companies were driven to bankruptcy.[11]

The surviving railroad companies had substantial pricing power. Farmers, who relied on the railroads to transport their goods to market, were angered by seemingly extortionate rail prices on routes served by only one rail company, without alternative transportation by water. Even on routes served by multiple carriers, price-fixing arrangements in which carriers coordinated to raise prices were common.[12] Farmers despised the "robber baron" railroad men and their oligopoly, and they wanted lower, more stable rail rates.

In response to the demands of the Grange movement, state legislatures in Minnesota, Iowa, Wisconsin, and Illinois passed "Granger laws," setting maximum prices for railroads and grain elevator companies. The Grangers also wanted Congress to pass federal regulation on railroad prices. The state legislation, and the prospect of federal legislation, raised a number of constitutional issues.

Price Regulation, Interstate Commerce, and Antitrust

The constitutionality of the state Granger laws was questioned on two grounds: first, that they violated due process, and second, that they interfered with Congress's power to regulate interstate commerce. Recall that the interpretation of the Fifth Amendment's due process clause was at stake in the Legal Tender Cases. The due process clause of the Fifth Amendment applied only to the federal government. The Fourteenth Amendment, adopted in 1868, also restricted state governments from depriving people of life, liberty, or property without due process. The commerce clause—Article I, Section 8, Clause 3 of the Constitution—gives Congress the power to "Regulate Commerce with foreign Nations, and among the several States."

The constitutionality of the price controls imposed by the Illinois Granger laws was upheld in 1877 in the Supreme Court case *Munn v. Illinois.*[13] The Court considered whether the Granger law interfered with Congress's power to regulate interstate commerce and determined that it did not. The Court also determined that the state regulation of private grain warehousers did not violate the due process clause:

> Under the powers inherent in every sovereignty, a government may regulate the conduct of its citizens toward each other, and, when necessary for the public good, the manner in which each shall use his own property. It has, in the exercise of these powers, been customary in England from time immemorial, and in

> this country from its first colonization, to regulate ferries, common carriers, hackmen, bakers, millers, wharfingers, innkeepers, &c., and, in so doing, to fix a maximum of charge to be made for services rendered, accommodations furnished, and articles sold. Down to the time of the adoption of the fourteenth amendment of the Constitution of the United States, it was not supposed that statutes regulating the use, or even the price of the use, of private property necessarily deprived an owner of his property without due process of law. Under some circumstances, they may, but not under all. . . .
>
> The controlling fact is the power to regulate at all. If that exists, the right to establish the maximum of charge, as one of the means of regulation, is implied. We know that this is a power which may be abused; but that is no argument against its existence. For protection against abuses by legislatures the people must resort to the polls, not to the courts.[14]

Before *Munn*, in 1874, Congress had considered but failed to pass a bill sponsored by the Iowa Republican George Washington McCrary. The bill "forbade unreasonable [freight] charges and provided for a board of railway commissioners with power to make a schedule of reasonable maximum rates."[15] The *Munn* case convinced some previously skeptical members of Congress that federal regulation of railroad prices could also be constitutional, and it prompted the introduction of new federal Granger bills. In particular, the Texas Democrat John Reagan was encouraged by the Court's decision to introduce a new bill for federal regulation of rail prices. The Reagan bill passed the House, but for several years, it could not be reconciled with a bill in the Senate sponsored by the Illinois Republican Shelby Cullom.

The impetus for congressional action came in 1886, when the Supreme Court, in *Wabash v. Illinois*, overturned *Munn v. Illinois*, ruling that the Illinois Granger law did place a burden on interstate commerce.[16] Thus, if Congress wanted price controls on the railroads, it would have to pass them at the federal level. Congress passed the Interstate Commerce Act early the next year. This act, signed by Democrat Grover Cleveland, created the Interstate Commerce Commission (ICC) and required the railroads to charge rates that were "reasonable and just." It forbade railroads from charging higher rates than long-haul trips for shorter hauls, in response to farmers' and small business owners' complaints that the railroads were price gouging.[17]

The ICC was the country's first independent regulatory authority. A century later, it was described as "one of the earliest instances we can point to where the federal government intervened directly in the economy to protect the economically weak from the economically strong."[18] But Congress's failure to clearly define the roles and authorities of the ICC posed a challenge for its effectiveness in its early years. The agency could not compel obedience to its orders when railroad companies refused to comply, and it was compelled to seek judicial enforcement, which was quite burdensome.[19]

The authority of the ICC to impose maximum prices was also questioned. The act gave the ICC authority to review rates and identify those that were unreasonable. The ICC inferred that from that authority, it should also be able to fix maximum prices. In *ICC v. Cincinnati, New Orleans and Texas Pacific Railway*, the Supreme Court rejected the ICC's interpretation, noting that "it would be strange if an administrative body could by any mere process of construction create for itself a power which Congress had not given to it."[20] This decision greatly limited the ability of the ICC to effectively regulate prices until 1906, when the Hepburn Act explicitly gave the ICC the power to fix maximum prices.[21]

Three years after passing the Interstate Commerce Act, Congress passed the Sherman Antitrust Act of 1890, again calling on its authority from the commerce clause to regulate against monopolies and trusts, which could charge above-competitive prices. Congress authorized the Department of Justice to bring suits against alleged violators of the act. Like the Interstate Commerce Act, the Sherman Antitrust Act was challenged in court. In 1895, the Supreme Court decided in *United States v. E. C. Knight Co.* that state governments, not Congress, had the authority to regulate manufacturing monopolies.[22] This effectively dismantled the act until 1905, when *Swift and Co. v. United States* ruled that parts of the manufacturing process could fit under Congress's commerce authority.[23]

The McKinley Tariff and the Sherman Silver Purchase Act

While the Granger laws, Interstate Commerce Act, and Sherman Antitrust Act attempted to protect farmers and consumers from the pricing power of railroads and trusts, another debate concerned how and whether to protect American interests through tariff policy. Recall that protectionism had been a cornerstone of the American System during the era of the Second Bank of the United States. Protective tariffs, which raised prices for imported and domestically produced manufactured goods, had angered the Southern agricultural states and led to the nullification crisis in 1832. Since the Civil War, the government had relied on high tariff rates, to the continued dismay of the Democrats, and the tariff debate remained along established party lines.

Tariff reduction, for President Cleveland, was a more appealing approach to helping farmers than other methods that had been suggested. For example, he vetoed the Texas Seed Bill, which would have given federal aid to Texas farmers suffering from the drought of 1885.[24] The veto reflected his distaste for government paternalism, "the bane of republican institutions and the constant peril of our government by the people. . . . It undermines the self-reliance of our people and substitutes in its place dependence upon governmental favoritism."[25] Cleveland also resisted the growing pressure from the free-silver movement that intensified in the 1880s, especially after six Western states with strong silver movements joined the Union. Here, he disagreed with many of his fellow Democrats, who supported free coinage of silver.

President Cleveland devoted his entire annual message to Congress in 1887 to "our present tariff laws, the vicious, inequitable, and illogical source of unnecessary taxation."[26] High tariffs were "vicious" and "inequitable," Cleveland thought, because they raised prices not only for imported goods subject to the duty but also for domestically produced goods, "because they render it possible for those of our people who are manufacturers to make these taxed articles and sell them for a price equal to that demanded for the imported goods that have paid customs duty. So it happens that while comparatively a few use the imported articles, millions of our people, who never used and never saw any of the foreign products, purchase and use things of the same kind made in this country, and pay therefor nearly or quite the same enhanced price which the duty adds to the imported articles."[27]

The high tariffs were also "unnecessary," he argued, because the federal government was already running large surpluses, making the Treasury "a hoarding place for money needlessly withdrawn from trade and the people's use, thus crippling our national energies, suspending our country's development, preventing investment in productive enterprise, threatening financial disturbance, and inviting schemes of public plunder."[28] Representative William McKinley, who would later become president, and other Republicans on the Ways and Means Committee agreed that government surpluses should be reduced, but they proposed the exact opposite solution. They argued that higher tariff rates would reduce imports enough that the net effect would be a reduction in the government's revenue.[29]

President Cleveland was defeated by the Republican candidate Benjamin Harrison in 1888 in a close election focused heavily on the tariff issue. According to the economist Frank Taussig: "The Republican victory probably was not due to any strong popular preference for the Protectionist policy. The ties of party attachment, which are immensely strong in the United States, held many thousands to the Republican party merely by force of tradition. These voters have been Protectionists because they are Republicans, not Republicans because they are Protectionists."[30]

Beholden to their campaign pledges, the Republicans passed

the McKinley Tariff in 1890, sharply increasing average import duties. As part of a political compromise to pass the McKinley Tariff, the Sherman Silver Purchase Act was passed in the same year.[31] That act was brokered by Senator John Sherman, an Ohio Republican who had been instrumental in the Coinage Act of 1873 and may have been one of the few to recognize that the Coinage Act would demonetize silver.[32] The Sherman Silver Purchase Act required the Treasury to more than double its monthly silver bullion purchases and took a partial step back toward bimetallism by committing the government to coining a limited amount of silver.[33]

As some Republicans had feared, the McKinley Tariff was unpopular in many parts of the country, and the Republicans lost their House majority in the 1890 midterms.[34] Soon after the tariff was enacted, labor interests claimed that it was causing prices to rise much more quickly than wages. A Senate resolution in 1891 instructed the Senate Committee on Finance to study the effects of the Tariff Act on prices and wages to determine whether this claim was correct. To facilitate the study, Republican Senator Nelson Aldrich, of Rhode Island, asked the Bureau of Labor to produce indexes of wages and prices. The bureau had been established a few years earlier, in 1884, in response to growing demand for unbiased information about labor-market conditions as the industrial labor force grew and began to organize, foreshadowing the growing role of government-collected economic data in industry and policy making.[35] To construct the price indexes, a group of researchers collected data on thousands of prices, stretching back to 1860. Using these indexes, Aldrich's committee determined that prices had indeed risen by more than wages after the tariff, eroding workers' purchasing power, although over a longer time horizon, workers had prospered.[36]

The tariff was also challenged at the Supreme Court in the 1892 case *Field v. Clark*, in which several importers contended that the tariff represented an unconstitutional delegation of power to the president, as it allowed the president to impose trade restrictions on countries imposing "duties or other exactions upon the agricultural or other products of the United States, which . . . he may deem to be reciprocally unequal and unreasonable." The Court disagreed with the importers, claiming, "Nothing involving the expediency or the just operation of such legislation was left to the determination of the president."[37]

By the time of the 1892 presidential election, the Republicans continued to face the fallout of the McKinley Tariff's unpopularity. Running on tariff reduction, Cleveland defeated Harrison, becoming the only president to serve two nonconsecutive terms. Cleveland's campaign had focused more on tariff reduction than on his monetary views—his opposition to free silver—which were denounced by much of his own party. In 1891, following passage of the Sherman Silver Purchase Act, Cleveland had warned: "If we have developed an unexpected capacity for the assimilation of a largely increased volume of this currency, and even if we have demonstrated the usefulness of such an increase, these conditions fall far short of insuring us against disaster if, in the present situation, we enter upon the dangerous and reckless experiment of free, unlimited, and independent silver coinage."[38] Cleveland repeated this sentiment in his Second Inaugural Address, arguing, "Nothing is more vital to our supremacy as a nation and to the beneficent purposes of our Government than a sound and stable currency . . . the danger of depreciation in the purchasing power of the wages paid to toil should furnish the strongest incentive to prompt and conservative precaution."[39] Cleveland convinced Congress to repeal the Sherman Silver Purchase Act in 1893, alienating the agrarian wing of his party.[40] For this and other reasons, the Democratic Party did not nominate Cleveland for another term in 1896.

Honest Money and the Cross of Gold

The 1896 election, much more than the 1892 election, was focused on monetary issues. At the 1896 Democratic National Convention, the "free silver" supporter William Jennings Bryan received the party's nomination after a speech focused on free silver and an end to the gold standard. "If they ask us why it is that we say more on the money question than we say upon the tariff question," he explained, "I reply that if protection has slain its thousands, the gold standard has slain its tens of thousands."[41] Bryan called back to revolutionary ideals to counter circulating arguments that bimetallism should only be adopted as part of an international agreement:

> It is the issue of 1776 over again. Our ancestors, when but three millions in number, had the courage to declare their political independence of every other nation; shall we, their descendants, when we have grown to seventy millions, declare that we are less independent than our forefathers? . . . If they say bimetallism is good, but that we cannot have it until other nations help us, we reply that, instead of having a gold standard because England has, we will restore bimetallism, and then let England have bimetallism because the United States has it. If they dare to come out in the open field and defend the gold standard as a good thing, we will fight them to the uttermost.[42]

One objection to monetary expansion was its effects on contracts: inflation would erode the real value of dollar-denominated debts. When a New York delegate proposed an "amendment to the platform providing that the proposed change in our monetary system shall not affect contracts already made," Bryan countered: "If [the New York delegate] means to say that we cannot change our monetary system without protecting those who have loaned money before the change was made, I desire to ask him where, in law or in morals, he can find justification for not protecting the debtors when the act of 1873 was passed, if he now insists that we must protect the creditors."[43] Bryan famously concluded, "You shall not press down upon the brow of labor this crown of thorns; you shall not crucify mankind upon a cross of gold."[44] Bryan subsequently also received the nomination of the Populist Party, a third party of free-silver supporters that had replaced the Greenback-Labor Party. This effectively ended the third-party role of the Populist Party, as many of the party's members followed Bryan into the Democratic Party.

In his speech accepting the Democratic Party's nomination, Bryan emphasized that his aim was not to raise prices but to stabilize them (which, given the recent deflation, implied a period of inflation). "An absolutely honest money," he proclaimed, "would not vary in its purchasing power; it would be absolutely stable, when measured by average prices. A dollar which increases in purchasing power is just as dishonest as a dollar which decreases in purchasing power."[45]

Bryan's references to purchasing power and average prices reflected a relatively new way at the time of thinking about stabilization that was beginning to gain traction. On a commodity standard, like the gold standard, the currency is stabilized with respect to a single commodity, like gold. When multiple countries are on a gold standard, each stabilizing its currency with respect to gold, the foreign exchange rates between the countries are also stabilized. What is not necessarily stabilized is the purchasing power of the currency. Changes in the supply or demand of gold lead to changes in its relative price, and thus to changes in the amount of other goods and services that the currency can buy. Bryan preferred to stabilize the currency with respect to its overall purchasing power—with respect to not just gold but also some larger basket of goods.

The phrase "honest money" that Bryan used was from the title of a book published the previous year by Arthur Fonda. Fonda's monetary proposal would require a commission of government statisticians to select a set of commodities and keep track of their prices and their share in consumer expenditures (as the Bureau of Labor had recently demonstrated that it could feasibly do, following the investigations into the effects of the McKinley Tariff). Fonda wrote that "from these data a table should be prepared showing the amount one dollar would have purchased."[46] The book proposed that the government issue paper currency and manage its circulation with the explicit aim of stabilizing the amount that a dollar could purchase. Bryan liked the idea of stabilizing the purchasing power of money, but he perhaps thought that Fonda's scheme was politically untenable. Instead, he advocated a bimetallic standard as a more familiar and palatable means of achieving a similar end.

Bryan ran unsuccessfully against McKinley in the general election. Despite the unpopularity of McKinley's tariff, the Republicans were able to convince many voters that Bryan was a dangerous radical. Although Bryan was defeated, his campaign highlights the swell of populist sentiment in that era, driven in no small part by the unfavorable price conditions facing farmers. The distribution of Bryan votes in 1896 is revealing: "Populism had only three compact centers. . . . Each was dominated by a product whose price had catastrophically declined: the South, based chiefly upon cotton; a narrow tier of four Northwestern states, Kansas, Nebraska, and the two Dakotas, based upon wheat; and the mountain states, based chiefly upon silver."[47]

President McKinley, less susceptible to populist appeals for monetary expansion, signed the Gold Standard Act of 1900, which set a ratio of $20.67 per ounce of gold, formalizing the US gold standard. But inflation came nonetheless. New gold discoveries in South Africa, Alaska, and Colorado, and advancements in mining and refining, allowed the world's gold stock to more than double from 1890 to 1913—a much quicker rate of increase than had occurred in previous decades.[48] The falling prices that had followed the Crime of '73 were replaced by rising prices.[49] This trend reversal brought an end to the intense focus on the money question and the free-silver movement. And ironically, Bryan's defeat ushered in an era of rising crop prices and agricultural prosperity.

Purchasing Power

We have seen in this chapter how the government attempted to manage prices after the Civil War through regulatory, fiscal, and monetary policies in order to promote its conception of economic justice. The new inflationary environment that began in the 1890s provided further impetus for government action. In particular, after the severe Panic of 1907, food prices grew more rapidly, heightening political conflicts between consumers and food producers.[50] As Republican President William Taft noted in his first annual message to Congress, "The high prices which such products bring mean great prosperity for the farming community, but on the other hand they mean a very considerably increased burden upon those classes . . . whose yearly compensation does not expand with the improvement in business."[51]

Politicians faced the difficult task of appearing responsive to consumers without antagonizing farmers. Editorial cartoons frequently blamed intermediaries and "food speculators," rather than farmers themselves, for the "exorbitant prices" of beef, pork, and eggs.[52] Processors, wholesalers, and retailers were accused of price gouging. Progressive reformers blamed the moneyed "trusts"—large corporations that consolidated their power over particular industries or products—for using their market dominance to artificially inflate prices.

Blaming the trusts was a natural response for Americans in the Progressive Era, who by and large "wanted economic success to continue to be related to personal character, wanted the economic system not merely to be a system for the production of sufficient goods and services but to be an effectual system of incentives and rewards. The great corporation, the crass plutocrat, the calculating political boss, all seemed to defy these desires."[53] We will see in the next chapters that the "popular clamor" to blame inflation on trusts, price gougers, and profiteering recurred in subsequent decades.

The American public did not attribute rising prices to the expansion of world gold production until at least 1910, when this idea spread from the London *Economist* to US popular media.[54] A 1910 opinion in the *Independent* made the case that none of the commonly cited causes of rising prices could explain the broad-based worldwide inflation:

> To say that the present high prices are due to trusts will not explain the similar rise of prices in cases where there are no trusts in those particular commodities of this country, or no trusts at all in other countries where the rise of prices is also well marked. To say that high prices are due to the tariff does not explain the similar rise of prices in England, where there is no protective tariff. To say that high prices are due to labor unions does not explain the rise of prices in the Orient, where there are no labor unions. To say that the rising prices are due to the growth of population, or to the pressure upon the means of subsistence, does not explain the rise of prices in those manufactures where the raw material has only slightly risen in price, and where the wages cost is relatively low; nor does it explain the falling prices of a decade ago, when population increased at virtually the same rate.[55]

Having discounted these possible explanations, the author concluded that "a general rise of prices must therefore mean a depreciation of gold. . . . Unless there is some change in the supply of (or the demand for) gold, there can be no change in the general price level."[56] Another opinion piece in the same publication similarly attributed inflation to gold rather than trusts, drawing an analogy to the Revolutionary War era: "The gold inflation is world-wide and prices everywhere have moved upward in response. . . . At the present time popular clamor seeks to fix the responsibility upon the trusts, just as in Washington's day a similar agitation resulted in laws against 'forestallers and monopolists,' whereas the true cause lay in the depreciating continental currency. 'Not worth a continental' in the future may be substituted by the phrase 'Not worth a gold dollar'; for, how serious the situation may become nobody knows."[57] This period of rising prices, just like the earlier period of falling prices, prompted further consideration of monetary reforms to stabilize the purchasing power of the dollar, most notably by Irving Fisher, one of the most influential economists of the twentieth century. Fisher was a professor of political economy at Yale, a prolific writer, and a progressive activist. Fisher's monetary theories reflect a strong influence of David Hume, and Fisher is credited with formalizing Hume's quantity theory. As did Hume, Fisher recognized that increasing the quantity of money could boost output and improve business conditions in the shorter run, but could only raise prices in the longer run.

In 1911, he published a treatise, *The Purchasing Power of Money*, to "set forth the principles determining the purchasing power of money and to apply those principles to the study of historical changes in that purchasing power, including in particular the recent change in 'the cost of living,' which has aroused world-wide discussion."[58] In that book, Fisher considered "the claim of advocates of a bimetallic standard that such a standard would tend to steady prices"—that is, Bryan's claim—and found it lacking. He argued that bimetallism, "even could it be maintained, would offer but an indifferent remedy for the variations in the price level," because gold and silver prices had been similarly unstable since the seventeenth century. He used a colorful analogy: "Two variable metals joined through bimetallism may be likened to two tipsy men locking arms. Together they walk somewhat more steadily than apart, although if one happens to be much more sober than the other, his own gait may be made worse by the union." Fisher also considered whether irredeemable paper money could stabilize the price level, as proposed by Fonda. He ruled this theoretically possible but practically unlikely: "It is true that the level of prices might be kept almost absolutely stable merely by honest government regulation of the money supply with that specific purpose in view. . . . But sad experience teaches that irredeemable paper money, while theoretically capable of steadying prices, is apt in practice to be so manipulated as to produce instability. In nearly every country there exists a party, consisting of debtors and debtor-like classes, which favors depreciation. A movement is therefore at any time possible, tending to pervert any scheme for maintaining stability into a scheme for simple inflation." Fisher added, "Even if, in times of peace, these persistent pleas for inflation could be resisted, it is doubtful if they could be resisted in time of war." Instead, Fisher proposed a "compensated dollar" plan, in which the dollar would still be redeemable in gold, but the gold weight of the dollar would vary to offset changes in the price index. His plan was influenced by a paper written in 1879 by the astronomer Simon Newcomb, who argued that "if we could, from time to time, increase or diminish the amount of the metal in the dollar, so that it would always exactly fulfill the required condition, we should have all that we want." Newcomb recognized that frequently changing the metallic content of coins was not feasible, but he proposed that an equivalent effect could be achieved by issuing "a paper currency which shall be redeemable, not in gold dollars of fixed weight, but in such quantities of gold and silver bullion as shall suffice to make the required purchases."[59]

Thus, despite the similarities between the monetary theories of Fisher and Hume, their policy prescriptions were quite different. Unlike Hume, who described the inherently stabilizing and equilibrating properties of an international gold standard, Fisher thought better price stabilization could be achieved in the hands of a central bank, which could be operated using the best available scientific knowledge and statistical tools. In Fisher's view, "economic science offered the prospect of keeping the politics out of money even while embracing centralization and active management."[60] Plans for a central bank for the United States were already underway. In the years to come, as described in the next chapters, Fisher would remain active in the "stable money" movement and would see some of his ideas put to the test.

FIVE

THE FEDERAL RESERVE ACT AND WORLD WAR I

> Prices mean the same thing everywhere now. They mean the efficiency or inefficiency of the nation, whether it is the government that pays them or not. They mean victory or defeat. They mean America will win her place once for all among the foremost free nations of the world, or that she will sink to defeat and become a second rate power alike in thought and action.
>
> WOODROW WILSON, "Address to Fellow Countrymen"[1]

The Creature from Jekyll Island

The previous chapters have shown how financial booms and busts can lead to highly disruptive price fluctuations. At least eight banking panics occurred in Manhattan, the center of the financial system, from 1863 to 1913, and several of them, in 1873, 1893, and 1907, became national panics.[2] The panics tended to occur in the fall, when farmers needed currency and credit to bring their crops to market. These seasonal increase in currency demand put the banking system under considerable strain, as the currency supply was not "elastic"—that is, it could not easily expand or contract in accordance with the needs of industry.[3] Under the national banking system, national banks needed federal government bonds as collateral for note issue, so the supply of currency was linked to the value of federal government debt, which resulted in currency inelasticity.

The Panic of 1907 helped raise public support for a central banking authority that could stabilize the banking system and provide an elastic currency. With the Aldrich-Vreeland Act of 1908, Congress established the National Monetary Commission to study reforms to the nation's money and banking system. Nelson Aldrich, who by then had become a Republican senator, led the commission's investigations of the monetary and banking systems of European countries (Aldrich, recall, had led a study of the effects of the McKinley Tariff on prices and wages in 1891). After the investigations, in November 1910, Aldrich and a small group of men—most with ties to Wall Street—secretly convened at the exclusive Jekyll Island Club off the coast of Georgia to discuss the findings and formulate a plan for a new system for the United States.

One of the attendees, Paul Warburg, was a former German banker who had immigrated to the United States. He convinced Aldrich that the "discount system" used by central banks in Germany, France, and England played a vital role in promoting financial stability. In those countries, the central bank served as a lender of last resort, lending to commercial banks at a facility called the discount window to help meet their liquidity needs.[4]

Aldrich then wrote his plan to establish the private and highly centralized National Reserve Association of the United States. The commission's final report emphasized that the National Reserve Association would "answer the exacting requirements of American conditions that would meet the needs of a progressive nation, with its hundred millions of energetic and enterprising people, whose development has been impeded by a defective and inefficient monetary system. The plan we propose is essentially an American system, scientific in its methods, and democratic in its control."[5] The American Bankers Association and most of Aldrich's fellow congressional Republicans endorsed the plan. But Democrats feared placing "vast and growing control over money and credit" in the hands of a private "money trust" and limiting the government's authority over money issuance.[6]

When the National Monetary Commission convened in 1908,

Republicans controlled both the House and the Senate. Had Aldrich formulated his plan more quickly, it might have passed without too much struggle. But Aldrich spent much of 1908 and 1909 tied up in passing the Payne-Aldrich Tariff Act of 1909, which greatly increased tariff rates and led to a rift in the Republican Party. Democrats took control of the House in the 1910 midterms and gained ground in the Senate. In the end, neither the Democrats nor the Republicans supported Aldrich's bill in the Senate.[7]

The Democrats also won the presidency when Woodrow Wilson was elected in 1912. President Wilson enlisted Congressman Carter Glass, a Democrat from Virginia, to draft a plan for a more decentralized system of regional reserve banks. The discount rate—the short-term interest rate on loans to commercial banks at the discount window—could vary across regions according to regional needs. Glass explained, "In the United States, with its immense area, numerous natural divisions, still more numerous competing divisions, and abundant outlets to foreign countries, there is no argument, either of banking theory or of expediency, which dictates the creation of a single central banking institution, no matter how skillfully managed, how carefully controlled, or how patriotically conducted."[8]

The Glass bill passed in the House with relatively little discussion of how its proposed changes to the monetary system would affect prices and inflation.[9] Rather, it was understood that, in accordance with the Gold Standard Act of 1900, participation in the international gold standard would determine prices in the United States. Thus, maintaining convertibility of the dollar to gold would limit the ability of a new reserve system to pursue price stabilization as an objective. But a different bill, passed in the Senate, would have made price stability the primary objective of monetary policy. That bill was sponsored by Senator Robert Owen, Democrat from Oklahoma, who had been a delegate at the 1896 convention that elected William Jennings Bryan following his "cross of gold" speech.

Senator Owen was well-acquainted with Irving Fisher's compensated-dollar plan, and he agreed with Fisher on the importance of stabilizing the purchasing power of the dollar.[10] Fisher, in a 1912 paper, promoted his compensated-dollar plan as "a more stable gold standard," although in fact it would have been quite different. Under the plan, dollar coins would still have been convertible to bullion on demand but at a rate that could vary, not a fixed rate. Because other countries were on the gold standard, the plan would imply that the exchange rate would vary. This was a major difference from the Glass proposal, which kept monetary policy committed to maintaining the gold standard and prioritized exchange-rate stability over domestic price stability.

Reconciling the Glass and Owen bills required long debate and countless compromises leading up to the passage of the Federal Reserve Act of 1913. On the issue of the gold standard, Glass prevailed, and language that would have committed the Federal Reserve to promoting price stability was removed. The Federal Reserve Act stated: "Federal reserve notes, to be issued at the discretion of the Board of Governors of the Federal Reserve System . . . shall be obligations of the United States and shall be receivable by all national and member banks and Federal reserve banks and for all taxes, customs, and other public dues. They shall be redeemed in lawful money on demand at the Treasury Department of the United States, in the city of Washington, District of Columbia, or at any Federal Reserve bank."[11] Owen's and Fisher's proposal that the Fed should pursue price stabilization, which seemed fairly heterodox at the time, would come up time and again in the following few decades, sometimes at the impetus of Owen and Fisher themselves, as coming chapters will discuss.

On the question of the discount rate, the act granted each reserve bank the authority to set its own rate of discount, "subject to review and determination of the Federal Reserve Board."[12] That is, the board could choose to veto the discount rate chosen by a reserve bank. Any member banks could borrow at the discount window using "eligible paper," which included short-term commercial and agricultural loans, as collateral. By April 1914, the Reserve Bank Organization Committee announced the twelve cities that would have Federal Reserve Banks and the boundaries of their districts.[13] The reserve banks opened and began preparing for business soon after World War I broke out in Europe.[14]

The New Freedom

The establishment of the Federal Reserve System was just one part of Wilson's economic agenda, the "New Freedom," which had been the basis of his 1912 campaign. In that campaign, Republican support was initially split between Theodore Roosevelt and President William Howard Taft. Roosevelt's supporters created a new party, the Progressives or "Bull Moose" Party, with a platform named "new nationalism."[15] Wilson's New Freedom and Roosevelt's New Nationalism shared a distaste for monopolies and trusts, and a desire to support labor interests. But the candidates proposed different approaches to dealing with these issues. Wilson favored breaking up the monopolies entirely, whereas Roosevelt called for tighter regulation of monopolies and a minimum wage for women.

A minimum wage is, of course, a form of price control: it is a floor on the price of labor. Interest in minimum-wage laws, both at the state and at the federal level, had been growing in the Progressive Era, but the constitutionality of such laws was not immediately clear. Article I, Section 10, Clause 1 of the Constitution prohibits state governments from passing any "Law impairing the Obligation of Contracts." It is possible to interpret this clause as restricting the states from interfering even with future contracts. In that case, a minimum-wage law would violate the clause by limiting the types of labor contracts that businesses and workers could potentially make.

Beginning with the *Knox v. Lee* legal tender case (see chapter 3), which held that "no obligation of a contract can extend to the defeat of a legitimate governmental authority," states began to interpret the restrictions of the clause less strictly and making laws that could be interpreted as interfering with contract obligations.[16] The courts typically upheld these laws. For example, in *Holden v. Hardy* in 1898, the Supreme Court upheld a maximum-hours law for underground miners, declaring that states could interfere with freedom of contract to enforce reasonable health or safety measures.[17]

An important exception came in *Lochner v. New York*, in which the Supreme Court in 1905 held that a New York law setting a maximum number of hours per week that bakers could work was unconstitutional: the maximum-hours law was an unjustified interference with freedom of contract, because there was no evidence that the law protected public health.[18] Labor activists and progressives were outraged, although as it turned out, the *Lochner* decision held less sway than *Holden* until the 1920s.[19] We will see in the next few chapters, though, that the *Lochner* case became more influential in the 1920s and 1930s.

The earliest minimum-wage laws in the United States were enacted by state and local governments and applied to women's and children's labor. It was easier to justify minimum-wage laws for women and children, who had weaker bargaining power than men and were more likely to receive below-subsistence wages. But Wilson expected that Roosevelt's hope to establish a minimum wage for women "is not in the long run meant to be confined in its application to women only." Wilson also predicted that a federal minimum-wage law would counterproductively *reduce* wages, as "the great majority of employers would take occasion to bring their wage scale as nearly as might be down to the level of that minimum."[20]

Wilson won with 42 percent of the popular vote; Roosevelt and Taft captured 27 percent and 23 percent, respectively. With Roosevelt's electoral defeat, aspirations for a federal minimum-wage law were put on hold. But economics journals had begun to more actively discuss the merits of a minimum wage for all workers, not just women and children. Massachusetts enacted such a law in 1912, and Oregon followed in 1913.[21] The Oregon law was upheld by a 4–4 Supreme Court decision a few years later in *Stettler v. O'Hara*.[22] Many other states adopted minimum-wage laws in the following few years.

In his first years in office, Wilson began implementing his New Freedom agenda. In addition to the Federal Reserve Act, Wilson also signed the Underwood-Simmons Act of 1913, reducing tariff rates; the Clayton Antitrust Act of 1914; and the Federal Trade Commission Act of 1914. In 1913, the Department of Agriculture, with the support of farmers and housewives, established the Office of Markets to help farmers market their food in more sanitary conditions with less reliance on middlemen. All of these reforms, which aimed to mitigate inequality and unfair business conditions, came from Wilson's belief that a proactive government, with an efficient bureaucracy, could address social and economic problems.

Wilson, who had a PhD in political science, had published a journal article in 1887 called "The Study of Administration." Administrative study, he wrote, had the object "to discover, first, what government can properly and successfully do, and, secondly, how it can do these proper things with the utmost possible efficiency and at the least possible cost either of money or of energy to put forth its characteristic flower of systematic knowledge."[23] Wilson argued that administrative study had, to that point, been neglected by political writers, who "had thought, argued, dogmatized only about the constitution of government; about the nature of the state, the essence and seat of sovereignty, popular power and kingly prerogative; about the greatest meanings lying at the heart of government, and the high ends set before the purpose of government by man's nature and man's aims. . . . Amidst this high warfare of principles, administration could command no pause for its own consideration."[24]

He did not view the expansion of administration as a threat to democratic principles or self-governance. To the contrary, he argued: "Our peculiar American difficulty in organizing administration is not the danger of losing liberty, but the danger of not being able or willing to separate its essentials from its accidents. Our success is made doubtful by that besetting error of ours, the error of trying to do too much by vote. Self-government does not consist in having a hand in everything, any more than housekeeping consists necessarily in cooking dinner with one's own hands. The cook must be trusted with a large discretion as to the management of the fires and the ovens."[25]

As soon as the war broke out, Wilson began several efforts to reduce food prices and increase food production. The war also gave him an unprecedented opportunity to expand the administrative state. He expanded the Department of Agriculture's educational and scientific programs for improving agricultural productivity, and he ordered the attorney general to investigate whether middlemen were taking "advantage of such circumstances to increase the price of food and the difficulties of living."[26] By 1916, however, aware that these programs were unpopular with farmers who benefited from higher prices, Wilson cut the programs back to improve his chances of reelection. He was reelected in 1916.[27]

Prices on the Home Front

In President Wilson's second term, international issues took precedence over the domestic aspects of the New Freedom agenda. Treasury Secretary William McAdoo, well versed in Civil War history, did not want to finance the war through paper money issues, for fears of the inflationary impact.[28] Instead, he planned to finance the war primarily through taxation. But the sixfold increase in effective income-tax rates from 1916 to 1918 was still far from sufficient to offset the increase in government expenditures, so the Treasury ran large deficits.[29]

The new Federal Reserve System supported the Treasury in financing the war. The Treasury ended the independent Treasury, designating the New York Fed as its fiscal agent.[30] The reserve banks reduced discount rates so that low interest rates could reduce the cost of the Treasury's debt finance; they also set more favorable discount rates on loans secured by government bonds to encourage member banks to purchase Treasury securities and helped sell Liberty bonds to the public.[31]

Wartime disruptions made Europe more reliant on imports from the United States and gave US banks a larger role in financing international trade.[32] Most of the belligerent nations suspended the gold standard and used their gold to pay for purchases from the United States, leading to large gold inflows, which the Federal Reserve System did not offset.[33] The combination of low interest rates, credit expansion, and monetary expansion from gold inflows contributed to rising inflation in the United States.[34]

Inflation in food prices was especially severe and troublesome. Food prices rose 46 percent from July 1916 to April 1917 as the British, French, and Italian governments increased their purchases of American agricultural products.[35] The most important wartime food product was wheat, because it was highly transportable, easy to store, and a major component of European and American working-class diets. The wheat harvest in 1916 was especially bad—just 636 million bushels, compared to 1 billion bushels the previous year.[36]

In April 1917, the *Independent* published excerpts of letters from readers about "the high cost of living." The article noted, "It is the salaried man who is hardest hit by the recent advance in prices." Readers recognized that high food prices benefited farmers, but they mostly viewed that benefit as a good thing. A minister's daughter from Boone, North Carolina, for example, wrote: "If prices are high, some one is getting more money to spend on comforts. . . . I am glad that the farmers are gaining wealth and position, and I believe that as a nation, we will gain the benefit of it."[37]

A farmer from Hanford, Washington, wrote that he "took to the soil" to support his growing family; that farmers' "willingness to wear overalls, our passing up of glittering, cheap pleasures . . . brings greater reward. There is nothing like an abundant harvest to dispel worry; nothing like the work of producing it to cure insomnia, appendicitis, and other aristocratic ailments. . . . High cost of living will provide a blessing for the American people if it makes them practical as it did me."[38]

Many blamed not the farmers themselves, but other causes. An opinion piece in *Business World* discussed several reasons for rising prices: "We are literally oozing gold as a country. . . . How does that make us poorer? It doesn't make us poorer; but it makes the cost of living soar and soar and soar; so that unless your wages go up in proportion, you are poorer for that great plenty of gold. Hence, we have the universal social unrest and the pressure up and up and up for higher wages."[39] According to this article, the "strongest force pump of them all" was "the Universal Trust in All Food Products": "If you are a householder living in a big city or a hotel man or a hotel guest, look over the food products on your table . . . you cannot lay your hand on a single article of food which the Trust has not enclosed in an iron fence of manipulation, to keep the producers from reaching the consumer, the city man from reaching the farmer; and the Trust takes toll with both hands on both sides of the fence."[40] The progressive urge to blame intermediaries, trusts, speculators, and price gougers for rising food prices was strong. For Wilson, "daily newspaper reports of middlemen purchasing large amounts of food, storing it for future use, and later making fortunes when Allied buying agents bought every grain in sight convinced him, and other Americans, that hoarders had caused bread prices to go up."[41]

Some interest groups, including the American Federation of Labor, urged President Wilson to impose an embargo on wheat and other food products. The idea was to reduce exports of foodstuffs, increasing domestic availability—a divisive proposal. Senator Porter J. McCumber, of North Dakota, noted: "Consumers are for it; producers are against it! Town people are for it; country people are against it! Laborers are for it; farmers are against it!"[42] Embargo legislation was introduced in December 1916, but without Wilson's backing, it was held up in committee and never passed.[43]

By January 1917, Secretary McAdoo urged Wilson to ask Congress for "legislation which will put it in the power of the Government to suppress extortionate prices during the continuation of the war in Europe."[44] Wilson resisted, fearing that establishing price controls could be seen as war mobilization and disrupt his ongoing mediation initiative. But the public demanded some sort of government action to reduce the cost of living. A "Living Cost Exhibit" in New York City featured exhibits "intended to show that, to cut the cost of living, there must be a readjustment of taxes, Federal control of railroads and natural resources, city-owned public utilities, and distribution of foodstuffs by cities."[45]

When news reached America of a new British government program to expand wheat production by guaranteeing British farmers a minimum wheat price for seven years, consumers in New York, Boston, and Philadelphia began rioting, looting, and demanding price controls and an end to wheat exports.[46] These "food riots" immediately became an important topic of discussion in the Senate. The *Washington Post* reported: "Discussing the recent food riots in New York, Representative Meyer London, Socialist, of New York, urged Congress to pass his bill for a national system of controlling supply and distribution of food. Declaring that 'food speculators have the public by the throat,' Mr. London said the crowning shame of our civilization had been exemplified in the New York food riots." London pointed to "speculators who were rolling in luxury while poor people at their very doors lacked food and shelter."[47]

When the United States entered the war on April 6, 1917, President Wilson pledged to provide abundant food to support the Allies. The Allies reported that they needed at least 190 million bushels of wheat from the United States and Canada to avert famine. To mobilize American agriculture and guarantee sufficient production, some congressmen suggested imposing a minimum guaranteed price for wheat in order to protect farmers from overproduction. Wilson again resisted the call for price controls, recognizing that the complicated task of designing and imposing them could distract Congress from other wartime legislative tasks.[48]

But the Senate requested that Secretary of Agriculture David Houston begin making plans for agricultural mobilization. Meeting with farm organization leaders, Secretary Houston found greater-than-expected resistance to agricultural price floors, as farmers anticipated that they could easily lead to other forms of price controls, including price ceilings.[49] After all, farmers already expected food prices to continue rising, so price floors seemed unnecessary and price ceilings highly undesirable.

For several months, Houston worked with Representative Asbury Lever, a South Carolina Democrat, to design a bill that could satisfy Wilson and the farm representatives. During this time, Wilson turned to a wealthy mining engineer named Herbert Hoover to advise him on agricultural mobilization. Hoover had earned a reputation as a food expert from his chairmanship of the Commission for Relief in Belgium, an international organization that supplied food to occupied Belgium during the war. Hoover assured Wilson that he could stabilize prices by regulating the supply of crops—via negotiations between industry and government and restrictions on exports—rather than by imposing direct controls. In other words, he would "manage" rather than "control" prices. And he urged Wilson to put him in charge of an independent temporary agency, outside of the Department of Agriculture, responsible for such price management efforts.[50]

Some of Hoover's recommendations made their way into the Food and Fuel Control Act, also called the Lever Act, that Congress passed in August 1917. The act established the US Food Administration and set a minimum price of $2 per bushel for wheat, but it did not explicitly set any other prices. Instead, the act prohibited charging prices that produced "excessive" profits or holding food back from the market to increase prices.[51]

Price Controls in Action

At the Food Administration, Hoover quickly earned the moniker of "food czar."[52] He had broad powers to enforce the provisions of the Lever Act: he could seize firms' products or even the firms themselves, or, most commonly, revoke a firm's license for alleged noncompliance. In cases of alleged violations, the burden of proof was on the merchant—a standard that is not the norm in peacetime.[53] The Wilson administration also relied on other newly created, independent agencies to manage other prices. For example, the Fuel Administration, which was also authorized by the Lever Act, regulated coal and coke prices, which had risen rapidly in 1917.

Representatives of the new agencies met frequently with President Wilson.[54] Of particular note is the War Industries Board, which was established by the Council of National Defense in July 1917. The War Industries Board, and later its Price-Fixing Committee, were tasked with developing a pricing system for strategic goods, such as coal, copper, iron, steel, and lumber. Initially, the Price-Fixing Committee concerned itself only with the prices that the government paid for strategic goods, but its role expanded to also protect the public in their purchases of materials and textiles.[55] Of course, the committee's powers to requisition goods or take over plants gave it the upper hand in these agreements.[56]

Bernard Baruch, the financier and progressive Democrat who headed the War Industries Board, later wrote: "We used a good many euphemisms during the war for the sake of national morale, and this one of 'price fixing by agreement' is a good deal like calling conscription 'Selective Service' and referring to registrants for the draft as 'mass volunteers.' Let us make no mistake about it: we fixed prices with the aid of potential Federal compulsion and we could not have obtained unanimous compliance otherwise."[57] In some cases, the committee fixed prices without industry agreement or consultation, such as when it set a maximum price for woolen rags in August 1918.

As the committee negotiated prices, one challenge it faced was that different producers had different costs. A particular price might ensure large profits for lower-cost producers but not cover the costs of higher-cost producers.[58] One option was to set a single price that was high enough to cover the costs of higher-cost producers. Another option was to set lower prices for lower-cost producers and higher prices for higher-cost producers. A third alternative was to nationalize the industry. The committee decided on a single-price system to minimize the administrative burden. They worried, however, that lower-cost producers, which received the same price as higher-cost producers, would make "unreasonable" profits. Thus, Congress introduced an act in 1917 that taxed corporations' "excessive" profits at a high rate.[59] The Revenue Act of

1918 supplemented the excessive profits tax with a war-profits tax on earnings more than three thousand dollars above a company's average annual net income from 1911 to 1913. These taxes would be repealed after the war with the Revenue Act of 1921.

The World War I price controls were able to have much larger effects than the Revolutionary War price controls because of the administrative growth that occurred in the interim, especially under Wilson. Despite this administrative development, which allowed the government to commit substantially more men and money, the government still faced substantial difficulties in its efforts to replace the free operation of the price system in World War I. The Price-Fixing Committee and the Food Administration both faced the extremely complicated task of resource allocation. In a free market, price signals determine the allocation of resources, but with price signals suppressed, Baruch implemented a "priorities system." When different agencies like the US Army, the Railroad Administration, and the War Shipping Board all wanted to have their contracts for industrial materials filled first, all contracts went through the War Industries Board, which set the priority for each contract. The priorities system was in place for too short a time to really test its strengths or weaknesses.[60] (We will see that problems became more apparent when a similar priorities system was implemented in World War II.)

The resource allocation problem sometimes manifested as unintended, even perverse, consequences of price controls. For example, as a contemporary observer wrote, price ceilings on wheat "made it more profitable to feed wheat than corn to hogs . . . when the world was urgently calling for bread. In other words, the regulations of the food commission, instead of accomplishing one of its chief purposes—namely, an increased production of wheat for human consumption, tempted the farmer as a matter of self-preservation to divert his wheat to his stock."[61]

Still, under the wartime price controls, the production of munitions in American factories increased, other wartime objectives were achieved, and the US economy expanded. Compliance with price controls, according to economists' estimates at the time, was generally good.[62] And even though inflation was high—more than 17 percent per year in 1917 and 1918—hyperinflation was avoided.[63] This is likely attributable to the effects of controls on expectations. By alleviating fears of hyperinflation, the controls prevented hyperinflation from becoming a self-fulfilling prophecy.[64]

At the time, commentators argued that controls worked because of the patriotic cooperation of business and labor. The economic historian Hugh Rockoff hastens to add: "Behind much of the 'voluntary' compliance lay the threat of seizure. It was not so much the willingness of Americans to comply that made controls work, but their willingness to tolerate extraordinary interference with traditional rights" in wartime. Rockoff also notes: "While the creation of more bureaucracies, and their resort to extreme threats, is clearly alien to the American spirit, the heart of the case against controls, as it is usually developed, is that controls are an extremely imperfect substitute for the market."[65] In the special circumstances of the war, he argues, the inefficiencies of price controls were relatively smaller than they would have been in peacetime:

> The most important functions of the market are to reveal information about people's tastes and preferences. What kind of automobiles should we make, what kind of clothing should be manufactured, even what kind of sports should be played? These are all questions that in peacetime most people are willing to leave to the market because it responds to 'dollar votes.' Consumers get what they really want. But in wartime this information becomes superfluous. The needs of the military are relatively obvious, and in any case, cannot be clarified by market activity. Thus, in wartime the balance of virtues swings in favor of central planning; while in peacetime, because of the information it generates, the balance favors the market.[66]

After the Armistice

The Armistice of November 1918 ended fighting on the western front, bringing about a major reduction in government military expenditures. But as a Bureau of Labor Statistics report later noted, "With sudden victory came confusion and lack of direction."[67] The government planned to quickly demobilize four million servicemen, who would have difficulty finding employment in the midst of a raging and deadly influenza pandemic.

Wholesale prices had doubled from 1914 to 1918, and the money supply had increased by 70 percent.[68] But after the Armistice, prices were expected to return to somewhere near their prewar levels, as had happened after other major wars. The price collapse, many feared, would be especially severe and disruptive, for several reasons.[69] First, the War Department canceled $3.8 billion worth of contracts with industry and found itself in possession of far more supplies, like canned goods, wool, and lumber, than it could possibly use in peacetime.[70] Industry feared that the government would sell its surpluses, flooding the market and reducing prices, despite Baruch's assurances that nonperishable surpluses would be held until they could be sold without disrupting markets. Second, agricultural, industrial, and mining capacity had been greatly expanded to meet wartime needs, and excess capacity was expected to put downward pressure on prices.

Certain industries did experience price declines in the post-Armistice recession that ensued from August 1918 to March 1919. In particular, textile prices, which had risen sharply during the war, fell sharply after the Armistice.[71] But overall, the expected deflation failed to materialize. The economy recovered from the recession with prices still well above their prewar levels. In fact, from the end of the war to the start of 1920, prices increased 16 percent, a result of continued money and credit expansion—the money supply grew 18 percent over the same period.[72] This expansion reflected the Federal Reserve's continued support of the Treasury's finances and in particular its facilitation of the sale of Victory bonds. The

Fed maintained low interest rates and easy credit conditions, which fueled consumer and business borrowing and inflation.[73]

This continued inflation meant that gold began to flow out of the United States. The United States, unlike the other major world powers, had remained on the gold standard during the war, with dollars redeemable for gold at a rate of $20.67 per ounce, but Wilson had imposed an embargo on the export of gold in September 1917. This embargo was lifted in June 1919, allowing gold to leave the country. The Federal Reserve Act required that the reserve banks maintain a minimum ratio of gold reserves to currency and deposits. During the War, the reserve banks had substantially more than the minimum required gold reserves, but by late 1919, reserves fell troublingly close to the minimum.[74]

Several of the reserve banks grew alarmed by the rapid decline in their gold reserves and proposed discount rate increases to reverse the flows. Raising the discount rate tends to increase other interest rates, encouraging domestic consumers to deposit their funds in banks and foreigners to invest in the United States, increasing the amount of gold in the vaults of the Fed and its member banks. But the Federal Reserve Board, pressured by the Treasury, vetoed the reserve banks' requests to raise interest rates, so inflation and gold outflows continued.[75] The Federal Reserve's governor W. P. G. Harding later wrote in his memoir that "all legitimate steps were taken by the Federal Reserve Board to restrict expansion, inflation, speculation, and extravagance during the year 1919, except one—a sharp advance in the discount rates. . . . The Board felt that it was its duty to cooperate with the Treasury authorities."[76]

President Wilson and others tended to blame the postwar inflation on business practices, rather than monetary policy, and thus argued that the country was not ready for an end of wartime price controls. They pointed to how sellers had adopted strategies for keeping prices up without coming afoul of antitrust laws. For example, some firms made guarantees that they would not cut prices in the future in order to dissuade prospective customers from waiting to make a purchase in the hope of lower prices to come.[77]

In August 1919, Wilson claimed: "There is now neither peace nor war. . . . There can be no peace prices so long as our whole financial and economic system is on a war basis."[78] He added: "The prices the people of this country are paying for everything that it is necessary for them to use in order to live are not justified by a shortage in supply, either present or prospective, and are in many cases artificially and deliberately created by vicious practices which ought immediately to be checked by law. They constitute a burden upon us which is the more unbearable because we know that it is wilfully imposed by those who have the power and that it can by vigourous public action be greatly lightened and made to square with the actual conditions of supply and demand."[79] Over the subsequent months, Wilson continued to call Congress's attention to "the widespread condition of political restlessness in our body politic," brought on, he claimed, by "heartless profiteering resulting in the increase of the cost of living." He urged Congress to pass "legislative measures which would be effective in controlling and bringing down the present cost of living," including an extension of the Food Control Act.[80] He also proposed a variety of regulations on goods destined for interstate commerce—for example, that they be "plainly marked with the price at which they left the hands of the producer"—to prevent "unconscionable" profits. "There can be no doubt of either the necessity of the legitimacy of such measures," Wilson claimed.[81]

Indeed, for many Progressives, a "halo of victory encircled everyone who rose to the top and every policy that survived to the end of the war."[82] Baruch, for example, thought that the records of the War Industries Board and other wartime agencies had demonstrated that a "strong guiding hand" of government in the economy was necessary in wartime and beneficial in peacetime as well.[83] (Baruch, who was awarded an Army Distinguished Service Medal for his contribution to the wartime mobilization, will reappear throughout the next few chapters, for he remained a highly influential government adviser in the 1920s and during the New Deal and World War II.) But others called for a return to freer markets, with prices determined by supply and demand, unencumbered by controls. A New York newspaper, for example, wrote: "In times of stress and under martial law government makes arbitrary rules by which men abide as a temporary expedient, just as the law of habeas corpus is occasionally suspended; but no government or no emergency can suspend the natural law of supply and demand, which is the basis of all prices."[84] Even some members of the administration, such as Julius Barnes, the director of the US Grain Corporation, argued that "price fixing by law has always failed and always will fail."[85]

The next chapter begins with the depression and severe deflation that occurred when the Federal Reserve Board finally agreed to raise discount rates. It describes how, in the courts and at the ballot box, the remaining wartime price controls were dismantled and a new international monetary order was built.

SIX

DEFLATION AND STABILIZATION

> It is not pretended that to stabilize the purchasing power of the dollar would banish all complaint in the financial, business, and industrial world, much less serve as a substitute for progressive economies. A stable monetary unit would be no more a substitute for the fertility of the soil than a stable bushel basket. Yet a reliable bushel will indirectly help even the tilling of the soil; and a reliable dollar would remove a heavy handicap now put on our productive energy and so indirectly help all production. Dependable weights, measures, and standards eliminate those enormous wastes which come from uncertainty, and, of all the possible wastes from uncertain units used in commerce, those from an uncertain dollar are by far the greatest and the gravest.
>
> IRVING FISHER, *Stabilizing the Dollar*[1]

The Return to Normalcy and the Recession of 1920–1921

We previously saw, in the postbellum era, three types of policies proposed to deal with falling prices and their effects on farmers: tariff increases, monetary reforms, and regulatory changes. In this chapter, we will see that deflation in the early 1920s again hit farmers hard, and prompted similar types of policy proposals. The deflation came when the Fed finally raised interest rates. During and after World War I, the Federal Reserve Board, at the behest of the Treasury, had kept discount rates low, even as inflation increased and gold flowed out of the country. By the end of 1919, several successful Treasury issues improved the Treasury's financial position enough that the Treasury withdrew its opposition to increases in the discount rate; in fact, the Treasury came to agree with the reserve banks that higher discount rates would help curb excessive speculation.[2] The Federal Reserve Board, at last, approved requests by the reserve banks for substantial discount rate increases. The recession that followed, in 1920 and 1921, was accompanied by the most severe deflation on record for the US economy: the price level fell by around 15 percent from 1920 to 1921.[3]

Milton Friedman and Anna Schwartz describe the increase in discount rates in January 1920 as "not only too late but also probably too much."[4] Their view was shared by contemporary observers, especially in the agricultural sector. European agricultural production recovered more quickly than expected after the war, reducing European demand for American crops.[5] Thus, farm prices collapsed more severely than consumer prices in the recession—a price index of farm products fell 53 percent from 1920 to 1921—so the deflation and recession hit farmers especially hard, and many banks in rural areas failed.[6] The 1921 Joint Congressional Commission of Agricultural Inquiry, established to investigate the deflation, concluded: "The commission believes that a policy of sharp advances in discount rates should have been inaugurated in the first six months of 1919, and can not excuse the action of the Federal Reserve Board and the Federal reserve banks in this period in failing to take measures to restrict the expansion, inflation, speculation, and extravagance, which characterized the period."[7] In the midst of this recession, Republican Warren G. Harding campaigned for president in 1920 on the promise of a "return to normalcy."[8] Normalcy, for Harding, entailed a reduction of government activism. In a Boston speech, he proclaimed:

> If we put an end to false economics which lure humanity to utter chaos, ours will be the commanding example of world leadership today. If we can prove a representative popular government under which a citizenship seeks what it may do for the government rather

> than what the government may do for individuals, we shall do more to make democracy safe for the world than all armed conflict ever recorded. The world needs to be reminded that all human ills are not curable by legislation, and that quantity of statutory enactment and excess of government offer no substitute for quality of citizenship. The problems of maintained civilization are not to be solved by a transfer of responsibility from citizenship to government.[9]

Harding's words resonated, and he won the election with more than 60 percent of the popular vote. His landslide victory marked the end of popular support for some of the interventionist government policies introduced during the war. The wartime measures were also dismantled in court. For example, an October 1919 amendment to the Food Control Act had added a penalty of fine or imprisonment for making "any unjust or unreasonable rate or charge in handling or dealing in or with any necessaries." The Cohen Grocery Company was charged with violating this part of the act for the prices it charged for sugar. When the Supreme Court heard *United States v. Cohen Grocery Co.* in 1920, the defendant argued that the statute was "so indefinite as not to enable it to be known what was forbidden, and therefore amounted to a delegation by Congress of legislative power to courts and juries to determine what acts should be held to be criminal and punishable." The defendant also held that "as the country was virtually at peace Congress had no power to regulate the subject with which the section dealt." The Court agreed; the majority opinion noted that, "because the law is vague, indefinite, and uncertain, and because it fixes no immutable standard of guilt, but leaves such standard to the variant views of the different courts and juries which may be called on to enforce it, and because it does not inform defendant of the nature and cause of the accusation against it, I think it is constitutionally invalid."[10]

A joint resolution of Congress declared a formal end of the wartime emergency in March 1921, repealing the Food Control Act and other measures that had been authorized for war.[11] Congress and the voters were clear: it was time for a "return to normalcy"—but what would the new normal look like? The war had changed the United States' role in the global economy. When the war began, the United States was a debtor nation; by the Armistice, it was a creditor, and New York a leading world financial center.[12] And thanks to the Underwood-Simmons Act of 1913, part of Wilson's New Freedom agenda, the United States had low tariff rates that encouraged international trade.

One of the earliest effects of the deep deflation was to increase farmers' support for higher tariffs. President Wilson warned farmers that high tariffs would hurt them, as they needed foreign markets to sell their surplus. But farmers grew desperate for protection from foreign competition. The Republican senator Porter McCumber pushed for much higher tariff rates on wheat to protect farmers in his state, North Dakota, from lower-priced Canadian wheat. The Emergency Tariff Act of 1921 passed Congress, but Wilson vetoed it at the end of his presidential term.[13] Shortly after Harding took office, Congress passed the Emergency Tariff Act again and secured President Harding's signature. Several months later, Congress passed the even more protectionist Fordney-McCumber Tariff of 1922.[14] The Fordney-McCumber Tariff was hugely unpopular with America's trade partners who relied on exports to the US market to make payments on their war loans from the United States; many passed retaliatory tariffs. Thus, the return to normalcy included a return to protectionism and a reduction in trade openness.

The Federal Reserve's higher discount rates did, as intended, attract gold inflows to the United States, restoring the Federal Reserve System's reserve position, and by the spring of 1921, the Fed Board and governors of the reserve banks (now called presidents) began debating whether reductions in the discount rate were warranted. In April, President Harding told reporters that "the Federal Reserve Board has to lower rates generally and help the farmers."[15] Not wanting to appear overly influenced by the president, most of the reserve banks waited until the following month to begin the reductions in the discount rate that would bring the recession to an end.

Near the end of the recession, President Harding had the opportunity to appoint four Supreme Court justices, including former President William Howard Taft, who became chief justice. The new, more conservative Court revived the freedom-of-contract doctrine, which had been "virtually moribund" since the war.[16] Recall that earlier in the Progressive Era, laws on minimum wages and maximum hours were typically upheld by the courts; the main exception was the 1905 *Lochner* ruling that a New York law setting the maximum hours that bakers could work was an unconstitutional violation of freedom of contract.

The important *Adkins v. Children's Hospital* case in 1923 made *Lochner* less anomalous.[17] In *Adkins*, the Court ruled against Washington, DC's minimum-wage law for women on due process grounds, announcing that "freedom of contract is . . . the general rule and restraint the exception; and the exercise of legislative authority to abridge it can be justified only by the existence of exceptional circumstances."[18] Similarly, a DC rent control statute that had been upheld in the 1921 case *Block v. Hirsh* made its way back to the Court in 1924, in *Chastleton Corp. v. Sinclair*.[19] This time, the Court unanimously struck down the statute, as the emergency that had "justified interference with ordinarily existing property rights" had passed (we later will see how other decisions in this spirit threatened to undermine key New Deal policies in the mid-1930s).[20]

Open-Market Operations and the Interwar Gold Standard

The recession of 1920 to 1921 changed the role of the Fed by revealing the power of a new tool for economic stabilization. During the recession, the reserve banks' transactions with member banks slowed so significantly that the reserve banks risked earning too little to meet their expenses. From October 1921 to May 1922, the individual reserve banks, in an uncoordinated manner, purchased around $400 million in government securities to try to improve their earnings.[21] They began to realize that these purchases affected conditions in the market for government securities and in turn affected credit and economic conditions more broadly.

The reserve banks decided it would be beneficial to coordinate their purchases and sales of government securities in response to credit conditions—a tool known as *open-market operations*. In 1923, the Open-Market Investment Committee was established for this purpose. The Open-Market Investment Committee was chaired by Benjamin Strong, who since 1914 had been governor of the Federal Reserve Bank of New York. Strong, a banker who had attended the Jekyll Island retreat and supported the Aldrich plan, was perhaps the most powerful man in the Federal Reserve System in the 1920s. Strong had opposed the Fed Board's subservience to the Treasury in 1919, urging an earlier rise in the discount rate.[22]

Strong's policy making at the Fed was underpinned by his "internationalist" views, shared by much of the East Coast elite at the time, who favored expanding the economic and diplomatic role of the United States. Those with this viewpoint tended to be Anglophiles, admiring British governance and hoping for tighter cooperation between the United States and Britain.[23] Strong had developed close ties with British bankers during the war and envisioned the Fed as an even greater international financial power that could assist with postwar European financial rehabilitation—which, in his view, required a return to the gold standard.

Indeed, a return to postwar normalcy, for much of the world, meant a return to the international gold standard. Recall that governments of many of the belligerent nations had financed the war by suspending specie payments, exporting gold, borrowing, and printing money. The departure from gold was intended to be temporary—countries had abandoned the gold standard in previous wars and returned after. This time, the return to gold was especially complicated because of the massive inflation and gold shipments that had occurred during the war. There was far more currency relative to gold reserves than before the war, so less gold was available to back each unit of currency. The supply of gold had been fairly stagnant since the beginning of the war, and experts did not predict that any major new gold discoveries were forthcoming. Many governments believed that returning to gold at prewar parity was critical for the credibility of their commitment to the gold standard but knew that it would lead to major deflation and general economic turmoil.[24]

Representatives of thirty-four nations met at the Genoa Conference in 1922 to try to resolve the challenges facing the international economic order, including the challenge of returning to gold. It seemed impossible that central banks could obtain enough gold to provide sufficient reserve backing for their money supplies.[25] Thus, they came up with a new system to economize on gold: the gold exchange standard. The idea was that countries would maintain convertibility between their currency and gold, but central banks would supplement their reserves with foreign exchange. That is, they could hold less gold and more foreign currencies, especially dollars and pounds, as reserves.[26]

The difference in reserves was not the only difference between the prewar "classical" gold standard and the interwar gold exchange standard. Another major difference was that the prewar gold standard was inherently stable because central banks were credibly committed to it. That is, as the economic historian Barry Eichengreen explains, "there was little doubt that the authorities ultimately would take whatever steps were required to defend the central bank's gold reserves and maintain the convertibility of the currency into gold." This faith was self-fulfilling: "If one of these central banks lost gold reserves and its exchange rate weakened, funds would flow in from abroad in anticipation of the capital gains investors in domestic assets would reap once the authorities adopted measures to stem reserve losses and strengthen the exchange rate. Because there was no question about the commitment to the existing parity, capital flowed in quickly and in considerable volume . . . and stabilizing capital flows minimized the need for government intervention."[27] This credible commitment to gold, moreover, was international, and international cooperation could be counted on. After World War I, this credibility and cooperation became substantially weaker because central banks' commitment to prioritizing maintenance of the gold standard above all other goals became far less politically feasible.[28] As politicians and the public came to recognize the power of monetary policy to pursue domestic objectives, like employment and price stabilization, central banks were increasingly subject to political pressure to pursue these goals even when such pursuit conflicted with the prescriptions of the gold standard: "The decisions of central bankers, long regarded as obscure, became grist for the political mill."[29]

For example, under the classical gold standard, if a central bank were losing gold reserves, it would increase the interest rate (tighten monetary policy) to attract more gold reserves. During the interwar period, the central bank might have faced pressure to avoid tightening monetary policy so as not to reduce domestic prices and employment.[30] As a result, capital no longer automatically flowed between countries in stabilizing directions in response to economic shocks. In Europe, the pressure to pursue domestic goals with monetary policy arose largely from the spread of unionism, the extension of franchise, and new political parties representing the interests of the working class.[31] These forces put a new political emphasis on employment goals.

In the United States, the labor movement was weakened in the early 1920s and union membership declined. Still, Governor Strong recognized the importance of price stability for minimizing labor unrest. During the Great Railroad Strike of 1922, he wrote a letter to the editor of the *Station Agent*, the publication of the Order of Railroad Station Agents: "Labor disputes are rarely very serious, long extended or disorderly, except when they have to do with compensation, and compensation disputes almost always arise when prices are rising. Periods of falling prices give rise to demands for fiat money and Government subsidies of this industry or that. Therefore, is not the fundamental condition of industrial and national tranquillity that of reasonable stability of prices, as from 1909 till toward the close of 1915?"[32] With open-market operations, the Fed could stabilize domestic prices even as the United States ran a trade surplus and gold flowed into the country. The Fed could sterilize these gold flows by selling government securities on the open market so that money supply and domestic prices didn't rise as much as they otherwise would have. Although this policy contrasted with the "rules of the game" of an international gold standard by preventing the functioning of the price-specie-flow mechanism, it worked well for a time. Reparations payments flowed from Germany to the Allies, who in turn sent funds to the United States to repay war debts. The United States' lending to the rest of the world kept the flow of funds precariously balanced and the gold standard viable.[33]

Despite the relative stability of prices after the 1920 to 1921 recession, farmers remained unsatisfied with monetary policy and with their relative economic position. Remember that farmers and their representatives had opposed the gold standard during the deflationary period beginning in the 1870s and had pushed for monetary expansion via silver or paper money. The deflation of 1920 and 1921 provoked similar sentiment. William Jennings Bryan, the populist politician who gave the "cross of gold" speech at the 1896 Democratic National Convention, continued to advocate on behalf of the farmer, about whom he wrote that "higher prices alone will save him from the injustice done him by falling prices." Bryan thought that the Fed, beholden to Wall Street, was ignoring the plight of the farmers:

> The Federal Reserve Bank that should have been the farmer's greatest protection has become his greatest foe. The deflation of the farmer was a crime deliberately committed, not out of enmity to the farmer but out of indifference to him. . . . While the Federal Reserve Bank Law is the greatest economic reform achieved in the last half-century, if not in our National history, it would be better to repeal it, go back to old conditions and take our chances with individual financiers, then to turn the Federal Reserve Bank over to Wall Street and allow its tremendous power to be used for the carrying out of the plans of the Money Trust.[34]

The Goldsborough and Strong Stabilization Bills

That the Fed could and should do more to help farmers seemed obvious to some politicians, many of whom were influenced by Irving Fisher. Fisher had updated and expounded upon his compensated-dollar plan in a 1920 book, *Stabilizing the Dollar: A Plan to Stabilize the General Price Level without Fixing Individual Prices.* The "crux of the plan," as he summarized, was to use an "adjustment rule by which the index number regulates the dollar's weight": "To keep the dollar from shrinking in value we make it grow in weight, thus recognizing that a depreciated dollar is a short-weight dollar; and, reversely, to keep the dollar from growing in value we make it shrink in weight, thus recognizing that an appreciated dollar is an over-weight dollar. Or, in alternative terms, since a heavier or lighter dollar simply means a lowered or raised price of gold, we may say that: To keep the price level of other things from rising or falling we make the price of gold fall or rise."[35] For Fisher, price stabilization was a social justice issue; as he argued, "With each change in the purchasing power of money (in other words, with each change in the price level), some people lose what properly belongs to them and others gain what does not properly belong to them."[36] These losses and gains, or "social pocket-picking," came from contracts fixed in nominal terms, from the slow adjustment of salaries and wages to price changes, and from the mistakes induced by *money illusion,* or people's tendency to confuse real and nominal values.

He highlighted the social injustice of price fluctuations in order to emphasize the legitimacy of congressional action to minimize them: "We, the people, neglect the problem, and therefore Congress which, under the Constitution, has the power to regulate the value of money, neglects it also. . . . Stabilizing the dollar would directly and indirectly accomplish more social justice and go farther in the solution of our industrial, commercial, and financial problems than almost any other reform proposed in the world today; and this it would do without the exertion of any repressive police force, but as simply and silently as setting our watches."

Fisher appeared before the House Banking and Currency Committee in 1922 to speak on behalf of a bill introduced by Representative Thomas Goldsborough, a Maryland Democrat. The Goldsborough bill would have implemented Fisher's proposal to stabilize the purchasing power of the dollar. The *New York Times,* reporting on the bill, quoted Fisher's explanation: "The gold dollar is now fixed in weight and therefore variable in purchasing power. What we need is a gold dollar fixed in purchasing power and therefore variable in weight."[37]

Although the Goldsborough bill did not pass, similar proposals came up again and again. The Fed's stabilization powers impressed Congressman James Strong, a Kansas Republican (of no relation to Benjamin Strong), who hoped to formalize them through legislation similar to the Goldsborough bill. The Strong bill proposed that "all of the powers of the Federal reserve system shall be used for promoting stability in the price level."[38] It is worth emphasizing what the Goldsborough and Strong proposals implied. If the Federal Reserve was to use all of its powers to stabilize the price level, it would not be able to use its powers to manage the gold standard. Domestic price stabilization would take full precedence. Before World War I, countries on the classical gold standard did have fairly stable price levels over the longer run, but that price stability over the shorter run was not the objective of the central bank. In that sense, the proposal was highly unorthodox.

However, a price stabilization mandate for the Fed would not imply a complete departure from the Fed's de facto behavior since the discovery of open-market operations. Under Governor Strong's leadership, and using its new policy tool, the Fed was able to stabilize prices throughout the mid-1920s, and recessions in 1923–1924 and 1926–1927 were very mild. And some leading Fed figures, such as Carl Snyder, head of the Statistical Department at the New York Fed, wondered why "we still cling to the fetish of a 'gold standard,' despite the fact that for more than a century many of our ablest economists and approved financial writers have seriously considered other and more stable standards of value."[39] He pointed to the impressive development of price indexes that had occurred since the government began constructing them in the 1880s, which would make price stabilization more technically feasible: "In the quite astonishing array of index numbers which we now possess, of wholesale and retail prices, wages, production, employment, wholesale and retail trade, volume of goods transported, etc., coupled with most exhaustive bank statements for the whole country, we now have a far more accurate and reliable guide for automatic determination of the currency issue than the foreign exchanges could possibly be; so accurate, indeed, that we now know definitely when and at what rate our currency is depreciating or appreciating, and have little or no need to refer, for this, to the foreign exchanges."[40] When Congressman Strong presented his price stabilization bill before the House in 1926, he urged Congress to "declare for stability." Price stabilization, he thought, could address the farm problem in the way that was "the most nearly just, as between debtors and creditors, taking into account the conditions as a whole": "For now the sixth year a crisis has existed for the farming population, and one of the remedies is for Congress to instruct the Federal reserve officials to promote stability. Why should we not seek to stabilize the general price level for the good of all, business, agriculture, and industry? Is it not time to take the money question out of politics or any special class?"[41] Congressman Strong claimed to have sent out form letters to more than five thousand financiers and economists across the country to solicit their opinions about price stabilization. The results convinced him that the Federal Reserve, through its open-market operations and discount rate and credit policies, had the power to stabilize the purchasing power of the dollar:

> It is a tremendous power. No greater power was ever given by any government in the history of the world than these powers, except perhaps the power of life and death and liberty. The Constitution directed Congress to "coin money" and to "regulate the value thereof," and while we have complied with the direction so far as

> the coinage of money is concerned, we have so far only complied with the direction to regulate the value of money by defining the number of grains of gold that shall constitute the dollar, without making any effort to determine and fix the value of the gold. So that direction of the Constitution has not been very well carried out, and I doubt if we ever had an opportunity to carry it out until the creation of the Federal reserve system with the great powers that have been placed in its hands.[42]

Fisher testified on behalf of the Strong bill. Another key supporter was Henry A. Wallace, who would later become vice president in the Roosevelt administration and who testified that the bill would promote agricultural interests. Wallace's father, Henry C. Wallace, was the secretary of agriculture from 1921 until his death in 1924. The younger Wallace explained that he had been interested in Fisher's compensated-dollar scheme "since 1913 or 1914," when "my grandfather said to me, 'You must get interested in this subject.'"[43] He viewed the price stabilization bill as a preferable alternative to staying on the gold standard and gradually allowing the price level to fall back to its prewar level: "I can say, from a political standpoint, that if we do take that long, slow, painful, grinding deflation toward the 1913 price level, the difficulty of farmers in paying interest on their mortgage indebtedness will bring about a political situation somewhat similar to that which existed in the eighties and nineties, of farmers to some extent striking out rather blindly in their wrath to find if they can not do something."[44] Another supporter of the bill who testified in Congress was George Shibley, a lawyer and populist reformer. Shibley had supported the Bryan campaign in 1896, the same year that he published a book advocating "governmental control of paper money in order to secure a stable measure of prices—stable money."[45] He was also a good friend of Senator Owen, who had pushed for a price stabilization mandate at the founding of the Fed.[46] In the 1926 hearings, he told Congress that "the business interests have aimed at and secured inflation" and "the creditor class have aimed at and secured deflation. Both deflation and inflation have injured the masses, as contrasted with the effects from stable money, and the masses are again to insist on stable money."[47] The Strong bill, Shibley argued, would remove what he saw as the Fed's excessive discretionary authority "to deflate the people's money and bank credit, or inflate, as the majority of the board may decide from time to time." Instead, "the index number of the price level will be publicly known each week and the law will be obeyed."[48]

Governor Benjamin Strong, despite his crucial role in developing the Fed's stabilization powers, did not support the proposed legislation. In contrast to Shibley, he thought that the bill, by removing the discipline of the gold standard, would give more discretion to Federal Reserve officials and increase the possibility of policy errors. Strong asked, "What safeguards are we going to introduce in regard to ignorance, stupidity, and bad judgment in the exercise of this power? How are we to deal with the problem of divided counsels in the system, where no action is possible because of differences of opinion? Is it possible to guard the misuse of these powers for selfish or even improper purposes, or even political objects, if you please?"

Governor Strong's reluctance also came from concerns about how the public would interpret the bill. First, he expressed "doubts about the effect of the bill on the minds of people who are not economists, and who really can not distinguish between individual prices and general prices." He feared that people would confuse stabilization of the general price level with the *fixing* of individual prices, and would believe thus that Congress had issued a mandate to the Fed to fix prices. He told Congress:

> Now, I can not believe that any such power to fix prices would prove acceptable to the people of this country or to the people of any democracy . . . I do not think that any such power exists or can be created to fix prices. . . . Much of the discussion of prices recently has arisen from the great misfortune which the farmers of the country have-suffered, which we all recognize and deplore. If the Federal

> reserve act is amended in these words, is it possible that the farmers of the country will be advised, or will be led to believe upon reading it, that a mandate has been handed to the Federal reserve system to fix up this matter of farm prices?[49]

When Democratic congressman Otis Wingo, of Arkansas, replied that "the farmer already thinks that you have that power and already thinks you are exercising it," Governor Strong responded: "Yes. Well, can we not disabuse his mind of that?" Wingo retorted, "I doubt it very seriously; although Mr. Strong, the author of the bill, is quite a farmer himself."[50] Governor Strong also offered a behavioral economics argument against a price stabilization mandate:

> For instance, take the laboring man. When he is working in the factory during the day, he is a believer in advancing prices. He thinks that will aid him in giving him constant employment at good wages. He goes home, however, and then his character changes. He is a consumer then, and he is liable to complain about the amount of rent that he has to pay, or his wife is complaining about the cost of sugar, and his whole attitude toward the regulation of prices changes. It seems to me that if the Federal reserve system is recognized as a price regulator it is going to be somewhat in the position of the poor man who tried to stop a row between an Irishman and his wife. They both turned in and beat him.[51]

In other words, people like higher prices for the things they sell or for their labor, but not for the things they buy, without recognizing that these go together—an insight that was later confirmed by the Nobel Prize winner Robert Shiller.[52] The bill was eventually defeated, as was a second Strong bill in 1928, but later chapters detail how the Fed eventually received a mandate to pursue price stability. Years after the Goldsborough and Strong bill debates, Fisher recollected "two startling things" from his conversations with Governor Strong about these bills: "First, that the power that he and his colleagues had was so great that he shuddered to think of how it could be abused and how it could really be prevented from being abused. Second, that he did not want to have any legislative guidance for fear that in exercising the powers he and his colleagues might not be able to measure up to the requirements of law."[53]

Farm Price Parity

The deflation of the 1920s led not only to protectionist tariffs and proposals for monetary reform but also to proposals for agricultural price supports through government interventions in production, distribution, and credit. Interventions to decrease or control the volume of agricultural production, farmers thought, could raise prices.[54] Farmers pointed to a "wide discrepancy between the prices farmers receive for their products and the prices charged for the things which the farmer must purchase, including both manufactured articles and labor."[55] They remembered how the government had intervened in the war to keep prices down and argued that similar interventions "can be used now to keep the price of grain up."[56]

Bernard Baruch, who had been so influential in the Wilson administration and remained a prominent public figure, was a major proponent of government intervention to support farm prices. In 1921, he wrote: "The war showed convincingly how dependent the nation is on the full productivity of the farms. . . . We ought not to forget that lesson when we ponder on the farmer's problems. They are truly common problems, and there should be no attempt to deal with them as if they were purely the selfish demands of a clear-cut group, antagonistic to the rest of the community."

Baruch believed that solving the "farmer's problems" required "prudent and orderly adjustment of production and distribution in accordance with consumption," so that "production should be sure, steady, and increasing, and that distribution should be in proportion to the need." Government intervention in agricultural production and distribution was necessary, according to Baruch, because

"The unorganized farmers naturally act blindly and impulsively and, in consequence, surfeit and dearth, accompanied by disconcerting price-variations, harass the consumer."[57]

At the War Industries Board, Baruch had worked with George N. Peek, who served as the industrial representative to the board. Before his service in Washington, Peek was an executive at the Moline Plow Company in Illinois.[58] After the Armistice, Peek attributed the troubles of his near-bankrupt business to the farmer's problem: "You can't sell a plow to a busted customer."[59] Peek thought that President Harding's tariffs protected industry more than agriculture. Farmers, he believed, were more in need of protection, because they were forced to produce surpluses to insure against unpredictable crop failures and inclement weather. Farm surpluses, in turn, drove farm prices down.

Peek and General Hugh S. Johnson, a businessman and former army officer, wrote that "the doctrine of protection must be revised to insure agriculture equality of tariff protection" through "some plan, in respect of surplus crops, to equalize supply with demand on the domestic market[,] . . . to protect that value by a tariff, and to divert surplus to export and sell it at world price."[60] In particular, they thought that domestic crop prices should be fixed at their average levels from 1910 to 1914, and that the government should establish an export corporation to buy any surpluses and sell them at a loss in international markets.[61] This would be a "two-price" system, because domestic prices would be higher than international prices. The plan would also impose an equalization fee, or a tax on farmers to cover any losses incurred by the export corporation from selling the surplus crops abroad.

With the support of Baruch, Peek proposed his plan at the National Agricultural Conference in January 1922, organized by Secretary of Agriculture Henry C. Wallace. During the initial years of the farm crisis, Wallace was staunchly opposed to direct government intervention in farm markets.[62] But Secretary Wallace saw that the Department of Agriculture needed to act to improve farmers' conditions and to satisfy the demands of the growing congressional farm bloc. Thus, Peek was able to persuade the National Agricultural Congress to include the following in its final report: "Agriculture is necessary to the life of the Nation; and, whereas, the prices of agricultural products are far below the cost of production, so far below that relatively they are the lowest in the history of our country; therefore it is the sense of this committee that the Congress and the President of the United States should takes such steps as will immediately reestablish a fair exchange value for all farm products with that of all other commodities."[63] In the years that followed, this "fair exchange value" goal came to be known as *parity*. The parity goal referred to restoration of the prewar price ratio of agricultural products to consumer goods. As the historian James H. Shideler notes: "'Parity' was soon equated with justice and fairness, and parity prices could be determined by one or another formula through simple calculation. Continuing disparity, improved techniques for measuring it, and especially advancement of dramatic reform proposals aiming toward the achievement of parity put the concept permanently into the business thinking of farmers, into their politics, and into the economic study of agriculture."[64] Between 1922 and 1923, Peek persuaded Secretary Wallace of the viability of his plan. But the Peek plan met resistance from former "food czar" Herbert Hoover. Hoover had supported Harding in his 1920 campaign and was rewarded with an appointment as secretary of commerce. Hoover agreed with Peek's diagnosis that overproduction and surplus were the causes of farmers' eroding purchasing power. But he disagreed with the cure, fearing that anti-price-fixing legislation would politicize the economy and prompt extensive lobbying in Congress while benefiting large agricultural producers more than small farmers.[65] Hoover said of government price-fixing: "I have done more of it than any other man who lives . . . and I would not propose price-fixing in any form short of again reentering the trenches in a World War."[66]

Hoover also questioned the jurisdiction of the Department of Agriculture in regulating foreign purchases and sales, stating in 1921 that the "functions of the Department of Agriculture should end when production on the farm is complete and movement therefrom starts, and at that point the activities of the Department of Commerce should begin."[67] Hoover instead pushed for expanding the use of voluntary farm marketing cooperatives, which he thought could allow farmers to better diversify and market their crops to reduce the need for farm surpluses.[68] Secretary Wallace, while touring rural American farmlands with President Harding, observed the farm cooperatives and found them insufficient. "I thoroughly agree with those who insist that what is needed is fair prices," he told the president.[69]

When President Harding died in August 1923, Hoover was reappointed as commerce secretary by the new president, Calvin Coolidge, who shared Hoover's views on farm relief. Wallace tried to convince the president that farm cooperatives, though meritorious, were not effective enough to give farmers "that control over supply which is necessary substantially to influence price."[70] Instead, Wallace continued to push for the Peek proposal of a government export corporation "to restore, so far as possible, the prewar ratio between wheat, and other farm products of which we export at surplus, and other commodities." Such a corporation, he acknowledged, "necessarily would need rather broad powers."[71]

Peek's plan also found supporters in Congress. In January 1924, Senator Charles L. McNary and Representative Gilbert N. Haugen—both Republicans—introduced a version of the plan in the McNary-Haugen bill. Supporters included the American Farm Bureau Federation and the National Board of Farm Organizations. The bill was opposed by a broad coalition, including Coolidge, Hoover, and business allies in Congress. It was also opposed by Southern agricultural interests, because at the time cotton prices were higher than parity prices, so the bill would have implied a reduction in cotton prices.

In 1924 the McNary-Haugen bill failed in the House by a vote of 223–155, but it was resurrected three times.[72] In 1926 it was defeated again by a slightly closer margin. In 1927, lower cotton prices garnered more Southern support for the bill, and it passed both the House and the Senate. But Coolidge vetoed the bill on Hoover's advice.[73] The same happened again the following year. Coolidge argued that "the equalization fee was not a true tax but instead represented an unconstitutional delegation of the taxing power of Congress, and was a tax for an arbitrarily selected class of citizens."[74]

Thus, Peek's vision did not become law—although elements of it would be resurrected in the New Deal. But by the end of the decade-long struggle over farm relief, farmers came to equate parity prices with fairness and justice and to accept a growing power of government that could intervene in agricultural production to achieve the price stability that they so prized.[75]

The Roaring Twenties

While the Goldsborough, Strong, and McNary-Haugen bills were being debated, the economy overall was booming. The Federal Reserve, like the First and Second Banks of the United States, was originally established with a twenty-year charter, set to expire in 1934. But by 1927, after several years of strong growth and rising gold reserves, the Fed was seen as such a success that Congress re-chartered the Fed into perpetuity with the McFadden Act.[76]

Governor Strong, whose health was deteriorating following recurrent bouts of tuberculosis, continued to lead the Federal Reserve Bank of New York and to support and lend to European central banks that were returning to the gold standard. In 1927, he favored a policy of low interest rates in the United States to facilitate the Bank of England's return to gold. The idea was that low interest rates would prompt less gold to flow into the United States and more into England, where investors could get higher returns.[77] The Federal Reserve Bank of New York's annual report for 1927 argued that what was good for Europe was good for America (and American farmers): "The reduction in discount rate was made at a time when domestic business was beginning to show some recession and the financial position of Europe was such that considerable financial stringency was threatened by the continuance of a four per cent discount rate in New York. A general increase in interest rates in Europe during the fall season would undoubtedly have restricted foreign purchases of American farm products."[78] Strong exhorted the other reserve bank governors to reduce discount rates as well. Chicago Governor James McDougal dissented, writing to Strong: "It seems to me that the desired result has already been attained through the reduction in your rate . . . up to the present time we are not convinced as to the necessity of having a uniform rate in all districts."[79] In September 1927, the Federal Reserve Board ordered McDougal to reduce the Chicago Fed's discount rate. McDougal reluctantly complied. Although Strong preferred that the other reserve banks lower rates, he opposed the board's attempt to seize control over discount rate policy. A struggle for control between the board and the reserve banks continued into the next year, when the mild recession was over and the stock market was booming.

By early 1928, members of the Federal Reserve Board and the Federal Reserve Bank of New York agreed that excessive speculation in the stock market was a concern, but they disagreed about how to discourage it. The board, wary of a repeat of the recession and deflation that had followed sharp discount rate increases in 1920, hoped that speculative excesses could be curbed without substantial rate increases through a policy of direct pressure on member banks—that is, dissuading them from speculative activity while leaving interest rates low for "productive" uses.[80] Strong worried that the direct pressure would cause "disastrous" credit rationing, and he instead pushed for increases in the discount rate.[81]

The Federal Reserve Board did approve of several discount rate increases in 1928, from 3.5 percent in January to 5 percent in July, before Strong's death in October shifted the balance of power from the New York Fed to the board and put the rate hikes on hold. At the same time that the Fed was raising discount rates, it also conducted substantial contractionary open-market operations, selling government securities to reduce member banks' reserves. This monetary policy, though highly contractionary, was not enough to put a damper on the booming stock market.[82] Market interest rates were rising in response to strong demand for loans to invest in the stock market. Because the discount rate did not rise as quickly as market interest rates, member banks still had an incentive to borrow from the Federal Reserve System so they could make loans at even higher interest rates.[83] Over the course of 1928, equity prices rose 39 percent and dividend payments also increased significantly, despite deteriorating economic conditions in other parts of the world that were beginning to weaken US exports.[84]

The next chapter explains how the Federal Reserve Board's hopes of avoiding another recession were soon dashed—and resoundingly. It also highlights the parallels between the Great Depression and the earlier 1920s recession, especially with respect to the price stabilization debates.

SEVEN

THE GREAT DEPRESSION AND THE NEW DEAL

> Values have shrunken to fantastic levels; taxes have risen; our ability to pay has fallen; government of all kinds is faced by serious curtailment of income; the means of exchange are frozen in the currents of trade; the withered leaves of industrial enterprise lie on every side; farmers find no markets for their produce; the savings of many years in thousands of families are gone. More important, a host of unemployed citizens face the grim problem of existence, and an equally great number toil with little return. . . . It is to be hoped that the normal balance of executive and legislative authority may be wholly adequate to meet the unprecedented task before us. But it may be that an unprecedented demand and need for undelayed action may call for temporary departure from that normal balance of public procedure.
>
> FRANKLIN DELANO ROOSEVELT, "First Inaugural Address"[1]

Golden Fetters and Goldsborough's Return

The Great Depression, one of the greatest disasters in US economic history, had much in common with the recession of 1920–1921. Both began with a monetary tightening intended to curb speculation. Both were highly deflationary. And in both, reduced international demand put downward pressure on agricultural prices, hitting farmers especially hard. So naturally, some of the same policy proposals, like the Goldsborough bill and the plan for farm price parity, were resurrected. But the Depression was much longer lasting, and it ultimately had a larger and more enduring impact on economic policy and economic thought.

Recall that by late 1928, there were signs that the Roaring Twenties were coming to a close. Exports were slowing and commodity prices were falling, reflecting weak global demand. But the stock market continued to boom, so the Federal Reserve Board finally allowed the Federal Reserve Bank of New York to increase the discount rate to 6 percent in August.[2] The short-run effects of this rate hike were dramatic. Industrial production fell by a full percentage point from July to August.[3] The booming stock market collapsed at the end of October: the Dow Jones Industrial Average fell around 13 percent on Black Monday, October 28, and another 12 percent on Black Tuesday, October 29, kicking off a nearly three-year decline.[4] Macroeconomic consequences were even more shocking. The price level fell 25 percent, and real and nominal gross national product declined 33 percent and nearly 50 percent, respectively, from 1929 to 1933. The unemployment rate shot up from less than 4 percent to more than 25 percent, and it remained above 10 percent until World War II.[5]

It is notable that, to rein in the stock market, Fed officials were willing to increase discount rates in 1929 despite declining commodity prices.[6] According to Friedman and Schwartz, the monetary policy tightening that began in 1928 and continued into 1929 was a grave mistake, which arose when "in the absence of any single well-defined statutory objective, conflicts developed between discretionary objectives of monetary policy. . . . The bull market brought the objective of promoting business activity into conflict with the desire to restrain stock market speculation."[7] Had either the Goldsborough or the Strong bill passed earlier in the decade, committing the Fed to using all of its powers to stabilize the price level, this action would not have been warranted.

International trade linkages and the gold exchange standard meant that the increase in the discount rate in the United States had large international repercussions. World War I had strengthened the United States' balance-of-payments position relative to that of the European economies, so a gold flow from the United States to Europe was critical for keeping current accounts "tenuously balanced" and preventing a large accumulation of gold in the United States.[8] But the discount rate hike attracted gold into the United States, curtailing lending to Europe and Latin America. To stay on the gold standard and continue making external debt payments, many countries had to increase their own interest rates and cut government spending, despite weak domestic macroeconomic conditions.[9]

The rules of the gold standard, in other words, called for deflation to improve these countries' trade balances and bring the international system back to equilibrium. Hume, remember, had recognized that equilibration under the price-specie-flow mechanism could take some time because of price inflexibility in the short run. That price inflexibility was exacerbated by the spread of unionism and other labor-market developments that made wages difficult to adjust.[10] As the failure of wages to decline led to rising unemployment, the United States' trade partners entered recessions. The downturn in the United States was so severe because the international depression reduced foreign demand for US exports at the same time that the Fed's contractionary monetary policy reduced domestic demand. Producers could not sell their goods at home or abroad, and instead they curtailed production.

For agricultural goods, curtailing production in response to weak demand was not always feasible. Farm products have nearly inelastic supply—that is, their supply is determined by farmers' past planting decisions and can't be quickly adjusted. Thus, beginning in early 1930, farm prices, especially of traded products like wheat, cotton, and tobacco, fell much more rapidly than other prices. Because farmers were already highly indebted, the fall in their income resulting from agricultural price declines led them to sharply reduce their consumption, and the demands for farm relief that had continued throughout the 1920s intensified.[11]

Herbert Hoover, while secretary of commerce, had opposed the McNary-Haugen bill of 1924 and its agricultural parity plan, preferring the expansion of farm cooperatives to "price fixing." When Hoover became president in 1929, he followed through with his campaign pledges to help farmers through cooperatives and protective tariffs. The Agricultural Marketing Act of 1929 established the Federal Farm Board with a $500 million fund to help stabilize agricultural prices. The board helped create nationwide cooperative marketing corporations for grain, wool, and cotton, and it could lend to these cooperatives to support farmers in "holding back" crops when prices were believed to be unduly low. For example, in late 1929, the board encouraged farmers not to sell their grain until prices had risen.[12] But the Agricultural Marketing Act provided very little relief for farmers or for the overall economy. The Smoot-Hawley Tariff of 1930, which increased tariffs on thousands of imported goods, also failed to help, as trading partners imposed retaliatory tariffs, and imports and exports plummeted.[13]

Nor did monetary policy stem the contraction. In what is now widely recognized as one of the biggest mistakes in Federal Reserve history, the Fed allowed the money stock to fall by failing to act as lender of last resort when a series of banking panics began in 1930. As in the early 1920s, rural banks were most likely to fail, as farmers couldn't make their loan repayments. The banking crisis worsened the depression and contributed to deeper deflation as fearful depositors withdrew their funds, reducing banks' reserves and forcing banks to contract their loans. The money and credit contraction reduced spending, production, employment, and prices. Deflation made it harder for households and firms to repay debts, leading to defaults and bankruptcies, and prolonging the financial distress.

Substantial monetary expansion would have required abandoning the gold standard, and policy makers around the world were tremendously reluctant to do so. "Beholden to the gold-standard mentality," Eichengreen and Peter Temin explain, they "refused to question the advisability of pursuing the deflationary route": "The Victorian and Edwardian virtues of thrift, reliability, stability, and cosmopolitanism were invoked ritually as attributes of the monetary system. Gold was moral, principled and civilized; managed money the opposite. The former was preserved by deflation, and the rhetoric of deflation was to cut wages. Only 'speculators' disagreed. This rhetoric delegitimized the arguments of those who dared question the merits of gold convertibility."[14] Nonetheless, the international gold standard began to unravel. Britain, which had returned to the gold standard in 1925, finally suspended it in September 1931, as speculative attacks on sterling drained Britain's gold reserves and forced a devaluation of the pound.[15] The rest of the British Empire and the Scandinavian countries devalued their currencies soon after, and some countries in Latin America had done so even before Britain. Countries that stayed on the gold standard longer tended to have more severe deflation and depression.[16]

The United States remained on the gold standard, but Irving Fisher—who famously failed to foresee the Great Crash coming—led another charge for monetary reform. The Depression reinforced his belief in the tremendous social benefits of price stabilization. And he saw that "the evils of deflation and liquidation through bankruptcy and default manifest themselves more malevolently in agriculture than in any other great industrial group."[17] Fisher was inspired by the Swedish Riksbank, the central bank of Sweden, which after leaving the gold standard in 1931, pledged to use all of its power to stabilize the purchasing power of the Swedish krona, making use of a weekly government-constructed index of consumer prices.[18]

With Fisher's encouragement, Representative Goldsborough introduced another price stability bill, which would have amended the Federal Reserve Act to make it "the policy of the United States that the average purchasing power of the dollar as ascertained by the Department of Labor in the wholesale commodity markets for the period covering the years 1921 to 1929, inclusive, shall be restored and maintained by the control of the volume of credit and currency."[19] The bill would have authorized the Federal Reserve Board to raise or lower the official price of gold if necessary for stabilizing the price level. Senator Duncan Fletcher, a Florida Democrat, introduced a similar bill in the Senate.

Henry A. Wallace and other representatives of farm interests again spoke in favor of the price stabilization bill, as did a representative of the American Federation of Labor. Former Senator Robert Owen, who had supported a price stabilization mandate at the founding of the Fed, also lent his backing. The bill was opposed by the New York Merchants' Association, who thought it would "help debtors by the destruction of creditors through the issuance of fiat money."[20] Federal Reserve officials also had strong reservations. Governor Eugene Meyer, for example, approved of the goal of price stabilization but argued: "You cannot accomplish it by law because it is a matter of judgment. You cannot supply judgment by law." He added: "If it were possible to take your resolution and put it into effect and accomplish the result you have in mind—I would like to say absolutely this is the thing for you to do and I will do my best to help to carry out every purpose. . . . But this bill contemplates, it seems to me, that a small group of men will understand things in the future that men nowhere understood within the last 10 years."[21] The board's Adolph Miller insisted that a legislated price stabilization mandate would lead to "a disaster, a breakdown," and that the Depression would have been even worse had such legislation been in place. He did not trust index numbers as a guide to policy, claiming: "The average of commodity prices does not mean anything. It is merely a metaphysical concept, something that has been invented by economists. It has no counterpart in actuality—it can not be traded in, bought, or sold. It is purely a figment of the mind."[22]

In the end, the Goldsborough bill easily passed in the House by a vote of 289–60. In the Senate, however, the bill was successfully blocked by Senator Carter Glass, who had helped author the Federal Reserve Act years earlier and had opposed Senator Owen regarding the price stabilization mandate.[23]

The Banking Crisis and Banking Holiday

The failure of the Goldsborough bill kept the Fed legally committed to the gold standard. But other legislation passed in 1932 broadened the Fed's emergency lending authority and enabled it to pursue more expansionary monetary policy. First, in January, President Hoover signed the Reconstruction Finance Corporation Act at the behest of Governor Meyer and made Meyer the chair of the new Reconstruction Finance Corporation. The quasi-public corporation was modeled after the War Finance Corporation of World War I and could extend loans to financial institutions with wide discretion as to the type of collateral that was acceptable.[24] The Reconstruction Finance Corporation essentially took on the lender-of-last-resort role on behalf of the Fed and provided loans to more than half the banks in the United States.[25] The Emergency Relief and Construction Act of 1932, which amended the Reconstruction Finance Corporation Act, added Section 13(3) to the Federal Reserve Act, expanding the Fed's authority to lend to a broader set of institutions in "unusual and exigent circumstances."[26]

The Banking Act of 1932 gave the reserve banks the authority to lend to member banks using types of assets that were not previously eligible for discount and to use government securities (rather than just gold and commercial paper) as collateral for Federal Reserve notes. Right away, the financial community understood that the Banking Act was intended to be inflationary. The *Commercial and Financial Chronicle* wrote that "the purpose is perfectly plain, the country is to be flooded with credit and with currency on the idea that thus it will be possible to stop deflation."[27]

With its new Banking Act authorities, the Fed began buying government securities in great volume. Between April and August, its purchases totaled about 2 percent of gross domestic product.[28] This open-market purchase program more than doubled the Fed's holdings of government debt. Although the Fed did not publicly announce its intentions for the open-market purchase program, the way it has with more recent programs of asset purchases, the public did quickly become aware of the program and understand its aims. For example, the *New York Times* reported on May 3, 1932, that "the Federal Reserve is engaged in the most determined effort to bring about a rise in the price level ever undertaken by any central bank."[29] The effort was successful while it lasted. Had the program lasted beyond August, the economy likely would have recovered more quickly.[30] It doesn't seem that the Fed was forced to stop the monetary expansion in order to stay on the gold standard, as exchange rate data give no indication that market participants began to doubt the Fed's commitment to the gold standard. Nor did Fed officials express much concern that the program would lead to a speculative attack on the dollar. Rather, the Fed thought the program had accomplished its goals, and the reserve banks couldn't maintain consensus to continue the program.[31]

When the program ended, the crisis was clearly not over; deflation continued, and the banking system remained fragile. Deflation and financial fragility built on each other, as deflation made borrowers less solvent and banks became less willing to extend credit in an environment of financial distress.[32] Hence the push for agricultural relief and monetary reform continued and became an important issue in the 1932 presidential campaign between President Hoover and his challenger, the Democrat Franklin Delano Roosevelt. In Roosevelt's campaign, he emphasized the "interdependence" between industry and agriculture, proclaiming, "Industrial prosperity can reach only artificial and temporary heights as it did in 1929 if at the same time there is no agricultural prosperity." He added that interdependence "applies also to the relationship between the different parts or our country. If in the South a cotton-raising population goes into bankruptcy because the price or cotton is so low that it does not pay for the cost of production, you in the wheat belt or in the corn belt are directly affected by a tragedy a thousand miles away."[33]

Roosevelt's promise that the government could play a more expansive role in agricultural and economic recovery appealed to a country still facing an unemployment rate near 25 percent. He won in a landslide, and Democrats gained large majorities in the House and Senate. In the lame-duck period between Roosevelt's election and inauguration, Congress continued to debate farm relief plans but made little progress. In October 1932, a drastic decline in livestock prices led to the near failure of a dozen banks in Nevada, as livestock raisers defaulted on loan repayments and the Nevada governor Fred Balzar declared a banking holiday.[34] During hearings over the proposed Agricultural Adjustment Relief Plan, Edward O'Neal, president of the American Farm Bureau Federation, warned that "unless something is done for the American farmer we will have revolution in the countryside within less than 12 months."[35]

One way that many hoped that Roosevelt would help the farmer was to devalue the dollar—to make it worth less in terms of gold, raising the price level. In January 1933, the president-elect suggested: "If the fall in the price of commodities cannot be checked, we may be forced to an inflation of our currency. This may take the form of using silver as a base, or decreasing the amount of gold in the dollar. I have not decided how this inflation can be best and most safely accomplished."[36]

Also in January, advocates for devaluation established the Committee for the Nation to Rebuild Prices and Purchasing Power. The committee's first interim report, circulated to leaders in industry, agriculture, and government, recommended a plan much like the one Fisher had long been advocating, in which "our dollar, instead of calling for redemption in a fixed number of grains of gold might call for a varying number of grains, so calculated as always to keep the price index at a practically fixed level."[37] Henry A. Wallace, Roosevelt's pick for secretary of agriculture and a well-known advocate of devaluation, was part of the committee's executive committee.[38]

The prospect that the president-elect would devalue undermined confidence in the dollar, which had been on shaky grounds since President Hoover, in a campaign speech in Des Moines, Iowa, revealed that the country had come close to defaulting on its dollar payments months earlier.[39] Foreign and domestic depositors, fearing impending devaluation, began to convert dollars to gold by withdrawing dollars from commercial banks and presenting them to the New York Fed for payment in gold. By February 1933, a major run on the dollar had ensued. Following Nevada's precedent, Michigan closed its banks, and other states followed in either closing their banks or limiting withdrawals. As gold drained out of the New York Fed, leaders of the New York Fed urged President Hoover to declare a national banking holiday, but Hoover was concerned about the legality of such action. His advisers suggested he could use the wartime authorities granted to the President by the Trading with the Enemy Act of 1917, but he ultimately resisted taking action.[40]

Roosevelt took office in the depths of the banking crisis. In his inaugural address on March 4, 1933, he announced that he would ask Congress for "broad Executive power to wage a war against the emergency, as great as the power that would be given to me if we were in fact invaded by a foreign foe." Extension of executive power in the face of emergency, Roosevelt argued, was no threat to "the future of essential democracy. . . . The people of the United States have not failed. In their need they have registered a mandate that they want direct, vigorous action."[41]

Convinced that the solution to the nation's problems was to reverse the deflation that so plagued the nation, Roosevelt moved with unprecedented speed to implement his New Deal policies, calling Congress to a special three-month session, which he coined his "first 100 days."[42] His first major action, on March 6, was to proclaim a four-day bank holiday, closing the banks and prohibiting sale or export of gold. On March 9, Congress passed the Emergency Banking Act, which amended the Trading with the Enemy Act so that presidential authority to restrict trade extended not only to wartime but also to "any other period of national emergency declared by the President."[43] The president extended the bank holiday to March 13. The night before the banks reopened, he gave his first fireside chat, promising that only sound banks would be reopened and explaining, "The new law allows the twelve Federal

Reserve banks to issue additional currency on good assets and thus the banks that reopen will be able to meet every legitimate call."[44]

When the banks reopened, depositors lined up to redeposit their gold despite continued fears of dollar devaluation. Some may have been motivated by patriotism or a newfound confidence inspired by Roosevelt's fireside chat and the de facto deposit insurance that the Emergency Banking Act created. But more likely, they redeposited their gold out of fear of retribution rather than a desire to hold paper. The Emergency Banking Act gave Roosevelt the authority to fine or imprison anyone caught violating prohibitions against gold hoarding or exporting.[45] The president issued several executive orders in April strengthening the prohibitions against gold exporting and hoarding, ensuring that most of the nation's gold was in the Fed's vaults and unable to leave the country. His April 20 proclamation formally suspended the gold standard. The Committee for the Nation boasted that the steps taken in March and April, which stopped the banking crisis, were ones they had recommended.

A New Deal for Monetary Policy

The president gained additional monetary authority with the Agricultural Adjustment Act (AAA), signed on May 12, 1933, "to relieve the existing national economic emergency by increasing agricultural purchasing power." The AAA was spearheaded by Secretary Wallace, whose father, Henry C. Wallace, had supported the McNary-Haugen bill on farm price parity. The AAA aimed to "reestablish prices to farmers at a level that will give agricultural commodities a purchasing power with respect to articles that farmers buy, equivalent to the purchasing power of agricultural commodities in the base period . . . August 1909–July 1914."[46]

The Thomas amendment of the AAA, also called the inflation amendment, gave the president an astonishing range of new monetary powers: it authorized him to issue greenbacks, to change the gold content of the dollar, and to remonetize silver. The amendment that Senator Elmer Thomas, Democrat of Oklahoma, originally introduced would have required the president to pursue inflation by issuing paper money, but Roosevelt insisted that be a discretionary authority.[47] The inflation amendment had huge implications for the Federal Reserve: it had to cooperate with the Treasury, lest the president simply issue greenbacks. Although most Federal Reserve officials disagreed with Roosevelt's goal of raising prices to 1926 levels, they began a program of open-market purchases "more to appease the President and the Congress and to forestall more drastic action than to attain some clearly defined monetary objective which they regarded as desirable."[48]

Near the end of the "first hundred days," representatives from sixty-six countries met in London to discuss economic recovery and currency stabilization. But on July 3, President Roosevelt issued his "bombshell" declaration: "The sound internal economic system of a nation is a greater factor in its well being than the price of its currency in changing terms of the currencies of other nations. . . . Let me be frank in saying that the United States seeks the kind of dollar which a generation hence will have the same purchasing and debt-paying power as the dollar value we hope to attain in the near future. That objective means more to the good of other Nations than a fixed ratio for a month or two in terms of the pound or franc."[49]

Among the United States delegates to the London Economic Conference was James Warburg, the son of Paul Warburg, the banker who had helped Aldrich design the Federal Reserve System. The younger Warburg intended to work for the reestablishment of an international gold standard. When the president made it clear that this was not his own aim, Warburg quietly resigned, hoping to privately "convince the President that it would be a mistake to continue his policy of monetary uncertainty and experimentation."[50]

By September, Warburg came to believe: "The tide could not be turned by a tolerated opposition from within. Public opinion would have to become aroused and articulate." In a public speech addressed to Fisher and Senator Thomas at the American Academy of Political and Social Science, speaking for what he saw as a "latent articulate majority," Warburg explained that, "given the political influences to which a democratic form of government will always be subject, I do not believe that as a practical matter there can be any such thing as a dollar of constant purchasing power. If human intelligence and human integrity were unable in the past to manage the comparatively simple mechanism of the gold standard, I can see no reason to suppose that the same human intelligence and human integrity will be able to cope with the vastly more complicated mechanism of the managed commodity dollar."[51]

Warburg argued that the American Revolution and the Civil War had taught that "controlled inflation" could not exist. But even if it could, he thought that "to raise the price level alone is, to my mind, not a proper aim of a recovery program":

> Unless a rise in prices is accompanied by a rise in incomes, I cannot see that it does any one any good. There is only one way that I know of to bring about a rise in prices together with a rise in national income, and that is by increasing the amount of business done in the expectation of a reasonable profit. There can be no increase in business activity so long as there is any uncertainty as to the future of the monetary unit. . . . Depreciation of the currency, and I am speaking now about "controlled depreciation," hurts every one who is more creditor than debtor, and aids only those who are preponderantly debtors. If inflation breaks away from control, it ruins all alike.[52]

But Warburg's arguments did not dissuade the president. In his October 1933 fireside chat, President Roosevelt repeated his intention to restore the price level and then "establish and maintain a dollar which will not change its purchasing and debt paying power during the succeeding generation." He announced that he was authorizing the Reconstruction Finance Corporation to buy gold in the United States or on the world market, establishing a government market for gold: "My aim in taking this step is to establish and maintain continuous control. This is a policy and not an expedient. It is not to be used merely to offset a temporary fall in prices. We are thus continuing to move towards a managed currency."[53] The mastermind behind the gold purchase program was Roosevelt's adviser, George Warren, a longtime scholar of farm prices, whom Irving Fisher admired as "one of the foremost proponents of stable money in this country."[54] Through gold purchases, which depreciated the dollar, Warren believed that commodity prices would rise. But investors didn't know just how far the dollar would fall until January 1934, when Roosevelt formally devalued the dollar, setting its price at $35 per ounce of gold. At that point, foreign capital began to pour into the United States, although this likely had more to do with the deteriorating political situation in Europe as Adolph Hitler came to power in Germany than with the dollar devaluation.[55]

Prices and industrial production grew rapidly under Roosevelt's reflationary policies. Just as traded crop prices fell the most in 1930, they grew the most quickly in 1933 as the dollar depreciated, and because farmers spent a large share of their additional earnings, the recovery in farm income contributed to broader recovery.[56] Irving Fisher commended the president, writing, "The fact that immediate reversal of deflation is easily achieved by the use, or even the prospect of use, of appropriate instrumentalities has just been demonstrated by President Roosevelt." He added: "If reflation can now so easily and quickly reverse the deadly down-swing of deflation after nearly four years, when it was gathering increased momentum, it would have been still easier, and at any time, to have stopped it earlier. . . . It would have been still easier to have prevented the depression almost altogether."[57]

To ensure that price stabilization would be pursued consistently in the future, Fisher and the Committee for the Nation supported Senator Goldsborough in introducing legislation to create the centralized Federal Monetary Authority, with total jurisdiction over the nation's monetary gold and sole authority to issue legal tender currency. The authority's directors, appointed by the president, would use their powers to promote stabilization of the price level.[58]

Explaining this plan in a letter to Senator Goldsborough, James Rand Jr., the chairman for the Committee for the Nation, wrote: "No government should permit such coercive power over its own credit to be held by any one group or class as the privately owned Federal Reserve System holds today. No government should delegate to private interests the control over the purchasing power of money." He continued: "President Roosevelt wisely asked and the Congress granted emergency powers which the Secretary of the Treasury can exercise until a permanent control mechanism can be devised and perfected. These emergency powers give to one man the constitutional authority of the Congress to regulate the value of money. Such permanent control should be lodged in an institution responsible to Congress and safeguarded from undue political and financial influence. . . . Our Government has been backward in recognizing that its sovereignty over coined money should be extended to paper currency, and has delegated to private interests this most important function."[59] At the Senate hearings on the bill, economics professor Willford King pointed out: "I do not think it is so surprising that the Federal Reserve Board has failed to regulate the price level, because the [Federal Reserve] act does not tell it to do so. . . . The purpose of this [Goldsborough] bill, as I understand, is to see to it that . . . somebody will be on hand whose specific duty it is to control the price level."[60]

Plans for the Federal Monetary Authority never came to fruition, but the Federal Reserve Act was amended to centralize some of the Fed's monetary authority. The Banking Act of 1935 transferred certain powers of the reserve banks to the Federal Reserve Board and changed the title of reserve bank leaders from *governor* to *president*, signifying their reduced control over monetary policy. It also vested control of open-market operations in the Federal Open Market Committee (FOMC), consisting of the seven members of the Board of Governors, the president of the Federal Reserve Bank of New York, and four other reserve bank presidents on a rotating basis, rather than all twelve reserve bank presidents.[61]

During the Senate hearings on the initial version of the bill,

James Warburg and members of the American Bankers Association expressed concern about the centralization of monetary policy in Washington and its potential inflationary consequences. To appease these critics, the Senate amended the bill to reduce the political influence over monetary policy, for example, by removing the Treasury secretary and the comptroller of the currency from the board.[62] One of the principal authors of the Banking Act was Marriner Eccles, a banker then working at the Treasury. Upon passage of the act, Roosevelt appointed Eccles as chairman of the Board of Governors, where Eccles acted as "virtually an assistant secretary of the Treasury for monetary affairs."[63] Eccles believed that fiscal spending could solve the Depression and that monetary policy should support fiscal expansion by keeping interest rates low.[64]

New Deal Price and Wage Controls

Another critical piece of New Deal legislation was the National Industrial Recovery Act (NIRA) of June 1933, partially modeled on the War Industries Board of World War I, which sought to promote industrial recovery and fair competition through several types of controls on prices and production. It suspended antitrust laws with the intent of facilitating higher prices through cartelization. The NIRA authorized the president to approve "codes of fair competition," overseen by the National Recovery Administration (NRA). The codes were supposed to strengthen workers' right to collective bargaining and to establish minimum wages.[65]

In his statement on the NIRA, President Roosevelt contended that "no business which depends for existence on paying less than living wages to its workers has any right to continue in this country." He explained that all employers should subscribe to an "industrial covenant":

> The idea is simply for employers to hire more men to do the existing work by reducing the work-hours of each man's week and at the

> same time paying a living wage for the shorter week. No employer and no group of less than all employers in a single trade could do this alone and continue to live in business competition. But if all employers in each trade now band themselves faithfully in these modern guilds—without exception—and agree to act together and at once, none will be hurt and millions of workers, so long deprived of the right to earn their bread in the sweat of their labor, can raise their heads again.[66]

Roosevelt also urged industry not to raise prices as rapidly as wages, asking "that managements give first consideration to the improvement of operating figures by greatly increased sales to be expected from the rising purchasing power of the public. . . . The aim of this whole effort is to restore our rich domestic market by raising its vast consuming capacity. If we now inflate prices as fast and as far as we increase wages, the whole project will be set at naught."[67]

Under the leadership of the NRA's director Hugh Johnson, more than five hundred codes were negotiated for individual industries, and around 80 percent of them included controversial provisions establishing price floors.[68] Roosevelt knew that such a massive increase in state involvement in economic activity—the NRA employed around 4,500 staff members—would require strong public buy-in, and he launched a campaign to encourage the public to do business with companies that displayed a "blue eagle" on their storefronts as a sign of cooperation with the NRA. But despite these efforts, many complained that the NRA codes made it easier for big businesses to collude to limit production and raise prices.[69]

Some of the criticism of the NRA came from within the Roosevelt administration. Gardiner Means was a Harvard economist on the Consumer Advisory Board of the NRA and served as an economic adviser to Secretary Wallace. Means wrote a report called "Industrial Prices and Their Relative Inflexibility," which Wallace transmitted to the Senate in January 1935. In this report, Means distinguished between market prices, set as a result of supply and demand as buyers and sellers interact, and administered prices, set by administrative action and quite inflexible.[70] Industrial prices were more likely than agricultural prices to be administered, he found. Means thought that the industry-written NRA codes exacerbated the tendency to administer higher prices and thus harmed consumers' purchasing power and delayed recovery.[71] Means's "administered price" thesis became highly influential and was used to discredit the NRA.

In January 1935, the NRA's new chairman, Samuel Williams, held hearings about industry price fixing. *Time Magazine* reported: "Chairman Williams told them plainly that, unless they could prove it would damage business, NRA was going to put an end to price control. Said he: 'Greater productivity and employment would result if greater price flexibility were attained.' . . . Of the 2,000 businessmen on hand probably 90 percent opposed Mr. Williams' aim. . . . Hence man by man, hour by hour, Business rose to argue and protest against what NRA proposed."[72]

Despite a variety of court challenges to the NRA and other New Deal legislation, discussed in the next section, Roosevelt asked Congress to pass additional legislation, sometimes called the Second New Deal, as he prepared to run for reelection. Among this legislation was the National Labor Relations Act of 1935, commonly called the Wagner Act, which reestablished labor's right to collective bargaining and created the National Labor Relations Board to enforce wage agreements. Wages, unionization rates, and strike activity increased substantially as a result.[73] By enforcing higher wages, the Wagner Act likely slowed the pace of labor-market recovery as businesses paid higher wages to their existing employees instead of hiring new employees.[74] The unemployment rate in late 1936 was still around 13 percent, even though industrial production had grown more than 20 percent that year.[75]

The New Deal in Court

The courts scrutinized New Deal policies for their potential to interfere with freedom of contracting and due process. Recall that the Granger laws of the 1870s, which set maximum prices charged by railroads and grain elevator companies, were scrutinized on similar grounds. The Court's 1877 decision in *Munn v. Illinois* suggested that state governments had a relatively broad scope to regulate the prices of businesses "affected with a public interest." Then, in the Progressive Era, the Court frequently upheld state laws that interfered with freedom of contracting. The 1905 case *Lochner v. New York* was an important exception.[76] But in the 1920s, the more conservative Court revived the *Lochner*-style freedom-of-contract jurisprudence, ruling against laws on a minimum wage and rent control that interfered with freedom of contract.[77]

The Great Depression turned the tide of public opinion, as many Americans blamed the Hoover administration's laissez-faire policies for the economic crisis; commitment to liberty of contract seemed less pressing than allowing the government to take action.[78] The Supreme Court, at first, shared this sentiment. In *Nebbia v. New York* in 1934, the Court ruled that a New York law fixing the price of milk was, in fact, constitutional.[79] The Court cited *Munn*, writing: "The phrase 'affected with a public interest' can, in the nature of things, mean no more than that an industry, for adequate reason, is subject to control for the public good. . . . There can be no doubt that upon proper occasion and by appropriate measures the state may regulate a business in any of its aspects, including the prices to be charged for the products or commodities it sells."[80] In other words, state regulation of prices would satisfy the requirements of due process so long as "the laws passed are seen to have a reasonable relation to a proper legislative purpose, and are neither arbitrary nor discriminatory," without the need to consider interference with freedom of contract.[81] This case, according to a legal scholar of the time, "refuted the contention that control of prices is *per se* unreasonable and unconstitutional."[82] This was a close decision, 5–4. The justices who dissented were nicknamed "the four horsemen." One of them, Justice James McReynolds, wrote:

> Regulation to prevent recognized evils in business has long been upheld as permissible legislative action. But fixation of the price at

> which A, engaged in an ordinary business, may sell, in order to enable B, a producer, to improve his condition, has not been regarded as within legislative power. This is not regulation, but management, control, dictation—it amounts to the deprivation of the fundamental right which one has to conduct his own affairs honestly and along customary lines. The argument advanced here would support general prescription of prices for farm products, groceries, shoes, clothing, all the necessities of modern civilization, as well as labor, when some Legislature finds and declares such action advisable and for the public good. . . . And if it be now ruled that one dedicates his property to public use whenever he embarks on an enterprise which the Legislature may think it desirable to bring under control, this is but to declare that rights guaranteed by the Constitution exist only so long as supposed public interest does not require their extinction. To adopt such a view, of course, would put an end to liberty under the Constitution.

Freedom of contract and due process were also the key issues in the "gold clause" cases, which captivated the nation in 1935.[83] It had long been standard practice for contracts to have "gold clauses," stipulating that repayments would be made in gold dollars. As part of the effort to devalue gold, in June 1933, Congress had passed a joint resolution declaring gold clauses in private and government contracts null and void.[84] In the gold clause cases, creditors opposed the abrogation of gold clauses, alleging that abrogation "operated to deprive plaintiff of his property without due process of law."[85] The plaintiffs also argued that contract abrogation was not among Congress's enumerated powers.[86]

Roosevelt knew that a decision in favor of the creditors, which would greatly increase the real value of national and private debt, would be economically and politically disastrous. Roosevelt was facing a growing challenge from the populist Louisiana senator Huey Long, who thought the New Deal didn't go far enough in helping the vulnerable. If the president were to enforce contract repayment in gold dollars, Senator Long would be given "a golden opportunity to tie the Administration to Wall Street."[87] The decisions came out in Roosevelt's favor, with the same 5–4 split as in *Nebbia*. Revelations later surfaced that President Roosevelt had prepared a radio address that he would have delivered in the case of an adverse decision explaining why he would not comply with it. The president likely made it known to the Court, ahead of the decision, that he would not comply if the gold abrogation unconstitutional was found unconstitutional.[88] Facing the threat of presidential noncompliance, which would have created a major political spectacle, the justices seem to have set aside their best interpretation of the Constitution to avert a crisis of legitimacy.[89]

The Court was less favorable to the New Deal in two 1935 cases, *Panama Refining Co. v. Ryan* and *A. L. A. Schechter Corp. v. United States*, which reviewed the NRA's delegation of power to the president.[90] The Court relied on the intelligible principle, set forth in the 1928 case *J. W. Hampton Jr. & Co. v. United States*, which allows Congress to delegate legislative power only if it lays out boundaries and limits to guide its delegee.[91] In both *Panama Refining* and *Schechter*, the Court ruled that the NIRA's broad, unprecedented, and nearly unfettered delegation of legislative power to the executive was unconstitutional.

In *Schechter*, the Court also ruled that small poultry slaughterhouses did not qualify as interstate commerce, so fell outside of Congress's commerce powers. A similar interpretation of the commerce clause undermined other New Deal legislation. In 1936, for example, the Court ruled in *Carter v. Carter Coal Co.* that the Bituminous Coal Conservation Act, which created the Bituminous Coal Commission to set prices and minimum wages in the coal industry, was unconstitutional because coal mining also was not interstate commerce.[92] That same year in *United States v. Butler*, the Supreme Court ruled that the AAA "invades the reserved rights of the states. It is a statutory plan to regulate and control agricultural production, a matter beyond the powers delegated to the federal government."[93] This decision at least temporarily dashed Roosevelt's hope that the AAA would "pass from the purely emergency phases necessitated by a grave national crisis to a long-time more permanent plan for American agriculture."[94]

After Roosevelt's sweeping electoral victory in 1936, he unveiled a "court-packing plan," the Judicial Procedures Reform Bill of 1937, which proposed to change the makeup of the Court that had recently ruled against the NIRA and AAA. This plan would have allowed the president to appoint up to six new justices, one for each member of the Court older than age seventy. In a fireside chat, Roosevelt accused the Court of "acting not as a judicial body, but as a policy-making body" when it opposed his policies.[95] Roosevelt's court-packing plan did not have the support he had hoped for in Congress. Senator Carter Glass deplored the plan, explaining: "We are simply given to understand that the President has a 'mandate from the people' to so reconstitute the Supreme Court as to have it sanction whatever the White House proposes to an agreeing Congress. . . . The predominant question is whether the practice of a century under an independent judiciary is to be abruptly terminated by authorizing the President to seize the court by the process of packing, in order to compel agreement with the Executive views. Should this be done without 'a mandate from the people?'"[96] While the plan was still under consideration, in March 1937, the Supreme Court ruled, in a surprising 5–4 decision, that a state minimum wage for women was constitutional. This case, *West Coast Hotel Co. v. Parrish*, overturned *Adkins v. Children's Hospital.*[97] *West Coast Hotel* is sometimes called the "switch in time that saved nine," because Justice Owen Roberts, who had voted with the conservative justices in the *Schechter* case, "switched" to join the side more favorable to the New Deal. The Court also supported the New Deal in *National Labor Relations Board v. Jones & Laughlin Steel Corp.*, which upheld the constitutionality of the Wagner Act.[98] These cases reduced Roosevelt's impetus to pass the Judicial Procedures Reform Bill, which failed in Congress later that year.

The Double-Dip Recession and the Purchasing Power School

By the spring of 1937, prices remained below their pre-Depression levels but were rising steadily. Consumer prices increased by about 5 percent from May 1936 to May 1937 while producer prices increased by around 12 percent.[99] President Roosevelt, who had spent most of his first term trying to reflate prices, started worrying that prices would grow too rapidly. He turned to his economic advisers, including Means, who continued to believe in the economic harms of "administered" prices. Caroline Ware, Means's wife, left her position teaching history at Vassar College to work in consumer affairs positions in the administration. Another adviser, Leon Henderson, also left academia to work for the New Deal. Henderson had served in World War I before studying and then teaching economics at the University of Pennsylvania's Wharton School and then directing the NRA's research and planning division.

Henderson, Means, and Ware were leaders of the influential "purchasing power school" of economists; they interpreted the Great Depression as being caused by underconsumption. They believed that the key to national prosperity was for the state to regulate against administered high prices and low wages so that consumers would have enough disposable income to purchase all of the nation's manufactured goods.[100] In March 1937, Henderson wrote Roosevelt a memo warning of an imminent downturn, noting that rising prices were eroding consumers' purchasing power.[101] Henderson's prediction soon came to pass, boosting his reputation.[102]

The recession that began in 1937 is sometimes called the double-dip recession, because it began while the recovery from the Great Depression was still underway. This recession was severe, with a 32 percent decline in industrial production from May 1937 to May 1938. The unemployment rate climbed back up to 20 percent.[103] Although the causes of the double-dip recession are still debated, recent work has attributed it to tax increases, unionization, and especially monetary contraction, imposed because of the Fed's and the Treasury's fear of imminent inflation.[104]

The wide influence the purchasing power school was apparent in contemporaneous interpretations of the recession. “Buying Power is Prosperity’s Key,” read a newspaper headline in February 1938.[105] The article described extreme confusion about whether the recession was attributable to prices that were too high or too low. On the one hand, it said: “Prices are too high. Few families are able to pay them. They have to skimp like everything. Consequently merchandise accumulates on retailers’ hands. . . . We call it over-production, but it is not that. It is under-consumption. Such is present-day White House reasoning, as clearly explained by President Roosevelt, to account for our current business recession.” On the other hand: “Oh no, prices are not high enough. They are so low that capital refuses to invest itself in industrially productive enterprises. . . . Farmers cannot sell their crops for enough to pay for raising them. . . . Most of our industrial magnates agree on this proposition, speaking for big business. Agriculture Secretary Wallace indorses it in behalf of the farmers. That is to say, according to their reckoning, we should have inflation.” The article pointed out that the Roosevelt administration—with the exception of Secretary Wallace, who still thought higher prices would promote agricultural interests—was supporting lower prices to boost purchasing power and consumption, so long as this could be accomplished without lower wages or salaries. The problem, in Roosevelt’s philosophy, was that “Big Business trims [workers’] pay anticipatorily” when prices fall.[106]

The tendency of big business to keep wages low and prices high, Roosevelt claimed, threatened democracy itself: “The liberty of a democracy is not safe if the people tolerate the growth of private power to a point where it becomes stronger than their democratic state itself. That, in its essence, is Fascism—ownership of Government by an individual, by a group, or by any other controlling private power.”[107] Thus, he urged Congress to “stop the progress of collectivism in business and turn business back to the democratic competitive order.”[108]

In response, Congress took two main actions in 1938 to prevent big businesses from eroding purchasing power. It passed the Fair Labor Standards Act, imposing the first federal minimum wage in the United States. And it established the Temporary National Economic Committee to study and make recommendations concerning industrial concentration and monopoly power. Henderson was the committee's executive secretary. Henderson will reappear in the next chapter, as he played a central role in the administration of price controls in World War II. Until the war began, consumer prices, which fell during the recession of 1937 to 1938, remained low, and unemployment remained high. Producer prices continued falling even after the recession ended.

EIGHT

WORLD WAR II AND THE OFFICE OF PRICE ADMINISTRATION

> Price and other controls are often opposed out of fear that such measures will concentrate power in the Government and threaten our freedom. By inclination I, too, am opposed to Government controls. But the gravest threats to the preservation of the American system today are not Government controls. They are military defeat abroad and further inflation at home.
>
> BERNARD BARUCH, *Hearing before the Senate Committee on Banking and Currency*[1]

The Office of Price Administration

When World War II broke out in September 1939, economists in Roosevelt's administration turned their attention to the likely effects of the war on the economy and prices. In December, Leon Henderson, who was still at the Temporary National Economic Committee (TNEC), called for the TNEC to hold a series of hearings on the war and prices. At the hearings, Henderson questioned businessmen about their views on inflation and price controls in wartime. Many, he found, were quite supportive of the idea of price controls, and emphasized their willingness to support the president in the war effort.[2] These hearings would provide the foundations for the price-control efforts during the war. The TNEC members would have been well aware that other countries, beginning with the fascist countries, had instituted price controls of their own leading up to the war.[3]

In May 1940, President Roosevelt reestablished the Council of National Defense, which was previously established in World War I, and made Henderson the head of the price stabilization division of its National Defense Advisory Commission (NDAC). At first, Henderson and his staff attempted to secure voluntary agreements with producers to restrain price increases. As in World War I, voluntary agreements were not always effective, nor were they truly voluntary. For example, Henderson threatened to seize lumber inventories to slow the advance of lumber prices.[4]

In February 1941, Henderson and the NDAC issued Price Schedule No. 1, which provided formulas for the maximum prices that could be charged for machine tools, which were rising in price because they were necessary for producing munitions. The ceilings might not have been legally enforceable, but the price schedule noted that violations would be publicized and implied that other government agencies would retaliate against violators.[5]

President Roosevelt, using his war powers, issued an executive order in April 1941 to merge the NDAC's price stabilization and consumer protection divisions to form the Office of Price Administration and Civilian Supply (OPA). He named Henderson the administrator, directing him "to prevent price spiraling, rising costs of living, profiteering, and inflation resulting from market conditions caused by the diversion of large segments of the Nation's resources to the defense program, by interruptions to normal sources of supply, or by other influences growing out of the emergency."[6] This is when Henderson earned his "price czar" moniker.

Although the OPA had more legal authority than the NDAC to impose price controls, the OPA still desired a formal mandate from Congress to strengthen its authority. Congress began discussing proposals for price-control legislation, and passed the Emergency Price Control Act (EPCA) in January 1942, the month after the United States entered the war. The EPCA made the OPA an independent agency and gave its administrator (still Henderson) considerable discretion to set price controls and enforce compliance, for example through revoking licenses.[7]

The EPCA also created an Emergency Court of Appeals, a temporary federal court that was given exclusive jurisdiction over cases regarding the validity of the OPA's price controls and regulations. The only way to bring a complaint to the Emergency Court of Appeals was to file a complaint with the administrator. If the complaint were denied, the aggrieved party could go to the Emergency Court, but only within sixty days of the issuance of the protested regulation. The regulation in question would remain in full force until and unless the Emergency Court found it invalid. Harvey Mansfield, who wrote *A Short History of OPA* in 1948, explains: "These provisions of the law prevented a regulation from being held valid in one Federal district and invalid in another. The consequences of such inconsistency of decisions would have been disastrous not merely to effective price control but also to the orderly marketing and distribution of goods."[8]

But the Emergency Court of Appeals process, Mansfield admits, was "open to certain serious criticisms. Assuming the Administrator had abused his power, a man could have been convicted and jailed for violation of a regulation which was in fact invalid, and this without an opportunity to be heard in the criminal court on the question of validity. Moreover, unless such a man had had the foresight to protest the regulation within 60 days of its issuance he would forever be foreclosed from making that contention anywhere."[9] This Emergency Court process, we will see, became one of the most contentious features of the EPCA.

The EPCA did set some important restrictions on the OPA's authority, however. Most notably, the OPA could not set agricultural prices "below the highest of (1) 110 percent of parity, (2) the market price as of October 1, 1941, (3) the market price as of December 15, 1941, and (4) the average market price during the period July 1, 1919 to June 30, 1929."[10] This provision, which was included in the act to ensure support of the farm bloc, meant that some agricultural commodities could have very high price ceilings. The OPA also did not have the authority to regulate wages, which were the domain of the National War Labor Board, established by Roosevelt's executive order, also in January 1942.

Clearly, the Roosevelt administration intended to rely on controls, not monetary policy, to manage wartime inflation. In April 1942, the Fed committed to supporting the war effort by maintaining an interest rate of .375 percent on Treasury bills, accomplishing the pegged interest rate by purchasing any Treasury bills offered at that rate. The Fed also established a 2.5 percent ceiling for long-termer term government securities, also by purchasing bonds and bills as needed.[11] These policies greatly expanded the Federal Reserve System's balance sheet and the monetary base.[12] To counter the inflationary impact of easy monetary policy, the Fed issued Regulation W, which attempted to limit consumer spending credit to buy durables by imposing large down payments and short maturities on loans. But this credit policy would have a limited ability to stabilize prices, so price controls would shoulder the largest burden of stabilization.

Public opinion polls from early 1942 show that the public strongly supported broad price controls. In April 1942, perhaps in response to this public sentiment, the OPA issued the General Maximum Price Regulation (known as General Max), which froze most prices at the highest level reached as of March 1942. General Max was not easy to enforce. Because different sellers might have charged different prices for the same item in March 1942, they could charge different prices under General Max. This made it difficult for consumers to tell whether a particular seller was overcharging. The OPA soon began issuing "dollars-and-cents" ceilings, which were easier to enforce.[13]

These price controls did not take individual sellers' costs into account, so higher-cost producers could be driven out of business. In this respect, the controls were much different from those in World War I, when the emphasis was on ensuring that profits were not excessive. Bernard Baruch, who had directed the War Industries Board during the war, unsuccessfully advocated that the OPA should set price controls on a "cost-plus" basis.[14] Businesses would have preferred Baruch's plan over Henderson's, and Henderson knew it: he predicted that it was "only a matter of time till I shall be the most damned man in the country."[15]

The historian Andrew Bartels describes the EPCA as a "prime example of the administrative New Deal in wartime," founded on "the New Deal assumption that the government should directly intervene and 'administer' economic affairs."[16] And like earlier New Deal legislation, its constitutionality was called into question—Meg Jacobs notes that "few federal agencies have stood closer to the center of the twentieth-century debate over government regulation of the American economy than the Office of Price Administration" (major legal debates surrounding the EPCA are discussed later in this chapter).

But Roosevelt could be more confident in 1942 than in 1935 that the Court would uphold the legislation he supported. Roosevelt had appointed eight of nine Supreme Court justices. And in the noteworthy 1942 case *Wickard v. Filburn*, the Court unanimously upheld the Agricultural Adjustment Act of 1938, which was passed after the earlier Agricultural Adjustment Act had been ruled unconstitutional.[17] In this case, the Court took an expansive interpretation of the commerce clause, ruling that commercial activity could be regulated as interstate commerce even if its effects on interstate commerce were only indirect.

Hold the Line and the Little OPAs

By the fall of 1942, it became clear that the OPA would have major difficulty restraining inflation if it could not set tighter controls on agricultural prices. In a September 1942 fireside chat, President Roosevelt reminded the country that the parity standard "was established as our national policy way back in 1933. It means that the farmer and the city worker are on the same relative ratio with each other in purchasing power as they were during a period some thirty years before—at a time then the farmer had a satisfactory purchasing power. 100 percent of parity, therefore, has been accepted by farmers as the fair standard for the prices they receive." The EPCA, by forbidding ceilings below 110 percent of parity on farm products, was an "act of favoritism for one particular group in the community." He added: "Our experience with the control of other prices during the past few months has brought out one important fact—the rising cost of living can be controlled, providing that all elements making up the cost of living are controlled at the same time. I think that also is an essential justice and a practical necessity."[18]

The next month, Roosevelt signed the Stabilization Act of 1942, sometimes referred to as the Inflation Control Act. It amended the EPCA to limit agricultural prices to 100 percent of parity or their maximum reached from January 1 to September 15, 1942. The act also extended the EPCA's expiration date by one year, to June 30, 1944, and authorized the president to issue orders on price and wage stabilization. The next day, the president issued an executive order imposing tighter wage and salary controls and directing the OPA administrator to "determine price ceilings in such a manner that profits are prevented which in his judgment are unreasonable or exorbitant."[19]

Despite the tightening of wage and price controls, prices continued to rise because of evasion and exceptions. And meanwhile, the OPA fell out of favor with the business community. Rockoff notes that "opposition from the business community to the 'professors' at the OPA eventually soured relationships between OPA on the one hand, and business, the Congress, and perhaps the public on the other, to such an extent that a change of administration seemed the only practical course." Henderson resigned and was replaced by Prentiss Brown, a former Democratic senator from Michigan who "did not want the job. . . . But when the White House put the job up to him as a patriotic duty, conscientious Prentiss Brown had no choice."[20]

In another effort to rein in price increases, President Roosevelt signed Executive Order No. 9328 on Prices and Wages, known as the "hold-the-line" order, in April 1943. Roosevelt proclaimed:

> To hold the line we cannot tolerate further increases in prices affecting the cost of living or further increases in general wage or salary rates except where clearly necessary to correct substandard living conditions. The only way to hold the line is to stop trying to find justifications for not holding it here or not holding it there. No one straw may break a camel's back, but there is always a last straw. . . . Some groups have been urging increased prices for farmers on the ground that wage earners have unduly profited. Other groups have been urging increased wages on the ground that farmers have unduly profited. A continuance of this conflict will not only cause inflation but will breed disunity at a time when unity is essential. . . . Inflation has been slowed up. Now we must stop it.

The hold-the-line order made it much more difficult for industries to receive approval to increase prices. Tighter price controls normally result in shortages because prices are below the market-clearing rate. Thus, the government relied more heavily on a rationing system when "hold the line" was put in place. Still, hold the line seems to have improved public perceptions of the OPA, since a more uniform price-control policy was seen as more fair than a policy that allowed a variety of exceptions.[21]

Administrator Brown, eager to leave the OPA and return to his law practice, found a suitable replacement in the wealthy advertising executive Chester Bowles. A *Time* article called "OPA Must Be Lovable" wrote of Bowles: "Reporters took a long, sympathetic look at an able new man in a jinxed job. After two years of rationing, OPA was still unworkable, still unlovable."[22]

Bowles set out to restore public and congressional support for OPA while "holding the line" on prices. Bartels notes that Bowles's "background in advertising made him sensitive to public opinion, public relations, and symbolism. Bowles shared many of the New Deal values of his predecessors. . . . However, his commitment was not to the ideal of an expert and apolitical price administration, although he appreciated and preserved the expertise in OPA. Instead, he stressed the importance of public participation and a committed public constituency for supporting the program politically."[23]

To improve relations with key interest groups, Bowles created new agricultural and consumer advisory groups and expanded the already-existing labor and industry advisory committees to the OPA. According to Mansfield, the OPA was able to "secure widest acceptance" for its price regulations when "a broad balance of regulation and benefit, an economic and political balance of relative interests, seemed to have been achieved among the major economic interests in the country: farm, labor, and business."[24]

The OPA also enlisted more than one hundred thousand volunteers to serve on local price-control boards, or "little OPAs," in nearly every county. Mansfield describes how the little OPAs' "members were drawn from all walks of life-farmers, housewives, merchants, artisans, professional men, and wage earners."[25] The predominantly female volunteers could publicize and explain controls to their local communities and monitor local stores for violations. Jacobs explains: "Price controls instituted by the Office of Price Administration relied not only on a vast regulatory state administered by technocratic planners but also on a dense web of popular participation and mobilization . . . which, in part, explains both consumers' heightened sense of state legitimacy and the ferocious opposition that controls engendered. Members of the OPA believed in a very invasive form of management democratized, they hoped, by mobilizing citizens in local communities to enforce rationing and controls."[26]

Indeed, because of this decentralized, broad public participation and mobilization, Bowles referred to the OPA's work as "big democracy in action."[27] The "big democracy in action" idea was one that Bowles and Roosevelt shared. Bowles helped Roosevelt author his January 1944 inaugural address, in which the president laid out a new vision for American democracy in which the "one supreme objective for the future" was "summed up in one word: Security."[28]

Roosevelt proclaimed: "This Republic had its beginning, and grew to its present strength, under the protection of certain inalienable political rights. . . . They were our rights to life and liberty. As our Nation has grown in size and stature, however—as our industrial economy expanded—these political rights proved inadequate to assure us equality in the pursuit of happiness. We have come to a clear realization of the fact that true individual freedom cannot exist without economic security and independence. . . . People who are hungry and out of a job are the stuff of which dictatorships are made."[29]

Challenges and Extension of Controls

Bowles's approach at the OPA was successful in restoring the confidence of businesspeople, Congress, and the public. Despite the public support that Bowles secured for the OPA, the legitimacy of its "radical model of state management" did not go unchallenged.[30] According to the legal scholars James Conde and Michael Greve, "The EPCA enshrined the New Dealers' institutional commitments—foremost, an abiding faith in bureaucratic expertise and a corresponding, unremitting hostility to markets, interloping courts, and the separation of powers," and each of these features was reviewed in court.[31]

First, the act severely restricted freedom of contract. The EPCA made it "unlawful, regardless of any contract, agreement, lease, or other obligation heretofore or hereafter entered into, for any person to sell or deliver any commodity, or in the course of trade or business to buy or receive any commodity" in violation of the price regulations of the OPA.[32] Recall that the Constitution forbids states from passing laws that impair contract obligations, but it places no such restriction on Congress, as long as the law is part of congressional exercise of its constitutional powers and does not violate due process. The most relevant constitutional powers, in the case of the EPCA, were the commerce and war powers. After *Wickard v. Fil-*

burn, the commerce power was interpreted broadly. Nonetheless, legal scholars at the time noted:

> There are definite limitations to that power which would preclude basing the validity of the Emergency Price Control Act upon the commerce clause. . . . If the power to regulate interstate commerce is the source of the power of the federal government to regulate practically all prices for commodities and services, and to fix rents in specific localities, in order to make such price-fixing effective . . . the commerce clause and the implied powers thereunder must stretched to such an extent as to do away completely with any limitation upon the power of Congress to regulate strictly intrastate activities.[33]

Instead, the EPCA's interference with contract obligations was more firmly supported by Congress's war power. The war power, in Article I, Section 8, "is the most far-reaching of all powers delegated to Congress. It is an authority which is always present but which can only operate in an emergency. This power in no way abrogates the restrictions of the Constitution, but it, like the commerce clause or any other power given to Congress, makes possible legislation which without this grant of power would be unconstitutional."[34] The legal scholar Joseph Aidlin explained in 1942 why the war powers supported the constitutionality of the EPCA:

> The war in which we are now engaged is a struggle for the preservation of our very existence as a democratic nation. . . . Every economic factor, every instrument of production, every hour worked, every item sold and service rendered, every material used bears directly upon the effectiveness of the prosecution of the war. . . . It cannot be questioned that "in the interest of national defense and security and necessary to the effective prosecution of the war" the stabilization of prices, prevention of speculation and of unwarranted and abnormal increases in prices and rents, the elimination and prevention of profiteering and hoarding, and the other

stated objectives of the Emergency Price Control Act are vitally necessary.[35]

Another controversial aspect of the EPCA was the Emergency Court of Appeals, which was given exclusive jurisdiction over cases regarding the validity of the OPA's price controls. Congress set up the appeals court knowing that if the regulations and orders issued by the OPA could be challenged in district courts, consistent enforcement of price controls across the country would be nearly impossible. The court was staffed with New Deal judges who almost always sided with the administrator, and it was subject to review only by the Supreme Court.[36] Conde and Greve explain that "the EPCA channeled all regulatory challenges through an administrative procedure that was designed to delay judicial relief. . . . The EPCA placed the regular courts at OPA's disposal for enforcement purposes, even while the regulations were being challenged through the administrative process or in the Emergency Court. The provisions made OPA's regulations binding in the courts, even in criminal cases, without a meaningful opportunity for judicial review."[37]

In the 1943 Supreme Court case *Lockerty v. Phillips*, a group of wholesale meat sellers challenged this feature of the EPCA. The Court upheld the EPCA, finding that Congress was not required to provide federal district courts to review complaints about the act: "There is nothing in the Constitution which requires Congress to confer equity jurisdiction on any particular inferior federal court. All federal courts, other than the Supreme Court, derive their jurisdiction wholly from the exercise of the authority to 'ordain and establish' inferior courts. . . . Article III left Congress free to establish inferior federal courts or not as it thought appropriate. It could have declined to create any such courts, leaving suitors to the remedies afforded by state courts, with such appellate review by this Court as Congress might prescribe."[38]

The role of the Emergency Court of Appeals was questioned again in *Yakus v. United States*, a 1944 case in which the plaintiff, Albert Yakus, was criminally prosecuted for selling beef above the price ceiling. The OPA's prosecution of meat packers was particularly intense, intended to suppress a growing black market for meat. Unregulated livestock prices kept rising while regulated wholesale and retail prices could not, forcing meat dealers to violate the price ceiling or go out of business.[39] The Supreme Court considered whether the Emergency Court of Appeals' review procedure afforded "a reasonable opportunity to be heard and present evidence." The Supreme Court ruled: "It is irrelevant to suggest that the Administrator or the Court has in the past or may in the future deny due process. Action taken by them is reviewable in this Court and if contrary to due process will be corrected here." It added: "In any event, we are unable to say that the denial of interlocutory relief pending a judicial determination of the validity of the regulation would in the special circumstances of this case, involve a denial of constitutional right. If the alternatives, as Congress could have concluded, were war-time inflation or the imposition on individuals of the burden of complying with a price regulation while its validity is being determined, Congress could constitutionally make the choice in favor of the protection of the public interest from the dangers of inflation."[40]

Perhaps the biggest constitutional challenge to the EPCA concerned its delegation of legislative power. This, too, was considered in *Yakus*. In 1935 the Court had ruled that the NIRA's delegation of legislative power to the president was unconstitutional, relying on the intelligible principle from the 1928 *Hampton* case.[41] In *Yakus*, the Court decided that the EPCA satisfied the intelligible principle, as the standards prescribed by the act "are sufficiently definite and precise to enable Congress, the courts and the public to ascertain whether the administrator, in fixing the designated prices, has conformed to those standards. . . . Hence we are unable to find in them an unauthorized delegation of legislative power." The Court added that "Congress is not confined to that method of executing its policy which involves the least possible delegation of discretion to administrative officers."[42]

In *Yakus* and other cases, like the 1944 case *Bowles v. Willingham*, the Supreme Court upheld the EPCA just as it was set to expire in June 1944.[43] Policy makers, including the Federal Reserve's Chairman Eccles, called for extension of price controls. Eccles argued that "inflationary dangers can only be avoided if the powers of the administrator are in no way weakened." He added:

> If the public is assured by the extension of this legislation for a sufficient length of time, without crippling amendments, that the line will be held against inflationary forces, the problem of financing the war and refunding the public debt will continue to be met successfully. If the public is led to believe, however, that the price, wage, and rationing controls are going to be weakened, or not continued as long as may be necessary, confidence can not be maintained in the purchasing power of our money. Without that confidence, not only would the successful prosecution of the war be jeopardized, but an orderly transition to a peacetime basis would be out of the question.[44]

The EPCA was, indeed, extended for another year by the Stabilization Extension Act of 1944, signed by President Roosevelt on June 30. Bartels notes that the House and Senate "renewed the price control acts in 1944 with few changes and considerable praise for Bowles and his program. OPA received unqualified endorsement from business groups . . . and labor and consumer groups lobbied hard for the program. In 1945, when OPA again came up for reauthorization, farm groups like the American Farm joined OPA's boosters."[45] The second extension moved the EPCA's expiration date to June 30, 1946.

Reconversion and Regimented Chaos

President Harry Truman, formerly Roosevelt's vice president, became president after Roosevelt's death in 1945, a few months before the war ended. The OPA and its price controls, though established on the basis of the war powers, enjoyed broad popular support and were not immediately stripped away.[46] Instead, in a radio address, President Truman urged the country to "continue to hold the price line." He called back to the end of the previous world war, when "we simply pulled off the few controls that had been established, and let nature take its course," urging: "The result should stand as a lesson to all of us. A dizzy upward spiral of wages and the cost of living ended in the crash of 1920."[47]

Truman recognized that with the end of war production, there was "no longer any threat of an inflationary bidding up of wage rates by competition in a short labor market."[48] Thus he authorized businesses to increase wages without approval of the War Labor Board, as long as the wage increases were not accompanied by price increases. Wage increases combined with price increases still needed approval. Soon after, Walter Reuther, vice president of the United Auto Workers (UAW), sent a letter to the president of General Motors (GM) declaring the UAW's "hearty agreement" with Truman's relaxation of the wage stabilization policy. Reuther demanded that GM agree to both a 30 percent increase in hourly wages and a freeze on automobile prices, which had been rising rapidly during demobilization. He wrote: "We have maintained all along that the public interest demands effective, stringent price control; and we in the ranks of organized labor are proud of the role we have played in protecting the consumer interest against the pressure of war profiteers. . . . Our proposal for maintaining high labor income without any increase in prices is imperative if we are to achieve an economy of Full Production, Full Employment, and Full Distribution and Consumption."[49] When GM and the union met for negotiations on October 19, 1945, the union presented a brief, "Purchasing Power for Prosperity," that was later sent widely to members of Congress and the press. The brief explained that the union's demands would "actively promote the public interest. The easy way to get wage increases is to conspire with industry to get price increases from OPA, getting wage demands met out of prices at the expense of the general public. This is the philosophy of 'The public be damned!' . . . We do not want our wage demands met out of price increases."[50] GM representatives insisted that the company could not afford such a large wage hike or give up the ability to set its own prices. The UAW, which had maintained a no-strike pledge during the war, went on strike from November 21, 1945, to March 13, 1946.

The position of UAW was weakened when the United Steelworkers, also on strike, accepted a 17.5 percent raise in exchange for favorable price concessions from the Truman administration—that is, steel prices were allowed to increase more than OPA had deemed appropriate. The UAW also received a 17.5 percent raise, and no concessions about product pricing. The Truman administration's willingness to compromise with the steelworkers, allowing a price increase to end the steel strike, helped weaken congressional support for the OPA. For many in Congress, the bigger fear was not an upward spiral of wages and prices, but just the opposite: that depression and deflation would follow the war as government military expenditures declined.[51] This made a strong OPA seem less necessary.

In June 1946, a few days before the EPCA was set to expire, Congress passed a bill that would have extended but drastically weakened the OPA. President Truman vetoed the bill, hoping to maintain a strong OPA. Instead, the OPA and its controls were allowed to expire, and prices immediately began to rise, especially for food. A doubling of meat prices in a month infuriated consumers, who organized boycotts. Labor leaders like Walter Reuther also organized protests and urged Congress to restore the OPA to end profiteering. Congress and the president reinstituted a weak version of the OPA with price controls on meat.[52]

In response, meat producers chose to hold their product back from market rather than be subject to the controls. Consumers, facing bare shelves, grew frustrated with the apparent inefficiencies and invasiveness of the controls. The National Association of Manufacturers leaned into this frustration, campaigning against the "regimented chaos" of the OPA. In the "beefsteak elections" of 1946, voters blamed the OPA for the scarcity of meat and voted Republicans back into control of Congress. Jacobs explains that the meat scarcity "generated the political animus and frustration that led to the decline of a form of state building predicated on a cross-class mobilization of consumers and, more broadly, to the post-war delegitimization of an interventionist New Deal state."[53] She adds: "By uniting consumers, labor, and the state in pursuit of a 'just price,' OPA drew its strength from a sea of forces that was at once too wide and too shallow. Precisely because OPA mobilized consumers and gave them a sense of entitlement, it came under severe attack from producers and, as it turned out, from the very same people from whom it drew its support. Consumers, once empowered, could not be controlled."[54] The president ordered the removal of controls in October 1946.

The previous chapter described how, in responding to the Great Depression, President Roosevelt expanded what is sometimes called the "administrative state," much like President Wilson did in World War I.[55] The proliferation of regulatory agencies with limited oversight, particularly in the Second New Deal, caused some consternation especially among conservatives in Congress and the American Bar Association. Roosevelt himself expressed concern about the "overlapping, duplication, and contradictory policies" of the agencies, which seemed poised to become "a fourth branch of government for which there is no sanction in the Constitution."[56] He requested a report on administrative procedure confirmed the explosion of new federal agencies, especially after 1930, and recommended standardizing the procedures that these agencies should follow. Progress on implementing these recommendations stalled during the war, as the scope and power of the agencies grew. But after the war, the Administrative Procedure Act of 1946 was passed to provide more constraints on agency rulemaking.[57]

Postwar Monetary Policy

According to Friedman and Schwartz, the Great Depression, New Deal, and World War II led to "a sharply changed climate of opinion about the role of government in economic affairs," as they "bequeathed both an increased sensitivity to fluctuations in economic activity and a widespread acceptance of the view that government had a direct responsibility for the maintenance of something approximating 'full employment,' a view that found legislative expression in the Employment Act of 1946."[58]

The Employment Act declared that it was "the continuing policy and responsibility of the federal government to use all practicable means . . . to promote maximum employment, production, and purchasing power." But the act did not prescribe any specific monetary or fiscal policy actions that should be used to achieve these goals.[59] The international monetary system was still in a transition process. Delegates from the Allied Nations had met in Bretton Woods, New Hampshire, in 1944, where they agreed to a new monetary arrangement that would in some respects resemble a gold standard, but it would be years before the Bretton Woods monetary system became operational (the workings of the system are described in the next chapter).[60]

The Treasury continued to require the Fed to peg interest rates as it had during the war, intending that fiscal policy, rather than monetary policy, be the primary stabilization tool. This type of arrangement, in which a central bank uses monetary policy to reduce the government's debt-servicing costs and support the prices of government securities, is known as *fiscal dominance*. This situation reflected the Keynesian consensus, which viewed fiscal policy as a more powerful tool than monetary policy.[61] As Friedman and Schwartz explain: "As a result of the Great Contraction, of the widespread success of the Keynesian revolution in academic economic thought, and of the experience with wartime controls which succeeded in suppressing some of the manifestations of the accumulation of money balances, the view was accepted that 'money does not matter,' that the stock of money adapted itself passively to economic changes and played a negligible independent role. Further, the major postwar problem was widely assumed to be prevention of deflation and depression, not inflation."[62] But debate began to brew within the Fed about whether to challenge the Treasury on the pegged interest rate, especially when consumer price inflation exceeded 17 percent in 1947.[63] The Federal Reserve Bank of Philadelphia, for example, advocated abandoning the peg and raising interest rates to reduce inflation. Even Chairman Eccles, who had supported the peg during the war, came to believe that the policy was no longer justified after the war, perceiving that it "fed the inflationary fires; and these fires slowly consumed the real purchasing power of the dollar."[64] Because of this stance, President Truman did not reappoint Eccles as Fed chair when his tenure ended in 1948, although Eccles remained on the board. Instead, Truman appointed Thomas McCabe, who had taken leave from his role as president and chief executive officer of Scott Paper to serve several roles in the Roosevelt administration.

The appropriate level of cooperation between the Fed and the Treasury continued to be debated. President Truman appointed a Commission on Organization of the Executive Branch of the Government and named former president Herbert Hoover as chair. In a 1949 report, the commission wrote that monetary policy "cannot be realistically viewed apart from Government fiscal and debt policy. The impact of the Federal budget on the level of production, prices, and employment is now widely recognized. Federal Reserve monetary policy is now seen as probably subsidiary in importance to the Federal budget in mitigating general economic instability. Moreover, the huge volume of Government debt outstanding means that Federal Reserve assistance to the Treasury will long be essential to efficient handling of the debt."[65]

The committee thought it "obvious that effective Government economic policy requires close cooperation between the monetary and fiscal authorities" and that "the Government (the Executive and Congress) will not, and should not, tolerate obstructionist action by the central bank against Government policies. A truly independent central bank, free to control the Nation's money supply counter to the wishes of the President and Congress, is unrealistic in the modern world." The committee noted that the Fed had nearly always "gone along with the Treasury," as "Federal Reserve officials, as responsible Government servants, would never be willing to flatly disrupt or destroy the Government's fiscal policy on important matters . . . and ultimately it is the Chief Executive, who, within the limits imposed by Congress, establishes the Government's monetary-fiscal policy."[66]

The problem the committee saw with this arrangement was that "domination by the Secretary of the Treasury, as is now prevalent in monetary-fiscal policy, would continue the age-old Treasury bias in favor of too-easy money in inflation periods, against effective monetary restriction."[67] The report recommended that "means must be found to give a more equal voice to the central bank in the process of Government policy formation."[68] It suggested that the Federal Reserve chair be made a more intimate adviser of the president and that monetary policy-making power be consolidated in a new, smaller Board of Governors. These recommendations were not enacted. But the relationship between the Fed and the Treasury did change dramatically a few years later, as discussed in the next chapter.

NINE

THE KOREAN WAR AND THE TREASURY-FED ACCORD

Is it really tolerable in a democracy to have so much power concentrated in a body free of democratic control?

MILTON FRIEDMAN, "Should There Be a Monetary Authority?"[1]

The Office of Price Stabilization

World War II was still fresh in the public memory when the North Korean invasion of South Korea, on June 25, 1950, kicked off another long and destructive conflict. The United Nations Security Council swiftly condemned the invasion, and President Truman sent US troops to the Korean Peninsula, explaining his conviction that "if the Communists were permitted to force their way into the Republic of Korea without opposition from the free world, no small nation would have the courage to resist threat and aggression by stronger Communist neighbors."[2]

The start of the Korean War brought immediate fears of inflation and shortages. Consumers rushed to the stores to buy goods before they rose in price or became scarce. The media urged consumers to resist "scare buying" goods that had been scarce during the previous war. For example, the *Economist* reported in August 1950 that "the new programmes of military expansion need cause no serious trouble unless Congress and the public between them make trouble inevitable. If the public chooses to show a little self-control, other controls will be unnecessary."[3] A contemporary observer wrote: "The increased prices exacted during this period were mostly speculative and unjustified. . . . Consumer goods and services were still in plentiful supply . . . [but] consumers manifested in the market their anticipations of future shortages and price increases and thus, in large measure, brought about with their fears the very conditions against which they sought to insure themselves. . . . As a nation, we were reacting to the facts of 1950 with the fears and impulses of 1944."[4] As soon as the war started, the public also favored a wage and price freeze. A Gallup poll found that 55 percent of Americans wanted a freeze in June 1950 and 63 percent in October.[5] Rockoff explains: "Popular support for controls flowed partly from some simple economic ideas. Frequently, people see that inflation reduces the value of the increments in income they earn, but not that their income grows, in part, as a result of inflation. The favorable attitude toward controls also reflected favorable memories of how well controls worked during the hold-the-line phase in World War II."[6]

Congress, facing an upcoming election, shared this favorable attitude toward controls, especially after Bernard Baruch, who had administered price controls in World War I, emphasized their necessity for the mobilization effort.[7] Thus, with the Defense Production Act of September 8, 1950, Congress granted President Truman broad powers to impose price, wage, credit, and production controls. The *Economist* described the legislation as an "astonishing spectacle of Congress trying to thrust on the President more and greater powers than he had asked or wanted."[8]

Indeed, although Truman created the Economic Stabilization Agency and Wage Stabilization Board by executive order the next day, he was reluctant to immediately impose controls. Why the reluctance? First, his administration was not sure that controls were necessary, as prices had started to stabilize after the initial wave of scare buying. Second, it was not clear that members of the public would accept controls as readily as they had in 1942, because patriotic fervor and support for US involvement in the war effort was not as strong.[9]

The Federal Reserve Board immediately reinstated the Regulation W credit controls that had been implemented in World War II.[10] President Truman hoped that the credit controls, combined with voluntary agreement by industry to avoid raising prices, would restrain inflation. Voluntary pricing standards were issued on December 19, 1950, along with a threat of mandatory controls if they were not followed. But many sellers were not persuaded to comply, and prices continued to rise.

The Economic Stabilization Agency established the Office of Price Stabilization (OPS) in January 1951. The OPS issued a price freeze on January 26, 1951, largely at the urging of the price stabilization director Michael DiSalle, who, much like Chester Bowles, was astute in mustering support for controls.[11] Prices for individual sellers were frozen at the highest level they had reached between December 19, 1950 and January 25, 1951. But the OPS faced major difficulties. An obvious one was that sellers who had complied with the voluntary pricing standards issued the previous month had their prices frozen at lower levels than the sellers who had disregarded the voluntary pricing standards and increased prices in December. This penalized the more "patriotic" sellers who had complied earlier. The OPS sought to address some of the unfairness and distortions of the original price freeze by tailoring its price regulations for particular industries.

Many amendments soon added to the Defense Production Act weakened the ability of OPS to control prices. For example, the Capehart amendment allowed manufacturers to apply for a price ceiling equal to the highest price received for item from January 1 to June 24, 1950, plus an adjustment for additional cost increases that had been incurred. The president and his congressional allies fought against these amendments, which they saw as emblematic of the power of special interests, but they were unable to prevent their passage.[12] Concerning these amendments, the legal scholars William Burt and William Kennedy wrote in 1952 that "the role of the Congressman dealing with price control legislation is not a happy one": "He is besieged by delegations from industries affected by price regulations; he receives telegrams and letters from scores of influential constituents; he is under constant, relentless and unceasing pressure to protect the interests of particular constituents within his Congressional district. On the other hand, he receives little pressure to vote in favor of price control except that he realizes that it will be a general issue in any campaign in which he engages."[13] Moreover, Congress "did not confine itself to resolving the general political problems raised by price control. It decided the most detailed and technical questions," even when it lacked sufficient technical expertise.[14] In this respect, congressional review of OPS was quite different from judicial review of the administrative agencies. The courts, they claimed, "have recognized that they have neither the staff nor the facilities to do the job of the administrative agencies. Consequently, most courts have limited their function to the correction of actions which are clearly wrong, either because they are arbitrary or discriminatory or because they are unsupported by facts, and to cases where the procedure of the administrative agency is unfair to the participants . . . Congress, unlike the courts, made no effort to maintain a balance between the job of the non-expert reviewer and the expert administrator."[15]

Intense public dissatisfaction with price controls for meat alarmed DiSalle, who believed that reducing beef prices was critical for gaining public support of the whole program. Beef was an especially salient price for most households at the time, accounting for about 12 percent of consumers' food budgets.[16] DiSalle ordered a rollback in beef prices in April 1951, infuriating beef producers, who brought their case to Congress. The day before the Defense Production Act was set to expire on July 31, 1951, Congress passed the Defense Production Act Amendments, which extended the act and its controls but also greatly weakened them. In particular, the amendments prohibited the OPS from setting any agricultural price ceilings below the price that prevailed on May 19, 1951.

This effectively prevented further rollbacks of beef prices. President Truman reluctantly signed the amendments to avoid expiration of the controls, but he disapproved of how the controls were weakened, telling Congress: "If we can hold down the prices of the things we have to buy, and maintain the purchasing power of the American dollar, we can carry out this vast defense effort and make our country secure. But if we encourage prices to rise, if we allow the value of our dollar to be eaten away by inflation, then we will jeopardize our whole program of defense."[17] By 1952, public and congressional support for the OPS and its price controls was weaker still. This reflected both the moderation of inflation and lower public support for the war effort: in early 1952, about half of Americans reported on a Gallup poll that American involvement in the war was a mistake.[18] Burt and Kennedy note: "The 1951 legislative fight had been largely concerned with the character of the controls which OPS might impose. The 1952 fight centered on the question of whether controls were needed at all."[19]

Republican Dwight Eisenhower was elected president in 1952, having run on a promise to end the war in Korea.[20] Seven months after his inauguration, the war ended. President Eisenhower's executive order on February 6, 1953, ended the price and wage controls, and OPS was dismantled at the end of April. Rockoff notes that price increases after the controls were removed were "nothing to compare with the price explosion that had followed the removal of controls in 1946; the Korean War controls ended not with a bang but a whimper."[21]

The Treasury-Fed Accord and the Phillips Trade-Off

The Korean War inflation was accompanied by a shift in public views about the respective roles of monetary and fiscal policy as macroeconomic stabilization tools. The post–World War II view that fiscal policy was most effective—that "money does not matter"—seemed less tenable when the fiscal policy stance was so largely determined by wartime spending needs.[22] If neither price controls nor fiscal policy would be effectively used to reduce inflation, that left monetary policy as the remaining option.

In the first months of the Korean War, the Federal Reserve continued to peg short- and long-term interest rates at low levels to support the Treasury in financing the war debts, just as it had during World War II. But as inflation picked up, Fed officials became concerned that interest rates were too low and called for an end to the peg. President Truman called the FOMC to the White House for a meeting and then released a statement claiming that the FOMC had promised to "maintain the stability of Government securities as long as the emergency lasts."[23] But Eccles, still on the Fed's board though no longer chairman, told the press that Truman's statement was false. Members of Congress, who had for a few years urged that the Fed should have "primary power and responsibility" over the cost of credit, were dismayed by the Truman administration's apparent dismissal of their stated preferences and insisted that the Fed and Treasury negotiate an agreement.[24]

The result was the Treasury-Fed Accord of March 3, 1951, which allowed the Fed to phase out the peg and use interest rate policy to stabilize economic conditions. The accord was an agreement, in other words, to end the system of fiscal dominance and begin a system of monetary dominance, in which the central bank pursues price stability regardless of the government's fiscal stance. Friedman and Schwartz note that "few episodes in American monetary history have attracted so much attention in the halls of Congress and in academic quarters, alike" as the dispute and accord between the Fed and the Treasury.[25] Shortly after the accord, Chairman McCabe resigned from the Fed, and President Truman appointed William McChesney Martin to replace him. Martin had played an important role in negotiating the accord while serving as assistant secretary of the Treasury, and he would end up serving as Federal Reserve chair under five presidents, until 1970.

Under Martin's leadership, inflation declined immediately after the accord. The Consumer Price Index had risen more than 9 percent from March 1950 to March 1951, but it rose only 2 percent from March 1951 to March 1952. Chairman Martin and the other Fed officials were highly inflation averse, viewed low and stable inflation as a top priority for monetary policy, and had a pretty good understanding of how to achieve it.[26] In particular, Fed minutes from the 1950s reveal that Martin and other members of the FOMC recognized that in the short run, allowing the economy to run above capacity could boost output and reduce unemployment, though at a cost of higher inflation.[27] They also understood that there was no positive long-run trade-off between output and inflation; that is, high inflation would adversely affect both employment and output if sustained.[28]

The short-run trade-off between inflation and output or unemployment is now called the Phillips curve, named for New Zealand economist A. W. Phillips. In 1958, Phillips published a famous paper presenting a downward-sloping relationship between wage inflation and unemployment in the United Kingdom.[29] When unemployment was higher, wages grew more slowly. Later, other economists showed that a similar relationship held in the United States and using price inflation instead of wage inflation. Although Phillips is credited with "discovering" the curve that bears his name, credit is more appropriately due to none other than Irving Fisher. In 1973, the *Journal of Political Economy* republished a long-lost paper written by Fisher in 1926 in which Fisher wrote that "between 1915 and the present-changes in the purchasing power of the dollar may very largely explain changes in employment."[30] He explained: "When the dollar is losing value, or in other words when the price level is rising, a business man finds his receipts rising as fast, on the average, as this general rise of prices, but not his expenses, because his expenses consist, to a large extent, of things which are contractually fixed. . . . The business man, therefore, finds that his profits increase. In fact, during such periods of rapid inflation, when profits increase because prices for receipts rise faster than expenses, we nickname the profit-taker the 'profiteer.' Employment is then stimulated-for a time at least."[31] Fisher argued that he had uncovered "a genuine and straightforward causal relationship; that the ups and downs of employment are the effects, in large measure, of the rises and falls of prices, due in turn to the inflation and deflation of money and credit. . . . If this conclusion be sound, we have in our power, as a means of substantially preventing unemployment, the stabilisation of the purchasing power of the dollar."[32] Today, economists don't think about causality running from prices to employment. Rather, the Phillips curve relationship comes about because strong aggregate demand boosts both employment and prices. This was also the understanding of FOMC policy makers in the 1950s: as the economy moved near capacity and unemployment fell, they expected that inflation would begin to rise. For example, in 1955, the FOMC member Watrous Irons commented, "The economy was moving nearer capacity in many respects, and as this point approached less efficient means of production would be utilized and prices would tend to rise."[33]

When Irons said this, the unemployment rate was 4.3 percent, and inflation in the Consumer Price Index (CPI) over the previous year had been just 0.4 percent. But the Martin Fed readied to respond to impending inflation. "Inflation is a thief in the night and if we don't act promptly and decisively we will always be behind," Martin told the FOMC in 1955.[34] As unemployment hovered near 4 percent, inflation did, in fact, pick up. The CPI increased by 3.7 percent from April 1956 to April 1957. In response to this inflation, the Fed began tightening monetary policy by increasing the discount rate several times in 1956 and 1957 and conducting open-market operations, with Martin describing the Fed's role as "leaning against the winds of deflation or inflation, whichever way they are blowing."[35]

Uneasy Independence

By many accounts, the Treasury-Fed Accord marks the start of the era of central bank independence for the Fed. The Fed gained some degree of independence from the Treasury, but not total insulation from politics. The Fed's pursuit of price stability was especially challenged when a sharp but brief recession, from September 1957 through April 1958, followed its rate hikes. The Fed's willingness to tighten monetary policy in response to higher inflation, and the administration's tolerance of the Fed's actions, outraged many voters and Democrat politicians, who did not want to make the apparent trade-off of higher unemployment for lower inflation.

A contemporary observer, the political scientist Richard Gable, wrote: "The Republican perception of the recession and the action taken were rooted in a conservative economic philosophy, a laissez-faire view of government, and a fear of inflation. The conservative position is less interested in economic growth and more interested in stabilizing the purchasing power of the dollar."[36] Many voters shared Gable's dissatisfaction with the Republican approach, and the Republicans suffered large losses in the 1958 congressional elections.

Neither Martin nor Eisenhower was dissuaded from the pursuit of price stability. In early 1959, as the economic recovery was progressing, Martin warned the largely unreceptive Joint Economic Committee of Congress, chaired by Senator Paul Douglas, a Democrat of Illinois, of "a real possibility of serious increase of the price level" later that year. Douglas, in turn, reminded Martin that Article I, Section 8 of the Constitution gave Congress the power to coin money and regulate its value and that Fed officials were to "act as agents of Congress . . . and not as agents of the Executive."[37]

Douglas also pointedly noted that the Employment Act of 1946 made it the policy of the federal government to promote maximum employment, production, and purchasing power, asserting: "To you the all-important matter is the stability in prices. That is important to us too, but growth is also important to us and comparatively full employment is also important to us." To this, Martin responded: "The growth that you are talking about comes through stability. Stability is not an end in itself—it is a means to a better standard of living, and I believe we would have had much more growth over the last 10 years and much more permanent growth, if there had been more stability in the economy and there had not been this recurrent instability in both employment and prices."[38]

In the 1959 Economic Report of the President, Eisenhower echoed Martin's commitment to price stability as the foundation of economic growth.[39] He called, unsuccessfully, for an amendment to the Employment Act of 1946 making price stability an explicit federal goal.[40] He also created the Cabinet Committee on Price Stability for Economic Growth, chaired by Vice President Richard Nixon. The committee's 1959 report rejected the "misconceptions" that "a small amount of inflation is no cause for concern," that "inflation will stimulate economic growth," and that "a little inflation is inevitable, relax and enjoy it."[41]

The report noted, "For the past quarter of a century the price increases which characterize periods of rising prosperity have not been offset at other times."[42] Accumulated increases in the cost of living over time, the report noted, "inflict unjust hardships on the many families whose incomes or pensions are fixed in dollars, or do not rise in proportion to prices," "violate our standards of fair play by harming families whose incomes are average or below-average," and "contradict promises implied when people put aside income in insurance, government bonds, retirement funds, and other forms of saving; for when the money is returned it fails to buy the goods and services that people were led to expect when they put the income aside."[43]

The committee recommended tax reform, removal of inefficient regulations, lifting of farm price supports, and "sound" monetary policy to promote price stability. Price controls, the report emphasized, "would do more harm than any amount of inflation that we have ever experienced or are likely to experience in peacetime. While reasonable stability of the *average level* of prices is desirable, variability of *individual* prices is essential, because that controls the efficiency and the progress of our dynamic economy." The report added that "price control inevitably leads to wage control. The two together inevitably lead to rationing goods and regulating jobs and working conditions. The resulting loss of freedom would ultimately prove even more disastrous than the loss in living standard."[44]

In January 1960, *Businessweek* published a long feature on Chairman Martin and the political battles he was sure to face heading into the presidential election. The article described Martin as a highly orthodox central banker "in the thick of a looming political fight over tight money. . . . The administration feels that tight money is essential if the United States is to achieve a balanced budget and a stable dollar. But the Democrats are anxious to do battle on the ground that these policies may prevent the Nation from attaining the added growth needed to meet the Russian challenge."[45] The article noted that Martin faced "a continual threat that Congress will step in and limit his freedom. . . . [H]e has frequently annoyed Congress, but never to the point of a showdown."[46]

If anyone was up for a showdown with Martin, it was Representative Wright Patman, a Texas Democrat who served twenty-four consecutive terms from 1929 to 1976. At the 1960 hearings of the Joint Economic Committee, Patman told Martin that "every time you have a decision to make and one alternative is on the side of the people and low interest, and the other alternative is on the side of the bankers and high interest, you have chosen the side of the bankers and high interest." Patman also accused Martin of making his decisions "from a Republican political campaign basis" instead of an economic basis.[47]

Martin adamantly defended himself against this accusation, responding: "I have called my shots and the Federal Reserve Board has called their shots, whether wise or unwise, according to their lights as they saw them in terms of the best interest of the people of this country without any thought of political benefit. I am not running for office and I do not intend to run for office." Patman retorted: "I wish you were. If you were, your decisions would probably be different."[48]

Patman's fears that Martin would help the Republicans in the following election were misplaced. A recession began in April 1960, and Vice President Nixon lost his presidential bid to Senator John F. Kennedy, a Democrat.

The Cold War and the Great Society

Kennedy's campaign, which promised to "get America moving again," focused on the escalating tensions between the United States and the Soviet Union and on the ailing economy, which was still suffering the effects of a prolonged steel industry strike in 1959.[49] The United States transitioned from a net exporter of steel to a net importer. This contributed to the first current account deficit for the United States since 1953 and an outflow of gold from the United States.[50]

This deficit and gold outflow was a cause of some concern under the newly operational Bretton Woods system, in which the dollar was convertible to gold at $35 per ounce. At the time of the Bretton Woods conference in 1944, the United States held the majority of the world's gold. A full return to the interwar gold standard seemed infeasible because other countries would have needed gold reserves of their own to back their currency with gold. Instead, other currencies were pegged to the dollar but adjustable if necessary to correct a "fundamental disequilibrium" in the balance of payments.[51] By the early 1960s, the United States was losing gold reserves at a rate that threatened to undermine confidence in the continued convertibility of the dollar at a constant gold price, and the stability of the whole Bretton Woods system.[52]

The Kennedy administration and the Federal Reserve had to take these international considerations into account in their response to the 1960 recession. The Federal Reserve cut the discount rate moderately but did not want to "excessively depress short-term interest rates and thus add to the United States' balance of payments difficulties."[53] If short-term interest rates were too low, currency arbitrageurs would convert dollars to gold in order to invest in higher-yielding European assets. To stimulate the economy further, the Treasury and the Fed cooperated to conduct Operation Twist—named for the popular dance from that year—to reduce longer-term interest rates without reducing shorter-term interest rates by purchasing long-term bonds and selling short-term Treasury bills.[54] The recession ended in February 1961 and was followed by a long expansion, although gold reserves continued to decline.[55]

Inflation remained low—under 2 percent—for the for the first half of the decade, even as the recovery accelerated.[56] But partly for national security reasons, President Kennedy was concerned with a particular price: the price of steel. When steel executives announced a price increase of $6 per ton in 1962, Kennedy held a press conference in which he described the increase as "a wholly unjustifiable and irresponsible defiance of the public interest" in the midst of "grave crises in Berlin and Southeast Asia." He added:

> The American people will find it hard, as I do, to accept a situation in which a tiny handful of steel executives whose pursuit of private power and profit exceeds their sense of public responsibility can show such utter contempt for the interests of 185 million Americans. . . . It would seriously handicap our efforts to prevent an inflationary spiral from eating up the pensions of our older citizens, and our new gains in purchasing power. It would add, Secretary McNamara informed me this morning, an estimated one billion dollars to the cost of our defenses, at a time when every dollar is needed for national security and other purposes. It would make it more difficult for American goods to compete in foreign markets, more difficult to withstand competition from foreign imports, and thus more difficult to improve our balance of payments position, and stem the flow of gold.[57]

His concern almost brought about a revival of wage and price controls. When a member of the press asked whether Kennedy was "thinking in terms of requesting or reviving the need for wage-price controls," Kennedy responded that he was "very interested in the prospective investigations that will be conducted in the House and

Senate, and whether we shall need additional legislation, which I would come to very reluctantly. But I must say the last 24 hours indicates that those with great power are not always concerned about the national interest."[58]

The steel companies complied with President Kennedy's verbal pressure, or "jawboning," by quickly rolling back prices. Earnings and profits, unsurprisingly, also fell, furthering the domestic steel industry's decline. Roger Blough, the chief executive officer of US Steel, told his shareholders that "this concept is incomprehensible to me—the belief that Government can ever serve the national interest in peacetime by seeking to control prices in competitive American business, directly or indirectly, through force of law or otherwise."[59]

Vice President Lyndon B. Johnson became president in 1963, when Kennedy was assassinated. He was reelected in 1964, running on his Great Society policy agenda that promised poverty reduction, urban renewal, health-care reform, and expanded voting rights.[60] Johnson passed a major tax cut that had been proposed by Kennedy. He also signed the Social Security Amendments of 1965, which created Medicare and Medicaid, which Kennedy had also endorsed.[61] Medicare and Medicaid provide public health insurance for older people and people with low income. The idea of a national health insurance program can be traced back to the 1920s, when the rising cost of hospital and physician care became a concern to progressive reformers.[62]

Johnson also took office just as US military involvement in Vietnam was escalating. Johnson and his advisers wanted the Fed to keep interest rates low to support the Great Society programs and Vietnam War financing. Patman, who had become chairman of the House Financial Services Committee, worried that the Fed would not comply with the administration's wishes. Patman thought that Chairman Martin was determined to destroy the "incredible economic record under President Johnson." Price stability, Patman claimed in 1965, was "as firm as a weight lifter's muscle," yet Martin was "the man who can't stand prosperity. . . . The cogs in his head click one way—tight, tight, tight money, high, high, high interest rates."[63] Patman claimed to be receiving phone calls all over the country asking:

> "What is this 'blank, blank' Martin trying to do?" "Who's back of him?" "What can we do to stop-him from ruining our economy?" . . . "Is it right for an American official to have the authority to make our economy plummet?" . . . "What can you do to make the Federal Reserve responsible to the President of the United States?" . . . "How can you have the Fed going one way and the government the other and come out whole?" "Must we have two governments in Washington—one elected and the other carefully selected by a few bankers?"[64]

Patman also leaned into growing criticism of the Fed's "penchant for secrecy."[65] Senator William Proxmire, a Democrat from Wisconsin, complained "that trying to find out why and how the Federal Reserve makes its decisions is like 'trying to paste a custard pie on a wall.'"[66] Patman hoped to make the Federal Reserve more accountable to elected officials by increasing its transparency. The Cold War had catalyzed a push for transparency in government, more broadly, as growing government secrecy threatened to undermine public trust and the legitimacy of government. Representative John Moss, a Democrat from California, warned: "The present trend toward government secrecy could end in a dictatorship. The more information that is made available, the greater will be the nation's security."

Moss, who viewed transparency as a pillar of democracy, had spent more than a decade pushing for transparency reforms. When he took office in 1952, access to government records was governed by the Administrative Procedure Act of 1946, which gave agencies considerable discretion regarding publication of government records. His efforts culminated in the Freedom of Information Act (FOIA) of 1966, which amended the Administrative Procedure Act to make government records more open. FOIA allows private citizens to request records from federal agencies and requires agencies to comply unless the requested information is subject to one of several exemptions. The purpose of FOIA is to "ensure informed citizens, vital to the functioning of a democratic society."[67]

When FOIA was under consideration in the Senate, the Federal Reserve Board of Governors wrote a letter commenting on the bill. The governors noted their belief that "premature disclosure of certain records of the Board and of the Federal Open Market Committee . . . would have an adverse impact on the Board's ability to carry out its responsibilities, including the effectuation of sound monetary policy."[68] In response to the passage of FOIA, Fed officials began splitting the FOMC meeting minutes into two sections: brief "Minutes of Action," recording attendance and general information, that could be used to satisfy FOIA requests, and lengthier Memoranda of Discussion that were protected by a FOIA exemption. The Fed did, thanks to Patman's efforts, begin to use an independent firm (though not the Government Accountability Office) to audit its books. Much larger steps toward Federal Reserve transparency came later and will be discussed in subsequent chapters.

The Seeds of Inflation

Although Patman wanted to "bring the money power back to the highest elected officials of the United States government and the Congress," Martin still believed in the value of an independent central bank and was determined to resist pressure for easier monetary policy.[69] In the fall of 1965, Martin learned that government spending on the increasingly unpopular Vietnam War was much higher than official numbers revealed.[70] Expecting this spending to contribute to inflation, Martin cast the deciding vote in a 4–3 decision by the Board of Governors to increase the discount rate in December. Johnson called Martin to a meeting at his ranch, where Martin held firm against the president's attempts to change his mind.[71] As it turned out, the December rate hike was not enough.

Inflation in the CPI, which had been below 2 percent in the early 1960s, rose to 3 percent in 1966.

Despite Martin's resistance to Johnson's pressure, Milton Friedman, who had praised Chairman Martin's policy making for most of the 1950s, began warning that the Martin Fed was allowing the money supply to expand too rapidly.[72] Friedman thought that the Fed could best promote macroeconomic and price stability by following a monetary growth rule (or *k-percent rule*) in which the money supply would increase at a constant rate. In 1965, he warned members of the Federal Reserve Board that there was "real danger of accelerated price rise if the present rate of monetary expansion continues."[73]

Friedman's warning was prescient, as inflation continued to rise. Martin urged Johnson's advisers to convince the president to raise taxes to counteract the inflationary effects of the Great Society and Vietnam War spending. In 1967, Martin lowered the discount rate, hoping that Johnson would comply with a tax increase. But Johnson and Congress did not pass a tax increase until spring 1968, after Johnson announced that he would not run for reelection.

The rise in inflation in the final years of Martin's chairmanship was accompanied by a reduction in unemployment, from 4.9 percent in January 1965 to 3.4 percent in January 1969. For some in the Johnson administration and on the Board of Governors, it seemed that the economy was moving to a better point on the Phillips curve. Johnson's economic advisers thought the Fed should try to keep unemployment around 4 percent, even if it meant allowing the modestly higher inflation to persist.[74] Martin, remember, seems to have understood that policy makers could not simply trade off somewhat higher inflation for permanently lower unemployment.[75]

Friedman formalized Martin's perspective in his remarkable 1967 presidential address to the American Economic Association.[76] (Edmund Phelps made similar arguments at around the same time.)[77] Friedman's argument hinged on the role of inflation expectations in the Phillips curve. Friedman was aware that Fisher "discovered" the Phillips curve in 1926 and described Fisher as "without question the greatest economist the United States has so far produced."[78] Like Fisher, he assumed that inflation expectations were typically backward-looking—that is, as inflation starts to rise, people come to expect higher inflation in the future.[79]

Rising inflation expectations start to shift the Phillips curve, so that any given level of unemployment corresponds to a higher level of inflation. This means that there is no stable Phillips trade-off between inflation and unemployment that policy makers can simply choose from. In the long run, unemployment returns to its "natural rate." Attempts to hold unemployment below its natural rate, by using loose fiscal and/or monetary policy to run the economy above capacity, eventually lead to higher and higher inflation.

TEN

THE GREAT INFLATION

Inflation is our domestic public enemy No. 1.

GERALD FORD, Address to Joint Session of Congress and the Nation[1]

A Monetary Phenomenon

Milton Friedman's presidential address to the American Economic Association is one of the most influential academic lectures in macroeconomics. It put the role of expectations at the forefront of macroeconomic thought and encouraged a greater focus on the long-run effects of macroeconomic policies.[2] The impact on modern macroeconomics can hardly be overstated. Friedman also had substantial influence in the policy realm at the time, but not enough to prevent the Great Inflation that defined the late 1960s through the early 1980s.

Friedman was an economic adviser to Richard Nixon as Nixon ran again for president, this time successfully, in 1968. *Time* reported in December 1969 that Friedman's ideas were "highly regarded within the Administration," and that Paul McCracken, chairman of Nixon's Council of Economic Advisers, described himself as "Friedmanesque."[3] Nixon's choice to replace Martin at the Fed, Arthur Burns, had been Friedman's professor; the two were close friends and shared a strong appreciation of free markets. Friedman hoped that the Fed chairmanship would be "a worthy capstone to Arthur Burns's distinguished career."[4]

In 1965, remember, Friedman had warned that overly rapid monetary expansion would cause inflation. By 1969, though, with consumer price inflation rising above 5 percent, the Fed had reversed course. This also was concerning to Friedman. *Newsweek* reported that since mid-1969, the Fed had "permitted no growth at all" in the money supply and that, "ironically, Friedman's principal complaint is that the Federal Reserve is overdoing the restraints in its effort to cure inflation. 'If the board continues to keep the growth of money at zero for another two months, I find it hard to see how we can avoid a severe recession,' he says."[5]

A mild recession did occur from December 1969 through November 1970. In the midst of it, Friedman wrote a *Newsweek* op-ed advising Burns:

> Because of the delay between monetary actions and their effects, *what happens to the economy during most of 1970—insofar as that is affected by monetary policy—is already determined.* What the Fed can do is shift promptly to a less restrictive policy and thereby build now a base for a healthy recovery from the recession. The real test will come during the next six months or so. . . . The temptation will then be strong for the Fed to overreact as it has so often in the past, to go from too slow a rate of monetary growth to too high a rate. If it acts in that way, it will simply set off another round of inflation. Let us hope that the Fed will this time have the foresight, the patience and the courage to hold to a steady and moderate course, to keep the quantity of money expanding at a rate high enough to encourage recovery from the recession but low enough to avoid renewed inflation.[6]

At first, Burns did just what Friedman recommended, easing monetary policy to allow the economy to recover from the recession. But in the recovery period, the relationship between Burns and Friedman grew strained. Very rapid money growth in early 1971 prompted Friedman to write in the *Sunday Bulletin* that "the money supply is being managed ineptly."[7] Burns's diagnosis of the causes of inflation began to contrast quite sharply with Friedman's famous profession that inflation "is always and everywhere a monetary phenomenon."[8]

In Burns's view, continued high inflation was not a result of his mismanagement of the money supply. Throughout 1971, even though the recession was over, unemployment remained high—around 6 percent—and inflation declined only slowly. Burns testified to Congress in August 1971: "A year or two ago it was generally expected that extensive slack in resource use, such as we have been experiencing, would lead to significant moderation in the inflationary spiral. This has not happened, either here or abroad. The rules of economics are not working in quite the way they used to."[9] Burns adopted a *cost-push* interpretation of inflation, in which inflation was driven by nonmonetary, supply-side forces like rising input costs and union-led wage increases.[10] Friedman protested that "the trade unions have no responsibility for inflation; rather, they react to it."[11]

Burns's cost-push view of inflation meant that he saw a very limited role for either fiscal or monetary policy in addressing it. Instead, in a shift away from his earlier free-market views, he came to believe that more direct government intervention in goods and labor markets was needed. He believed that price and wage controls, or "incomes policies," would be more effective than monetary policy for reducing inflation.[12] As inflation rose, to Friedman's frustration, the public increasingly shared Burns's view.[13]

The Nixon Shock

President Nixon was initially highly reluctant to impose the price and wage controls that his Fed chair recommended. Years earlier, he had worked as a lawyer at OPA, where he "found such an extension of government power frightening" and "regarded his fellow employees as 'slide-rule boys' and 'snoopsters.'"[14] In 1959, he had chaired the Cabinet Committee on Price Stability for Economic

Growth, which emphasized the dangers of price and wage controls. Nixon initially dismissed price controls as a "socialist scheme, a scheme to socialize America." In a meeting with his advisers, he referenced the authoritarian, intrusive nature of the World War II price-control system, with "50,000 OPA cops, you know running around, telling everybody, messing in your face and so forth."[15]

But the president grew increasingly frustrated with the slow recovery from the 1970 recession and stubborn inflation, which undermined his own reelection chances and the stability of the Bretton Woods system. The prolonged inflation meant that the dollar was overvalued at the official convertibility rate of $35 per ounce of gold. By the middle of 1971, investors began speculating against the dollar, fearing it would be devalued. Holders of dollars began converting dollars to gold, draining US gold reserves.[16] Nixon's response was a three-pronged Economic Stabilization Program, announced in a speech on August 15, 1971.

First, the president devalued the dollar and closed the gold window, severing the link between the dollar and gold and effectively ending the Bretton Woods arrangement. Foreign currencies were appreciated by varying amounts against the dollar, with the goal of improving the US trade balance. Nixon tried to reassure the public that "the effect of this action . . . will be to stabilize the dollar": "If you want to buy a foreign car or take a trip abroad, market conditions may cause your dollar to buy slightly less. But if you are among the overwhelming majority of Americans who buy American-made products in America, your dollar will be worth just as much tomorrow as it is today."[17] Second, he announced a ninety-day price and wage freeze, known as Phase I, which would be followed by a period of controlled increases, known as Phase II. The initial freeze in Phase I would give policy makers time to plan the Phase II controls without prompting a rush of anticipatory price increases in the meanwhile. In this respect, it was effective, with minimal evidence of price increases for prices that were covered by the freeze (some prices, like for agriculture, imports, and exports, were exempt).

The controls were seen as necessary to support the third component of the Economic Stabilization Program, an expansionary fiscal package that included tax reductions to promote business recovery. The Council of Economic Advisers wrote in its annual report that "action to make fiscal policy more expansive had been limited by the need to avoid intensifying any inflationary expectations and stepping-up the inflation. The establishment of the direct wage-price controls created room for some more expansive measures, because it provided a certain degree of protection against both the fact and the expectation of inflation."[18]

The economist Phillip Cagan explains that the purpose of the controls was "to hold down price increases made in anticipation of further inflation. . . . Given the objective of influencing anticipations, an elaborate enforcement agency was not necessary and indeed was economically impractical—in addition to being politically repugnant to the administration. The idea was to do little to disrupt the economy."[19] Thus, in contrast to the World War II price controls, which relied on sixty thousand government employees and thousands of volunteers, the Nixon controls relied on a much smaller apparatus. The seven-member Price Commission and fifteen-member Pay Board, each with staff of a few hundred, administered the controls, and around three thousand Internal Revenue Service employees handled public inquiries and enforcement.[20]

The limited enforcement apparatus focused on the largest firms and unions, reflecting the popular view, shared by Chairman Burns, that these large firms and unions were "pushing" inflation by driving up costs. Unsurprisingly, these larger firms and unions were the quickest to challenge the controls. In the 1971 case *Amalgamated Meat Cutters v. Connally,* decided by the US District Court for the District of Columbia, the meat cutters' union challenged the constitutionality of the Economic Stabilization Act, which they saw as a "naked grab of authority" that gave the president "unbridled legislative power" to determine "the scope, manner and timing" of controls.[21] The judges, relying on the 1944 *Yakus* decision, held that no declaration of an emergency or even evidence of sharply rising prices was needed to justify economy-wide controls.

By early 1972, inflation and wage growth seemed to be decelerating. With an election coming later in the year, the administration hoped to speed up the business and labor market recovery. Nixon pressured Burns for monetary expansion to improve his reelection chances.[22] Burns did ease monetary conditions in 1972, although it may not have been the direct result of Nixon's pressure. Instead, it likely reflected Burns's own belief that the incomes policy was the most effective means of keeping inflation at bay.

At first, Nixon's economic policies were overwhelmingly popular, and Nixon won reelection in a landslide.[23] It came as something of a surprise, then, when in January 1973 Nixon unveiled Phase III, which the *New York Times* described as "a far bigger shift than many people were expecting." By announcing "nothing less than the removal of mandatory controls from most of the economy and their replacement with a system of voluntary compliance," the president took "an unexpectedly long step back towards an uncontrolled economy."[24] The *Times* attributed the shift to the president's free-market ideals and distaste for controls, which he had imposed only reluctantly in 1971. The remaining controls were on food, health care, and construction.[25] Health-care price controls, in particular, were kept in place because of the rapid rise in health-care costs since the beginning of Medicare and Medicaid in 1965.

With decontrol and continued monetary expansion, prices quickly began to rise. By June, with year-over-year consumer price inflation reaching 6 percent, the administration imposed a new sixty-day freeze on retail prices and promised that a new Phase IV, with tighter, mandatory controls, would follow. This freeze, according to the *Times*, was both an admission that Phase III had failed and a "response to those critics who have contended that the White House's preoccupation with the Watergate scandal has paralyzed the Administration's ability to cope with major problems at home and abroad."[26]

The announcement of the freeze brought immediate criticism from business and labor leaders and from consumer advocates. Douglas Kenna, president of the National Association of Manufacturers, warned that the controls would create "chaotic conditions in the production and distribution of essential commodities." The UAW's president Leonard Woodcock warned it would "not solve the nation's problem," and Ethel Roseman, a consumer advocacy group leader, dismissed the controls as "a hoax," "no more than an attempt to pacify the citizens of this country because of his embarrassment over Watergate."[27]

The Nixon administration's reliance on controls, rather than monetary restraint, was also criticized by economists at the time. Cagan explained: "Despite the inequities and inefficiencies of controls, the general public still finds them more appealing than open inflation. Until monetary policy can subdue the inflationary pressures, controls in some form are likely to straddle the economy. The danger in this prospect is that controls divert attention from monetary policy and may encourage a postponement of the restraint which is necessary to curb inflation."[28] Friedman, likewise, thought that the controls were Nixon's "biggest mistake" but believed that monetary reform was just as important as decontrol.[29] He testified to Congress in June 1973 that monetary growth had been "decidedly too high" in the previous eighteen months and that the Fed bore "a great deal of responsibility for an economic climate which underlies the rapid price explosion in the first few months of this year."[30]

This lack of monetary restraint, combined with major supply-side shocks, led to strong upward pressure on prices. A five-month Arab oil embargo began in October 1973 and led to a quadrupling of oil prices, and several major crop failures around the world pushed up food prices. Imposing controls on top of these pressures led to shortages that made the economic distortions of price controls more obvious to the public.[31] Thus, the second freeze and Phase IV controls were much less popular than Phases I and II.

The Fed's mismanagement of monetary policy was also scrutinized. Senator William Proxmire, the Wisconsin Democrat who had long criticized the Fed's lack of transparency, asked Burns to address the extent to which the Fed was responsible for rapid inflation. Burns responded in a November 1973 letter to Senator Proxmire that "special influences" like high farm prices due to global crop failures, supply bottlenecks, and energy shortages were to blame, adding, "Partial decontrol in early 1973 and the subsequent freeze failed to bring the results that were hoped for."[32]

In Friedman's own letter to Senator Proxmire, he wrote: "The only justification for the Fed's vaunted independence is to enable it to take measures that are wise for the long run even if not popular in the short run. That is why it is so discouraging to have [Burns's reply to Senator Proxmire] consist almost entirely of a denial of responsibility for inflation and an attempt to place the blame elsewhere." The Fed, he argued, had "the power to prevent the sharp acceleration in monetary growth," which was responsible for rising inflation. Friedman concluded:

> There is literally no way to end inflation that will not involve a temporary, though perhaps fairly protracted, period of low economic growth and relatively high unemployment. Avoidance of the earlier excessive monetary growth would have had far less costly consequences for the community than cutting monetary growth down to an appropriate level will now have. But the damage has been done. The longer we wait, the harder it will be. And there is no other way to stop inflation. . . . If the Fed does not explain to the public the nature of our problem and the costs involved in ending inflation; if it does not take the lead in imposing the temporarily unpopular measures required, who will?[33]

Whip Inflation Now

Most of the Nixon price controls, except for those on petroleum prices, were lifted in April 1974, and Nixon resigned that August following the Watergate scandal.[34] When Gerald Ford took office, the economy was in a recession and entering the throes of stagflation: the unemployment rate was 5.5 percent and rising, and CPI inflation was above 10 percent.[35] Ford had taken several economics courses at the University of Michigan, where he developed a strong interest in economics and belief in the value of free markets and deregulation.[36] Thus, Ford hoped to address inflation by encouraging citizens to take voluntary actions rather than by reimposing mandatory price controls.

Congress and the president held the large Conference on Inflation in September 1974. Ford summarized his takeaway from the conference in his famous "Whip Inflation Now" (WIN) speech on October 8, which kicked off a campaign of the same name: "We found, I would say, very broad agreement that the Federal Government imposes too many hidden and too many inflationary costs on our economy."[37] The president noted: "Food prices and petroleum prices in the United States are primary inflationary factors. America today partially depends on foreign sources for petroleum, but we can grow more than enough food for ourselves." He called upon farmers to "produce to full capacity" and on Congress to remove regulations that limited production or otherwise contributed to high prices. He directed the newly formed Council on Wage and Price Stability (CWPS) "to find and to expose all restrictive practices, public or private, which raise food prices" and "to be the watchdog over inflationary costs of all governmental actions."[38]

President Ford also required that "all major legislative proposals, regulations, and rules emanating from the executive branch of the Government will include an inflation impact statement that certifies we have carefully weighed the effect on the Nation. I respectfully request that the Congress require a similar advance inflation impact statement for its own legislative initiatives."[39] The WIN campaign is best remembered (and ridiculed) for the bright red WIN pins that people wore to express their support of the campaign. The White House had twelve million pins produced, but only one hundred thousand were requested by the public.[40]

Ford initially thought that tighter fiscal policy could help address the inflation problem. In October 1974, he proposed a tax hike and reductions in government spending. But with unemployment rising and growth slowing, fiscal stringency was politically unpalatable. By January 1975, Ford instead proposed a tax cut to boost economic activity. Congress passed a bill that included a tax cut larger than the president suggested, along with increased government spending, which Ford was compelled to sign, although he vetoed subsequent attempts to raise government spending further.[41]

President Ford also sparred with Congress over the appropriate response to continued high energy prices. Ford wanted to end the price controls on domestic oil, reduce US dependence on foreign oil, and promote the conservation of energy resources, even if that meant accepting higher prices for a time. He suggested that a "windfall profits" tax on domestic oil producers could help appease the public, who would otherwise oppose decontrolling the "greedy" oil companies.

In January 1975, he signed a proclamation increasing the import fee on petroleum by $1 per barrel and announced plans for further $1 per barrel increases in February, March, and April.[42] By raising the price of foreign oil, he hoped to stimulate domestic oil production, reducing prices in the longer run. Democrats in Congress immediately accused him of abusing presidential power and passed legislation suspending his authority to impose additional import fees for ninety days. Ford vetoed the bill but agreed to wait sixty days for Congress to come up with an alternative plan for energy before proceeding with additional import fee increases.[43] When four months had passed with no satisfactory action from Congress, Ford announced an additional import fee.

Negotiations between the president and Congress culminated in the Energy Policy and Conservation Act of December 1975, which, in many respects, was a victory for the Democrats. The new import fees on foreign oil were removed, and domestic oil prices were reduced by 12 percent. Petroleum price controls were not lifted, although there were provisions for decontrol to begin after forty months. The act also created the Strategic Petroleum Reserve and imposed gasoline mileage standards on auto manufacturers.[44] The *New York Times* reported that Ford "faced pressures from both directions in deciding whether to sign or veto the energy bill":

> He was lobbied intensively by oil and automobile companies who strongly urged a complete removal of price controls, mandatory standards and other restraints. Many of the Southern conservatives in the Republican Party, whose support he needs to win the nomination next year, had urged veto. A number of his own aides reportedly wanted him to-allow the price mechanism of the free market to determine fuel prices, a position that Mr. Ford is sympathetic to ideologically. But if he vetoed the bill and allowed fuel costs to jump, the results could have helped touch off a new wave of inflation. In the Northeastern states, including New Hampshire, where he faces an important primary election in February, passage of the energy bill was a major issue.[45]

With lower oil prices, inflation and unemployment both declined in the year following the Energy Policy and Conservation Act, but the respite was only temporary.

Stop-Go Monetary Policy and the Full Employment and Balanced Growth Act

Ford's WIN speech barely mentioned monetary policy, and the Fed made no lasting effort to fight inflation. Rather, the Fed followed what is often called a "stop-go" pattern, tightening policy only until unemployment began to rise, then easing again, allowing inflation to ratchet up over time. Burns later explained, in a 1979 speech, "The Anguish of Central Banking," that "the Federal Reserve was still willing to step hard on the monetary brake at times—as in 1966, 1969, and 1974—but its restrictive stance was not maintained long enough to end inflation. By and large, monetary policy came to be governed by the principle of undernourishing the inflationary process while still accommodating a good part of the pressures in the marketplace."[46]

Burns admitted that "the Federal Reserve System had the power to abort the inflation at its incipient stage fifteen years ago or at any later point, and it has the power to end it today. At any time within that period, it could have restricted the money supply and created sufficient strains in financial and industrial markets to terminate inflation with little delay. It did not do so because the Federal Reserve was itself caught up in the philosophic and political currents that were transforming American life and culture."[47] He traced the origins of these "currents" to the Great Depression, New Deal, and World War II, when "a great and growing body of problems and hardships became candidates for governmental solution."[48]

Burns focused in particular on the Employment Act of 1946, noting: "Inflation came to be widely viewed as a temporary phenomenon—or, provided it remained mild, as an acceptable condition. 'Maximum' or 'full' employment, after all, had become the nation's major economic goal—not stability of the price level. That inflation ultimately brings on recession and otherwise nullifies many of the benefits sought through social legislation was largely ignored."[49] The Fed, he felt, was obligated to "accommodate" the government's policies, including its growing spending and deficits, lest it end up "frustrating the will of the Congress, to which it was responsible—a Congress that was intent on providing additional services to the electorate and on assuring that jobs and incomes were maintained, particularly in the short run."[50]

More recent legislation that had been in the works for much of the decade would place even more emphasis on full employment as a national priority. The most ardent supporters of full employment legislation in Congress were Representative Augustus Hawkins, of California, and Senator Hubert Humphrey, of Minnesota, both Democrats. Hawkins, an author of the Civil Rights Act of 1964, was troubled by the much lower labor-force participation rates and higher unemployment rates of black people compared to white people. He wanted the government to guarantee a right to employment for anyone willing and able to work. He rejected the idea of a Phillips trade-off—that drastically reducing unemployment would increase inflation—arguing instead that finding jobs for minorities would alleviate "inflationary shortages and bottlenecks."[51] Humphrey, who served as vice president under Lyndon Johnson, also thought that monetary and fiscal policy guided by the Phillips trade-off view led to harmful consequences for the poor.[52]

In 1976, Humphrey and Hawkins introduced a bill, the Full Employment and Balanced Growth Act, which called for a 3 percent unemployment rate goal, with the federal government as employer of last resort. Humphrey and Hawkins did not expect the bill to pass but wanted it to become part of the Democratic platform for the November elections. Jimmy Carter, who gained the nomination, was the least supportive of the bill among the Democratic candidates, for he feared that it would, in fact, cause inflation.[53] After Carter's election, the Carter administration and Republicans in Congress negotiated with Humphrey and Hawkins to pass the Full Employment and Balanced Growth Act (or Humphrey-Hawkins Act) in 1978. The act set highly ambitious goals of 3 percent unemployment for adults twenty and older and no inflation (0 percent) within a decade, but it gave precedence to the unemployment goal.

The Humphrey-Hawkins Act also required the Fed to submit a semiannual monetary policy report to Congress to report on progress with respect to the goals.[54] This was important progress toward the transparency goal that Patman had pushed for in the 1960s. The Watergate affair and the Vietnam War had further increased public concern over government secrecy, and over Ford's veto, Congress amended the Freedom of Information Act of 1966 to strengthen transparency in government.[55]

Shortly after, a law student named David Merrill filed a FOIA request to obtain some Federal Reserve documents that were released with a delay. He wanted immediate rather than delayed disclosure of the policy directives and memoranda of discussion produced after each FOMC meeting. The FOMC denied this request, arguing that immediate release "would undermine the effectiveness of the agency's policy."[56] The district court and the court of appeals sided in Merrill's favor, determining that the documents were statements of policy and thus not subject to any FOIA exemptions. But the Supreme Court, in *Federal Open Market Committee of the Fed-*

eral Reserve System v. Merrill, determined that "the sensitivity of the commercial secrets involved, and the harm that would be inflicted upon the Government by premature disclosure, should continue to serve as relevant criteria in determining the applicability" of FOIA exemption privileges.[57]

The Supreme Court did not make a ruling on whether the immediate release of the policy directives would "significantly harm the Government's monetary functions or commercial interests," making delayed release permissible, but rather remanded that question to the district court.[58] There, the FOMC argued that "prompt disclosure would allow private investors to anticipate FOMC action resulting in exaggerated market response," and also "would primarily benefit large investors who are capable of promptly assessing the impact of FOMC policy and would place them at a competitive advantage over smaller investors."[59] But other experts prepared affidavits expressing the view that prompt disclosure would actually enhance monetary policy effectiveness.

The district court finally decided that "the dispute among the experts in this case is not one over facts in any objective sense but rather is a dispute over economic theory. It may in fact be finally reducible to a dispute over proper monetary policy. . . . It is at once apparent that this Court is an inappropriate forum for weighing the wisdom of the FOMC's choice."[60] Thus, delayed disclosure was allowed to continue, although the balance of expert opinion regarding proper monetary policy was beginning to shift in favor of greater transparency.[61]

The courts proved similarly unwilling to adjudicate against the Fed in other cases that challenged the Fed's policy making in the 1970s. Two cases brought by Congressman Henry Reuss, a Democrat from Wisconsin, and by Senator Donald Riegle Jr., of Michigan, also a Democrat, challenged the participation of the reserve bank presidents on the FOMC as a violation of the appointments clause of the Constitution (Article II, Section 2, Clause 2).

Reuss had introduced legislation in 1976 that would have required that the five reserve bank presidents with FOMC seats be appointed by the president and confirmed by the Senate rather than by their private-sector boards of directors. When this legislation failed, Reuss brought suit in the US District Court for the District of Columbia, where he claimed that "improper delegation of responsibilities to the FOMC resulted in a usurpation of his powers, under article I, section 8, of the Constitution, to coin and regulate the value of money, to regulate commerce, and to borrow money on the credit of the United States."[62] As a bondholder, he also "maintained that actions taken by the FOMC might result in his being deprived of property without due process of the law."[63] This property deprivation, Reuss argued, could occur whether the FOMC chose to tighten or to loosen monetary policy: "By voting to increase the availability of money and credit, the defendant individuals can reduce the purchasing power of the dollar, thereby diminishing the value in so-called constant dollars or real terms of the plaintiffs bonds. . . . By voting to decrease the availability of money and credit, the defendant individuals can bring about a general reduction in economic activity sufficient to impair the ability of the obligors on the plaintiff's bonds to make payment of interest or principal or both, thereby diminishing or extinguishing their value."[64] The district court decided that Reuss lacked standing to sue, as he "failed to allege any causal connection between the allegedly improper selection of the Reserve Bank representatives . . . and any possible impact on the value of his securities." His claims to standing as a legislator were "remote, conjectural and insufficient."[65] Senator Riegle brought a similar suit in 1979. Riegle claimed that his position as a Senator gave him a stronger standing case than Reuss because his power to vote to confirm appointees was impaired.[66] This time, the appeals court held that Riegle did have standing, in part because "Riegle's inability to exercise his right under the Appointments Clause of the Constitution is an injury sufficiently personal to constitute an injury-in-fact."

But they still dismissed the Senator's case, arguing that, "where a congressional plaintiff could obtain substantial relief from his fellow legislators through the enactment, repeal, or amendment of a statute, this court should exercise its equitable discretion to dismiss the legislator's action."[67] In other words, because Congress itself could choose to amend the Federal Reserve Act, the court wanted to avoid "thwarting Congress's will by allowing a plaintiff to circumvent the processes of democratic decisionmaking."[68] This "equitable discretion doctrine" also led to the dismissal of later attempts by members of Congress to sue the Fed.[69]

The Carter Program

Economic conditions at the start of Carter's presidency were far from the goals for unemployment and price stability set by the Humphrey-Hawkins Act. Troublingly, inflation continued to rise throughout 1978 despite high unemployment. When Carter announced his anti-inflation program in October 1978, he emphasized the necessity of inflation reduction for full employment: "If we do not get inflation under control, we will not be able to reduce unemployment further, and we may even slide backward."[70] He wanted to avoid imposing "a complicated scheme of Federal government wage and price controls," which he saw as "too extreme," or engineering "a deliberate recession which would throw millions of people out of work."

Carter's economic advisers, like Barry Bosworth, who directed the CWPS from 1977 to 1979, thought that "sole reliance on fiscal or monetary restraint" to reduce inflation would be "simply too costly in terms of unemployment. . . . If measures are taken to bring the current inflation down to half of what it is now within the next two years, the levels of unemployment will be of double-digit magnitudes, an extremely high price to pay."[71] Monetary and fiscal restraint reduce inflation by reducing aggregate demand. But Bosworth thought that "broad institutional changes in the structure of the American economy" had made it "possible today for wages and prices to be determined not by competitive pressures in the marketplace or the interaction of supply and demand." He explained that "the organization of labor unions, the technological changes in production, and the growing role of government in the economy were responses to specific problems. But as a result of these actions, people have more and more discretion to dictate to some extent what their own wage or price increases will be."[72]

The Congressional Budget Office concurred that "the on-going price advance results principally from various interest groups using their economic and political power to maintain their traditional rates of real income growth." They also noted that "the continued momentum of inflation during periods of high unemployment is rooted in self-fulfilling expectations—held by workers, business and consumers—about future high rates of price increase."[73] Thus, Carter thought that the solution to inflation would "involve action by government, business, labor, and every other sector of our economy." He added:

> Some of these factors are under my control as president—especially government actions—and I will insist that the government does its part of the job. But whether our efforts are successful will finally depend on you as much as on me. Your decisions—made every day at your service station or your grocery store, in your business, in your union meetings—will determine our nation's answer to inflation as much as decisions made here at the White House or by the Congress on Capitol Hill. . . . We know that government is not the only cause of inflation. But it is one of the causes, and government does set an example. Therefore, it must take the lead in fiscal restraint.

Carter gave the CWPS responsibility for implementing a voluntary program of price and wage standards. The CWPS had no legal authority to enforce these standards but could apply some pressure by publicizing lists of companies that failed to comply and excluding them from government contracts.[74] Bosworth described the Carter anti-inflation program as an effort to "create an environment with fiscal and monetary policy that will be conducive to a moderation of inflation and then to try to use some voluntary measures to see if the rate of wage increases and price increases can be reduced at less cost in terms of unemployment than would otherwise be the case."[75]

The Federal Reserve chairman G. William Miller, who had replaced Burns in March 1978, described Carter's anti-inflation program as "a constructive step toward breaking the inflationary patterns and psychology that today are so firmly entrenched." As did Carter, he claimed that "the job of containing inflation requires a concerted effort on the part of all Americans," and he pledged that the Fed would "play its part in supporting the President's initiative by exercising appropriate restraint in the provision of bank reserves, credit, and money."[76] But Miller did not view the Fed as primarily responsible for price stability, for he believed that inflation was largely out of the Fed's control. Thus, he did little to rein in inflation during his chairmanship.

The Carter anti-inflation program had its share of critics, such as Carl Madden, who served as chief economist for the Chamber of Commerce from 1966 to 1976. It was not the case, Madden thought, that monetary and fiscal policy makers had tried and failed to reduce inflation; rather, they had not tried. He wrote that "other objectives of monetary and fiscal policy have taken precedence over anti-inflation. To be sure, a society that strives for rapid economic growth and full employment need not therefore give up price stability. But the United States has done so." He added that "the inflation-unemployment trade-off has worsened. . . . The trade-off makes the prospective cost of reducing inflation appear higher than earlier. That cost, of course, is lost output and employment. The converse is also argued; that is, stimulative measures intended to reduce joblessness and spur growth may accelerate inflation more than earlier."[77]

The Government Accountability Office published two reports in 1980 that criticized the tactics and efficacy of the CWPS. One highlighted the failure to focus on encouraging productivity improvements as a method of reducing inflation, despite congressional desire that it do so. Productivity growth was much slower in the 1970s than in the previous two decades. The report recommended that CWPS "should place more emphasis on its statutory responsibilities to focus attention on the need to increase productivity and to stimulate productivity in the design and monitoring of the wage and price standards . . . and should provide wage and price exceptions for programs that are documented to improve productivity."[78]

The other report focused more specifically on the failure to restrain massive oil and energy price increases, attributing the failure to "limitations in the [price] standards' coverage, monitoring, and enforcement" and concluding that "the Council's inability to do very much about oil product price increases raises deep issues concerning the Council's mission and responsibility."[79] The CWPS set price standards for many different petroleum products, but not for crude oil, which was still subject to controls imposed during the Nixon administration. These controls had evolved over the years into a complex and, in Friedman's words, "perverse and irrational" system, with a lower price ceiling for "old oil" from existing domestic producers and a higher price for "new oil" from foreign and new domestic producers.[80] The two-tiered price controls were meant to prevent domestic producers from reaping "windfall" profits as a result of higher world oil prices while still allowing sufficient imports to meet domestic needs and incentivizing new production. But the effect was to stifle domestic oil production and increase reliance on petroleum imports.[81]

A sharp decrease in oil production following the Iranian Revolution of 1979 led to a large increase in foreign oil prices, and as a result, consumers faced fuel shortages and long lines at gas stations. The Energy Policy and Conservation Act of 1975 had given the president the authority to phase out oil price controls beginning 1979. Carter wanted to use that authority, but he knew that the more liberal wing of the Democratic Party would oppose decontrol because of concern about oil industry price gouging. Thus, he announced a proposal for a windfall profit tax on domestically produced crude oil, to make decontrol politically palatable and raise revenue to reduce the deficit.[82] Congress passed the windfall profit tax in 1980, but revenues were lower than projected, and the tax was eventually repealed in 1988.[83]

When Miller left the Fed to become Treasury secretary, President Carter appointed Paul Volcker, then president of the New York Fed, as the new Fed chair. Volcker began his term in August 1979. Volcker was much more committed to reducing inflation than either Burns or Miller had been. Chair Volcker emphasized to Congress and to the press his intention to slow the growth of the money supply to fight inflation. But it was hard to convince the public, and the markets, that he would stay the course with monetary tightening. Many expected that the Fed would reverse course as soon as unemployment, which was already beginning to rise, reached 7.8 percent by the end of a brief recession in 1980. Because of the low credibility of the Fed's inflation-fighting commitment, inflation expectations remained high, so inflation continued to climb.[84]

Inflation was a key issue in the 1980 campaign. In the primaries, Carter was challenged from the left by Senator Edward Kennedy, of Massachusetts, who called for a wage and price freeze followed by formal wage and price controls and a large stimulus package. Kennedy announced his proposal in Pennsylvania steel-mill country, where he "lambasted the administration anew for allegedly failing to protect the domestic steel industry from unfair import competition" and pledged to do a better job than the president of supporting steel prices.[85] Kennedy's challenge was unsuccessful, but it embarrassed the president and the Democratic Party.[86]

Republican candidate Ronald Reagan also challenged Carter's approach to inflation. "I think this idea that has been spawned here in our country, that inflation somehow came upon us like a plague and therefore it's uncontrollable and no one can do anything about it, is entirely spurious, and it's dangerous to say this to the people," he said in a debate. President Carter, Reagan claimed, had "blamed the people for inflation, OPEC, he's blamed the Federal Reserve System, he has blamed the lack of productivity of the American people, he has then accused the people of living too well. . . . We don't have inflation because the people are living too well. We have inflation because the Government is living too well. . . . Yes, you can lick inflation by increasing productivity and by decreasing the cost of Government to the place that we have balanced budgets and are no longer grinding out printing press money, flooding the market with it because the Government is spending more than it takes in."[87]

ELEVEN

THE VOLCKER DISINFLATION AND THE GREENSPAN STANDARD

> In those circumstances, the monetarist refrain that inflation is, after all, in the end a monetary phenomenon struck an increasingly responsive chord among the body politic. In effect, central banks began to have a stronger platform for effective action.
>
> PAUL VOLCKER, "The Triumph of Central Banking?"[1]

Decontrol and Disinflation

Ronald Reagan defeated Carter by a landslide in the 1980 election, ending the era of New Deal liberalism and ushering in a new era of American conservativism. Reagan was committed to what he called "free play of wages and prices."[2] Thus, one of Reagan's first official acts as president, in February 1981, was to remove the remaining controls on oil prices.[3] He also eliminated the wage and price standards of the Council on Wage and Price Stability. Reagan's decontrol measures reflected public appetite for deregulation: two-thirds of respondents to a 1981 public opinion poll agreed that government regulation of business and interference with free enterprise had gone too far.[4] But the president's critics faulted him for acting on his own, "without formal counsel from Congress and the public," and congressional Democrats warned that decontrol would make the United States more vulnerable to price increases by the Organization of Petroleum-Exporting Countries, or OPEC.[5]

In early 1981, Paul Volcker began another attempt to restrain inflation through monetary tightening, although unemployment remained high after the 1980 recession. Volcker defended the approach against charges that it was inconsistent with the directives of the Humphrey-Hawkins Act: "We will not be successful, in my opinion, in pursuing a full employment policy unless we take care of the inflation side of the equation while we are doing it. I think that philosophy is actually embodied in the Humphrey-Hawkins Act itself. I don't think that we have the choice in current circumstances—the old tradeoff analysis—of buying full employment with a little more inflation."[6] Volcker faced enormous pressure to reverse course as interest rates soared and another, deeper recession began in 1981. Home builders mailed two-by-four wooden planks to the Fed to protest the high interest rates had hurt their business. Representative Henry Gonzalez, a Texas Democrat, accused Volcker of having "legalized usury beyond any limits imaginable," and threatened to impeach him.[7] Reagan's Treasury secretary, Donald Regan, was also a vocal critic of Volcker, although Reagan himself promised to "do nothing to undermine" Federal Reserve independence.[8]

Volcker's most ardent critics today decry his support of Reagan's union-busting policies.[9] Writing for *The Week*, Jeff Spross claims that "Volcker explicitly viewed breaking the power of organized labor as a critical piece of his anti-inflation crusade."[10] During the Professional Air Traffic Controllers Organization (PATCO) strike of August 1981, members of PATCO, a public union, demanded better working conditions and higher wages. Because PATCO members were federal government employees, their strike was illegal. The president ordered the air-traffic controllers to return to work and fired more than eleven thousand who refused. This watershed moment in US labor relations was followed by declining union membership and greater reluctance to use strikes as a bargaining tactic.

Volcker supported Reagan's strategy of reducing inflation by moderating wage demands and later reflected that "one of the major factors in turning the tide on the inflationary situation was the controllers' strike," which "had a profound effect on the aggressiveness of labor at that time, in the midst of this inflationary problem."[11]

By the end of the recession, in November 1982, unemployment had reached 10.8 percent, and CPI inflation had at last fallen below 5 percent. From there, both unemployment and inflation steadily declined. In 1983, President Reagan reappointed Volcker for a second four-year term, remarking: "He is as dedicated as I am to continuing the fight against inflation. And with him as chairman of the Fed, I know we'll win that fight."[12]

Volcker did continue the fight, despite substantial resistance. In 1983, a group of around eight hundred individuals and private businesses challenged the monetary authority of the Fed in the DC district court, alleging "that they suffered serious financial damage as a result of monetary instability and high interest rates in recent years."[13] In *Committee for Monetary Reform v. Board of Governors of Federal Reserve System*, the plaintiff argued that Congress had unconstitutionally delegated its power to coin money and regulate its value to the FOMC. As in the earlier *Reuss* and *Riegle* cases, it also argued that the reserve bank presidents serving on the FOMC should be appointed by the president, according to the appointments clause. To establish standing, the plaintiff needed to demonstrate that the alleged constitutional violations had led to their personal injuries. They argued that the reserve bank presidents contributed to FOMC decisions to restrict the growth of the money supply, leading to higher interest rates. The court concluded that the argument was too speculative. The court of appeals concurred:

> Moreover, in light of the complexity of the modern economy, it is also highly uncertain whether and to what extent such policies were responsible for the adverse economic conditions that allegedly resulted in harm to the appellants. Similarly, the appellants have given no indication as to how they can succeed in estab-

> lishing that an overly broad delegation of power to the Federal Reserve System has had the consequence of undermining economic certainty and thereby increasing interest rates. . . . We think that courts lack both the competence and the authority to determine such abstract issues, which are better addressed through political and economic debate over the role of monetary policy in the national economy.[14]

The Triumph of Central Banking?

Inflation remained low throughout Volcker's second term while unemployment and interest rates began to fall. By the time of the 1984 presidential campaign, Reagan could run successfully on the strength of the economy. The famous "Morning in America" television spot for Reagan declared: "With inflation at less than half of what it was just four years ago, they can look forward with confidence to the future. It's morning again in America, and under the leadership of President Reagan, our country is prouder and stronger and better."[15]

Volcker's own popularity also improved. At the end of his term, in 1987, the *New York Times* reported that Volcker was "considered almost a national hero for chopping inflation from an average rate of 12.8 percent in 1979 and 1980 to less than one-third that level for each of the past five years."[16] The *Los Angeles Times* wrote: "Even as late as 1984, Congress was seriously considering efforts to rein in the vaunted independence of the Fed. . . . Some lawmakers muttered about impeaching Volcker. How times have changed. Today, Volcker's stern visage, his gloomy lectures on the evils of deficit spending and the clouds of smoke from his ever-present cheap cigar have made him into something of a national folk hero, an American Crocodile Dundee—the man who slew the inflation dragon and stayed to preside over one of the longest economic expansions since World War II."[17] Despite his folk-hero status, Volcker did not serve a third term. Facing frequent conflict with the Reagan appointees on the Board of Governors, he submitted his resignation at the end of his term. A few years after leaving office, Volcker gave a lecture in the Per Jacobsson series, the same series in which Burns gave his lecture "The Anguish of Central Banking." Volcker playfully titled his lecture "The Triumph of Central Banking?" Although Volcker included a question mark in his title, in retrospect, most economists do consider the Volcker disinflation a triumph. In particular, it was a triumph of ideas: first, that low and stable inflation should be the remit of monetary policy, and second, that stabilizing longer-run inflation expectations is critical for stabilizing inflation itself.

Stabilizing longer-run inflation expectations requires some type of nominal anchor, or "constraint on the value of domestic money."[18] For much of US history, the dollar's nominal anchor came from a gold or bimetallic standard. The demise of the Bretton Woods system, which decoupled the dollar from gold, broke the dollar's nominal anchor, which allowed monetary policy makers much more discretion to expand the money supply. Senator Jesse Helms, a North Carolina Republican, remarked, "It is no coincidence that inflation of the dollar which precipitated the final break with gold, accelerated after the last vestige of gold's discipline was removed."[19]

Senator Helms was instrumental in 1980 legislation establishing the Gold Commission, chaired by economist Anna Schwartz, that studied the possibility of a return to the gold standard. The commission ultimately did not recommend returning to gold but suggested that the Congress and the Fed consider the adoption of a monetary policy rule.[20] A monetary policy rule, like the k-percent rule that Schwartz's coauthor Friedman had long favored, also provides a nominal anchor. By limiting monetary policy makers' discretion, a rule can help insulate them from political pressure to expand the money supply to boost output and employment in the short run. This boost to output and employment requires the monetary authority to surprise people with higher-than-expected inflation.

A key insight of the rational expectations revolution of the 1970s was that policy makers cannot surprise people repeatedly and indefinitely.[21] If people have rational expectations, so they "understand the policy maker's incentives and form their expectations accordingly," they will expect higher inflation.[22] Inflation will rise, but with no benefit to growth or employment. A formal rule for monetary policy improves the situation by eliminating the potential for, and the expectation of, higher inflation.

In a famous 1983 paper, the economists Robert Barro and David Gordon pointed out that "reputational forces can substitute for formal rules."[23] In other words, if a central bank manages to establish credibility, or the reputation for being committed to low inflation, the private sector will realize that it will be unlikely to attempt to create an inflation surprise, because of the immense reputational cost it would entail. Credibility, then, can serve as another form of nominal anchor. Volcker's Fed did not adopt a formal rule for monetary policy, but it did use reputational forces as a substitute. Once Volcker established his tough-on-inflation reputation, inflation expectations became "anchored."

Following Volcker's death in 2019, Ben Bernanke told the *New York Times* that Volcker "personified the idea of doing something politically unpopular but economically necessary."[24] Volcker reflected on this popularity issue in his "Triumph" lecture. Central banks around the world, he noted, were enjoying much greater reputations than they had in prior decades. He explained that "at a certain point in the inflationary process, public opinion will support strong policies to restore stability even though those policies seem to entail a harsh short-term cost."

But he argued that "the best results will be achieved if an inflationary threat is dealt with at an early stage, before the public is fully alarmed."[25] In other words, central banks cannot wait to gain public support before responding to inflationary threats. Thus, he made a case that a central bank should enjoy "substantial autonomy in its operations and with insulation from partisan and passing political pressures." He also suggested that "the recurring difficulty in acting before inflation builds momentum could be reduced if central banking statutes in the United States and other countries stated more explicitly that the main continuing purpose of monetary policy should be the stability of prices." He added: "No doubt the manner and intensity with which that goal is pursued at specific times will and should be influenced by surrounding circumstances. For that reason, I don't have much faith in setting out specific targets for reducing inflation; the pseudo-precision implied would risk undermining rather than reinforcing credibility. But, the experience of recent years, does suggest that vacuous admonitions that a monetary authority be all things to all men—for growth, full employment, and stability—risk confusion and misunderstanding about what a central bank can really do."[26] Volcker's mention of "specific targets" alluded to growing interest in inflation targeting around the world. In 1990, the year of his lecture, the Reserve Bank of New Zealand became the first central bank to adopt a formal inflation target. The Bank of England, the Bank of Canada, and the Swedish Riksbank soon followed. Bernanke and Frederic Mishkin explain that the inflation-targeting approach "is characterized, as the name suggests, by the announcement of official target ranges for the inflation rate at one or more horizons, and by explicit acknowledgment that low and stable inflation is the overriding goal of monetary policy."[27]

In many countries, the adoption of inflation targeting reflected public recognition that "the central bank is the best place to make the technical decisions necessary to achieve price stability and to make judgments about whether the pursuit of other objectives is consistent with this goal."[28] The ascendancy of inflation targeting reflected a desire to avoid a repeat of the Great Inflation by providing a nominal anchor that could stabilize longer-run inflation expectations. The growing ranks of inflation-targeting central banks around the world, as a whole, had positive experiences in their early years of the new framework—inflation was lower and less volatile, with no apparent adverse effects on output. But the United States, as the next chapter covers, was a latecomer to inflation targeting.

Fedspeak and the Greenspan Standard

President Reagan selected Alan Greenspan as Volcker's replacement. The *New York Times* reported: "Economists and other analysts said Mr. Greenspan, in taking a job that is sometimes described as the second most influential in the nation, was unlikely to pursue a policy markedly different from Mr. Volcker's. Mr. Greenspan shares the free-market views of the White House and has long been an important presence both in Washington and the Wall Street community."[29]

Chairman Greenspan, sometimes called the "maestro," presided over the so-called Great Moderation, from 1987 to 2006. During this time, he faced only two recessions, each lasting less than a year, and inflation nearly always remained below 5 percent. Greenspan was a Republican and gave Reagan high praise for his "wholehearted embrace of capitalism and a rule of law," noting: "The President understood the self-correcting tendencies of free markets and the fundamental wealth-creating capacity of capitalism. He trusted Adam Smith's invisible hand to stimulate creativity and innovation and to produce outcomes that he perceived as generally fair." Like Volcker, he approved of Reagan's handling of the air-traffic controllers' strike.

Early in Greenspan's chairmanship, Representative Stephen Neal, a Democrat from North Carolina, led a push within Congress for an inflation target and rules-based monetary policy. In 1989, Neal introduced an unsuccessful resolution that would have directed the FOMC maintain an inflation rate of 0 percent.[30] Throughout his chairmanship, members of Congress continued to push for the Fed to pursue something more like inflation targeting. In 1995, Senator Connie Mack of Florida and Representative H. James Saxton of New Jersey, both Republicans, introduced the Mack-Saxton bill, which would have made price stability the primary goal of monetary policy, repealing the Humphrey-Hawkins Act and the Fed's dual mandate of both price stability and maximum employment. The bill, which failed in 1995 and again in 1997, also would have required the Fed to provide a numerical definition of price stability, one of the hallmarks of an inflation-targeting framework.[31] Text from the bill was included in related bills in 1999, 2003, and 2005, but the legislation was not enacted.[32]

Opponents of the Mack-Saxton bill disliked giving price stability primacy over maximum employment. Representative Reuss (who, remember, unsuccessfully sued the Fed) and the economist John Kenneth Galbraith expressed their disapproval of the legislation in a 1996 *New York Times* piece. They wrote: "The Mack-Saxton Bill would legitimize the Federal Reserve's actual policies in recent years. Forgetting about jobs and growth, Mr. Greenspan has made his reputation by battling at Armageddon against an increasingly invisible inflation."[33]

Greenspan did tell Senator Mack that "having a primary goal of price stability is the most important thing which a central bank can contribute to a market economy," but Greenspan respected both parts of the dual mandate and preferred to use considerable discretion in choosing how to balance and pursue them.[34] Near the end of Greenspan's chairmanship, the economists Alan Blinder and Ricardo Reis wrote: "For years now, US monetary policy has been said to be on 'the Greenspan standard,' meaning that it is whatever Alan Greenspan thinks it should be. Similarly, the so-called nominal anchor for US monetary policy has been neither the money supply nor any sort of inflation target, but rather the Greenspan standard itself. . . . Federal Reserve policy under his chairmanship has been characterized by the exercise of pure, period-by-period discretion, with minimal strategic constraints of any kind, maximal tactical flexibility at all times, and not much in the way of explanation."[35] Blinder and Reis praised Greenspan's leadership of the Fed but warned: "The secret to Greenspan's success remains a secret. When the next leader of the Fed takes his seat behind the chairman's desk and opens the top drawer in search of Alan Greenspan's magic formula, he may be sorely disappointed."[36]

Chairman Greenspan initially resisted another key feature of the inflation-targeting approach, the embrace of a high degree of transparency. When Greenspan first became chairman, he believed, as did Volcker before him, that the Fed should communicate only rarely. The Fed at the time still did not announce its decisions on interest rates to the public, for fear of causing market overreactions.[37] When Greenspan did have to speak, especially in congressional testimony, he developed a form of cryptic communication known as "Fedspeak." Years later, Greenspan explained:

> As Fed chairman, every time I expressed a view, I added or subtracted 10 basis points from the credit market. That was not helpful. But I nonetheless had to testify before Congress. On questions that were too market-sensitive to answer, "no comment" was indeed an answer. And so you construct what we used to call Fed-speak. I would hypothetically think of a little plate in front of my eyes, which was the Washington Post, the following morning's headline, and I would catch myself in the middle of a sentence. Then, instead of just stopping, I would continue on resolving the sentence in some obscure way which made it incomprehensible.[38]

Janet Yellen, who later became Federal Reserve chair, explains: "For decades, the conventional wisdom was that secrecy about the central bank's goals and actions actually makes monetary policy more effective. . . . This secretiveness regarding monetary policy decisions clashed with the openness regarding government decisions expected in a democracy, especially since Federal Reserve decisions influence the lives of every American. And there were critics within the economics profession. James Tobin and Milton Friedman, both Nobel laureates, disagreed on almost every aspect of monetary policy, but they were united in arguing that transparency regarding central bank decisions is vital in a democracy to lend legitimacy to policy decisions."[39]

Representative Henry Gonzalez was particularly troubled by the Fed's lack of transparent communication with the public. Gonzalez had been mentored by Representative Wright Patman and shared Patman's concern about the Fed's lack of accountability.

"Like chairman Patman," he said, "I'm not worried about taking on an icon. The Federal Reserve has evolved into an entity in and unto itself and now believes it has no relationship to the rest of the Government."[40] In 1989, Gonzalez became chair of the House Banking Committee, which had oversight of the Fed. In 1993, Gonzalez's committee learned that the Fed possessed transcripts of FOMC meetings since 1976. This prompted what the *New York Times* called Gonzalez's "most vigorous offensive ever to inject more democracy and accountability into the Federal Reserve."[41] Gonzalez wanted the transcripts made public and future meetings to be recorded and broadcast with a sixty-day delay.[42] Gonzalez called Greenspan and other Federal Reserve officials to testify in October. At these hearings, Representative Lee Hamilton, a Montana Democrat, summarized his and Gonzalez's complaints about the Fed:

> The Federal Reserve occupies an anomalous position within the Government of the United States. It is an enormously powerful institution, but it does not conform to the normal standards of government accountability. Power without accountability simply does not fit into the American system of democracy. Through its control over monetary policy, the Federal Reserve affects the lives and well-being of all Americans. The path that the Federal Reserve sets for monetary policy and interest rates affects every business person, worker, consumer, borrower, and lender in the United States. The dilemma created by this concentration of power is that the independence which the Federal Reserve must have in order to insulate monetary policy from political pressures also serves to remove the Fed from the normal processes of accountability that apply to every other agency of government. Monetary policy is decided in secret, behind closed doors.[43]

Not all of Gonzalez's Democrat colleagues supported his reform efforts. New York's representative Charles Schumer, for example, said that "the Fed has done a good job. Monetary policy should be structured so it is not subject to the short-term vicissitudes of politics."[44]

Similarly, President Bill Clinton, who had reappointed Greenspan despite their political differences, said that the Fed "is functioning well and does not need an overhaul just now."[45]

Greenspan acknowledged that "the role of a central bank in a democratic society requires a very subtle balancing of priorities between the need for sound, far-sighted monetary policy and the imperative of effective accountability by policymakers," but he thought that Gonzalez's proposals got the balance wrong—they would make the Fed too susceptible to political pressure.[46] He warned, "If accountability is achieved by putting the conduct of monetary policy under the close influence of politicians subject to short-term election cycle pressures, the resulting policy would likely prove disappointing."[47] He also feared that making transcripts or videos public would turn the meetings into "a series of bland, written presentations. The advantages to policy formulation of unfettered debate would be lost."[48]

Nonetheless, other forces pushed the Fed in the direction of greater transparency. In October 1993, FOIA exemptions became more difficult to obtain.[49] Around that same time, there was also a series of press leaks about Fed policy directives. These circumstances convinced the FOMC to begin releasing full transcripts of its meetings with a five-year lag.[50] This strategy, they hoped, would satisfy public demand for greater transparency without stifling deliberation in the meetings. This concession fell far short of what Gonzalez desired, and he told *American Banker* that the Fed reminded him of Nixon and Watergate.[51]

Another step toward transparency came in early 1994, when the Fed was preparing to raise interest rates for the first time in around five years. At the February FOMC meeting, Greenspan told the FOMC that he wanted to take the unusual step of announcing the rate change to the public, to "make certain that there is no ambiguity about our move."[52] He told the committee that "this announcement of the move is not precedential. . . . There are certain individual events where periodically the Federal Reserve has made special statements; I'm merely stipulating that this is one of them."[53] The committee agreed and issued a short statement announcing that "the decision was taken to move toward a less accommodative stance in monetary policy in order to sustain and enhance the economic expansion."[54]

Although Gonzalez disapproved of the rate hike, he was glad to see the Fed announce the decision publicly. The announcement did, despite Greenspan's intentions, set a precedent. From then on, the FOMC issued statements immediately following meetings in which a policy change was made. In 1999, the FOMC began issuing statements following every meeting, even meetings without policy changes. Even though the Fed came to adopt transparent procedures reluctantly, Fed officials gradually began to embrace transparency as a desirable feature of their policy making. Vice Chair Alan Blinder remarked that "the central bank's independence carries with it a corollary of accountability. . . . In particular, the public has a right to know more about what the Federal Reserve is doing and why it is doing it."[55]

Health-Care Prices

The previous chapter on the Great Inflation, and this chapter on the Volcker disinflation, have described how price stabilization eventually came to be accepted as the responsibility of an independent central bank. The Volcker disinflation demonstrated the power of monetary policy to stabilize *aggregate* prices more effectively than other approaches, like Nixon's price controls or Ford's Whip Inflation Now program.

In many of the earlier chapters of the book, we saw policy makers and the public focus on the prices of *particular* goods or assets. Some of the most important price fluctuations were those of western land, farm products, and gold and silver. In part, this reflected the lack of reliable statistics on the aggregate price level until relatively late in American history. It also reflected the importance of certain prices for macroeconomic stability or for the interests of certain groups. Even after the responsibility for price stability was delegated to the Federal Reserve and aggregate prices were stabilized, certain prices continued to receive special attention from policy makers and were more likely to prompt calls for government intervention. In the Greenspan era, this was especially the case for health-care, energy, and housing prices.

The prices of medical goods and services receive special attention from policy makers because of the nature of health care. Paul Krugman explained in the *New York Times* in 2005: "We rely on free markets to deliver most goods and services, so why shouldn't we do the same thing for health care? . . . It comes down to three things: risk, selection and social justice."[56] *Risk* refers to the fact that a small minority of the population incur a large share of medical expenses in any given year. In 2002, Krugman noted, 5 percent of the US population accounted for half of medical costs. Health insurance protects people from the risk of incurring a crushingly high expense.

But health insurance markets are notoriously subject to an adverse selection problem: people who know they are less likely to have high medical costs are the least willing to pay for insurance. Unless private insurers heavily screen potential customers, denying coverage to customers with preexisting conditions or high risk of disease, they will end up insuring only those customers who are most likely to have high costs. Public health insurance programs, like the Medicare and Medicaid programs that began in 1965 as part of Johnson's Great Society, do not screen out people who are likely to incur high costs. Krugman explains: "Citizens of advanced countries—the United States included—don't believe that their fellow citizens should be denied essential health care because they can't afford it. And this belief in social justice gets translated into action, however imperfectly. Some of those unable to get private health insurance are covered by Medicaid. Others receive 'uncompensated' treatment, which ends up being paid for either by the government or by higher medical bills for the insured. So we have a huge private health care bureaucracy whose main purpose is, in effect, to pass the buck to taxpayers."[57] Recall that Nixon's controls on health-care prices had outlasted most other controls because of concerns about rising costs. Rising prices for prescription drugs were also a major contributor to increased spending of private health insurers, Medicare, and Medicaid, as well higher out-of-pocket costs for individuals. Prescription drug companies are able to charge monopoly prices because of patent protection, which is intended to incentivize the costly process of drug development.[58] High prices also reflect the price insensitivity of consumers toward drugs that are essential for their life and health.

The Drug Price Competition and Patent Term Restoration Act of 1984, or the Hatch-Waxman Act, amended patent laws related to pharmaceutical products to make it easier for generic drugs to be approved for market.[59] When President Bill Clinton took office in 1993, having campaigned heavily on health policy reforms, he denounced drug companies for raising prices at more than twice the inflation rate in the late 1980s and early 1990s, forcing some sick Americans to choose between buying food and medicine. The *New York Times* reported: "His proposals for revamping the medical system would fundamentally reshape the playing field for drug companies, pressuring them to hold down prices and in some ways treating them as much like a crucial social service or public utility as private profit-seeking businesses. For their part, the drug makers say the President is unfairly singling them out. They assert that his proposals would cripple research budgets, delaying the discovery of cures for scourges like AIDS, cancer and Alzheimer's disease."[60] President Clinton set up the Task Force on National Health Care Reform, headed by First Lady Hillary Clinton, to develop a plan to provide universal health care for all Americans. But the plan died in Congress in 1994, facing opposition from Republicans, the insurance industry, and pharmaceutical firms.[61] Note that when the Medicare program began, hospital costs were a greater concern than prescription drug costs, so the program covered only prescription drugs that were administered by a physician, not those that were administered by a patient at home.[62] Clinton's plan, had it passed, would have added outpatient coverage of prescription drugs to Medicare. The pharmaceutical firms opposed the plan in part because they worried that this drug benefit would be accompanied by the imposition of price controls.[63]

Incremental reform continued after the failure of Clinton's comprehensive reform, most notably with respect to Medicare coverage of prescription drugs. In December 2003, President George W. Bush signed the Medicare Prescription Drug, Improvement, and Modernization Act, which added prescription drug coverage through the new Medicare Part D. A controversial feature of the legislation was that it prevented the federal government from negotiating prices directly with drug manufacturers. According to the *New York Times*, "Critics argue that the Republicans were so sensitive to the drug industry's fear of price controls that they left the elderly exposed to a future of soaring drug costs."[64] As we will see, this feature of the law, and other drug-pricing provisions, have recently been amended by the Inflation Reduction Act of 2022.

Gas Prices and the Housing Bubble

Energy and housing prices were also of particular concern to policy makers and the public in the Greenspan era. Because oil is a global commodity, its price can fluctuate dramatically in response to international developments. The price of oil directly affects the price of gasoline and has an impact on the prices of many other goods and services that use energy as an input. An increase in oil prices is referred to as an adverse supply shock. It makes production more costly, raising prices and lowering output. An adverse demand shock, in contrast, lowers prices at the same time as it lowers output. Monetary policy can offset demand shocks. In the face of an adverse demand shock, the central bank can conduct expansionary monetary policy, which raises prices and raises output.

The monetary policy response to a supply shock is more complicated. If it pursues expansionary policy to offset the decline in output, it will exacerbate the rise in prices. If it pursues contractionary policy to offset the rise in prices, it will exacerbate the fall in output. A very strict inflation targeter, intent on keeping inflation at target even at short horizons, might respond by tightening policy, which would be very costly in terms of output and employment. And even if that action stabilized aggregate inflation, it would likely be the case that the relative price of oil and gas would be higher than before the oil shock. Another option is for the central bank to "look through" the supply shock, waiting out the temporarily higher inflation.[65] This is usually the preferable option, although it entails some risks and challenges.[66]

First, it is challenging to disentangle supply shocks and demand shocks in real time. Many different types of shocks can hit the economy at around the same time, and it is hard to tell exactly how much of any change in inflation, output, or unemployment is due to a particular shock. The central bank risks underresponding to a demand shock if it attributes too much of the change in conditions to a supply shock. The difficulty of distinguishing supply and demand shocks can also make it difficult for a central bank to explain its policy response to the public, which is related to the second risk—the risk that inflation expectations can become unanchored. If inflation rises in response to an oil shock, and in turn people come to expect higher inflation in the long run, it will become much more difficult for the central bank to stabilize inflation even after the supply shock fades away. In the 1970s, for example, policy makers attributed too much of the increase in inflation to oil shocks and kept monetary policy too loose. And inflation expectations were unanchored, so they rose with inflation, making the Volcker disinflation very costly.[67]

Because it is so difficult for monetary policy to respond to a rise in oil prices, the burden of response falls to fiscal and regulatory policy. The public usually demands a response, for several reasons. First, gas prices are very salient—many people see gas prices posted on signs multiple times per day and purchase gas frequently, so gas prices become an important driver of consumer sentiment.[68] Second, many people do not have much flexibility to reduce their consumption of gas, at least in the short run. People need a certain amount of gas to drive to work, and it is often not feasible to buy a more fuel-efficient vehicle, take public transportation, or move closer to work. Third, a rise in oil and gas prices tends to offend people's sense of justice, because it seems that the oil and gas companies reap undeserved benefits from higher prices that result from seemingly random global occurrences. Recall the persistence of petroleum price controls even after the other Nixon controls were lifted and the windfall profit tax of 1980.

When Hurricane Katrina disrupted national supply chains, including the energy infrastructure, in 2005, gas prices spiked from about $2.61 per gallon on August 22, the day before the hurricane hit, to $3.07 per gallon on September 5. President Bush directed the secretary of energy to sell thirty million gallons of oil from the Strategic Petroleum Reserve, set up in the Ford administration in response to the Arab oil embargo of 1973 to 1974, beginning on September 6. The Department of Energy also issued a waiver allowing the use of cheaper winter-blend gasoline instead of the more expensive summer blend that was normally required in September for environmental reasons. Both of these measures worked by increasing the supply of available oil or gas, thereby countering the effect that the reduction in supply had on prices. Gas prices did begin to decline almost immediately.

But some Democrats in Congress were concerned that the increase in price reflected not just the basic forces of supply and demand but also profiteering or price gouging by oil and gas companies that were taking unfair advantage of the state of emergency. Senator Carl Levin, of Michigan, told the *New York Times* on September 6, "We have a million people displaced and we have 100 million Americans that are opening up their hearts and homes to be of assistance and we have some people who are trying to take advantage of it for their own personal profit."[69] In Senate hearings, some Democrats openly called for price controls while others proposed imposing a windfall profit tax on gas or instituting a federal gas tax holiday, although none of the measures would counteract the supply shock leading to higher prices. A windfall profits tax, for example, increases production costs and is therefore itself an adverse supply shock. The Gas Price Stabilization Bill of 2005, which incorporated a variety of these measures, failed to pass.[70]

Later in September, Senator Maria Cantwell, a Democrat from Washington, introduced the Energy Emergency Consumer Protection Act of 2005, which also aimed to prevent price gouging for oil and gas. The bill would have allowed the president to declare an energy emergency, and during such an emergency would have made it "unlawful for any person to sell crude oil, gasoline, or petroleum distillates in, or for use in, the area to which that declaration applies at a price that—(A) is unconscionably excessive; or (B) indicates the seller is taking unfair advantage of the circumstances to increase prices unreasonably."[71] Again, the legislation failed to pass, as did similar legislation in 2007.[72]

Housing prices, like oil and gas prices, pose challenges for monetary policy makers but for different reasons. Houses are assets with volatile prices, and houses are frequently used as collateral in loans. This means that fluctuations in housing prices can cause financial and macroeconomic instability.[73] For homeowners, rising house prices increase wealth, and falling house prices do the opposite. For mortgage holders, falling house prices can put them "underwater" on their mortgage. The housing market is also particularly sensitive to monetary policy because house prices are so sensitive to interest rates.[74]

House prices grew rapidly in the early 2000s. By 2005, many economists were warning that the United States was in the middle of a housing bubble—in other words, that prices were rising as a result of speculative frenzy, rather than fundamentals.[75] Thus, when President Bush nominated Ben Bernanke, then chairman of the Council of Economic Advisers, to replace Greenspan at the Fed, market participants and members of Congress were eager to know how Bernanke would use monetary policy to respond to housing prices.[76] Many looked back to a speech he gave in 2002, in which he discussed why "leaning against the bubble" by raising interest rates is usually an ineffective strategy: "Understandably, as a society, we would like to find ways to mitigate the potential instabilities associated with asset-price booms and busts. Monetary policy is not a useful tool for achieving this objective, however. Even putting aside the great difficulty of identifying bubbles in asset prices, monetary policy cannot be directed finely enough to guide asset prices without risking severe collateral damage to the economy."[77] Bernanke, a renowned scholar of the Great Depression, presented the Fed's too-aggressive attempt to lean against a stock-market bubble in the late 1920s as a cautionary tale. A better approach, he suggested, was to use regulatory and supervisory policies to reduce the incidence and effects of bubbles. At Bernanke's nomination hearings in 2005, when questioned directly about the possibility of a bubble in the housing market, Bernanke again emphasized that supervision and regulation, particularly of riskier nontraditional mortgages, was preferable to using monetary policy. He also noted: "Housing prices will probably stabilize. Energy prices are an issue."[78]

Rising energy prices were an issue, he thought, because they were contributing to an increase in overall inflation—the Consumer Price Index had risen more than 4 percent over the past year.[79] Concern about rising inflation had led the Greenspan Fed to raise interest rates at each meeting since June 2004. Going into his chairmanship, Bernanke would also prioritize price stability, but as the next chapter discusses, he placed more emphasis on transparency than did Greenspan and pushed for the Fed to adopt an explicit inflation target.

TWELVE

INFLATION TARGETING AND THE GREAT RECESSION

Ultimately, the legitimacy of our policies rests on the understanding and support of the broader American public, whose interests we are working to serve.

BEN BERNANKE, closing remarks on the Centennial of the Federal Reserve Act[1]

Inflation Targeting before the Crisis

In Ben Bernanke's confirmation testimony in 2005, he promised to "maintain the focus on long-term price stability as monetary policy's greatest contribution to general economic prosperity and maximum employment," adding that "monetary policy is most effective when it is as coherent, consistent, and predictable as possible, while at all times leaving full scope for flexibility and the use of judgment as conditions may require." He also noted that "a more transparent policy process increases democratic accountability, promotes constructive dialogue between policy makers and informed outsiders, reduces uncertainty in financial markets, and helps to anchor the public's expectations of long-run inflation."[2]

Bernanke had been a proponent of inflation targeting since before becoming chairman. In 2003, while on the Board of Governors, he remarked that "discussions of inflation targeting in the

American media remind me of the way some Americans deal with the metric system—they don't really know what it is, but they think of it as foreign, impenetrable, and possibly slightly subversive."[3] The American media's skepticism of inflation targeting, Bernanke thought, reflected a misconception that inflation targeting would force the Fed to follow a strict rule or to ignore output and employment objectives. Rather, he explained, policy makers would still have flexibility and discretion to respond to output and employment as long as they stabilized inflation near the target over the longer run.

As evidence that the Fed had an "implicit" inflation target at the time, Bernanke pointed to the FOMC's statements after their meetings in May and August 2003, when the Fed expressed concern about the possibility of an "unwelcome substantial fall in inflation . . . from its already low level."[4] Bernanke explained that "the reference, beginning in May, to an 'unwelcome' fall in inflation contrasted starkly with Fed policy of previous decades, in which low or declining inflation had always been treated as desirable. Effectively, the Fed had publicly acknowledged that it had an inflation target, and that the target was greater than zero, even if it was not yet willing to give a precise number."[5]

Others at the Fed also became more vocal in their support for inflation targeting. For example, Marvin Goodfriend, while senior vice president and policy adviser at the Federal Reserve Bank of Richmond, argued that the Fed should adopt inflation targeting because "in a democracy a central bank should be fully accountable for the monetary policy that it pursues. . . . Adopting inflation-targeting procedures explicitly would improve the transparency of the policy process and the ability of Congress to hold the Fed accountable for monetary policy."[6]

As chair, Bernanke continued to favor the adoption of an explicit inflation target, and the FOMC discussed this possibility at several meetings before the Great Recession. At the FOMC's meeting in October 2006, Jeffrey Lacker, president of the Richmond Fed, noted that Bernanke's nomination hearings "appeared to provide the Congress with an opportunity to object, if they were so inclined, to unilateral adoption of an inflation target by the Federal Open Market Committee. I take the fact that they did not do so, at least publicly, as evidence that they would view a numerical inflation objective as broadly consistent with the wide latitude accorded to us by our existing legislative mandate."[7] Lacker supported announcing an explicit inflation objective, arguing that "as a matter of public accountability in a constitutional democracy, we owe it to the citizens of the United States to tell them this simple and yet very important implication of how we conduct monetary policy."[8]

At the same meeting, Frederic Mishkin, a member of the Board of Governors, also supported the adoption of an explicit numerical inflation goal. He explained that "the key to successful monetary policy is having a strong nominal anchor," and that "you don't have to do it with a long-run numerical inflation goal—the Federal Reserve has been very successful in doing it with an individual." In other words, the "Greenspan standard" had provided a nominal anchor based on Greenspan's *personal* credibility. Mishkin continued: "I feel we are very lucky to have had the Chairmen we have had. It could have come out quite differently. Having an explicit numerical definition of price stability, a long-run goal for inflation, means that the nominal anchor is less dependent upon who the Chairman is, and I think that's actually something that is very good." Still, he wanted the Fed to proceed cautiously:

> It is very important that we do not get too far ahead of the Congress on this. It is extremely important that we express a further definition of what we mean by price stability in a way that is absolutely consistent with the Federal Reserve Act and with the law and with the dual mandate. . . . A key part of the success of the Federal Reserve has been based on the fact that the Federal Reserve is clearly perceived by the public, the politicians, and the markets as having a weight on output fluctuations in our decisions. . . . This is a primary reason that we've had the support of the public and the politicians. We certainly don't want to lose that.

Mishkin was correct to worry that Congress might object to an explicit inflation target. In February 2007, Barney Frank, the Democratic chairman of the House Financial Services Committee, told the *Financial Times* that it would be a "terrible mistake" for the Fed to adopt an inflation target, which would "come at the expense of equal consideration of the other main goal, that is employment." The article noted that "Fed watchers say that, in order to make any such change, Mr. Bernanke would need at least the tacit consent of key figures in Congress. Mr. Frank's unequivocal statements suggest this consent will still be difficult to secure."[9]

Still, when the FOMC discussed inflation targeting again at its March 2007 meeting, Bernanke informed the committee that he had "consulted a bit with the Congress" and was "pretty encouraged by my discussions. I had the sense that—and this is a very important caveat—so long as our commitment to the dual mandate remains strong both in word and in deed, we will get a fair hearing if we decide to go forward. . . . I don't think that there are immediate barriers from the political side to prevent us from considering this."[10]

Many FOMC participants supported the adoption of a target for similar reasons as in the 2006 meeting. But others worried about the politics and the optics of such a move. Dallas's Fed president Richard Fisher, for example, was "not convinced that a numerical target is necessary at this stage":

> I do note that others have done this. . . . I'm not of the nature that I like to join the crowd for the sake of joining the crowd. . . . I am worried about whether or not we've accumulated sufficient political capital to sell this to the rest of the Congress and to the representatives of the people, and I'm a little concerned about the timing of our doing so. We spent the past two days talking about downside risk to the economy. Some of us feel, as I stated in our earlier discussion, that we may be just a revision away or perhaps a shock away from some economic turbulence, some economic weakness, and perhaps a recession. I wonder about the optics, Mr. Chairman,

of our dwelling on this subject at this time, given that there doesn't seem to be a compelling need.[11]

Boston's Fed president Cathy Minehan similarly wondered "why we want to spend our time and our political capital right now or anytime in the near future to ensure that we're conveying all the subtleties of an inflation target. . . . Neither the market nor the public needs to be told a number to believe that we seek low and stable rates of inflation. We have the credibility that comes from a long period of success on this front."[12] She and the Kansas City Fed president Thomas Hoenig also feared that setting a numerical inflation target would signal that the FOMC valued its price stability goal above its maximum sustainable employment goal.

Many of those in favor of a numerical objective thought that these concerns could be alleviated if the time horizon associated with the target was long and open ended. Janet Yellen, for example, said she would "find it very hard to support a numerical objective without a long-run horizon to provide a lot of flexibility to respond to output and employment considerations. I believe that a fixed time horizon is inconsistent with the dual mandate. The long-run nature of the inflation objective would have to be clearly explained to the public in the context of the dual mandate, and I think we would need to stress that we would always take the implications for near-term economic and financial stability into account when deciding how to move toward our inflation objective."[13]

Mishkin also considered it "absolutely critical that we make it clear that the horizon would sometimes have to be quite long. In fact, from a political viewpoint doing so is extremely important because by indicating that the horizon could be sometimes quite long we are actually indicating that we care about output fluctuations, which is a key element of the dual mandate. Politically it is also important because it makes it clear that we would be unwilling to beat the economy over the head with a baseball bat in order to get inflation down quickly."[14]

Discussions of inflation targeting at these meetings also focused on which price index would be targeted and what value or range of values to target. Some members felt that Consumer Price Index inflation was more familiar and easier for the public to understand than Personal Consumption Expenditures (PCE) inflation, but PCE inflation had some technical advantages. The bigger issue was not whether to target CPI or PCE inflation but whether to use a headline or core measure. Headline CPI and headline PCE include highly volatile food and energy prices, whereas core CPI and core PCE exclude them. The core measures are less noisy and a clearer signal of underlying price pressures. But as Yellen explained: "The public is quite skeptical, probably rightly so, of measures that exclude food and energy. Those are important out-of-pocket expenses. I agree with the argument that, if we have a long-run goal, there is an advantage to using a total rather than a core index."[15]

The Crisis and the Bernanke Doctrine

The committee's consideration of inflation targeting was put on hold as the "downside risk to the economy" that Fisher referred to materialized in an unprecedented way. Housing prices did not stabilize, as Bernanke predicted in his nomination hearings. They collapsed, helping to set off a severe financial crisis in 2007. Troubled subprime mortgages had been securitized into complex asset-backed securities, so when they started to perform poorly, so did many other private credit assets. Lenders became hesitant to accept these assets as collateral, drying up lending, and institutions that were exposed to these assets became nearly or fully insolvent.[16]

Looking back, Bernanke attributed the housing bubble not to mismanaged monetary policy but to insufficient regulation and supervision: "Stronger regulation and supervision aimed at problems with underwriting practices and lenders' risk management would have been a more effective and surgical approach to constraining the housing bubble than a general increase in interest rates. Moreover, regulators, supervisors, and the private sector could have more effectively addressed building risk concentrations and inadequate risk-management practices without necessarily having had to make a judgment about the sustainability of house price increases."[17] In a speech commemorating Milton Friedman's ninetieth birthday in 2002, Bernanke quipped: "I would like to say to Milton and Anna: Regarding the Great Depression. You're right, we did it. We're very sorry. But thanks to you, we won't do it again."[18] To avoid "doing it again," the Fed acted as a lender of last resort at the start of the crisis. The Fed invoked the emergency lending authority that Congress gave it during the Great Depression to provide loans and assistance to a variety of financial and nonfinancial firms. The Fed did not begin cutting interest rates at the start of the crisis, because it was not immediately clear that employment and growth were weakening. Moreover, energy prices were rising, so the Fed was concerned about inflation.

But as it became clear that the lender-of-last-resort measures, though unprecedented in scope and scale, would not be enough to stem the crisis, Fed officials grew more concerned about effects of continued financial distress on the macroeconomy. The FOMC cut the federal funds rate by one percentage point at the end of 2007 and made several more rate cuts in the first half of 2008. By the August 2008 meeting, financial conditions and growth seemed to be improving, and rising oil prices again raised concerns about inflation, so the FOMC paused its rate cuts. The FOMC also began to have trouble controlling the federal funds rate. Bernanke explains: "In our lender-of-last-resort role, we had been pumping hundreds of billions of dollars into the financial system. As the borrowers deposited the proceeds of the loans with their banks and the banks redeposited the funds in their Fed accounts, bank reserves swelled. With plenty of reserves available, the funds rate—the rate banks charge each other to borrow reserves—regularly fell below the FOMC's 2 percent policy target. In short, our provision of liquidity, in our role as lender of last resort, was interfering with our ability to conduct monetary policy."[19] The Fed's solution was to convince Congress to allow the Fed to pay interest on reserves beginning in

October 2008. Because banks would not want to lend to one another at a rate lower than the interest rate they could earn on reserves at the Fed, the interest rate on reserves would provide a "floor" under the fed funds rate.[20] The Fed continues to use interest on reserves to control the federal funds rate.

When the investment bank Lehman Brothers declared bankruptcy on September 15, 2008, the crisis intensified, and the "floor" under the fed funds rate became unnecessary. By December, the FOMC had reduced its target for the federal funds rate to virtually zero. In other words, the policy rate was at the "zero lower bound." The Fed was constrained from cutting its policy rate further, but the economy was still suffering from massively low aggregate demand. The unemployment rate was 7.3 percent in December 2008, and it continued to rise in 2009, peaking at 10 percent in October. Another sign of low aggregate demand was declining inflation. Inflation was relatively high in early 2008 because of rising oil prices, but in 2009, it turned slightly negative. In other words, there was mild deflation.

Bernanke had described this type of situation—deflation coupled with the zero lower bound—in yet another speech in 2002, in which he emphasized that "a central bank whose accustomed policy rate has been forced down to zero has most definitely not run out of ammunition." Here, too, his familiarity with the Great Depression shaped his beliefs about the role of monetary policy. He understood that deflation was at least as dangerous as inflation, spelling out what later became known as the Bernanke doctrine: "The Congress has given the Fed the responsibility of preserving price stability (among other objectives), which most definitely implies avoiding deflation as well as inflation. I am confident that the Fed would take whatever means necessary to prevent significant deflation in the United States and, moreover, that the US central bank, in cooperation with other parts of the government as needed, has sufficient policy instruments to ensure that any deflation that might occur would be both mild and brief." The financial crisis and Great Recession gave Bernanke the chance to put the Bernanke doctrine to the test. Some experts began to speculate that the Fed would announce an explicit inflation target as part of its deflation-fighting toolkit. The *Financial Times* reported in November 2008 that "risk of deflation could lead Ben Bernanke to approach the new administration and Congress next year about adopting an inflation target at the Federal Reserve."[21] Policy makers did discuss this possibility at the December 2008 FOMC meeting, but they decided instead to rely on a variety of unconventional monetary policies to stimulate the economy and avoid more severe deflation.[22] In late November 2008, Bernanke announced that the Fed would begin making large-scale purchases of mortgage-backed securities to stabilize conditions in housing and mortgage markets. The large-scale asset-purchase program (sometimes called *quantitative easing*, or QE) was later expanded to include purchases of longer-term Treasury securities.

The Fed also used forward guidance to stimulate the economy, following precedent from 2003, when concerns about deflation led the Greenspan Fed to state that "the Committee believes that policy accommodation can be maintained for a considerable period."[23] In December 2008, the FOMC noted that "weak economic conditions are likely to warrant exceptionally low levels of the federal funds rate for some time." Later, the FOMC made further clarifications to its forward guidance to convince people that policy would remain expansionary far into the future in an effort to boost inflation expectations.[24]

The deflation was, as Bernanke promised, mild and brief, although the labor market recovery was slow. The deflation was so mild and so brief, in fact, that economists began referring to a "missing disinflation puzzle" and the "death of the Phillips curve."[25] With unemployment so high, typical Phillips curve models predict that inflation should have fallen much more than it did in the United States and other advanced economies. Most "solutions" to the missing disinflation puzzle emphasize the role of inflation expectations.[26] Inflation expectations held relatively stable even as the labor market went into free fall, preventing inflation itself from falling.[27] Oil and gas prices were high and rising for much of 2007 and 2008, which helped keep households' inflation expectations elevated.[28] The Fed's unconventional monetary policies and its years of "implicit" inflation targeting may also have helped.

Some of the Fed's critics on the Right warned that the large-scale asset purchases would lead to hyperinflation. For example, Senator Chuck Grassley, a Republican from Iowa, warned in 2009 that "the Fed has the ability to put money out, it's got the ability to take money back in, and if they don't do that, we will have hyperinflation worse than we had in 1980 and '81." But Fed policy makers correctly predicted that inflation was more likely to remain quite low.

More bipartisan criticisms concerned the Fed's wielding of immense unelected power. The Fed's progress toward greater transparency and accountability, though welcome to many, was not sufficient, especially as the Fed expanded its balance sheet and came to play a much bigger role in the global economy. In 2009, Congressman Ron Paul, a Texas Republican, and Senator Bernie Sanders, and Independent from Vermont, introduced the Federal Reserve Transparency Act, known as Audit the Fed. The bill had support from an "unusual coalition," including members of the right-wing, fiscally conservative Tea Party movement and certain labor leaders and progressive economists.[29]

The bill has never been enacted, although it was reintroduced as recently as 2021. Bernanke said of a later version of the bill that the principal effect "would be to make meeting-by-meeting monetary policy decisions subject to Congressional review and, potentially, Congressional pressure. . . . The Fed should continue to strive to improve its transparency and accountability, and in particular to ensure that Congress has all the information it needs to fulfill its oversight responsibilities. However, this goal is not best achieved by overturning longstanding practice and effectively inserting Congress and the Government Accountability Office into monetary policy decisions, calling into question the Fed's independence."[30] Bernanke would continue to strive for greater transparency but through the Fed's communication strategy rather than through expanded auditing.

The Target and the Slow Recovery

The Fed lived up to Bernanke's promise to Friedman and Schwartz in the sense that the Great Recession was nowhere near as bad as the Great Depression. The unemployment rate peaked at 10 percent rather than 25 percent. Still, the recession was the most severe in decades and the labor market's recovery was slow. Bernanke, who was originally appointed by President George W. Bush, a Republican, was reappointed by President Barack Obama, a Democrat, in 2009.

In October 2011, with unemployment still at 8.8 percent, the economist Christina Romer, who had served as Obama's chair of the Council of Economic Advisers in 2009 and 2010, published a *New York Times* op-ed titled "Dear Ben: It's Time for Your Volcker Moment."[31] She wrote: "Inflation is still low, but unemployment is stuck at a painfully high level. And, as in 1979, the methods the Fed has used so far aren't solving the problem. Mr. Bernanke needs to steal a page from the Volcker playbook. To forcefully tackle the unemployment problem, he needs to set a new policy framework—in this case, to begin targeting the path of nominal gross domestic product."

Nominal gross domestic product, or NGDP, is the dollar value of the economy's output. NGDP growth is the sum of real GDP growth and inflation. If the normal growth rate of real GDP is 2.5 percent per year and inflation is 2 percent per year, then NGDP should grow around 4.5 percent per year. Romer explained that NGDP in 2011 was about 10 percent below where it would have been if it had grown 4.5 percent per year since 2007 and that the Fed could adopt NGDP targeting by "pledging to do whatever it takes to return nominal GDP to its pre-crisis trajectory." The Fed would subsequently loosen or tighten policy as needed to keep NGDP close to a path growing 4.5 percent per year. Romer argued that an NGDP target would help stimulate the economy by improving growth expectations and overall confidence:

> Another possible effect is a temporary climb in inflation expectations. Ordinarily, this would be undesirable. But in the current

> situation, where nominal interest rates are constrained because they can't go below zero, a small increase in expected inflation could be helpful. It would lower real borrowing costs, and encourage spending on big-ticket items like cars, homes and business equipment. Even if we went through a time of slightly elevated inflation, the Fed shouldn't lose credibility as a guardian of price stability. That's because once the economy returned to the target path, Fed policy—a commitment to ensuring nominal GDP growth of 4 1/2 percent—would restrain inflation. Assuming normal real growth, the implied inflation target would be 2 percent—just what it is today.[32]

She also noted: "Because it directly reflects the Fed's two central concerns—price stability and real economic performance—nominal GDP is a simple and sensible target for long after the economy recovers."

NGDP targeting, also called nominal income targeting, was not a new idea. It was discussed in the economics literature in the 1970s and 1980s, and in 1994, Hall and Mankiw wrote that "it seems fair to say that the consensus today favors nominal income as the most suitable object of monetary policy."[33] But inflation targeting, not nominal income targeting, was widely adopted around the world. The Fed, which still had not adopted an explicit inflation target, was perhaps best suited to choosing an NGDP target in 2011. A staff memo presented to the FOMC, titled "Alternative Monetary Policy Frameworks," discussed some of the same benefits of nominal income targeting that Romer had described, including the fact that it "explicitly recognizes both sides of the dual mandate" and "would likely be viewed by the public as suggestive of a similar degree of concern for both the price stability and employment objectives."[34]

The memo also noted that such a target could "provide effective forward guidance to reinforce market perceptions about the strength of the Committee's desire to keep interest rates low for an extended period, given that the gap between nominal income and target could initially be quite large," and that it would help keep inflation expectations anchored. It added, "Of course, the FOMC would need to make it clear to the public that the nominal income targeting framework is not in fact a cover for engineering a temporary or perhaps permanent rise in the inflation target; to this end, the Committee would want to demonstrate that the implicit gap in resource utilization underlying the initial nominal-income gap is reasonable."[35]

When the FOMC discussed the memo (and Romer's op-ed) at its November 2011 meeting, several participants were concerned that the communication challenges involved in adopting NGDP targeting would be too great and that such a move would, in fact, be viewed as opportunistic. This was not the universal view of the committee—for example, the Boston Fed's president Eric Rosengren believed that "an announcement that nominal GDP targeting was necessary to get much stronger growth in output is understandable to the public and could be effective if it was conveyed in conjunction with more aggressive actions."[36]

But the more common view was expressed by the Philadelphia Fed's president Charles Plosser, who worried that "switching to a new framework at this time could easily be viewed by some as an opportunistic way to inflate the economy. In an inflation environment where fiscal deficits loom large and well-respected economists are advocating inflating our way out of the problems, changing our framework now risks appearing opportunistic, and that will undermine our credibility over the long term."[37] Plosser preferred that the FOMC "concentrate on better explaining and strengthening our flexible inflation targeting framework that the Committee has been working toward for the past two decades."[38]

Governor Janet Yellen, who chaired the FOMC subcommittee on communications, thought that if the committee wished to pursue NGDP targeting, "it would only be prudent to develop, implement, and carefully communicate this approach over a course of a number of years. This is the approach that's been taken by the Bank of Canada, which has spent the past half-decade exploring alternative monetary policy frameworks in close consultation with the public and the Canadian parliament. In the near term, however, we might consider making more frequent references in our monetary policy communications to the level of nominal income and its relevance in guiding our thinking, in effect, turning it into a second pillar of policy."[39]

She noted that she continued to support announcing a numerical inflation target to improve transparency and public accountability, and she suggested that "a consensus statement about our policy framework could be an ideal means of enunciating an explicit inflation goal because such a statement of principles could emphasize our commitment to both parts of our dual mandate. The statement could specifically indicate our judgment that the mandate-consistent inflation rate is 2 percent. . . . In my view, it would be also essential to clarify that the time horizon over which inflation is expected to converge to the longer-run goal would depend on economic conditions and would reflect the Committee's judgments about the path of policy that most effectively promotes both parts of our dual mandate."[40]

Bernanke requested that Yellen's subcommittee draft such a statement for presentation in the December meeting. The draft became the basis for the "Statement on Longer-Run Goals and Monetary Policy Strategy" that the FOMC published in January 2012. The statement formalized a 2 percent target for headline PCE inflation:

> The inflation rate over the longer run is primarily determined by monetary policy, and hence the Committee has the ability to specify a longer-run goal for inflation. The Committee judges that inflation at the rate of 2 percent, as measured by the annual change in the price index for personal consumption expenditures, is most consistent over the longer run with the Federal Reserve's statutory mandate. Communicating this inflation goal clearly to the public helps keep longer-term inflation expectations firmly anchored, thereby fostering price stability and moderate long-term interest rates and enhancing the Committee's ability to promote maximum employment in the face of significant economic disturbances.[41]

As Yellen and others had insisted, the statement emphasized that the FOMC did not prioritize its price stability mandate over its employment mandate and did not commit to bringing inflation to target over any fixed time horizon: "In setting monetary policy, the Committee seeks to mitigate deviations of inflation from its longer-run goal and deviations of employment from the Committee's assessments of its maximum level. These objectives are generally complementary. However, under circumstances in which the Committee judges that the objectives are not complementary, it follows a balanced approach in promoting them, taking into account the magnitude of the deviations and the potentially different time horizons over which employment and inflation are projected to return to levels judged consistent with its mandate."[42] Thus, the new statement made the Fed's interpretation of price stability more explicit but without reducing policy makers' flexibility and discretion. Romer wrote her NGDP targeting op-ed when I was a new PhD student at UC Berkeley, and she taught one of my first macroeconomics classes. It took several years of following monetary policy closely before I also came to believe that a nominal income target could have been a better choice than an inflation target in 2012, for reasons that I explain in the next chapters.

Fed Up

In the years following the inflation-targeting announcement, the labor market gradually improved. Unemployment, for example, fell from 8.3 percent in January 2012 to 6.6 percent in January 2014. Inflation, meanwhile, remained below target. Many economists expected that inflation would pick up once unemployment fell below around 5 percent. The slow recovery was especially frustrating to progressive economists and left-wing populists, who thought that the Fed should direct more of its immense power toward addressing unemployment, underemployment, and labor-market disparities. The Fed's focus on price stability, many thought, was unnecessary, and benefited Wall Street at the expense of Main Street.

This sentiment was embodied by ten activists who appeared at the Fed's annual monetary policy conference in Jackson Hole, Wyoming, in August 2014, wearing green shirts reading "What Recovery?" They spoke with the Kansas City Fed's president Esther George, the host of the conference, for two hours about their hopes and concerns.[43] Many of these activists were unemployed and had been sent to Jackson Hole on behalf of a coalition of more than seventy left-leaning and populist advocacy groups, community organizations, and labor unions, including the Center for Popular Democracy. The coalition later called itself Fed Up and advocated for continued low interest rates, greater diversity at the Fed, and a stronger commitment by the Fed to address unemployment and racial disparities in the labor market.

Janet Yellen, who had been appointed Fed chair earlier that year, had a reputation as a monetary "dove" who highly valued the Fed's maximum employment mandate. When she met with Fed Up representatives in November 2014, they urged her to delay raising the federal funds rate until the labor market could improve further, especially for minority workers.[44] Fed Up also held a "countersummit" in Jackson Hole at the same time as the Fed's 2015 Jackson Hole meeting, met with reserve bank presidents throughout the year, and protested the rate hike that eventually came in December 2015, when unemployment was 5 percent and PCE inflation was just 1.1 percent.

Why did the FOMC raise the federal funds rate when inflation was still below target? As the FOMC statement explained: "The Committee judges that there has been considerable improvement in labor market conditions this year, and it is reasonably confident that inflation will rise, over the medium term, to its 2 percent objective. Given the economic outlook, and recognizing the time it takes for policy actions to affect future economic outcomes, the Committee decided to raise the target range for the federal funds rate."[45] In other words, because monetary policy works with a delay, central banks tend to raise interest rates in advance of rising inflation, to avoid getting "behind the curve."

This reasoning was unpopular among Fed Up and its sympathizers. Inflation, they pointed out, had been persistently below target for years and was showing no signs of rising. Why couldn't the Fed also tolerate a period of above-target inflation to allow a stronger labor market recovery? Even better, why couldn't the Fed raise the inflation target to something like 3 percent or 4 percent?[46] Fed officials also began to grow concerned as inflation remained below target even as unemployment fell below 5 percent. The Chicago Fed's president Charles Evans, for example, noted in a speech that prolonged low inflation had pulled inflation expectations below target, lowering nominal interest rates down and raising the risk of another zero-lower-bound episode.[47] Fed officials were not willing to raise the inflation target, but the FOMC did revise its Statement on Longer-Run Goals and Monetary Policy Strategy in 2016 to clarify that the target was "symmetric" in the sense that "the Committee would be concerned if inflation were running persistently above or below this objective."

The Fed Up coalition took it as a victory when, in her June 2016 congressional testimony, "Yellen responded to our demands and made history by finally acknowledging that Black and Latino communities are still experiencing significant economic struggles."[48] The FOMC held off on another rate hike until December 2016. Chair Yellen also regularly spoke about inequality and diversity, and the research staffs of the reserve banks began to direct more of their research efforts to those areas.[49]

Although Fed Up criticized the Fed throughout Yellen's chairmanship, the coalition became more supportive of her when it became clear that newly elected Republican president Donald Trump was unlikely to reappoint her. The Economic Policy Institute, Center for Popular Democracy, and Fed Up published a report urging Yellen to seek another term as chair and crediting her with rejecting "evidence-free warnings that low interest rates and large-scale asset purchases would spark runaway inflation and damage the economy. Economic outcomes—substantial and noninflationary improvements in employment and wages since the beginning of

2014—have vindicated her decisions."[50] The economists Stephanie Kelton and Paul McCulley wrote in the *New York Times*: "The Fed Chair should be a 'Principled Populist.'"[51] They likewise praised Yellen and expressed concern that President Trump's next appointee would be less committed to the pursuit of full employment.

As it turned out, President Trump appointed Jerome Powell, whom Obama had appointed to the board in 2012. Chairman Powell's monetary policies in the first years of his term were similar to those that Yellen likely would have pursued. Under Powell, the FOMC began very gradually raising the federal funds rate, making three twenty-five-basis-point hikes in 2017 and four in 2018. The rate increases were gradual enough that unemployment continued to decline, dropping below 4 percent. The puzzle of missing disinflation was replaced by a new puzzle of missing inflation, as inflation remained below target despite very low unemployment.

Despite low unemployment and inflation, the Fed was in a precarious position. President Trump vociferously criticized Powell on Twitter for raising rates, demonstrating that populist pressure on central banks can come from both the Left and the Right. The Fed made three twenty-five-basis-point rate cuts in August, September, and October 2019, leaving the federal funds rate around 1.5 percent. Trump criticized the Fed for not cutting interest rates all the way to zero, like some of its peers. Trump's tweets reflected his nationalist "America first" politics. For example: "the USA should always be paying the the [*sic*] lowest rate. No Inflation! It is only the naïveté of Jay Powell and the Federal Reserve that doesn't allow us to do what other countries are already doing. A once in a lifetime opportunity that we are missing because of 'Boneheads.'"[52] He also tweeted, "who is our bigger enemy, Jay Powel [*sic*] or Chairman Xi?"[53]

The *Financial Post* wrote, in response to Trump's tweets, "central banks everywhere were reminded that they are only one populist uprising away from losing the operational independence they so cherish, explaining why so many of them . . . are working harder to establish a bond with the public."[54] Establishing a bond with the public is not an easy task for a central bank. The Fed had been gradually revising its strategy for communicating with the public ever since the "transparency revolution" of the Greenspan era. Janet Yellen, as chair, had been especially devoted to ensuring that the Fed could communicate with the general public, not just sophisticated financial market participants. Most people, of course, don't listen to monetary policy makers' speeches or read Federal Reserve statements. Instead, their exposure to monetary policy news comes from the media, and coverage of Fed communication tends to be quite limited.[55]

The Yellen Fed ramped up its use of alternative communication channels, like social media, to try to reach broader audiences. Still, not many people want to follow the Fed on Twitter or Facebook, and public understanding of the Fed's mandate and policies remains limited.[56] In a survey I conducted with my student Alex Rodrigue in 2017, just a quarter of respondents knew that the Fed's inflation target was 2 percent. A few years later, awareness of the target was similarly low.[57]

Fed Listens and the Framework Review

Chair Jerome Powell, like his predecessor, expressed a desire to communicate directly with the public, a task that seemed more urgent in the face of presidential antagonism. Powell announced that the Fed would conduct a comprehensive review of monetary policy strategy, tools, and communications in 2019 and 2020. He explained, "With labor market conditions close to maximum employment and inflation near our 2 percent objective, now is a good time to take stock of how we formulate, conduct, and communicate monetary policy."[58] As part of the review, the Fed hosted a series of fourteen Fed Listens events across the country in 2019. According to Powell:

> The participants represented small businesses, employee groups and labor unions, state and local governments, schools and com-

> munity colleges, workforce development organizations, housing groups, community development financial institutions (CDFIs), and retirees. . . . Many of the participants in the events hailed from organizations representing historically disadvantaged populations or underserved communities. While members of the community affairs staff at the Reserve Banks regularly interact with such groups as part of ongoing outreach, the Fed Listens events were distinct in their focus. At the events, questions posed to the participants centered not only on the effects of monetary policy actions on them and the groups they represent, but also on how they view the relative economic importance of the dual-mandate goals.[59]

The Fed Listens report notes that in 2019, "there was less discussion at the Fed Listens events of inflation than there was of labor market conditions. Participants generally acknowledged that inflation was low and posed few challenges."[60] Although the unemployment rate was below 4 percent throughout 2019, "participants frequently noted that the national statistics were not representative of their own communities, where unemployment rates were still high. More pointedly, some participants questioned the characterization of labor market conditions as 'hot' in light of the still high unemployment in their communities."[61] The view underlying the Fed Listens report was gaining steam among politicians and the media too. Senator Elizabeth Warren, a progressive Democrat from Massachusetts who had campaigned for the Democratic presidential nomination, promised to "appoint Federal Reserve Board members who believe in full employment, who recognize that inflation fears have been overblown for years, and who are willing to let wages grow."[62]

Dylan Matthews wrote for *Vox* that "the Fed has deliberately chosen to keep hundreds of thousands, if not millions, of people from finding work that they could have found with looser policy, in the name of preventing inflation. . . . The Fed should be erring on the side of letting jobs proliferate, letting people enter the labor force, letting wages rise. It's erred too often on the side of fighting phantom inflation that never arose, and workers have paid the price. It's time for that calculus to change."[63] The calculus did change, as Fed officials also began to question just how "hot" the labor market really was. The FOMC cut the federal funds rate three times throughout 2019, with Powell explaining, "We can sustain much lower levels of unemployment than had been thought" without risk to price stability.

At the Cato Institute's annual monetary conference in 2019, called "Fed Policy: A Shadow Review," the Fed's vice chair Richard Clarida provided his thoughts on the Fed's review. He noted that given the years of below-target inflation, policy makers were evaluating "strategies that aim to reverse past misses of the inflation objective." Clarida explained:

> Under our current approach as well as the approaches of many central banks around the world, persistent inflation shortfalls of the target are treated as "bygones." . . . Persistent inflation shortfalls carry the risk that longer-term inflation expectations become anchored below the stated inflation goal. In part because of that concern, some economists have advocated 'makeup' strategies under which policy makers seek to undo past inflation deviations from target. . . . The success of makeup strategies relies on households and firms believing in advance that the makeup will, in fact, be delivered when the time comes—for example, that a persistent inflation shortfall will be met by future inflation above 2 percent.

At the same conference, I gave a talk on the benefits of NGDP level targeting, which also involves a makeup strategy: the Fed would choose a path for NGDP, or nominal income, and attempt to make up for past undershoots or overshoots.[64] Recall that Christina Romer recommended and the FOMC discussed this type of strategy in 2011. The FOMC had rejected NGDP targeting in 2011 because of concerns that it would be too difficult to communicate to the public and that it would signal too dramatic a break with the status quo. In 2019, I argued, a break from the status quo was a feature, not a bug. A Gallup poll that April found that just 6 percent and 42 percent of respondents, respectively, thought that the Fed was doing an excellent job or a good job.[65] For comparison, even during the Great Recession in 2009, 10 percent and 48 percent of respondents, respectively, thought the Fed was doing an excellent or good job."[66]

I pointed out that central banks around the world were facing "pressure to reduce their focus on inflation and increase their focus on other outcomes, especially as high inflation becomes a more distant memory and/or as populist movements gain strength. . . . A strong argument for adopting NGDPLT [level targeting] soon is that doing so could fend off populist urges to impose reforms that could be less effective. That is, willingness to break from an unpopular status quo could boost central banks' institutional legitimacy in the short term."[67]

An NGDP level target, I suggested, would allow the Fed to frame its policy decisions in terms of income, which many people have an easier time understanding than inflation. In a recession, the Fed conducts monetary policy to boost aggregate demand, increasing both inflation and nominal income. It is much easier to explain to the public that policies are intended to boost income rather than inflation. And most importantly, an NGDPLT would facilitate accountability by providing a single quantitative target for monetary policy. This would reduce the scope for political interference and increase public trust. A makeup strategy, but not an NGDPLT, was incorporated into the Fed's new framework, which I discuss in the next chapter.

At the same time that the Fed was conducting its framework review, a heterodox school of economic thought called modern monetary theory (MMT) was gaining mainstream attention. MMT advocates, mostly on the progressive Left, argue that a government that issues its own fiat currency cannot be forced to default on debt issued in that currency. They propose that the government should use deficit spending to ensure full employment (through a job guarantee program) and to address other social issues, like climate change.[68] The role of the central bank in MMT is simply to finance the budget deficit, much as the Fed did during World Wars I and

II and the Korean War before the Treasury-Fed Accord. In other words, MMT calls for a regime of fiscal dominance. Inflation targeting and central bank independence, remember, are premised on a regime of *monetary dominance*, in which the central bank pursues price stability regardless of the government's fiscal stance.

Representative Alexandria Ocasio-Cortez, a Democrat from New York, suggested an MMT approach to fund the "Green New Deal," a package of policies to address climate change and provide universal health care and guaranteed jobs.[69] Should high inflation appear, MMT advocates argued, fiscal policy makers could address it by raising taxes.[70] At the time, of course, inflation had been below target for years, and high inflation seemed an unlikely prospect.

THIRTEEN

THE PANDEMIC AND THE RETURN OF INFLATION

> So, clearly, people don't like inflation—a lot. And many people are experiencing it, really, for the first time, because we haven't had anything like this kind of inflation in 40 years. And it's really something people don't like. . . . And we understand that, and we understand the hardship that people are experiencing from high inflation, and we're determined to do what we can to get inflation back down. . . . Clearly, it's an incredibly unpopular thing, and it's very painful for people. I guess what I'm saying is, the question, the really critical question from the perspective of doing our job is making sure that the public does have confidence that we have the tools and will use them and they do work to bring inflation back down over time. It will take some time, we think, to get inflation back down, but we will do that.
>
> JEROME POWELL, press conference[1]

Pandemic Price Gouging

In February 2020, the unemployment rate was just 3.5 percent, and inflation was still below target. The 2019 novel coronavirus (COVID-19) was just beginning to be detected in the United States. The COVID-19 pandemic would have profound implications for the global economy and governance. In the United States, the pandemic itself and policy responses to the pandemic have affected both aggregate and relative prices. Later sections of this chapter discuss the response of the Fed and other macroeconomic policy makers and implications for aggregate inflation. This section discusses state-level and microeconomic policies concerning prices in the pandemic.

The pandemic created an extreme shock to the demand for specific goods like hand sanitizer and personal protective equipment, driving prices many times higher than before and sometimes prompting outrage.[2] A 2020 survey of city, county, and state consumer agencies across the country found that price gouging was the most commonly cited pandemic-related complaint reported to these agencies.[3] According to the American Bar Association: "Price gouging refers to the practice of raising the price of essential goods, services, or commodities to an unreasonable, unfair, or excessive level, typically during a declared state of emergency or, in some states, any 'external crisis.' As there is no federal anti-price-gouging law, the primary role of curbing this conduct traditionally has rested with state attorneys general."[4]

New York enacted the first anti-price-gouging law (APGL) in response to heating-oil shortages in 1979.[5] The statute says that "during any abnormal disruption of the market for goods and services vital and necessary for the health, safety and welfare of consumers or the general public, no party within the chain of distribution of such goods or services or both shall sell or offer to sell any such goods or services or both for an amount which represents an unconscionably excessive price."[6]

Other states passed APGLs in subsequent years in response to other emergencies. For example, Florida passed a price-gouging law following Hurricane Andrew in 1992, as did California following the Northridge earthquake in 1994.[7] Several others did so following the terrorist attacks in 2001 or Hurricane Katrina in 2006. Many statutes, like New York's, prohibit "unconscionable" price increases. Others, less ambiguously, prohibit price increases above a certain percentage of pre-emergency levels or prohibit any price increases at all for qualifying goods.

All fifty states declared active emergencies during the pandemic. In most states, the emergency declarations activated preexisting price-gouging statutes. Some states enacted new APGLs in response to the pandemic, and many states created portals where consumers could report instances of price gouging. In March 2020, thirty-three attorneys general coauthored a letter to large online retailers Amazon, Facebook, eBay, Walmart, and Craigslist, warning them to monitor and prohibit price gouging by third-party retailers on their sites.[8]

At the federal level, President Trump, invoking the Defense Production Act, issued three executive orders prohibiting hoarding and price gouging of goods on a list of critical supplies determined by the secretary of health and human services. The COVID-19 Hoarding and Price Gouging Task Force, in the Department of Justice, was charged with investigating and prosecuting cases of price gouging; it conducted hundreds of investigations. The head of the task force, Craig Carpenito, explains that "when the [Department of Justice] saw a reseller charge substantially higher prices, it inquired whether the legitimate costs of the reseller were high, and if the reseller must have sold at a high resale price to turn any profit or simply break even. . . . Whether the reseller is profiteering was the dominant inquiry. Despite such insight, however, neither the DOJ nor the Task Force provided any bright-line rules, largely leaving such questions to prosecutorial discretion."[9] Throughout the pandemic, several bills were introduced in Congress that would have given the federal government more comprehensive authority to combat price gouging, but none has passed.[10]

APGLs are a form of price control and as such are subject to many of the same economic and ethical debates about efficiency and equity. Much of the philosophy literature on price gouging is based on the highly contested notion of a *just* price.[11] One approach is to define any price set by consensual, nonfraudulent bargaining as just. Other more stringent definitions impose requirements concerning, for example, the informational symmetry between buyer and seller or the number of potential buyers and sellers. Still others argue that it is impossible to define a just price except on a case-by-case basis.[12] And even if people agree that a price is unjust, they may still disagree about whether such injustice warrants government intervention.[13]

Economists emphasize that APGLs impede markets from sending the right signals for producers to increase supply. This is more consequential in a long-lasting global pandemic than in a shorter, more localized emergency. The infectiousness of COVID-19 also means that APGL-induced shortages had major public health consequences.[14] A study by economists Rik Chakraborti and Gavin Roberts, using cellphone-tracked mobility data, finds that APGLs may have undermined COVID-19 mitigation efforts and increased mortality by causing customers to spend more time in commercial spaces searching for items in short supply. They estimate that increased social contacts during this searching time may account for about 25 percent of COVID-19 deaths in states with APGLs in early April 2020.[15]

Even before the pandemic, prescription drug prices in the United States continued to be subject to considerable policy debate. Recall that a controversial feature of the Medicare Prescription Drug, Improvement, and Modernization Act of 2003 was that it that it prevented the federal government from negotiating prices directly with drug manufacturers. The Elijah E. Cummings Lower Drug Costs Now Act, which passed the House in 2019 but not the Senate, would have changed this feature, requiring the Department of Health and Human Services to negotiate maximum prices for certain drugs.[16]

The pandemic, unsurprisingly, intensified the focus on drug prices, in particular prices for potential COVID-19 treatments and vaccines. For example, in April 2020, a group of congressional Democrats laid out a set of proposed guidelines for the pricing of COVID-19 drugs and vaccines that they hoped would be incorporated into COVID-19 relief legislation. Among these was the "stop profiteering" guideline: "Pharmaceutical companies must not be allowed to sell any COVID-19 vaccine, drug or therapeutic at an unreasonable price, whether or not it has been developed with US taxpayer dollars. An 'after the fact' enforcement mechanism is not efficient enough for a public health emergency—we must mandate up front that manufacturers agree to a reasonable price."[17] This proposal garnered substantial criticism from some economists, who feared it would stifle innovation, and from the pharmaceutical industry. In May, representatives from thirty-one mostly conservative organizations wrote a letter urging Congress to reject the drug-pricing guidelines.[18] Congress instead took other approaches to facilitate affordable access to treatments and vaccines. Notably, the federal government created an "advance market" for Pfizer and Moderna vaccines by making an initial purchase of one hundred million vaccine doses from each company, should their vaccines receive emergency use authorization from the Food and Drug Administration. After both manufacturers received authorization in December 2020, the government continued making purchases, for a total of over 1.2 billion doses, at an average price of $20.69 per dose, by late 2022.[19] The US population was able to receive these doses for free.

Average Inflation Targeting

Although the pandemic had obvious effects on certain specific prices, it was unclear, at first, how the pandemic would affect aggregate inflation. A pandemic is both a supply shock and a demand shock. It is a supply shock because people can't go to work and supply chains are disrupted, which increases costs and puts upward pressure on prices. It is a demand shock because people consume less, due to uncertainty, fear, and physical constraints, which puts downward pressure on prices. I ran a household survey on March 5 and 6, 2020, and found that respondents who were more worried about the pandemic also tended to have higher inflation expectations—that is, the general public thought of the pandemic as a supply shock, even though many policy makers and professional forecasters thought of it more like a disinflationary demand shock.[20]

At the start of the pandemic, policy makers acted aggressively to counter the unprecedented loss of jobs and income. The Fed quickly cut its policy interest rate, the federal funds rate, down to zero, and began engaging in large-scale asset purchases, forward guidance, and emergency lending programs.[21] Congress also passed a $2.2 trillion fiscal stimulus package, the Coronavirus Aid, Relief, and Economic Security (CARES) Act, signed by President Trump on March 27. For most households, a particularly salient part of the CARES Act was the stimulus payments of up to $1,200 per adult and $500 per child. Additional payments of up to $600 per adult and $600 per child came later in the year with the Tax Relief Act of 2020.[22]

Thanks to the massive fiscal and monetary stimulus, the COVID-19 recession was brief, officially ending in April 2020. This does not mean that the economy was anywhere close to fully recovered in April, so the Fed maintained interest rates at the zero lower bound and continued its asset purchases. The unemployment rate was 14.7 percent, and the labor-force participation rate was just 60.2 percent, compared to 63.4 percent before the pandemic. In other words, in addition to the many people who became unemployed, many others left the labor force altogether. PCE inflation did fall to around 0.4 percent in April, but deflation was avoided.[23]

That August, the Fed announced the key results of its framework review. The FOMC amended its Statement on Longer-Run Goals and Monetary Policy Strategy to adopt an average inflation targeting (AIT) framework. The revised statement explains that "the Committee seeks to achieve inflation that averages 2 percent over time, and therefore judges that, following periods when inflation has been running persistently below 2 percent, appropriate monetary policy will likely aim to achieve inflation moderately above 2 percent for some time."[24]

There are a few key points to note about the AIT framework. First, the new AIT framework, unlike the old inflation-targeting framework, includes a makeup strategy, which Vice Chair Clarida had alluded to in 2019. Before the Fed adopted AIT, the framework implied that policy makers would always aim for 2 percent inflation, regardless of past undershoots or overshoots of the target; it let bygones be bygones. Under the new framework, when inflation has been persistently below 2 percent, the Fed will aim for inflation above 2 percent so that inflation will average around 2 percent.

Second, the makeup strategy is asymmetric: the Fed will make up for past undershoots of the target, but not past overshoots. It lets bygones to the upside be bygones. It does not let bygones to the downside be bygones. In August 2020, this asymmetry seemed inconsequential. Inflation had been undershooting the target for years, and persistent overshoots were hard to fathom. AIT implied that monetary conditions could be easier for longer, to make up for past undershoots and ensure that longer-run inflation expectations didn't slip too far below target and make the zero lower bound less likely to bind in the future. Allowing a period of above-target inflation would also give the labor market more time to strengthen before the Fed began to reverse its expansionary policies, meaning that the Fed could more aggressively pursue maximum employment, which the amended statement describes as a "broad-based and inclusive goal."[25]

Third, the new framework, like the previous framework, is flexible, in the sense that it leaves policy makers full discretion with respect to how they choose to prioritize the two sides of the dual mandate whenever they come into conflict. Fourth, the phrase "inflation that averages 2 percent over time" does not specify a time horizon over which the "average" is computed, giving policy makers considerable discretion with respect to how quickly or slowly to respond to inflation. Shortly after the revised framework was released, the Cleveland Fed's president Loretta Mester said that AIT "isn't really tied to a formula," and Reuters reported that Fed policy makers would "do their own math on 'average' inflation."[26]

As I interpreted it at the Cato Annual Monetary Conference in 2021—the conference theme was "Populism and the Future of the

Fed"—the new framework reflected a broader political trend that political scientists Christopher Bickerton and Carlo Invernizzi Accetti call technopopulism.[27] They explain: "Political competition in advanced democratic states today is increasingly ordered around appeals to both 'the people' and to competence and expertise. Far from clashing with one another, these appeals are combined in multiple and complex ways."[28] In other words, although populism and technocracy are often thought of as opposites, they are in many ways complements. Both reflect dissatisfaction with representative democracy and its institutions, and are based on alternative appeals to legitimacy. Thus, we observe the growing power of unelected technocratic institutions (like central banks) at the same time that a variety of left- and right-wing populist movements are gaining ground.[29]

Technopopulism, I suggested, could help us understand why, despite increasingly urgent warnings of a "populist threat" to central bank independence, populist sentiment in the United States and other countries had not led to a narrower or more restricted role of central banks.[30] Instead, central bankers had gained greater power and discretion by combining technocratic and populist appeals.[31] Chair Powell's explanations for the new framework, for example, combined appeals to both expertise and to the popular will. He repeatedly cited not only the technical rationale but also how "the Fed Listens events helped us connect with our core constituency, the American people."[32] In short, by promising greater responsiveness to the popular will, the Fed obtained greater technocratic discretion, in turn likely making itself more susceptible to political pressure.

#TeamTransitory

When President Joe Biden, a Democrat, took office in January 2021, PCE inflation was 1.4 percent, similar to its typical value in 2019. The unemployment rate, at 6.4 percent, was still well above its prepandemic low of 3.5 percent.[33] In late January, President Biden announced his proposal for the American Rescue Plan (ARP), another large fiscal stimulus package. Policy analysts realized that even if the fiscal stimulus were to push inflation above target, the new AIT framework implied that the Fed would not immediately tighten monetary policy in response but would welcome a period of inflation temporarily above target.[34] Republican Senators, including Tim Scott of South Carolina, asked Chair Powell about the possible inflationary implications of the proposed stimulus bill during Powell's February 2021 Senate hearings. Powell explained: "We have all been living in a world for a quarter of a century and more where all of the pressures were disinflationary, you know, pushing downward on inflation. We have averaged less than 2 percent inflation for more than the last 25 years. Inflation dynamics do change over time, but they do not change on a dime, and so we do not really see how a burst of fiscal support or spending that does not last for many years would actually change those inflation dynamics."[35] Powell also noted:

> There perhaps once was a strong connection between budget deficits and inflation. There really has not been lately. That does not mean it will not return. . . . We may see upward pressure on prices as the economy fully reopens. A good problem to have. I do not think that those effects should either be large or persistent, and the real reason for that is that we have had decades of well-anchored inflation expectations, meaning that we have had a very volatile economy for the last 15 years, and inflation has just kind of done what it was going to do. It did not go up.[36]

The ARP passed Congress along strict party lines, with support from Democrats and opposition from Republicans, and President Biden signed it into law on March 11, 2021. One of the provisions of the ARP was sending $1,400 stimulus checks to most low- and middle-income households in mid-March. For context, fiscal spending in response to the pandemic, including the CARES Act and the American Rescue Plan Act, was more than four times as large as the American Recovery and Reinvestment Act of 2009, passed in response to the global financial crisis, and the budgetary cost of pandemic-related legislation was comparable to that of war production in 1943.[37]

As the stimulus checks boosted household income and spending, inflation began to rise. March 2021 was the first month since 2018 that year-over-year PCE inflation, at 2.5 percent, exceeded the 2 percent target. From there, it continued to grow. PCE inflation over the year ending in May 2021, for example, was 4 percent. Core PCE inflation, which excludes food and energy prices, was 3.5 percent.[38] That month, NPR reported that "the 1970s are starting to trend—for all the wrong reasons," explaining that rising prices were "raising concerns in some quarters about whether the United States is headed back to the awful economic days of the 1970s. . . . The Biden administration insists those concerns are far off the mark, and that the days when Americans sported campaign-style 'Whip Inflation Now' buttons on their wide lapels are long gone."[39]

Janet Yellen, Treasury secretary and former Fed chair, remarked: "I came of age and studied economics in the 1970s and I remember what that terrible period was like. No one wants to see that happen again."[40] For most of the year, Federal Reserve officials, including Chair Powell, also insisted that the high inflation would be transitory and that the comparison to the 1970s was off base. They had several reasons. First, a lot of the rise in inflation reflected increases of specific prices, like used cars, that were hit hardest by pandemic-induced supply-chain disruptions. Once the supply-chain issues were resolved, inflation pressures would ease, without the need for monetary tightening.

Second, the pandemic had shifted consumption away from services and into goods. Because people were not spending as much money eating out and buying other services, they had more to spend on goods. Production had not had time to adjust to this shift in consumption patterns, so goods prices were rising rapidly. Once consumption patterns returned to normal or production had time to adjust, inflation pressures would ease, again without the need for monetary tightening. Third, unlike in the 1970s, longer-run inflation expectations appeared well anchored; markets and professional forecasters expected inflation to return to target over a five- to ten-year horizon.[41] This meant that even a large fiscal stimulus might have only a small and temporary impact on inflation. San Francisco Fed researchers, for example, estimated that the ARP would raise core inflation by only about 0.3 percentage points per year through 2022.[42]

As the year progressed, though, there were signs that inflation might not be so transitory after all. Services inflation began to rise, and inflation became more broad based. Median consumer expectations for inflation in two to three years rose from 2.5 percent in 2019 to 4.2 percent in late 2021. Consumer inflation uncertainty, which had been at an all-time low just before the pandemic, began to climb.[43] Moreover, NGDP, which fell sharply at the start of the pandemic recession, had risen back up to its trend path by the middle of 2021 and then continued growing well above its precrisis trend.[44] Thus, an NGDP level target, as discussed in chapter 12, would have implied that monetary tightening was needed. This was a major contrast to the period following the Great Recession, when NGDP remained below its precrisis trend path for years, suggesting that monetary policy was too tight.[45]

Under the new average inflation-targeting framework, though, the appropriate stance of monetary policy was unclear. The framework gave the Fed enormous discretion with respect to how high it would allow inflation to rise before raising interest rates. Discussions about what the Fed *should* do became highly politicized. If inflation were indeed transitory in the sense that it would recede on its own when supply chains healed, then the Fed might be able to avoid monetary tightening altogether. Economists on Twitter, especially on the Left, used the hashtag #TeamTransitory to root for continued monetary accommodation and to criticize anyone who suggested otherwise—most notably, Larry Summers, the former Treasury secretary under President Clinton, who described the ARP as the "least responsible macroeconomic policy we've had in the last 40 years" and warned that one possible outcome was high inflation.[46]

The debates about whether inflation was transitory were so contentious because any suggestion that inflation was not transitory amounted to a suggestion that monetary tightening was needed—that the Fed needed to prioritize price stability over continued labor market expansion. The unemployment rate dropped below 5 percent that fall, but remained above its prepandemic low, and the labor-force participation rate was still low.[47] Much like in 2015, progressives wanted the Fed to tolerate somewhat higher inflation in the interest of full employment. And this time around, the Fed's framework gave it more leeway to do so.

By November 2021, though, with PCE inflation around 5.6 percent, Chair Powell admitted that it was time to "retire" the word transitory.[48] As inflation continued to rise in 2022, politicians and the public agreed that inflation was unacceptably high, but disagreed about the causes and the best solutions to the problem. In early 2022, for example, Senator Elizabeth Warren accused corporations of "jacking up prices for American consumers and driving inflation."[49] She warned Fed officials that "dealing with inflation requires the Fed to act if the problem is an overheated economy, but dealing with rising consumer prices also involves the [Federal Trade Commission], the Department of Justice, in breaking up monopolies and investigating crooked price-fixing schemes that also increase costs for hardworking families. . . . Today's price increases have many causes. And I hope the Fed treads carefully in using its tools to help lower prices for American families."[50]

The Russian Invasion

The inflation situation was complicated by the Russian invasion of Ukraine in February 2022. By executive order, and with bipartisan support, the president banned imports of Russian oil to reduce Russian president Vladimir Putin's ability to finance the war.[51] Supply shortages contributed to more rapid increases in already-rising oil prices. Gas prices, in turn, spiked. Russia and Ukraine are also major exporters of wheat and other agricultural products, so the war reduced the global food supply and increased food prices.

Remember that supply shocks, like these energy and food price shocks, are complicated for monetary policy makers. Typically, the best response is to "look through" supply-driven inflation, because monetary policy works by influencing aggregate demand. In early 2022, only part of the rise in inflation was attributable to oil price increases. Even core inflation, which excludes energy prices, was well above target. The Fed raised the federal funds rate by twenty-five basis points in March, a cautious first step in addressing excessive demand pressures. But clearly, even if the Fed were to bring aggregate inflation back toward its target—which seemed likely to take many months—the reduced supply of oil would keep relative oil and gas prices elevated.

The Fed alone, then, would not be able to ease the pain of higher prices at the pump, and this pain was damaging President Biden's approval ratings. To counter what he called "Putin's Price Hike," Biden authorized the largest-ever release of oil from the Strategic Petroleum Reserve (SPR).[52] The Treasury estimated that Biden's release from the SPR may have lowered gas prices by seventeen cents to forty-two cents per gallon in the short run.[53] As the war continued and the SPR dwindled, it became clear that continued releases would not be a sustainable way to more drastically reduce gas prices. Lutz Kilian, an energy economist at the Dallas Fed, noted: "The impact of the SPR on gasoline prices tends to be modest. The SPR is not well suited for managing global oil price risks. That would take a much bigger reserve. [It is] at its best in dealing with short-run supply disruptions such those caused by hurricanes or shipping accidents."[54]

President Biden also saw the SPR releases as just a temporary bridge to a longer-run goal of greater domestic energy production and energy independence. The White House claimed in March that "too many companies aren't doing their part and are choosing to make extraordinary profits and without making additional investment to help with supply. . . . Right now, the oil and gas industry is sitting on more than 12 million acres of non-producing Federal land with 9,000 unused but already-approved permits for production. Today, President Biden is calling on Congress to make companies pay fees on wells from their leases that they haven't used in years and on acres of public lands that they are hoarding without producing."[55]

Later, President Biden ramped up his criticism of domestic oil and gas companies, saying: "There is no question that Vladimir Putin is principally responsible for the intense financial pain the American people and their families are bearing. But amid a war that has raised gasoline prices more than $1.70 per gallon, historically high refinery profit margins are worsening that pain."[56] President Biden's public verbal pressure, or jawboning, quickly drew comparisons to President Kennedy's pressure on the steel industry in 1962, and many questioned whether it was fair to blame the companies, rather than government-imposed barriers, for low domestic production.[57]

For example, the Institute for Energy Research, a free-market-oriented energy think tank, wrote that "before allowing development on leases, the government conducts environmental analysis under the National Environmental Policy Act, which often takes years to complete, holding up many leases from becoming productive. Further, many leases are held up in litigation by environmental groups. . . . Some leases are awaiting other government approvals."[58] Similarly, Spencer Cox, the Republican governor of Utah, wrote to the president that it was "strikingly inconsistent for US policy to discourage European reliance on Russian-produced energy while simultaneously refusing the leasing and permitting of oil and gas development on our own federal lands." He noted that the Bureau of Land Management had issued an average of 115 and 81 leases per year, respectively, during the Trump and Obama administrations, for oil and gas development in Utah, but none during the Biden administration.[59]

Some Democrats in Congress used the geopolitical emergency and what they dubbed "greedflation" to motivate new calls for anti-profiteering or anti-price-gouging legislation.[60] In March, Senator Sanders introduced the Ending Corporate Greed Act, which would "impose a 95 percent windfall tax on the excess profits of major companies."[61] In May, Senator Warren and two of her colleagues introduced the Price Gouging Prevention Act of 2022, and Representatives Kim Schrier, of Washington, and Katie Porter, of California, both Democrats, introduced the Consumer Fuel Price Gouging Prevention Act.[62] Schrier argued: "Congress needs to be doing all it can to bring down costs for American families. . . . Gas and oil companies should be held accountable and should not be making the situation worse by gouging Americans at the pump."[63]

These bills did not garner sufficient support to pass. Most Republicans, and some Democrats, worried that they would cause shortages and have little lasting effect on inflation. Summers quipped, "The 'price-gouging at the pump' stuff, the more general price-gouging stuff, is to economic science what President Trump's remarks about disinfectant-in-your-veins was to medical science."[64]

Powell's Volcker Moment

Consumer polling in mid-2022 found that many blamed pandemic-related supply-chain disruptions, the Russian invasion, and corporate greed, rather than monetary policy, as the primary culprits of high inflation. Moreover, only 9 percent of Americans strongly agreed that the Fed had the power to control inflation; 56 percent agreed somewhat.[65] Yet the Fed needed to convince the public that it would and could restore price stability.

The FOMC raised rates by 50 basis points in May 2022, as core inflation remained elevated and unemployment was steady at 3.6 percent. At his press conference, Chair Powell noted: "The surge in prices of crude oil and other commodities that resulted from Russia's invasion of Ukraine is creating additional upward pressure on inflation. And COVID-related lockdowns in China are likely to further exacerbate supply chain disruptions as well."[66] The *New York Times* reporter Jeanna Smialek asked Powell to clarify what he meant to convey by referring to these supply-side inflation pressures. Powell responded: "Our tools don't really work on supply shocks. Our tools work on demand. And to the extent we can't affect, really, oil prices or other commodity prices or food prices and things like that, so we can't affect those. But there's a job to do on demand."[67]

At the press conference, Steve Matthews of *Bloomberg* noted: "You've recently spoken in great praise of Paul Volcker, who had the courage to bring inflation down with recessions in the 1980s. And while it's certainly not your desire—the soft landing is the big hope of everyone—would this FOMC have the courage to endure recessions to bring inflation down if that were the only way necessary?"[68] Powell affirmed his admiration for Volcker:

> We see restoring price stability as absolutely essential for the country in coming years. Without price stability, the economy doesn't work for anybody, really. And so it's really essential, particularly for the labor market. . . . In the last two, three years, you had the benefits of this tight labor market going to people in the lower quartiles. And it was, you know, racial, wealth, and income—not wealth, but income gaps were coming down, wage gaps. So it's a really great thing. We'd all love to get back to that place. But to get back to anything like that place, you need price stability. . . . And it's obviously going to be very challenging, I think, because you do have, you know, numerous supply shocks, which are famously difficult to deal with.[69]

Brian Cheung of *Yahoo Finance* asked about the "great pain" that came with the Volcker disinflation, to which Volcker responded that "yes, there may be some pain associated with getting back" to target, "but, you know, the big pain over time is in not dealing with inflation and allowing it to become entrenched."[70]

When the Fed began a series of more aggressive seventy-five-basis-point rate hikes in June and July, Senator Warren warned, in the *Wall Street Journal*, that the rate hikes would be not only "painful" but also "ineffective," costing millions of jobs. She praised President Biden's alternative approaches to inflation reduction, including SPR releases and efforts to "combat corporate monopolies using inflation as an excuse to pad their profits" by enabling more aggressive antitrust enforcement.[71] She added: "Congress should do its part to fight inflation. Investing in high-quality, affordable child care would lower costs by bringing more than a million parents into the workforce. Ending tax breaks for off-shoring and investing in American manufacturing would create good jobs and strengthen supply chains. Allowing Medicare to negotiate prices for prescription drugs would lower healthcare costs. And giving the Biden administration more tools to bolster competition policy would help crack down on price gouging by large corporations."

Some of these proposals made their way into the Inflation Reduction Act, which Congress passed and the president signed in August 2022. The act, which includes a range of climate, health, energy, and tax provisions, is projected to increase tax revenues more than it increases spending, eventually reducing the government budget deficit. The White House touted this deficit reduction, as well as specific provisions related to health care and energy, as anti-inflationary. The Inflation Reduction Act also includes provisions to reduce prescription drug prices. Most notably, it requires the secretary of health and human services to negotiate certain drug prices with manufacturers, ending the long-disputed ban on such negotiations. This drug-pricing provision becomes effective in 2026.

A YouGov poll found that 52 percent of Americans were in favor of the Inflation Reduction Act, with even greater shares supporting specific provisions. But only 12 percent thought it would reduce inflation, and 40 percent thought it would actually increase inflation.[72] As I argued in *The Hill*, though, if lawmakers are committed to an independent Federal Reserve and a regime of monetary dominance, they shouldn't describe the bill as either reducing or increasing inflation: "Congress has already delegated price stabilization to the Federal Reserve. Central bank independence requires that the Fed be allowed to pursue its price stability mandate—which it interprets as 2 percent annual PCE inflation—regardless of what Congress and the president do."[73]

Recall that modern monetary theory, which was growing in popularity before the pandemic, calls for raising taxes in response to higher inflation. The high inflation of 2021 and 2022 has highlighted the political infeasibility of this approach. Policy makers made a nod to raising taxes with the Inflation Reduction Act, but much of the tax increase was offset by spending increases, and the deficit reduction was too far in the future and too small to substantially reduce inflation. Leading MMT advocates, such as Stephanie Kelton, began calling for President Biden to "use the bully pulpit to urge conservation" and "use the bully pulpit to call on elected officials to make public transportation (trains, busses subways, etc.) free to all riders" to reduce energy and transportation prices.[74] She suggested a multipronged approach, including building housing, eliminating nonstrategic tariffs, providing Medicare for All, and cracking down on price gouging. Ultimately, she concluded, "The Federal Reserve isn't going to fix inflation."[75]

Chairman Powell begged to differ. Just ten days after Biden signed the Inflation Reduction Act, Powell emphasized that "central banks *can* and *should* take responsibility for delivering low and stable inflation. . . . We must keep at it until the job is done." This, he said, was a clear lesson of the Volcker disinflation, which "followed multiple failed attempts to lower inflation over the previous 15 years. A lengthy period of very restrictive monetary policy was ultimately needed to stem the high inflation and start the process of getting inflation down to the low and stable levels that were the norm until the spring of last year. Our aim is to avoid that outcome by acting with resolve now."[76]

The FOMC raised the federal funds rate by seventy-five basis points again at its September and November 2022 meetings, despite several letters from congressional Democrats urging the Fed not to put full employment at risk in its fight for price stability. For example, Senator Sherrod Brown, chairman of the Committee on Banking, Housing, and Urban Affairs, wrote to Powell, "We must avoid having our short-term advances and strong labor market overwhelmed by the consequences of aggressive monetary actions to decrease inflation, especially when the Fed's actions do not address its main drivers."[77]

The FOMC raised the federal funds rate by fifty basis points at its December 2022 meeting and by twenty-five basis points at its February 2023 meeting, as inflation was beginning to slow. Following the collapse of Silicon Valley Bank in March 2023, the FOMC raised rates by another twenty-five basis points, noting: "Recent developments are likely to result in tighter credit conditions for households and businesses and to weigh on economic activity, hiring, and inflation. The extent of these effects is uncertain. The Committee remains highly attentive to inflation risks."[78]

Subsequently, with continued signs that inflationary pressures were abating, the FOMC raised the federal funds rate by twenty-five basis points in May and July 2023. At his press conference following the July meeting—the most recent at the time I am completing this book—Powell commented, "We do have a shot, and my base case is that we will be able to achieve inflation moving back down to our target without the kind of really significant downturn that results in high levels of job losses that we've seen in some past instances . . . of tightening that look like ours . . . but it's a long way from assured and you know, we have a lot left to go to see that happen."[79] Even if this best case scenario comes to pass, inflation is likely to remain a highly charged political issue, and the legitimacy of our current monetary arrangements will continue to face scrutiny from across the political spectrum.

FOURTEEN

LOOKING BACK AND LOOKING AHEAD

> The delicate balance between private right and social control is independently weighed in an endless process of reappraisal of authority and liberty in our democratic society. The balance is never more difficult to maintain justly than in wartime.
>
> HARVEY MANSFIELD, *A Short History of OPA*[1]

Prices and Legitimacy in American Democracy

I wrote this book during a period in which inflation in the US and much of the rest of the world was unusually high. It was also a period of unusual circumstances, including a global pandemic and the Russian war against Ukraine. I hope that by the time you are reading this book, we are facing more stable macroeconomic, global health, and geopolitical conditions, although I hardly dare to make predictions about the next big shocks that may hit the economy and society. In this final chapter, I offer some reflections on the long sweep of history that this book has covered and thoughts about the future.

In the first chapter, I explained that this book would focus on evolving beliefs about the legitimate role of the state in managing and stabilizing prices. I borrowed a definition of legitimacy from the former central banker Paul Tucker, who explains that "legitimacy grounds and comprises the capacity of an agency to pursue its mandate as part of the broader state apparatus, without relying wholly on coercive power."[2] Tucker also explains that, "to be accepted as legitimate, a government institution's design and operation (in their broadest sense) must comport with a political society's deepest political values. . . . For constitutional democracies, those include the values of democracy, constitutionalism (including, importantly, the separation of powers), and of the rule of law."

This book has told the story of how American policy makers' and institutions' attempts to stabilize prices have reflected, shaped, and sometimes come into conflict with our political values. As American political values are neither homogeneous nor static, the legitimacy of a wide variety of state interventions in prices has been litigated and relitigated in the courts and the courts of public opinion.

When the framers of the Constitution gave Congress the power to "coin Money" and "regulate the Value thereof," money was much different from today (chapter 1). Distrust of unbacked paper money, like the Continental currency issued to finance the Revolution, was widespread, because paper money was susceptible to depreciation and inflation. The idea that a government might force creditors to accept depreciated money in repayment of debt conflicted with the Lockean consent-based view of legitimacy held by many of the founders. Many of the founders opposed price controls, which were also implemented during the Revolution, on similar grounds—they force sellers to sell at a particular price against their consent.

The framers sought to design monetary institutions that would be strong enough allow the new nation to flourish without risking excessive concentration of power that could lead to tyranny (chapter 2). A flourishing America, for Thomas Jefferson, was an agrarian, republican society of small farmers. For Alexander Hamilton, it required commercial prosperity, bolstered by a strong federal government. These two competing visions shaped early American politics and institutions, including the First and Second Banks of the United States and, later, the Federal Reserve System.

Because of America's agricultural origins, fluctuations in the prices of crops and land, sometimes driven by international developments, could be highly disruptive. Jacksonian Democrats, successors to the Jeffersonians, thought that "hard money," coined by the federal government, could best protect the "common man" from the dangers of price fluctuations (chapter 3). It was only later—especially after the Crime of 1873 and ensuing deflation—that progressives pushed for the government to help the common man by taking a more active role in monetary policy. In the Progressive Era, William Jennings Bryan and others pushed for monetary expansion, through "free silver" or greenbacks, to improve the plight of farmers by reducing the real value of their debts (chapter 4).

Around the same time, Irving Fisher began his decades-long advocacy of monetary policy focused on stabilizing not the price of gold but the purchasing power of the dollar. His proposal was not incorporated into the Federal Reserve Act of 1913, which kept the United States on the gold standard. The new Federal Reserve System was barely open for action when World War I broke out (chapter 5). World War I was the first time since the Revolutionary War that price controls were broadly implemented, and unlike in the Revolutionary War, the controls could be supported by a much more developed state administrative apparatus. Many of the controls focused on farm products, as food prices and production are so critical to any war effort. The war demonstrated the powerful ability of a crisis to reshape public views about the role of the state and expand the role of the executive.

Even as the war ended and the share of Americans on farms declined, fluctuations in farm prices were hugely consequential in American politics and prompted a variety of policy responses and proposals, ranging from monetary policy to tariffs to price regulations (chapter 6). Much of the later part of this book has focused on the evolving role of the Federal Reserve in securing (or failing to secure) price stability. Throughout the two great deflations in the 1920s, during the recession of 1920–1921 and the Great Depression, Fisher continued to advocate for a price-stability mandate for the Fed. Still, there was no widespread agreement that the Federal Reserve could or should be primarily responsible for price stability.

The Great Depression and World War II, even more than World War I, demonstrated how a crisis can increase support for government intervention in the economy and legitimize previously unthinkable policy responses and a larger role for the executive. When President Franklin Roosevelt took office in the midst of the Depression, he was quick to analogize the economic crisis to a war that might "call for temporary departure from that normal balance of public procedure."[3] He asked Congress for "broad Executive power to wage a war against the emergency, as great as the power that would be given to me if we were in fact invaded by a foreign foe," proclaiming that the people had "registered a mandate that they want direct, vigorous action."[4] Congress soon amended the Trading with the Enemy Act of 1917, which allowed the president to restrict trade in wartime, so that it also applied to peacetime emergencies.

Roosevelt used his executive authorities, including those awarded in the Thomas Amendment of 1933, to confiscate privately owned gold, halt gold outflows, abrogate gold contracts, and suspend the gold standard, as part of his plan for reflating the United States economy (chapter 7). Fisher applauded President Roosevelt's monetary actions in 1933, but others questioned their legitimacy. *The Economist* reported that "the country has exchanged a President with little effective power for a 'currency dictator.'"[5] The economist Edwin Kemmerer remarked that the Thomas Amendment gave the president and his appointees "a legal authority over the nation's currency that is almost complete. A Stalin or a Hitler could hardly have more."[6]

The legitimacy of President Roosevelt's price stabilization policies in World War II likewise faced scrutiny (chapter 8). The Emergency Price Control Act (EPCA) gave the administrator of the Office of Price Administration (OPA) a tremendous amount of discretion to set price controls and enforce compliance.[7] The EPCA also created an Emergency Court of Appeals exclusive jurisdiction over cases regarding price controls. The Supreme Court questioned whether the arrangements limited freedom of contracting and interfered with due process and whether they constituted an unconstitutional delegation of legislative power to the OPA. Ultimately, the Supreme Court upheld EPCA, largely on the grounds of Congress's war power.

At the start of the Korean War, the Fed remained subservient to the Treasury, and price controls were again used, though less effectively, to address inflation (chapter 9). Even after the Treasury-Fed Accord of 1951 gave the Fed greater monetary policy independence, there was not always sufficient political will to use monetary policy to reduce inflation. This became most apparent during the Great Inflation of the 1970s, which President Nixon's price controls, President Ford's Whip Inflation Now program, and President Carter's Council on Wage and Price Stability failed to subdue (chapter 10). This all changed with the Volcker disinflation—the "triumph of central banking" (chapter 11). The Volcker disinflation came at a high cost, but it demonstrated the power of monetary policy and the importance of central bank credibility and independence.

Central bank independence, as Volcker emphasized, "must not imply isolation. . . . A central bank operating in an open democratic society will need to develop and sustain its basic policies within some broad range of public understanding and acceptability."[8] Volcker's successors have attempted to improve public understanding and acceptance, mostly through communication and transparency reforms. The Fed adopted a 2 percent inflation target in 2012 as the economy was slowly recovering from the Great Recession (chapter 12). But public understanding and acceptance of the Fed's approach to inflation targeting has never been complete. In the years following the adoption of the target, inflation was persistently below target, and critics of the Fed urged the Fed to more aggressively pursue full employment, even if it meant allowing higher inflation. By the time the Fed held a series of Fed Listens events in 2019 as part of its framework review, high inflation was becoming a distant memory, and the Fed and other central banks were facing increasing pressure to stop "fighting phantom inflation" and focus on other social goals, like increasing employment and reducing inequality.[9]

The COVID-19 pandemic thrust the world back into crisis mode (chapter 13). In addition to activating anti-price-gouging laws and reigniting long-running debates about drug-pricing policies, the pandemic also provoked a massive fiscal and monetary policy response that staved off a long-lasting recession. The impressively quick recovery from the pandemic recession was soon followed by inflation pressures and exacerbated by supply-chain distress and the Russian war against Ukraine. Throughout most of 2021, policy makers insisted that inflation was transitory. Under the average inflation-targeting framework that the Fed adopted in 2020, the Fed could allow inflation to overshoot the 2 percent target and wait for it to subside.

Beginning in March 2022, however, the Fed began a series of interest rate hikes and emphasized its firm commitment to price stability, with Chairman Powell promising to "keep at it until the job is done."[10] It was a promise that not everyone believed he should keep. In the introduction, I suggested that the post-Volcker "consensus"—delegate price stability to the central bank, and give the central bank independence in the pursuit of that goal—was on shaky ground. In the remainder of this chapter, I'll reflect on the stakes of our national response to price stabilization in the years ahead.

Forging Ahead

In the months leading up to the 2022 midterm elections, several public opinion polls asked American voters about their top concerns. Most polls found that inflation was the leading issue on voters' minds, followed by the fate of American democracy.[11] I see these two concerns as fundamentally entwined. High and volatile inflation causes hardship for many families whose wages don't keep up with price increases. Inflation makes it harder for families to plan for the future, increasing uncertainty and anxiety as it erodes the standard of living.[12]

The costs of inflation, I believe, are even more than these. High inflation also erodes confidence in policy makers, institutions, and democracy itself: people look to their policy makers for assurance and solutions, and instead they find finger-pointing and false promises. They find a system that seems too dysfunctional to provide them with the basic security of stable purchasing power. And they question the legitimacy of the institutions and structures that govern their lives and livelihoods—institutions like the Federal Reserve System and the Congress that oversees it.

Amid this discontent, appeals for price controls as a "democratic" solution have gained ground. This book is not a total condemnation of price controls, but I do caution against their adoption in current circumstances. Todd Tucker, of the Roosevelt Institute, whose appeal for price controls in the *Washington Post* prompted me to write this book, points to at least three ongoing crises that might justify the imposition of a broad program of price controls: the climate crisis, the COVID-19 pandemic, and the crisis of health-care costs.[13] I agree with Tucker's basic premise that price controls are most likely to be effective during a crisis. In a crisis like a war, the public is more likely to support such government intervention in the economy, and price controls are most likely to have a beneficial stabilizing effect on expectations in the face of anticipated shortages. As Tucker writes: "There is no reward for speculation, as predictions that prices will go up reward buying low now to sell high later. Instead, price controls send a signal that this will not be tolerated."[14]

This potential beneficial effect of price controls through expectations is short-lived, however. Over chronic or longer-lasting emergencies, the allocative and informational inefficiencies of price controls are likely to far outweigh their benefits.[15] The implications of price controls for democracy are also troubling when emergencies are defined in an expansive and open-ended way. First, a price-control system would require a larger surveillance state with weaker privacy protections. Tucker notes that "many more officials would need to be hired" to administer price controls in today's more complex economy, and adds that "if we think future crises might merit price controls, expanding governments' abilities now to track prices throughout supply chains is a must."

Second, such a system would shift the balance of power and loosen the checks and balances in American government. To implement price controls as an emergency measure in World War II, Congress delegated substantial power to the executive. And as Tucker recalls, the decisions of the OPA "could not be reviewed by the normal court system at all. . . . Rather, jurisdiction was given to a new Emergency Court of Appeals—a specialized bench with industrial expertise that applied a deferential standard of review and allowed the price controls to go into effect while courts reviewed the lawsuits." Tucker suggests that similar "checks on business and courts" would be necessary for effective price controls today.

In short, price controls require an expanded administrative and surveillance state, enabled by weaker restrictions on executive authority and erosion of due process that can be justified only in a crisis. Political scientists Steven Levitsky and Daniel Ziblatt note that "crises are a time-tested means of subverting democracy." They explain that "autocrats love emergencies," because "crises—real and imaginary—loosen normal constitutional constraints."[16] Americans were willing to temporarily subject themselves to a "price czar" to fight World War II. I doubt they are prepared to do so to fight against a chronic crisis like climate change.

I don't think that we should consign ourselves to an economy and political system in permanent crisis mode—although, to some extent, we already have. Roosevelt's emergency declaration was not formally ended until 1977.[17] Since 1978, presidential declarations of national emergencies have been governed by the National Emergencies Act. Presidents declare emergencies frequently, and the emergencies are long lasting. A 2019 report by the Brennan Center for Justice found that sixty-two national emergencies had been declared since the passage of the National Emergencies Act, with the average declared emergency lasting 9.6 years.[18] The same report found that emergency authorities have accumulated over time, so that there are now 136 statutory powers available to the president during a national emergency, including substantial economic powers.

Presidential reliance on emergency powers reflects a larger, and troubling, trend in American democracy: the increasing reliance on executive action and technocratic executive agencies. The political writer Julius Krein attributes this tendency to the "weakness and unresponsiveness of nominally democratic institutions."[19] He explained that even populist politicians have come to rely on technocrats to make progress on their policy goals: "The executive bureaucracy has proved a more reliable instrument for translating populist causes into policy than nominally democratic institutions like Congress. . . . Technocratic bureaucracies—although they can certainly be captured—actually retain greater capacity for autonomous policymaking in the public interest than theoretically democratic institutions like legislatures. . . . Whatever incremental progress the administration made on the distinctive, populist elements of Mr. Trump's 2016 campaign . . . was almost entirely achieved through executive orders or technocratic agencies."[20] The reliance on executive action and technocratic agencies has continued during the Biden administration. In President Biden's first days in office, he issued dozens of executive orders and actions related to the pandemic, climate change, immigration, and other issues. The *New York Times* editorial board urged the president to "ease up on the executive actions. . . . This is no way to make law."[21] Another *Times* piece lamented that "the power to set government policy is becoming increasingly disconnected from public opinion."[22]

These tendencies toward long-lasting emergency declarations, executive actions, and reliance on technocratic agencies are closely related to the technopopulist political logic that I discussed earlier. In established democracies, political movements have *combined* technocratic and populist appeals in a variety of ways. Popular movements are not opposed to technocratic institutions but want "all institutions of society to jump into the social and political goals of the moment, regardless of boring legalities."[23] In their book on technopopulism, Bickerton and Accetti warn that technopopulism will not solve the crisis of political representation to which it responds. Instead, "Increasingly atomized individuals are bound to get a sense that political representation is being hollowed out, even if—or indeed precisely because—political actors claim to represent the substantive interests of society as a whole in a 'direct' and 'unmediated way.'"[24]

Technopopulism, as I discussed, has had major implications for the Federal Reserve, one of the world's most powerful technocratic agencies. As it has taken on more authority and discretion, it has begun appealing directly to the people and the popular will.[25] The "populist threat" to central bank independence that was so often warned of in the 2010s did not constrain the Fed but rather played a part in transforming its communication strategy and its monetary policy framework and expanding its power. With the return of high inflation, the Fed's recent decision to recommit itself to a sharply focused pursuit of price stability has put it under fire from critics who would prefer a stronger focus on full employment and social goals.[26]

To some extent, this criticism is reflected in recent suggestions that the Fed should simply raise its inflation target, say to 3 percent, rather than imposing the high labor-market costs of disinflating back to the 2 percent target. I think that this proposal makes the classic mistake of assuming that there is a long-run trade-off between inflation and unemployment—in other words, that higher inflation can help us "purchase" permanently lower employment (Chapter 10). And I agree with Federal Reserve Board member Philip Jefferson, who argues that raising the inflation target would carry the risk of leading people to fear that the target "could be changed opportunistically in the future," permanently damaging the Fed's credibility and unanchoring expectations.[27]

On the other side of the political spectrum are those who see the high inflation as a reason to vastly limit the Fed's monetary policy authority and its role in the pursuit of price stability. For example, in October 2022, Representative Alex Mooney, a Republican from West Virginia, introduced the Gold Standard Restoration Act, which would do just as its title suggests. Republicans introduced a similar bill in 1984, after the Great Inflation.[28] The text of the 2022 bill decries how "that Federal Reserve note has lost more than 30 percent of its purchasing power since 2000, and 97 percent of its purchasing power since the passage of the Federal Reserve Act in 1913."[29] Mooney claims that, under a gold standard, "prices would be shaped by economics rather than the instincts of bureaucrats. No longer would our economy be at the mercy of the Federal Reserve and reckless Washington spenders."[30]

This sentiment is shared by many enthusiasts of decentralized private cryptocurrencies that are not susceptible to purchasing power erosion through government overissuance. The most famous cryptocurrency, Bitcoin, is designed so that there will never be more than twenty-one million Bitcoins in circulation. The economist Robert Murphy has argued: "Economically, the chief attraction of Bitcoin is its mathematically guaranteed scarcity. . . . No external technological or physical event could cause Bitcoin inflation, and since no one is in charge of Bitcoin, there is no one tempted to inflate 'from within.'"[31]

A return to a gold standard or some new form of Bitcoin standard strikes me as both unfeasible and unwise. We saw that the equilibrating features of the gold standard work well only when monetary authorities are credibly committed to the "rules of the game," and that even if a gold standard provides price stability in the very long run, episodes of substantial inflation and deflation are possible in the short run. Bitcoin has had an enormously volatile purchasing power, making it unlikely to replace fiat currency as a widely used medium of exchange.[32] The benefits of a central bank that pursues price stability are too large for society to willingly relinquish. But how can these benefits be legitimately and effectively harnessed?

In 1926, when Congress was debating whether to mandate that the Fed stabilize prices, Governor Benjamin Strong commented: "The assumption that the Federal reserve system has powers of great magnitude in the control of prices ought to be considered not alone from the standpoint of economics, but from the standpoint of human nature to some extent. . . . What safeguards are we going to introduce in regard to ignorance, stupidity, and bad judgment in the exercise of this power? . . . Is it possible to guard the misuse of these powers for selfish or even improper purposes, or even political objects, if you please?"[33] Since then, history has shown that the Fed does have these great powers and has also demonstrated the necessity of safeguards. This is why I have come to believe that a single and clearly defined target for monetary policy, something like an NGDP level target, would make best use of this "power of great magnitude" while guarding against its misuse. As I have written, "A well-defined, quantitative target clarifies the meaning of accountability and helps distinguish accountability from responsiveness. Reducing technocratic discretion in this way reduces the impetus to work through the central bank to achieve a variety of policy goals that are better left to the political process."[34]

When I began advocating for an NGDP level target in 2019, I thought that the transition to this new framework could be quite smooth because the Fed had kept NGDP on a relatively stable growth path for several years. The Fed did not adopt NGDP level targeting in 2019, but it adopted a flexible average inflation target in 2021. Subsequently, NGDP rose well above its prepandemic trend path. In other words, monetary policy was looser under flexible average inflation targeting than it would have been under an NGDP level target. Adopting a new framework now, versus in 2019, would be more challenging. Central banks should not make frequent changes to their monetary policy frameworks, because the public needs to be able to rely on those frameworks guiding policy far into the future. Frequent framework changes risk damaging a central bank's credibility.

The economists David Beckworth and Patrick Horan suggest that the Fed could adopt something like NGDP level targeting by modifying, rather than totally scrapping, the average inflation-targeting framework.[35] Recall that the current average inflation target is asymmetric: the Fed makes up for past undershoots of inflation but not past overshoots. Beckworth and Horan provide the technical details of how a symmetric flexible average inflation target could be implemented in a way that would capture the important features of NGDP level targeting. In particular, it would allow the Fed to "look through" temporary supply shocks without the need to distinguish between supply and demand shocks in real time, it would stabilize inflation in the medium run, and it would reduce macroeconomic and financial instability. It would help the Fed achieve its dual mandate, but with less discretion and more accountability and transparency. Making average inflation targeting symmetric would also likely make inflation easier for the public to understand.

An NGDPLT would not be a panacea, either for the economy or for American democracy. But an independent but constrained central bank, committed to stabilizing nominal spending and aggregate prices, would help on both fronts. Aggregate price stability is a foundation for economic strength; its absence fuels political and social unrest. Aggregate price stability reduces the impetus to control relative prices through distortionary means, like tariffs and controls, that reduce efficiency, increase the role of lobbying, and have unintended consequences. Even if the Fed keeps its average inflation-targeting framework unchanged, it can emphasize its commitment to price stability, acknowledge the policy mistakes of 2021 and 2022, and be transparent about how it will avoid such mistakes in the future. I don't expect that all readers will agree with the policy suggestions that I have provided in this final chapter. Still, I hope that the historical context that this book provides will facilitate a more informed discussion and consideration of policy proposals aimed at addressing prices and inflation in years to come.

NOTES

Introduction

1. Office of Price Administration, Community Service Division, Information Department, "Historical Reports on War Administration" (May 1946).
2. Jeff Stein and Rachel Siegel, "What Should the White House Do to Combat Inflation? Experts Weighed in with 12 Ideas," *Washington Post*, January 26, 2022, https://www.washingtonpost.com/us-policy/2022/01/26/inflation-white-house-experts/.
3. Franklin D. Roosevelt, "Message to Congress on an Economic Stabilization Program," April 27, 1942, American Presidency Project, https://www.presidency.ucsb.edu/documents/message-congress-economic-stabilization-program.
4. Office of Price Administration, "Historical Reports on War Administration."
5. Isabella Weber, "Could Strategic Price Controls Help Fight Inflation?," *The Guardian*, December 29, 2021, https://www.theguardian.com/business/commentisfree/2021/dec/29/inflation-price-controls-time-we-use-it.
6. Friedrich Hayek, "The Use of Knowledge in Society," *American Economic Review* 35, no. 4 (1945): 519–30.
7. Jeffrey Jones, "Government Agency Ratings: CIA, FBI Up; Federal Reserve Down," Gallup, October 5, 2022, https://news.gallup.com/poll/402464/government-agency-ratings-cia-fbi-federal-reserve-down.aspx; Bill to Amend the Internal Revenue Code of 1986 to Impose an Income Tax on Excess Profits of Certain Corporations, 117th Cong. (2022), https://www.congress.gov/117/bills/s3933/BILLS-117s3933is.pdf.
8. Paul Tucker, *Unelected Power: The Quest for Legitimacy in Central Banking and the Regulatory State* (Princeton, NJ: Princeton University Press, 2019).
9. Milton Friedman, *Capitalism and Freedom* (Chicago: University of Chicago Press, 1962), 13.
10. Irving Fisher, *Stabilizing the Dollar: A Plan to Stabilize the General Price Level without Fixing Individual Prices* (New York: Macmillan, 1920), 55.
11. Robert Higgs, *Crisis and Leviathan* (Oxford: Oxford University Press, 2013).
12. Hugh Rockoff, "War and Inflation in the United States from the Revolution to the Persian Gulf War," in *Economic History of Warfare and State Formation*, ed.

Jari Eloranta, Eric Golson, Andre Markevich, and Nikolaus Wolf (Singapore: Springer, 2016), 159–95.

13. Juilliard v. Greenman, 110 U.S. 421 (1884).
14. Nathan Chapman, "Due Process of War," *Notre Dame Law Review* 94, no. 2 (2018): 639–708, at 645.
15. Block v. Hirsh, 256 U.S. 135, 156 (1921).
16. Anshu Siripurapu, "What Is the Defense Production Act?," Council on Foreign Relations, https://www.cfr.org/in-brief/what-defense-production-act.
17. Masood Ahmed, "The US Is Losing the Global War against COVID-19—And That Is a National Security Issue," Center for Global Development, July 28, 2021, https://www.cgdev.org/blog/us-losing-global-war-against-covid-19-and-national-security-issue.
18. Matthew Famiglietti and Carlos Garriga, "A Simple Evaluation of Two Decades of Inflation Targeting: Lessons for the New Monetary Policy Strategy," *Economic Synopses*, no. 1 (2021): 1–3; Ben Bernanke, Thomas Laubach, Frederic Mishkin, and Adam Posen, *Inflation Targeting: Lessons from the International Experience* (Princeton, NJ: Princeton University Press, 1998).
19. Mark Aldrich, "Capital Theory and Racism: From Laissez-Faire to the Eugenics Movement in the Career of Irving Fisher," *Review of Radical Political Economics* 7, no. 3 (1975): 33–42.
20. Irving Fisher, "The Debt-Deflation Theory of Great Depressions," *Econometrica* 1, no. 4 (1933), 337–57, at 346–47.
21. Ben Bernanke and Frederic Mishkin, "Inflation Targeting: A New Framework for Monetary Policy?," *Journal of Economic Perspectives* 11, no. 2 (1997): 97–116, at 97.
22. Irving Fisher, *The Purchasing Power of Money* (New York: Macmillan, 1911), available at https://www.econlib.org/library/YPDBooks/Fisher/fshPPM.html.
23. Meg Jacobs, "'How about Some Meat?': The Office of Price Administration, Consumption Politics, and State Building from the Bottom Up, 1941–1946," *Journal of American History* (1997): 910–41, at 912.

Chapter One

1. Arthur Sackley, "Coinage, Commodities, and Count Carli: An Account of the Inventor and the Computation of the Original Index Numbers," *Monthly Labor Review* 88, no. 7 (1965): 817–21.
2. Thomas Sowell, *Basic Economics*, 4th ed. (New York: Basic Books, 2010), ch. 25.
3. Adam Smith, *An Inquiry into the Nature and Causes of the Wealth of Nations* (1776), https://www.econlib.org/library/Smith/smWN.html.
4. David Hume, *Political Discourses: On Money, Part II, Essay III* (1752), https://www.econlib.org/book-chapters/chapter-part-ii-essay-iii-of-money/.
5. Hume, *Political Discourses.*
6. "Consumer Price Index Frequently Asked Questions," US Bureau of Labor Statistics, https://www.bls.gov/cpi/questions-and-answers.htm.

7. Hugh Rockoff, "On the Controversies behind the Origins of the Federal Economic Statistics," *Journal of Economic Perspectives* 33, no. 1 (2019): 147–64.
8. Arthur Sackley, "Coinage, Commodities, and Count Carli: An Account of the Inventor and the Computation of the Original Index Number," *Monthly Labor Review* 88, no. 7 (1965): 817–21.
9. Sackley, 818.
10. Martin Allen, "Currency Depreciation and Debasement in Medieval Europe," in *Money in the Western Legal Tradition: Middle Ages to Bretton Woods*, ed. David Fox and Wolfgang Ernst (Oxford: Oxford University Press, 2016), 41–52.
11. Ron Michener, "Money in the American Colonies," *EH.Net Encyclopedia*, ed. Robert Whaples, June 8, 2003, https://eh.net/encyclopedia/money-in-the-american-colonies.
12. Marion H. Gottfried, "The First Depression in Massachusetts," *New England Quarterly* 9, no. 4 (1936): 655–78.
13. Michener, "Money in the American Colonies."
14. Adam Smith, *The Wealth of Nations*, ed. Edwin Canaan (New York, 1937), 311.
15. Michener, "Money in the American Colonies."
16. Grubb, "Creating Maryland's Paper Money Economy, 1720–1739: The Role of Power, Print, and Markets" (Working Paper No. w13974, National Bureau of Economic Research, Cambridge, MA, 2008).
17. Leslie V. Brock, *The Currency of the American Colonies, 1700–1764* (New York: Arno Press, 1975).
18. Farley Grubb, *Benjamin Franklin and the Birth of a Paper Money Economy* (Philadelphia: Federal Reserve Bank of Philadelphia, 2006).
19. Benjamin Franklin, *A Modest Inquiry into the Nature and Necessity of a Paper Currency* (Philadelphia, 1729).
20. Grubb, *Benjamin Franklin and the Birth of a Paper Money Economy*.
21. Grubb, "Creating Maryland's Paper Money Economy."
22. Clarence P. Gould, "Money and Transportation in Maryland, 1720–1765," *Johns Hopkins University Studies in Historical and Political Science* 32 (1915): 9–176.
23. Grubb, "Creating Maryland's Paper Money Economy."
24. *Archives of Maryland* (Baltimore: Maryland Historical Society), 35:441, quoted in Grubb, "Creating Maryland's Paper Money Economy."
25. Grubb, "Creating Maryland's Paper Money Economy."
26. Charles Calomiris, "Institutional Failure, Monetary Scarcity, and the Depreciation of the Continental," *Journal of Economic History* 48, no. 1 (1988): 47–68.
27. Bruce D. Smith, "Some Colonial Evidence on Two Theories of Money: Maryland and the Carolinas," *Journal of Political Economy* 93 (1985): 1178–1211.
28. Grubb, *Benjamin Franklin and the Birth of a Paper Money Economy*.
29. "Adams's Original Draft, 24 September 1765," National Archives: Founders Online, https://founders.archives.gov/documents/Adams/06-01-02-0054-0002.
30. James Otis Jr., *The Rights of British Colonies Asserted and Proved* (1764), https://oll.libertyfund.org/page/1763-otis-rights-of-british-colonies-asserted-pamphlet.
31. Stamp Act Congress, "Declaration of Rights and Grievances" (1765).

32. John Locke, *Second Treatise of Government* (1690), https://www.gutenberg.org/files/7370/7370-h/7370-h.htm.
33. Locke.
34. Locke.
35. Hugh Rockoff, *Drastic Measures: A History of Wage and Price Controls in the United States* (Cambridge: Cambridge University Press, 1984), 25.
36. Calomiris, "Institutional Failure, Monetary Scarcity, and the Depreciation of the Continental."
37. Benjamin Franklin, *Memoirs of the Life and Writings of Benjamin Franklin: Comprising the Private Correspondence and Public Negotiations of Dr. Franklin, and a Selection from His Political, Philosophical, and Miscellaneous Works* (London: Henry Colburn, 1833), 3:106.
38. Benjamin Franklin, *Writings*, quoted in Rockoff, *Drastic Measures*, 27.
39. *The Articles of Association* (October 20, 1774), Records of the Continental and Confederation Congresses and the Constitutional Convention, Record Group 360, National Archives, https://catalog.archives.gov/id/6277397.
40. Rockoff, *Drastic Measures*, ch. 2.
41. Jonathan Grossman, "Wage and Price Controls during the American Revolution," *Monthly Labor Review* 96, no. 9 (1973): 3–10.
42. Murray Rothbard, *Conceived in Liberty*, vol. 4 (New Rochelle, NY: Arlington House Publishers, 1979).
43. Rockoff, *Drastic Measures*, 28.
44. "Act to Prevent Monopoly and Oppression," quoted in Grossman, "Wage and Price Controls during the American Revolution," 4.
45. Grossman, "Wage and Price Controls during the American Revolution," 5.
46. Quoted in Rockoff, *Drastic Measures*, 2930.
47. David R. Henderson, "John Locke," https://www.econlib.org/library/Enc/bios/Locke.html.
48. John Locke, "Some Considerations of the Consequences of the Lowering of Interest, and Raising the Value of Money" (1691), in *The Works of John Locke in Nine Volumes*, vol. 4 (London: Rivington, 1824), http://name.umdl.umich.edu/A48895.0001.001.
49. John Witherspoon, "Essay on Money," in *The Works of John Witherspoon* (Edinburgh: Printed for Ogle and Aiman, J. Pillans and Sons; J. Ritchie; and J. Turnbull, 1805), 9:38.
50. Witherspoon, 9:39.
51. *Papers of the New Haven Colony Historical Society* (New Haven, CT: Printed for the Society, 1882), 3:51.
52. Quoted in US Congress Joint Economic Committee, *Economic Report of the President*, 1977, 167.
53. Farley Grubb, "State Redemption of the Continental Dollar, 1779–90," *William and Mary Quarterly* 69, no. 1 (2012): 147–80.
54. Ballard C. Campbell, *Disasters, Accidents, and Crises in American History: A Refer-*

ence Guide to the Nation's Most Catastrophic Events* (New York: Infobase Publishing, 2008).

55. John Witherspoon, *Works of John Witherspoon* (1802), 4:222–23.
56. "From George Washington to Edmund Pendleton, 1 November 1779," National Archives: Founders Online, https://founders.archives.gov/documents/Washington/03-23-02-0113; "From George Washington to Jabez Bowen, 9 January 1787," National Archives: Founders Online, https://founders.archives.gov/GEWN-04-04-02-0428.
57. Alexander Hamilton, "Final Version of the Second Report on the Further Provision Necessary for Establishing Public Credit (Report on a National Bank)," December 13, 1790, National Archives: Founders Online, https://founders.archives.gov/documents/Hamilton/01-07-02-0229-0003.
58. Campbell, *Disasters, Accidents, and Crises in American History*.
59. David P. Szatmary, *Shays' Rebellion: The Making of an Agrarian Insurrection* (Amherst: University of Massachusetts Press, 1980).

Chapter Two

1. "Thomas Jefferson to Josephus B. Stuart, 10 May 1817," National Archives: Founders Online, https://founders.archives.gov/documents/Jefferson/03-11-02-0287.
2. Chester E. Eisinger, "The Influence of Natural Rights and Physiocratic Doctrines on American Agrarian Thought during the Revolutionary Period," *Agricultural History* 21, no. 1 (1947): 13–23; John Locke, *Second Treatise of Government* (1689), sec. 5, "Of Property."
3. A. Whitney Griswold, "The Agrarian Democracy of Thomas Jefferson," *American Political Science Review* 40, no. 4 (1946): 657–81, at 672.
4. "From Thomas Jefferson to James Madison, 20 December 1787," National Archives: Founders Online, https://founders.archives.gov/documents/Jefferson/01-12-02-0454.
5. Robert S. Hill, "Federalism, Republicanism, and the Northwest Ordinance," *Publius* 18, no. 4 (1988): 41–52.
6. Alexander Hamilton, "New York Ratifying Convention: Remarks (Francis Childs's Version), [24 June 1788]," National Archives: Founders Online, https://founders.archives.gov/documents/Hamilton/01-05-02-0012-0023.
7. M. J. C. Vile, *Constitutionalism and the Separation of Powers*, 2nd ed. (Indianapolis, IN: Liberty Fund, 1967), https://oll.libertyfund.org/title/vile-constitutionalism-and-the-separation-of-powers.
8. E. H. Scott, ed., *Journal of the Federal Convention Kept by James Madison* (Chicago: Albert, Scott and Co., 1893), 47.
9. "Madison Debates," August 16, 1787, Avalon Project, Yale Law School, https://avalon.law.yale.edu/18th_century/debates_816.asp.
10. "Madison Debates."

11. "Madison Debates."
12. "Madison Debates."
13. Joyce Appleby, "Commercial Farming and the 'Agrarian Myth' in the Early Republic," *Journal of American History* 68, no. 4 (1982): 833–49.
14. Thomas J. Weiss, "Revised Estimates of the United States Workforce, 1800–1860," in *Long-Term Factors in American Economic Growth*, ed. Stanley L. Engerman and Robert E. Gallman (Chicago: University of Chicago Press, 1986), 641–76; Robert C. Allen, "Economic Structure and Agricultural Productivity in Europe, 1300–1800," *European Review of Economic History* 4, no. 1 (2000): 1–26.
15. Appleby, "Commercial Farming and the 'Agrarian Myth' in the Early Republic."
16. George Washington, "Washington's Farewell Address to the People of the United States" (1796), available at https://www.senate.gov/artandhistory/history/resources/pdf/Washingtons_Farewell_Address.pdf.
17. David A. Hall and Matthew St. Clair Clarke, *Legislative and Documentary History of the Bank of the United States: Including the Original Bank of North America* (Washington, DC: Gales & Seaton, 1832), 55, available at https://fraser.stlouisfed.org/title/3632.
18. David J. Cowen, *The Origins and Economic Impact of the First Bank of the United States, 1791–1797* (New York: Garland Publishing, 2000).
19. Phil Davies, "The Bank That Hamilton Built," September 1, 2007, Federal Reserve Bank of Minneapolis, https://www.minneapolisfed.org/article/2007/the-bank-that-hamilton-built.
20. Andrew T. Hill, "The First Bank of the United States," Federal Reserve History, https://www.federalreservehistory.org/essays/first-bank-of-the-us.
21. Alexander Hamilton, "Final Report on the Establishment of a Mint, [28 January 1791]," National Archives: Founders Online, https://founders.archives.gov/documents/Hamilton/01-07-02-0334-0004.
22. George Selgin, "Salvaging Gresham's Law: The Good, the Bad, and the Illegal," *Journal of Money, Credit, and Banking* 28, no. 4 (1996): 637–49.
23. Larry White, *Better Money: Gold, Fiat, or Bitcoin?* (Cambridge: Cambridge University Press, 2023), ch. 2.
24. "Money in Colonial Times," Federal Reserve Bank of Philadelphia, http://www.philadelphiafed.org/education/teachers/resources/money-in-colonial-times/.
25. Hill, "First Bank of the United States."
26. "From George Washington to John Parke Custis, 26 May 1778," National Archives: Founders Online, https://founders.archives.gov/documents/Washington/03-15-02-0227.
27. Morris Bien, "The Public Lands of the United States," *North American Review* 192, no. 658 (1910): 387–402, at 391–92.
28. Murray Rothbard, *The Panic of 1819: Reactions and Policies* (New York: Columbia University Press, 1962).
29. Bray Hammond, *Banks and Politics in America: From the Revolution to the Civil War* (Princeton, NJ: Princeton University Press, 1957), 219–20.

30. Hammond, ch. 8.
31. Hammond, ch. 8.
32. Donald Kagin, "Monetary Aspects of the Treasury Notes of the War of 1812," *Journal of Economic History* 44, no. 1 (1984): 69–88.
33. Kagin, 71–72.
34. Kagin, 71–72.
35. Quoted in Kagin, 74.
36. Rothbard, *Panic of 1819*, 5.
37. Kagin, "Monetary Aspects of the Treasury Notes," 79.
38. Andrew T. Hill, "The Second Bank of the United States," Federal Reserve History, https://www.federalreservehistory.org/essays/second-bank-of-the-us.
39. Kagin, "Monetary Aspects of the Treasury Notes," 86.
40. Rothbard, *Panic of 1819*.
41. Clive Day, "The Early Development of the American Cotton Manufacture," *Quarterly Journal of Economics* 39, no. 3 (1925): 450–68.
42. Douglas Irwin, "Sectional Conflict and Crisis, 1816–1833," in *Clashing over Commerce: A History of US Trade Policy*, ed. Douglas Irwin (Chicago: University of Chicago Press, 2017), 125–75.
43. "Thomas Jefferson to Benjamin Austin, 9 January 1816," National Archives: Founders Online, https://founders.archives.gov/documents/Jefferson/03-09-02-0213.
44. Susan Hoffmann, *Politics and Banking: Ideas, Public Policy, and the Creation of Financial Institutions* (Baltimore: Johns Hopkins University Press, 2001), 48.
45. Federal Reserve Bank of Philadelphia, *The Second Bank of the United States: A Chapter in the History of Central Banking* (Philadelphia: Federal Reserve Bank of Philadelphia, 2021), https://www.philadelphiafed.org/-/media/frbp/assets/institutional/education/publications/second-bank-of-the-united-states.pdf.
46. Ralph C. H. Catterall, *The Second Bank of the United States* (Chicago: University of Chicago Press, 1903).
47. Leon M. Schur, "The Second Bank of the United States and the Inflation after the War of 1812," *Journal of Political Economy* 68, no. 2 (1960): 118–34.
48. Rothbard, *Panic of 1819*.
49. Rothbard, 14.
50. Rothbard, 16.
51. Charles Sellers, *The Market Revolution: Jacksonian America, 1815–1846* (Oxford: Oxford University Press, 1991), 136.
52. Frank W. Taussig, *The Tariff History of the United States* (New York: G. P. Putnam's Sons; London: Knickerbocker Press, 1892; rpt., Auburn, AL: Ludwig von Mises Institute, 2010), 65.
53. Taussig, 68.
54. McCulloch v. Maryland, 17 U.S. 316 (1819).
55. Arthur Fraas, "The Second Bank of the United States: An Instrument for Interregional Monetary Union," *Journal of Economic History* 34, no. 2 (1974): 447–67.

56. Fraas.
57. Quoted in H. W. Brands, *The Money Men: Capitalism, Democracy, and the Hundred Years' War over the American Dollar* (New York: W. W. Norton, 2010), 68–69.
58. Richard Sylla, "The Jacksonian Economy," Economic History Association, https://eh.net/book_reviews/the-jacksonian-economy/.
59. Merrill D. Peterson, *The Great Triumvirate: Webster, Clay and Calhoun* (New York: Oxford University Press), 206.
60. Taussig, *Tariff History of the United States*, 68.
61. Robert V. Remini, "Martin Van Buren and the Tariff of Abominations," *American Historical Review* 63, no. 4 (1958): 903–17.

Chapter Three

1. Andrew Jackson, "Farewell Address," March 4, 1837, American Presidency Project, https://www.presidency.ucsb.edu/documents/farewell-address-0.
2. James Roger Sharp, *The Jacksonians versus the Banks: Politics in the States after the Panic of 1837* (New York: Columbia University Press, 1970), 6.
3. Hill, "Second Bank of the United States."
4. "December 8, 1829: First Annual Message to Congress," Miller Center, https://millercenter.org/the-presidency/presidential-speeches/december-8-1829-first-annual-message-congress.
5. Stephen Campbell, "Nicholas Biddle," Economic Historian, May 23, 2021, https://economic-historian.com/2021/02/nicholas-biddle/.
6. "Andrew Jackson: Veto Message" (July 10, 1832), in Philip B. Kurland and Ralph Lerner, eds., *The Founders' Constitution* (Chicago: University of Chicago Press; Carmel, IN: Liberty Fund), doc. 20, https://press-pubs.uchicago.edu/founders/documents/a1_8_18s20.html.
7. Andrew Jackson, "Andrew Jackson to Cabinet," September 18, 1833, Correspondence of Andrew Jackson, ed. John Spencer Bassett, https://tile.loc.gov/storage-services/service/mss/maj/01083A//01083A_0290_0337.pdf.
8. John Calhoun, *South Carolina Exposition and Protest* (Columbia, SC, 1829), 5, https://dc.statelibrary.sc.gov/bitstream/handle/10827/21911/HOUSE_CR_Exposition_and_Protest_1828-12-19.pdf.
9. Andrew Jackson, "Proclamation No. 26: Respecting the Nullifying Laws of South Carolina" (December 10, 1832), *A Century of Lawmaking for a New Nation: US Congressional Documents and Debates, 1774–1875*, https://memory.loc.gov/cgi-bin/ampage?collId=llsl&fileName=011/llsl011.db&recNum=816.
10. Bray Hammond, "Jackson, Biddle, and the Bank of the United States," *Journal of Economic History* 7, no. 1 (1947): 1–23.
11. Jackson, "Farewell Address."
12. Editorial dated March 28, 1834, quoted in Paul O'Leary, "The Coinage Legislation of 1834," *Journal of Political Economy* 45, no. 1 (1937): 86–87.
13. O'Leary, 88–89.

14. Alfred Lee, "Bimetallism in the United States," *Political Science Quarterly* 1, no. 3 (1886): 389–90.
15. Jackson, "Farewell Address."
16. Richard Sylla, "The Jacksonian Economy," Economic Historian, https://eh.net/book_reviews/the-jacksonian-economy/.
17. John Joseph Wallis, "The Depression of 1839 to 1843: States, Debts, and Banks" (unpublished ms., University of Maryland and National Bureau of Economic Research), http://www.ltadvisors.net/Info/research/1839depression.pdf.
18. Catterall, *Second Bank of The United States.*
19. Peter Temin, *The Jacksonian Economy* (New York: W.W. Norton & Co., 1969).
20. Peter Rousseau, "Jacksonian Monetary Policy, Specie Flows, and the Panic of 1837," *Journal of Economic History* 62, no. 2 (2002): 457–88.
21. Rousseau.
22. Rousseau.
23. Martin Van Buren, *Message from the President of the United States, to the Two Houses of Congress, at the Commencement of the First Session, of the Twenty-fifth Congress* (Washington, DC: Printed at the Madisonian Office, September 5, 1837), 10.
24. Martin Van Buren, "September 4, 1837: Special Session Message," Miller Center, https://millercenter.org/the-presidency/presidential-speeches/september-4-1837-special-session-message.
25. Jeffrey Hummel, "Martin Van Buren: The Greatest American President," *Independent Review* 4, no. 2 (1999): 255–81. See William Gouge, *A Short History of Paper Money and Banking in the United States to Which is Prefixed an Inquiry into the Principles of the System* (Philadelphia: T. W. Ustick, 1833), https://cdn.mises.org/A%20Short%20History%20of%20Paper%20Money%20and%20Banking_2.pdf.
26. William Gouge, "Remarks," *Journal of Banking* (1841): 196.
27. William Gouge, *An Inquiry into the Expediency of Dispensing with Bank Agency and Bank Paper in the Fiscal Concerns of the United States* (Philadelphia: William Stavely, 1837).
28. Isaac Toucey, "Independent Treasury" (speech in the House of Representatives, June 23, 1838), in Cong. Globe, 25th Cong., 2nd Sess. 413 (1838), https://memory.loc.gov/cgi-bin/ampage?collId=llcg&fileName=005/llcg005.db&recNum=952.
29. Hummel, "Martin Van Buren."
30. Wallis, "The Depression of 1839 to 1843."
31. "August 16, 1841: Veto Message regarding the Bank of the United States," Miller Center, https://millercenter.org/the-presidency/presidential-speeches/august-16-1841-veto-message-regarding-bank-united-states.
32. James W. Cummings, *Towards Modern Public Finance: The American War with Mexico, 1846–1848* (London: Routledge, 2009).
33. Leonard L. Richards, *The California Gold Rush and the Coming of the Civil War* (New York: Knopf, 2008).
34. Robert Whaples, "California Gold Rush," in *EH.Net Encyclopedia*, ed. Robert Whaples, March 16, 2008, http://eh.net/encyclopedia/california-gold-rush/.

35. David A. Martin, "1853: The End of Bimetallism in the United States," *Journal of Economic History* 33, no. 4 (1973): 825–44, 830.
36. Austin Dean, *China and the End of Global Silver, 1873–1937* (Ithaca, NY: Cornell University Press, 2020).
37. Dean.
38. Martin, "End of Bimetallism in the United States," 826.
39. T. David Fosdick, "Interest or Money," *Hunt's Merchants Magazine* 22 (1850): 276, quoted in Martin, "End of Bimetallism in the United States," 826.
40. George Friedrich Knap, *The State Theory of Money* (London: Macmillan and Co., 1924), 32.
41. Martin, "End of Bimetallism in the United States," 836.
42. Neil Carothers, *Fractional Money: A History of Small Coins and Fractional Paper Currency of the United States* (New York: John Wiley & Sons, 1930; rpt., Wolfeboro, NH: Bowers and Merena Galleries, 1988), 108.
43. Senate Executive Document, US Senate, S. Exec. Doc. No. 31, 32nd Cong., 1st Sess., VII, No. 618, 2.
44. Andrew Johnson, Cong. Globe, 32nd Cong., 2nd Sess. 476 (1853), https://www.google.com/books/edition/The_Congressional_Globe/lEU4AQAAMAAJ?hl.
45. Johnson, Cong. Globe, 32nd Cong., 2nd Sess. 476 (1853)
46. Martin, "End of Bimetallism in the United States," 841.
47. Martin, 825.
48. "The Kansas-Nebraska Act" (May 30, 1854), US Senate, https://www.senate.gov/artandhistory/history/minute/Kansas_Nebraska_Act.htm.
49. James L. Huston, "Western Grains and the Panic of 1857," *Agricultural History* 57, no. 1 (1983): 14–32, at 20.
50. Charles Calomiris and Larry Schweikart, "The Panic of 1857: Origins, Transmission, and Containment." *Journal of Economic History* 51, no. 4 (1991): 807–34.
51. Calomiris and Schweikart.
52. Thomas Klitgaard and James Narron, "Crisis Chronicles: Defensive Suspension and the Panic of 1857" (2015), Liberty Street Economics, https://libertystreeteconomics.newyorkfed.org/2015/10/crisis-chronicles-defensive-suspension-and-the-panic-of-1857/; Huston, "Western Grains and the Panic of 1857," 16.
53. Huston, 16.
54. Huston, 22.
55. James Buchanan, "First Annual Message to Congress on the State of the Union," December 8, 1857, American Presidency Project, https://www.presidency.ucsb.edu/documents/first-annual-message-congress-the-state-the-union.
56. Buchanan.
57. Buchanan.
58. Buchanan.
59. David W. Lange, *History of the United States Mint and Its Coinage* (Atlanta: Whitman Publishing, 2005).

60. Bray Hammond, "The North's Empty Purse, 1861–1862," *American Historical Review* 67, no. 1 (1961): 1–18.
61. Quoted in Hammond, 8.
62. Hammond, 7.
63. Gerry Spaulding Elbridge, *History of the Legal Tender Paper Money Issued during the Great Rebellion, Being a Loan without Interest and a National Currency* (Buffalo, NY: Express Printing Company, 1869), 53, available at https://fraser.stlouisfed.org/files/docs/publications/books/1869histlegaltender/historyoflegaltender.pdf.
64. Murray Rothbard, "Aurophobia: or, Free Banking on What Standard?" *Review of Austrian Economics* 6 (1992): 97–108.
65. Quoted in Alexander McClure, *"Abe" Lincoln's Yarns and Stories* (New York: Western W. Wilson, 1901), available at https://www.gutenberg.org/files/2517/2517-h/2517-h.htm.
66. Abraham Lincoln, "Message to Congress" (1862), in *Collected Works of Abraham Lincoln*, ed. Roy P. Basler (New Brunswick, NJ: Rutgers University Press, 1953), 5:282–83.
67. "In His Own Words: Abraham Lincoln on Banking," Office of the Comptroller of the Currency, https://www.occ.treas.gov/about/who-we-are/history/founding-occ-national-bank-system/in-his-own-words-abraham-lincoln-on-banking.html.
68. Lincoln, "Message to Congress," 282–83.
69. George A. Selgin and Lawrence H. White, "Monetary Reform and the Redemption of National Bank Notes," *Business History Review* 68, no. 2 (1994): 205–43, at 207.
70. Abraham Lincoln, "December 6, 1864: Fourth Annual Message," Miller Center, https://millercenter.org/the-presidency/presidential-speeches/december-6-1864-fourth-annual-message.
71. Selgin and White, "Monetary Reform and the Redemption of National Bank Notes," 209.
72. Selgin and White, 207.
73. Michael Bordo, Christopher Erceg, Andrew Levin, and Ryan Michaels, "Three Great American Disinflations" (Board of Governors of the Federal Reserve System, International Finance Discussion Papers No. 898, 2007), https://www.federalreserve.gov/pubs/ifdp/2007/898/ifdp898.pdf.
74. Charles Calomiris, "Price and Exchange Rate Determination during the Greenback Suspension," *Oxford Economic Papers*, n.s., 40, no. 4 (1988): 719–50.
75. Marc Weidenmier, "Turning Points in the US Civil War: Views from the Grayback Market," *Southern Economic Journal* 68, no. 4 (2002): 875–90.
76. Quoted in Rockoff, "On the Controversies behind the Origins of the Federal Economic Statistics," 148.
77. "Chapter L: Price Indexes (Series L 1–52)," *Historical Statistics of the United States 1789–1945*, col. 1, 232, US Census Bureau, https://www2.census.gov/library

/publications/1949/compendia/hist_stats_1789-1945/hist_stats_1789-1945-chL .pdf.

78. Rockoff, *Drastic Measures*, 42.
79. Bernard Moses, "Legal Tender Notes in California," *Quarterly Journal of Economics* 7, no. 1 (1892): 1–25.
80. Gordon Bakken, "Law and Legal Tender in California and the West," *Southern California Quarterly* 62, no. 3 (1980): 239–59.
81. Moses, "Legal Tender Notes in California."
82. *Daily Alta California* 16, no. 5265 (August 2, 1864), https://cdnc.ucr.edu/?a=d&d=DAC18640802.2.13&e=-------en--20--1--txt-txIN--------.
83. Quoted in Bakken, "Law and Legal Tender in California and the West," 241.
84. Bakken, 243–44.
85. Quoted in Moses, "Legal Tender Notes in California," 18.
86. Bordo et al., "Three Great American Disinflations."
87. Ulysses S. Grant, "March 4, 1869: First Inaugural Address," Miller Center, https://millercenter.org/the-presidency/presidential-speeches/march-4-1869-first-inaugural-address.
88. Bordo et al., "Three Great American Disinflations."
89. Hepburn v. Griswold, 75 U.S. 603 (1869).
90. Richard Timberlake, "From Constitutional to Fiat Money: The US Experience," *Cato Journal* 32, no. 2 (2012): 349–62.
91. Legal Tender Cases, 79 U.S. 457 (1870).
92. Juilliard v. Greenman, 110 U.S. 421 (1884).
93. Legal Tender Cases, 79 U.S. 457 (1870).
94. Legal Tender Cases, 79 U.S. 457.
95. W. A. Croffut, "Bourbon Ballads," *York Tribune*, September, 1879, https://www.loc.gov/item/amss.as101480/.

Chapter Four

1. William Jennings Bryan, "Cross of Gold" (July 9, 1896), American Rhetoric, https://www.americanrhetoric.com/speeches/williamjenningsbryan1896dnc.htm.
2. Paul Stephen Dempsey, "The Rise and Fall of the Interstate Commerce Commission: The Tortuous Path from Regulation to Deregulation of America's Infrastructure," *Marquette Law Review* 95, no. 4 (2012): 1151–89, at 1155–56.
3. Oliver Hudson Kelley, *Origin and Progress of the Order of the Patrons of Husbandry in the United States; a History from 1866 to 1873* (Philadelphia: J. A. Wagenseller, 1875).
4. Milton Friedman, "The Crime of 1873," *Journal of Political Economy* 98, no. 6 (1990): 1159–94, at 1170.
5. Friedman, 1161.
6. Friedman, 1168–69.
7. Friedman, 1170.

8. Friedman, 1171–72.
9. Brandon Dupont, "'Henceforth, I Must Have No Friends': Evaluating the Economic Policies of Grover Cleveland," *Independent Review* 18, no. 4 (2014): 559–79, at 566.
10. Heather Cox Richardson, *West from Appomattox: The Reconstruction of America after the Civil War* (New Haven, CT: Yale University Press, 2007), 131.
11. Dempsey, "The Rise and Fall of the Interstate Commerce Commission," 1155–56.
12. Dempsey, 1155–56.
13. Munn v. Illinois, 94 U.S. 113 (1877).
14. Munn v. Illinois, 94 U.S. 114, 134 (1877).
15. Keith T. Poole and Howard Rosenthal, "Congress and Railroad Regulation: 1874 to 1887," in *The Regulated Economy: A Historical Approach to Political Economy*, ed. Claudia Goldin and Gary D. Libecap (Chicago: University of Chicago Press, 1994).
16. Wabash, St. Louis & Pacific Railway Co. v. Illinois, 118 U.S. 557 (1886).
17. "The Interstate Commerce Act is Passed," February 4, 1887, US Senate, https://www.senate.gov/artandhistory/history/minute/Interstate_Commerce_Act_Is_Passed.htm.
18. James C. Miller III, "Keynote Address to ICC Centennial Celebration" (1987), quoted in Dempsey, "The Rise and Fall of the Interstate Commerce Commission," 1162.
19. James W. Ely Jr., "The Troubled Beginning of the Interstate Commerce Act," *Marquette Law Review* 95, no. 4 (2012): 1131–34, at 1132.
20. ICC v. Cincinnati, New Orleans and Texas Pacific Railway, 167 U.S. 479 (1897).
21. Ely, "The Troubled Beginning of the Interstate Commerce Act," 1134.
22. United States v. E. C. Knight Co., 156 U.S. 1 (1895).
23. Swift and Co. v. United States, 196 U.S. 375 (1905).
24. Dupont, "'Henceforth, I Must Have No Friends,'" 560.
25. "Second Inaugural Address of Grover Cleveland" (March 4, 1893), Avalon Project, Yale Law School, https://avalon.law.yale.edu/19th_century/cleve2.asp.
26. Grover Cleveland, "December 6, 1887: Third Annual Message," Miller Center, https://millercenter.org/the-presidency/presidential-speeches/december-6-1887-third-annual-message.
27. Cleveland, "Third Annual Message."
28. Cleveland, "Third Annual Message."
29. Douglas A. Irwin, "Higher Tariffs, Lower Revenues? Analyzing the Fiscal Aspects of 'the Great Tariff Debate of 1888," *Journal of Economic History* 58, no. 1 (1998): 59–72.
30. Frank Taussig, "The McKinley Tariff Act," *Economic Journal* 1, no. 2 (891): 326–50, at 329.
31. Dupont, "'Henceforth, I Must Have No Friends,'" 564.
32. Walter T. K. Nugent, *Money and American Society, 1865–1880* (New York: Free Press, 1968).
33. Fisher, *Purchasing Power of Money*.

34. Taussig, "McKinley Tariff Act," 330.
35. H. M. Douty, "A Century of Wage Statistics: The BLS Contribution," *Monthly Labor Review* (1984): 16–28, at 17; Nicholas Eberstadt, Ryan Nunn, Diane Whitmore Schanzenbach, and Michael R. Strain, *"In Order That They Might Rest Their Arguments on Facts": The Vital Role of Government-Collected Data* (Washington, DC: Hamilton Project and American Enterprise Institute, 2017), https://www.brookings.edu/wp-content/uploads/2017/02/thp_20170227_govt_collected_data_report.pdf.
36. Rockoff, "On the Controversies behind the Origins of the Federal Economic Statistics," 149.
37. Field v. Clark, 143 U.S. 649 (1892).
38. Quoted in Dupont, "'Henceforth, I Must Have No Friends,'" 566.
39. Cleveland, "Second Inaugural Address."
40. Grover Cleveland, "Message on the Repeal of the Sherman Silver Purchase Act," August 8, 1893, American History: From Revolution to Reconstruction and Beyond, http://www.let.rug.nl/usa/documents/1876-1900/grover-cleveland-message-on-the-repeal-of-the-sherman-silver-purchase-act-august-8-1893.php.
41. Bryan, "Cross of Gold."
42. Bryan.
43. Bryan.
44. Bryan.
45. William Jennings Bryan, "Madison Square Garden, New York City, NY Speech," August 12, 1896, Railroads and the Making of Modern America, https://railroads.unl.edu/documents/view_document.php?id=rail.wjb.18960812.01.
46. Arthur I. Fonda, *Honest Money* (New York: Macmillan & Co., 1895), 159.
47. Richard Hofstadter, *The Age of Reform: From Bryan to FDR* (New York: Vintage Books, 1955).
48. Milton Friedman and Anna Schwartz, *A Monetary History of the United States, 1867–1960* (Princeton, NJ: Princeton University Press, 1963), 137.
49. Friedman and Schwartz, 138.
50. David I. Macleod, "Food Prices, Politics, and Policy in the Progressive Era," *Journal of the Gilded Age and Progressive Era* 8, no. 3 (2009): 365–406, at 368.
51. William H. Taft, "First Annual Message," December 7, 1909, American Presidency Project, https://www.presidency.ucsb.edu/documents/first-annual-message-17.
52. Macleod, "Food Prices, Politics, and Policy in the Progressive Era," 370.
53. Hofstadter, *Age of Reform.*
54. Macleod, "Food Prices, Politics, and Policy in the Progressive Era," 374.
55. Edwin Seligman, "High and Low Prices," *The Independent,* March 31, 1910.
56. Seligman.
57. J. Pease Norton, "The Remedy for the High Prices," *The Independent,* February 10, 1910.
58. Fisher, *Purchasing Power of Money.*

59. Simon Newcomb, "The Standard of Value," *North American Review* 129, no. 274 (1879): 223–37.
60. Perry Mehrling, "Economists and the Fed: Beginnings," *Journal of Economic Perspectives* 16, no. 4 (2002): 207–18, at 211.

Chapter Five

1. Woodrow Wilson, "Address to Fellow Countrymen," July 11, 1917, quoted in Rockoff, *Drastic Measures*, 43.
2. Gary Richardson and Tim Sablik, "Banking Panics of the Gilded Age," Federal Reserve History, https://www.federalreservehistory.org/essays/banking-panics-of-the-gilded-age.
3. F. M. Taylor, "Do We Want an Elastic Currency?," *Political Science Quarterly* 11, no. 1 (1896): 133–57, at 134.
4. Michael Bordo and David Wheelock, "The Promise and Performance of the Federal Reserve as Lender of Last Resort 1914–1933," in *The Origins, History, and Future of the Federal Reserve: A Return to Jekyll Island*, ed. by Michael D. Bordo and William Roberds (Cambridge: Cambridge University Press, 2013), 59–98.
5. Nelson Aldrich, *Publications of National Monetary Commission* (Washington, DC: Government Printing Office, 1912), 41.
6. Arsene Pujo, *Report of the Committee Appointed Pursuant to House Resolutions 429 and 504 to Investigate the Concentration of Control of Money and Credit* (Washington, DC: Government Printing Office, February 28, 1913), 130.
7. George Selgin, "New York's Bank: The National Monetary Commission and the Founding of the Fed," *Cato Policy Analysis*, no. 793 (2016), https://www.cato.org/publications/policy-analysis/new-yorks-bank-national-monetary-commission-founding-fed.
8. Carter Glass, *An Adventure in Constructive Finance* (New York: Doubleday, Page and Co., 1927), 82.
9. Allan Meltzer, *A History of the Federal Reserve*, vol. 1, *1913–1951* (Chicago: University of Chicago Press, 2003), 72.
10. Robert W. Dimand, "Competing Visions for the US Monetary System, 1907–1913: The Quest for an Elastic Currency and the Rejection of Fisher's Compensated Dollar Rule for Price Stability," *Cahiers d'Économie Politique* 2, no. 45 (2003): 101–21.
11. Federal Reserve Act of 1913, sec. 16 "Note Issues."
12. Federal Reserve Act of 1913, sec. 14, "Open-Market Operations."
13. David Wheelock, "The Fed's Formative Years," Federal Reserve History, https://www.federalreservehistory.org/essays/feds-formative-years.
14. Meltzer, *History of the Federal Reserve*, 74.
15. Saladin Ambar, "The Campaign and Election of 1912," Miller Center, https://millercenter.org/president/wilson/campaigns-and-elections.
16. George C. Leef, "The Lost Contract Clause," *Regulation*, Summer 2017, https://www.cato.org/regulation/summer-2017/contract-clause.
17. Holden v. Hardy, 169 U.S. 366 (1898).

18. Lochner v. New York, 198 U.S. 45 (1905).
19. David Bernstein, "Liberty of Contract" (George Mason Law and Economics Research Paper No. 08-51), in *Encyclopedia of the Supreme Court of the United States*, ed. David S. Tanenhaus, Kay P. Kindred, Felice Batlan, Alfred L. Brophy, and Mark A. Graber (Detroit: Macmillan, 2008), https://papers.ssrn.com/sol3/papers.cfm?abstract_id=1239749.
20. Woodrow Wilson, "On Labor," 1912, at "Hear Wilson's Speech on Labor," History Matters, https://historymatters.gmu.edu/d/5723/.
21. Price V. Fishback and Andrew J. Seltzer, "The Rise of American Minimum Wages, 1912–1968," *Journal of Economic Perspectives* 35, no. 1 (2021): 73–96.
22. Stettler v. O'Hara, 243 U.S. 629 (1917).
23. Woodrow Wilson, "The Study of Administration," *Political Science Quarterly* 2, no. 2 (1887): 197–222, at 197.
24. Wilson, 198.
25. Wilson, 214.
26. Quoted in Tom Hall, "Wilson and the Food Crisis: Agricultural Price Control during World War I," *Agricultural History* 47, no. 1 (1973): 32.
27. Hall, 31.
28. Paul Studenski and Herman Krooss, *Financial History of the United States* (Washington, DC: Beard Books, 1952), 286–87.
29. Meltzer, *History of the Federal Reserve*, 84.
30. Meltzer, 85.
31. Meltzer, 85.
32. Wheelock, "Fed's Formative Years."
33. Friedman and Schwartz, *Monetary History of the United States*, 212.
34. Meltzer, *History of the Federal Reserve*, 89.
35. Hall, "Wilson and the Food Crisis," 25.
36. Hall, 25.
37. "The High Cost of Living: What Our Readers Are Doing—and Thinking—about It," *The Independent*, April 7, 1917.
38. "The High Cost of Living."
39. Agnes C. Laut, "An Era of High Prices: The Cost of Living Increased a Hundredfold," *Business World* 61, no. 4 (October 1916): 273.
40. Laut, 273.
41. Hall, "Wilson and the Food Crisis," 34.
42. Quoted in Hall, 31.
43. Hall, 35.
44. Quoted in Hall, 36.
45. "Living Cost Exhibit Opens: Intended to Show Reasons for High Prices and the Remedies," *New York Times*, February 5, 1917.
46. Hall, "Wilson and the Food Crisis," 38.
47. "Contrast Food Riots and Revels as Senate Discusses Living Cost; French Revolution Is Recalled," *Washington Post*, February 22, 1917.

48. Hall, "Wilson and the Food Crisis," 40.
49. Hall, 40.
50. Hall, 42–45.
51. Rockoff, *Drastic Measures*, 51–52.
52. William E. Leuchtenburg, *Herbert Hoover: The American Presidents Series: The 31st President, 1929–1933* (New York: Henry Holt and Co., 2009), 33.
53. Rockoff, *Drastic Measures*, 51.
54. Rockoff, 43.
55. Paul Hannah, "Some Aspects of Price Control in Wartime," *Cornell Law Review* 27, no. 1 (1941): 21–55, at 22.
56. Hannah, "Some Aspects of Price Control in Wartime," 22–23.
57. Quoted in *Price-Control Bill: Hearings before the Committee on Banking and Currency, House of Representatives, Seventy-seventh Congress, First Session, on H.R. 5479* (Washington, DC: Government Printing Office, 1941), 228.
58. Rockoff, *Drastic Measures*, 47.
59. B. W. Patch, "Excess Profits Tax," *Editorial Research Reports II* (1950), CQ Researcher, http://library.cqpress.com/cqresearcher/cqresrre1950110300.
60. Hugh Rockoff, "Until It's Over, Over There: The US Economy in World War I," in *The Economics of World War I*, ed. Stephen Broadberry and Mark Harrison (Cambridge: Cambridge University Press, 2005), 310–43.
61. Martin Luther Pearson, *The Effects of Government Price-Fixing on Wheat* (Bloomington: Indiana University Press, 1920), 55.
62. Albert Merritt, *War Time Control of Distribution of Foods* (New York: Macmillan Co., 1920).
63. For these data, see "Consumer Price Index: All Items for the United States," FRED, https://fred.stlouisfed.org/series/M04128USM350NNBR.
64. Rockoff, *Drastic Measures*, 81.
65. Rockoff, 78.
66. Rockoff, 82.
67. *Historical Studies of Wartime Problems* (Washington, DC: Bureau of Labor Statistics, 1943), 1.
68. Leland Crabbe, "The International Gold Standard and US Monetary Policy from World War I to the New Deal," *Federal Reserve Bulletin* (1989): 423–40, at 427.
69. W. M. Persons, "The Crisis of 1920 in the United States: A Quantitative Survey," *American Economic Review* 12, no. 1 (March 1922, suppl.): 5–19.
70. Herbert E. Stats, "Termination of War Contracts," in *Editorial Research Reports* (Washington, DC: CQ Press, 1944), 1:339–53, http://library.cqpress.com/cqresearcher/cqresrre1944051600.
71. Board of Governors of the Federal Reserve System, *Federal Reserve Bulletin*, March 1919, https://fraser.stlouisfed.org/title/62/item/20587.
72. Crabbe, "International Gold Standard and US Monetary Policy from World War I to the New Deal," 427.
73. Crabbe, 427.

74. Crabbe, 427.
75. Friedman and Schwartz, *Monetary History of the United States*, 223–24.
76. W. P. G. Harding, *The Formative Period of the Federal Reserve System* (Boston: Houghton Mifflin, 1925), 223.
77. *Historical Studies of Wartime Problems*, 14.
78. Woodrow Wilson, "Address to Congress on the High Cost of Living," August 8, 1919, American Presidency Project, https://www.presidency.ucsb.edu/documents/address-congress-the-high-cost-living.
79. Wilson.
80. Woodrow Wilson, "Seventh Annual Message," December 2, 1919, Miller Center, https://millercenter.org/the-presidency/presidential-speeches/december-2-1919-seventh-annual-message.
81. Wilson.
82. Hugh Rockoff, "The Halo of Victory: What Americans Learned from World War," VoxEU, 2014, https://voxeu.org/article/us-learned-wrong-lessons-wwi.
83. Rockoff.
84. "An End of Price-Fixing," *Literary Digest*, May 24, 1919.
85. "Against Price Fixing," *Washington Post*, October 21, 1919.

Chapter Six

1. Fisher, *Stabilizing the Dollar*, 110.
2. Meltzer, *History of the Federal Reserve*, 103.
3. J. R. Vernon, "The 1920–21 Deflation: The Role of Aggregate Supply," *Economic Inquiry* 29, no. 3 (1999): 572–80, at 572.
4. Friedman and Schwartz, *Monetary History of the United States*, 231.
5. Gene Smiley, "The US Economy in the 1920s," *EH.Net Encyclopedia*, ed. Robert Whaples, June 29, 2004, https://eh.net/encyclopedia/the-u-s-economy-in-the-1920s/.
6. Lee Alson, Waye Grove, and David Wheelock, "Why Do Banks Fail? Evidence from the 1920s," *Explorations in Economic History* 31, no. 5 (1994): 409–31.
7. Quoted in Friedman and Schwartz, *Monetary History of the United States*, 228.
8. Warren Harding, "Readjustment," May 14, 2020, Miller Center, https://millercenter.org/the-presidency/presidential-speeches/may-14-1920-readjustment.
9. Harding.
10. United States v. Cohen Grocery Co., 255 U.S. 81 (1921).
11. Joint Resolution Declaring That Certain Acts of Congress, Joint Resolutions, and Proclamations Shall Be Construed as If the War Had Ended and the Present or Existing Emergency Expired, 41 Stat. 136 (1921).
12. Rockoff, "Until It's Over, Over There."
13. "Wilson Tariff Veto Sustained by House," *New York Times*, March 4, 1921.
14. Edward S. Kaplan, "The Fordney-McCumber Tariff of 1922," in *EH.Net Encyclopedia*, ed. Robert Whaples, March 16, 2008, http://eh.net/encyclopedia/the-fordney-mccumber-tariff-of-1922/.

15. Friedman and Schwartz, *Monetary History of the United States*, 234.
16. Bernstein, "Liberty of Contract."
17. Bernstein.
18. Adkins v. Children's Hospital, 261 U.S. 525 (1923).
19. Block v. Hirsh, 256 U.S. 135 (1921).
20. Chastleton Corp. v. Sinclair, 264 U.S. 543 (1924).
21. Friedman and Schwartz, *Monetary History of the United States*, 251.
22. Friedman and Schwartz, 226.
23. Priscilla Roberts, "Benjamin Strong, the Federal Reserve, and the Limits to Interwar American Nationalism," *Federal Reserve Bank of Richmond Economic Quarterly* 86, no. 2 (2000): 61–98.
24. Crabbe, "International Gold Standard and US Monetary Policy from World War I to the New Deal," 426.
25. Barry Eichengreen, *Elusive Stability: Essays in the History of International Finance 1919–1939* (New York: Cambridge University Press, 1990), 125–29.
26. Barry Eichengreen, *Golden Fetters: The Gold Standard and the Great Depression 1919–1939* (New York: Oxford University Press, 1992), 5.
27. Eichengreen, 5.
28. Eichengreen, 9.
29. Eichengreen, 9.
30. Eichengreen, 9.
31. Eichengreen, 9.
32. Benjamin Strong, in United States, Order of Railroad Station Agents, *The Station Agent: Official Publication of the Order of Railroad Station Agents* 3, no. 1 (August 1922): 19.
33. Eichengreen, *Golden Fetters*, 13.
34. William Jennings Bryan, *Hearst's International Magazine*, November 1923, 23.
35. Fisher, *Stabilizing the Dollar*, 105.
36. Fisher, 55.
37. Quoted in "Fisher Supports Bill to Stabilize the Dollar," *New York Times*, December 19, 1922.
38. *Stabilization: Hearings before the Committee on Banking and Currency on H.R. 7895, a Bill to Amend Paragraph (d) of Section 14 of the Federal Reserve Act, as Amended, to Provide for the Stabilization of the Price Level for Commodities in General*, 69th Cong. (1926).
39. Carl Snyder, "The Stabilization of Gold: A Plan," *American Economic Review* 13, no. 2 (1923): 276–85, at 279.
40. Snyder, 279.
41. *Stabilization: Hearings before the Committee on Banking and Currency on H.R. 7895*, 69th Cong. 5 (1926) (James Strong, "Amendment to the Federal Reserve Act," speech on February 20, 1926).
42. *Stabilization: Hearings before the Committee on Banking and Currency on H.R. 11806, a Bill to Amend the Act Approved December 23, 1913, Known as the Federal Reserve Act; to Define Certain Policies toward Which the Powers of the Federal Reserve*

System Shall Be Directed; to Further Promote the Maintenance of a Stable Gold Standard; to Promote the Stability of Commerce, Industry, Agriculture, and Employment; to Assist in Realizing a More Stable Purchasing Power of the Dollar; and For Other Purposes, 70th Cong. 4 (1928).

43. *Stabilization*, 70th Cong. 194.
44. *Stabilization*, 70th Cong. 194.
45. George Henry Shibley, *The Money Question: The 50% Fall in General Prices, the Evil Effects; the Remedy, Bimetallism at 16 to 1 and Governmental Control of Paper Money in Order to Secure a Stable Measure of Prices—Stable Money* (Chicago: Stable Money Pub., 1896).
46. Thomas Goebel, "'A Case of Democratic Contagion': Direct Democracy in the American West, 1890–1920," *Pacific Historical Review* 66, no. 2 (1997): 213–30.
47. *Stabilization*, 69th Cong. 16.
48. *Stabilization*, 69th Cong. 13.
49. *Stabilization*, 69th Cong. 292–93.
50. *Stabilization*, 69th Cong. 294.
51. *Stabilization*, 69th Cong. 295.
52. Robert Shiller, "Why Do People Dislike Inflation?," in *Reducing Inflation: Motivation and Strategy*, ed. Christina Romer and David Romer (Chicago: University of Chicago Press, 1997), 13–70.
53. Quoted in Thomas Cargill, "Irving Fisher Comments on Benjamin Strong and the Federal Reserve in the 1930s," *Journal of Political Economy* 100, no. 2 (1992): 1273–77.
54. Hofstadter, *Age of Reform*.
55. O. Kile, "Congress and the Farm Problem," *Editorial Research Reports II* (1926), CQ Researcher, http://library.cqpress.com/cqresearcher/cqresrre1926050300.
56. Arthur C. Townley, November 28, 1921, nonpartisan leader, quoted in Hall, "Wilson and the Food Crisis," 46.
57. Bernard Baruch, "Some Aspects of the Farmers' Problem," *The Atlantic*, July 1921, https://www.theatlantic.com/magazine/archive/1921/07/some-aspects-of-the-farmers-problems/646916/.
58. Gilbert C. Fite, *George N. Peek and the Fight for Farm Parity* (Norman: University of Oklahoma Press, 1954), 29.
59. Quoted in Fite, 38.
60. George N. Peek and Hugh S. Johnson, *Equality for Agriculture* (Washington, DC: H. W. Harrington, 1922), 3.
61. Murray R. Benedict, *Farm Policies of the United States, 1790–1950* (New York: Twentieth Century Fund, 1953), 212–13.
62. James H. Shideler, *Farm Crisis, 1919–1923* (Berkeley: University of California Press, 1958).
63. H.R. Doc. No. 195, at 171 (1922) (report of the National Agricultural Congress, Washington, DC, January 23–27, 1922).
64. Shideler, *Farm Crisis*, 199.

65. Joan Wilson, "Hoover's Agricultural Policies 1921–1928," *Agricultural History* 51, no. 2 (April 1977): 335–61, at 345.
66. Quoted in Wilson, 343.
67. Quoted in Wilson, 351.
68. Wilson, 343.
69. Shideler, *Farm Crisis*, 260.
70. Henry C. Wallace, *The Wheat Situation* (Washington, DC: Government Printing Office, 1923), 73.
71. Wallace, 74.
72. Benedict, *Farm Policies*, 216.
73. Wilson, "Hoover's Agricultural Policies," 358.
74. Benedict, *Farm Policies*, 228.
75. Shideler, *Farm Crisis*.
76. Gary Richardson, Daniel Park, Alejandro Komai, and Michael Gou, "The McFadden Act of 1927," Federal Reserve History, https://www.federalreservehistory.org/essays/mcfadden-act.
77. Tim Todd, *The Balance of Power: The Political Fight for an Independent Central Bank, 1790-Present* (Kansas City, MO: Federal Reserve Bank of Kansas City, 2012).
78. Federal Reserve Bank of New York, "Thirteenth Annual Report for the Year Ended December 31, 1927" (New York: Federal Reserve Bank of New York, 1927), 16, https://fraser.stlouisfed.org/files/docs/historical/frbny/1927_frb_newyork.pdf.
79. "Chicago Fed History: 1915–1939," Federal Reserve Bank of Chicago, https://www.chicagofed.org/Home/utilities/about-us/history/chicago-fed-history-1915-1939.
80. Friedman and Schwartz, *Monetary History of the United States*, 254.
81. Quoted in Friedman and Schwartz, 254.
82. James D. Hamilton, "Monetary Factors in the Great Depression," *Journal of Monetary Economics* 19 (1987): 145–69.
83. Friedman and Schwartz, *Monetary History of the United States*, 289.
84. Timothy Cogley, "Monetary Policy and the Great Crash of 1929: A Bursting Bubble or Collapsing Fundamentals?," *Federal Reserve Bank of San Francisco Economic Research*, no. 10 (1999), https://www.frbsf.org/economic-research/publications/economic-letter/1999/march/monetary-policy-and-the-great-crash-of-1929-a-bursting-bubble-or-collapsing-fundamentals/; Eichengreen, *Golden Fetters*, 15.

Chapter Seven

1. Franklin Delano Roosevelt, "First Inaugural Address," March 4, 1933, Miller Center, https://millercenter.org/the-presidency/presidential-speeches/march-4-1933-first-inaugural-address.
2. Friedman and Schwartz, *Monetary History of the United States*, 264.
3. For these data, see "Industrial Production: Total Index," FRED, https://fred.stlouisfed.org/series/INDPRO.

4. Gary Richardson, Alejandro Komai, Michael Gou, and Daniel Park, "Stock Market Crash of 1929," Federal Reserve History, 2013, https://www.federalreservehistory.org/essays/stock-market-crash-of-1929.
5. David Wheelock, "Monetary Policy in the Great Depression: What the Fed Did, and Why," *Federal Reserve Bank of St. Louis Review* 74, no. 2 (1992): 3–28.
6. For these data, see "Produce Price Index by Commodity: All Commodities," FRED, https://fred.stlouisfed.org/series/PPIACO; "Consumer Price Index: All Items for United States," FRED, https://fred.stlouisfed.org/series/M04128USM350NNBR.
7. Friedman and Schwartz, *Monetary History of the United States*, 297–98.
8. Eichengreen, *Golden Fetters*, 12.
9. Eichengreen, 15.
10. Barry Eichengreen and Peter Temin, "The Gold Standard and the Great Depression," *Contemporary European History* 9, no. 2 (2000): 183–207.
11. Joshua Hausman, Paul Rhode, and Johannes Wieland, "Farm Product Prices, Redistribution, and the Early US Great Depression," *Journal of Economic History* 81, no. 3 (2021): 649–87.
12. Benedict, *Farm Policies*, 239.
13. Robert Whaples, "Where Is There Consensus among American Economic Historians? The Results of a Survey on Forty Propositions," *Journal of Economic History* 55, no. 1 (1995): 139–54.
14. Barry Eichengreen and Peter Temin, "Ideology and the Shadow of History," in *The Economic Future in Historical Perspective*, ed. Mark Thomas and Paul A. David (Oxford: Oxford University Press, 2006), 13:357.
15. Barry Eichengreen, *Globalizing Capital: A History of the International Monetary System* (Princeton, NJ: Princeton University Press, 1996), 52.
16. Ben Bernanke and Harold James, "The Gold Standard, Deflation, and Financial Crisis in the Great Depression: An International Comparison," in *Financial Markets and Financial Crises*, ed. R. Glenn Hubbard (Chicago: University of Chicago Press, 1991), 33–68, at 44.
17. Irving Fisher, *Booms and Depressions* (New York: Adelphi, 1932), 202.
18. William T. Gavin, "In Defense of Zero Inflation" (Working Paper No. 9005, Federal Reserve Bank of Cleveland, Cleveland, OH, 1990).
19. *Restoring and Maintaining the Average Purchasing Power of the Dollar: Hearings before the Committee on Banking and Currency*, 72nd Cong. 1 (1932), available at https://fraser.stlouisfed.org/title/791.
20. Quoted in Irving Fisher, *Stable Money: A History of the Movement* (New York: Adelphi, 1934), 199.
21. Fisher, 120.
22. Quoted in Fisher, 202.
23. Jim Saxton, *Establishing Federal Reserve Inflation Goals* (Washington, DC: Joint Economic Committee, US Congress, 1997).
24. Michael Gou, Gary Richardson, Alejandro Komai, and Daniel Park, "Recon-

struction Finance Corporation Act," Federal Reserve History, https://www.federalreservehistory.org/essays/reconstruction-finance-corporation.

25. James Butkiewicz, "The Impact of a Lender of Last Resort During the Great Depression: The Case of the Reconstruction Finance Corporation," *Explorations in Economic History* 32, no. 2 (1995): 197–216.
26. Parinitha Sastry, "The Political Origins of Section 13(3) of the Federal Reserve Act," *Federal Reserve Bank of New York Economic Policy Review* 24, no. 1 (2018): 1–33.
27. Quoted in Chang-Tai Hsieh and Christina Romer, "Was the Federal Reserve Constrained by the Gold Standard During the Great Depression? Evidence from the 1932 Open Market Purchase Program," *Journal of Economic History* 66, no. 1 (2006): 140–76.
28. Michael Bordo and Arunima Sinha, "A Lesson from the Great Depression That the Fed Might Have Learned: A Comparison of the 1932 Open Market Purchases with Quantitative Easing," Working Paper No. 22581, National Bureau of Economic Research, Cambridge, MA, 2016), 3.
29. Quoted in Bordo and Sinha, 20.
30. Bordo and Sinha, 32.
31. Hsieh and Romer, "Was the Federal Reserve Constrained by the Gold Standard During the Great Depression?," 142.
32. Francesca Carapella, "Banking Panics and Deflation in Dynamic General Equilibrium," *Finance and Economics Discussion Series, Federal Reserve Board of Governors*, no. 18 (2015): 3; Bernanke and James, "The Gold Standard, Deflation, and Financial Crisis in the Great Depression," 34.
33. Franklin Delano Roosevelt, "Campaign Address in Topeka, Kansas on the Farm Problem," September 14, 1932, American Presidency Project, https://www.presidency.ucsb.edu/documents/campaign-address-topeka-kansas-the-farm-problem.
34. James S. Olson, "Rehearsal for Disaster: Hoover, the R. F. C., and the Banking Crisis in Nevada, 1932–1933," *Western Historical Quarterly* 6, no. 2 (1975): 149–61.
35. *Agricultural Adjustment Relief Plan: Hearings on H.R. 13991 before the Senate Committee on Agriculture and Forestry*, 72nd Cong. 15 (1933).
36. *Commercial & Financial Chronicle*, January 28, 1933, quoted in Barrie A. Wigmore, "Was the Bank Holiday of 1933 Caused by a Run on the Dollar?," *Journal of Economic History* 47, no. 3 (1987): 739–55, at 74.
37. Fisher, *Stable Money*, 120.
38. Wigmore, "Was the Bank Holiday of 1933 Caused by a Run on the Dollar?," 743.
39. Herbert Hoover, "Address at the Coliseum in Des Moines, Iowa," October 4, 1932, American Presidency Project, https://www.presidency.ucsb.edu/documents/address-the-coliseum-des-moines-iowa.
40. George Selgin, "The New Deal and Recovery, Part 5: The Banking Crisis," Cato at Liberty 2020, https://www.cato.org/blog/new-deal-recovery-part-5-banking-crisis.
41. Franklin D. Roosevelt, "First Inaugural Address," March 4, 1933, Miller Center,

https://millercenter.org/the-presidency/presidential-speeches/march-4-1933-first-inaugural-address.

42. Elmus Wicker, "Roosevelt's 1933 Monetary Experiment," *Journal of American History* 57, no. 4 (1971): 864–79, at 866.
43. George Selgin, "The New Deal and Recovery, Part 6: The National Bank Holiday," Cato at Liberty, 2020, https://www.cato.org/blog/new-deal-recovery-part-6-national-bank-holiday.
44. Franklin Delano Roosevelt, "Fireside Chat 1: On the Banking Crisis," March 12, 1933, Miller Center, https://millercenter.org/the-presidency/presidential-speeches/march-12-1933-fireside-chat-1-banking-crisis.
45. Selgin, "National Bank Holiday."
46. "Agricultural Adjustment Act of 1933," box 54, folder 1, William McChesney Martin Jr. Papers, FRASER, Federal Reserve, https://fraser.stlouisfed.org/archival-collection/william-mcchesney-martin-jr-papers-1341/agricultural-adjustment-act-1933-457089.
47. Wicker, "Roosevelt's 1933 Monetary Experiment," 867.
48. Wicker, 865.
49. Franklin D. Roosevelt, "Wireless to the London Conference," July 3, 1933, American Presidency Project, https://www.presidency.ucsb.edu/documents/wireless-the-london-conference.
50. James Warburg, "Reply to Senator Elmer Thomas and Professor Irving Fisher," *Annals of the American Academy of Political and Social Science* 171 (1934): 144–51, at 145.
51. James Warburg, "Reply to Senator Elmer Thomas and Professor Irving Fisher," *Annals of the American Academy of Political and Social Science* 171 (1934): 144–51, at 146.
52. Warburg, 148.
53. Franklin Delano Roosevelt, "Fireside Chat 4: On Economic Progress," October 22, 1933, Miller Center, https://millercenter.org/the-presidency/presidential-speeches/october-22-1933-fireside-chat-4-economic-progress.
54. Fisher, *Stable Money*, 61. On Warren, see Scott Sumner, "Roosevelt, Warren, and the Gold-Buying Program of 1933," *Research in Economic History* 20 (2001): 135–72.
55. George Selgin, "The New Deal and Recovery, Part 7: FDR and Gold," Cato at Liberty, 2020, https://www.cato.org/blog/new-deal-recovery-part-7-fdr-gold.
56. Joshua K. Hausman, Paul W. Rhode, and Johannes F. Wieland, "Recovery from the Great Depression: The Farm Channel in Spring 1933," *American Economic Review* 109, no. 2 (2019): 427–72.
57. Fisher, "Debt-Deflation Theory of Great Depressions," 346–47.
58. Fisher, *Stable Money*, 213.
59. *Hearings before the Subcommittee of the Committee on Banking and Currency on H.R. 7157 as Amended and Reintroduced as H.R. 8780, a Bill to Establish the Federal Monetary Authority and to Control the Currency of the United States*, 73rd Cong. (1934).

60. *Hearings before the Subcommittee of the Committee on Banking and Currency*, 73rd Cong. (1934).
61. Gary Richardson, Alejandro Komai, and Michael Gou, "Banking Act of 1935," Federal Reserve History, https://www.federalreservehistory.org/essays/banking-act-of-1935.
62. Richardson, Komai, and Gou.
63. Richard Timberlake, "The Tale of Another Chairman," *Federal Reserve Bank of Minneapolis* 13, no. 2 (1999): 32–35.
64. Timberlake, 32–35.
65. Barbara Alexander, "The National Recovery Administration," in *EH.Net Encyclopedia*, ed. Robert Whaples, August 14, 2001, http://eh.net/encyclopedia/the-national-recovery-administration/.
66. Franklin Delano Roosevelt, "Statement on the National Industrial Recovery Act," June 16, 1933, American Presidency Project, https://www.presidency.ucsb.edu/documents/statement-signing-the-national-industrial-recovery-act.
67. Roosevelt.
68. Alexander, "National Recovery Administration."
69. Alexander.
70. Gardiner Means, *Industrial Prices and their Relative Inflexibility* (Washington, DC: US Government Printing Office, 1935), 24.
71. Means, 25–29.
72. "Dollar Men and Prices," *Time Magazine*, January 21, 1935.
73. Harold L. Cole and Lee E. Ohanian, "New Deal Policies and the Persistence of the Great Depression: A General Equilibrium Analysis," *Journal of Political Economy* 112, no. 4 (2004): 779–816.
74. Christopher Hanes, "Explaining Anomalous Wage Inflation in the 1930s United States," *Journal of Economic History* 80, no. 4 (2020): 1031–70.
75. For these data, see "Industrial Production: Total Index," FRED, https://fred.stlouisfed.org/series/INDPRO; "Unemployment Rate for United States," FRED, https://fred.stlouisfed.org/series/M0892AUSM156SNBR.
76. Lochner v. New York, 198 U.S. 45 (1905).
77. Adkins v. Children's Hospital, 261 U.S. 525 (1923).
78. Bernstein, "Liberty of Contract."
79. Nebbia v. New York, 291 U.S. 502 (1934).
80. Nebbia v. New York, 291 U.S. 502.
81. Nebbia v. New York, 291 U.S. 502.
82. Bernard F. Grainey, "Price Control and the Emergency Price Control Act," *Notre Dame Law Review* (1943): 31–50.
83. Norman v. Baltimore & Ohio Railroad Co., with United States v. Bankers Trust Co., 294 U.S. 240 (1935); Nortz v. United States, 294 U.S. 317 (1935); Perry v. United States, 294 U.S. 330 (1935); David Glick, "Conditional Strategic Retreat: The Court's Concession in the 1935 Gold Clause Cases," *Journal of Politics* 71, no. 3 (2009): 800–816.

84. Gary Richardson, Alejandro Komai, and Michael Gou, "Roosevelt's Gold Program," Federal Reserve History, https://www.federalreservehistory.org/essays/roosevelts-gold-program.
85. Perry v. United States, 294 U.S. at 347.
86. Gerard N. Magliocca, "The Gold Clause Cases and Constitutional Necessity," *Florida Law Review* 64, no. 5 (2012): 1243–78.
87. Magliocca, 1259.
88. Magliocca, 1247.
89. Glick, "Conditional Strategic Retreat," 807.
90. Panama Refining Co. v. Ryan, 293 U.S. 388 (1935); Schechter Corp. v. United States, 295 U.S. 495 (1935).
91. J. W. Hampton Co. v. United States, 276 U.S. 394 (1928).
92. Carter v. Carter Coal Co., 298 U.S. 238 (1936).
93. United States v. Butler, 297 U.S. 1 (1936).
94. Franklin Delano Roosevelt, "Statement on a More Permanent Plan for American Agriculture," October 25, 1935, American Presidency Project, https://www.presidency.ucsb.edu/documents/statement-more-permanent-plan-for-american-agriculture.
95. Franklin D. Roosevelt, "Fireside Chat 9: On 'Court Packing,'" March 9, 1937, Miller Center, https://millercenter.org/the-presidency/presidential-speeches/march-9-1937-fireside-chat-9-court-packing.
96. Carter Glass, "Radio Address on Judicial Reorganization," March 29, 1937, Teaching American History, https://teachingamericanhistory.org/document/radio-address-on-judicial-reorganization/.
97. West Coast Hotel v. Parrish, 300 U.S. 379 (1937); Adkins v. Children's Hospital, 261 U.S. 525.
98. National Labor Relations Board v. Jones & Laughlin Steel Corp., 301 U.S. 1 (1937).
99. For these data, see "Producer Price Index by Commodity: All Commodities," FRED, https://fred.stlouisfed.org/series/PPIACO; "Consumer Price Index for All Urban Consumers: All Items in US City Average," FRED, https://fred.stlouisfed.org/series/CPIAUCNS.
100. Jacobs, "'How about Some Meat?,'" 915.
101. Michael Roberto, *The Coming of the American Behemoth: The Origins of Fascism in the United States, 1920–1940* (New York: NYU Press, 2018), 330.
102. Rockoff, *Drastic Measures*, 87.
103. For these data, see "Industrial Production: Total Index," FRED, https://fred.stlouisfed.org/series/INDPRO; "Unemployment Rate for United States," FRED, https://fred.stlouisfed.org/series/M0892AUSM156SNBR.
104. Joshua Hausman, "What Was Bad for General Motors Was Bad for America: The Automobile Industry and the 1937/38 Recession," *Journal of Economic History* 76, no. 2 (2016): 427–77; Patricia Waiwood, "Recession of 1937–38," Federal Reserve History, https://www.federalreservehistory.org/essays/recession-of-1937-38.
105. Charles P. Stewart, "Buying Power Is Prosperity's Key," *Henderson Daily Dispatch*,

February 4, 1938, 5, https://chroniclingamerica.loc.gov/lccn/sn91068401/1938-02-04/ed-1/seq-5/.

106. Stewart, "Buying Power Is Prosperity's Key," 5.

107. Franklin D. Roosevelt, "Message to Congress on Curbing Monopolies," April 29, 1938, American Presidency Project, https://www.presidency.ucsb.edu/documents/message-congress-curbing-monopolies.

108. Roosevelt.

Chapter Eight

1. *Defense Production Act of 1950: Hearings before the Committee on Banking and Currency on S. 3936, a Bill to Establish a System of Priorities and Allocations for Materials and Facilities, Authorize the Requisitioning Thereof, Provide Financial Assistance for Expansion of Productive Capacity and Supply, Strengthen Controls over Credit, Regulate Speculation on Commodity Exchanges, and by These Measures Facilitate the Production of Goods and Services Necessary for the National Security, and for Other Purposes*, 81st Cong. 99 (1950) (Bernard Baruch).
2. Geofrey T. Mills and Hugh Rockoff, "Business Attitudes towards Wage and Price Controls in World War II," *Business and Economic History* 12 (1983): 146–57.
3. Rockoff, *Drastic Measures*, 86.
4. Rockoff, 88.
5. Rockoff, 88.
6. Franklin D. Roosevelt, "Executive Order 8734 Establishing the Office of Price Administration and Civilian Supply, April 11, 1941, American Presidency Project, https://www.presidency.ucsb.edu/documents/executive-order-8734-establishing-the-office-price-administration-and-civilian-supply.
7. Emergency Price Control Act of 1942, Pub. L. No. 77-421, 56 Stat. 23 (1942).
8. Harvey Mansfield, *A Short History of OPA* (Washington, DC: Office of Temporary Controls, 1948), 275.
9. Mansfield, 276.
10. Rockoff, *Drastic Measures*, 91.
11. Robert L. Hetzel and Ralph F. Leach, "The Treasury-Fed Accord: A New Narrative Account," *Federal Reserve Bank of Richmond Economic Quarterly* 87, no. 1 (2001): 33–55, at 33.
12. Daniel Sanches, "The Second World War and Its Aftermath," Federal Reserve History, https://www.federalreservehistory.org/essays/wwii-and-its-aftermath.
13. Rockoff, *Drastic Measures*, 93.
14. Jacobs, "'How about Some Meat?,'" 916.
15. Quoted in Jacobs, 917.
16. Andrew H. Bartels, "The Office of Price Administration and the Legacy of the New Deal, 1939–1946," *Public Historian* 5, no. 3 (1983): 5–29.
17. Wickard v. Filburn, 317 U.S. 111 (1938).
18. Franklin D. Roosevelt, "Fireside Chat 22: On Inflation and Food Prices," Septem-

ber 7, 1942, Miller Center, https://millercenter.org/the-presidency/presidential-speeches/september-7-1942-fireside-chat-22-inflation-and-food-prices.

19. Franklin D. Roosevelt, "Executive Order 9250 Establishing the Office of Economic Stabilization," October 3, 1942, American Presidency Project, https://www.presidency.ucsb.edu/documents/executive-order-9250-establishing-the-office-economic-stabilization.
20. "US at War: Enter Grimly," *Time Magazine*, December 28, 1942, http://www.time.com/time/magazine/article/0%2C9171%2C886073%2C00.html.
21. Rockoff, *Drastic Measures*, 98.
22. "OPA Must Be Lovable," *Time Magazine*, August 9, 1943, https://content.time.com/time/subscriber/article/0,33009,766904,00.html.
23. Bartels, "Office of Price Administration and the Legacy of the New Deal," 19.
24. Mansfield, *A Short History of OPA*, 9.
25. Mansfield, 242.
26. Jacobs, "'How about Some Meat?,'" 912.
27. Bartels, "Office of Price Administration and the Legacy of the New Deal," 22.
28. Jacobs, "'How about Some Meat?,'" 920.
29. Franklin D. Roosevelt, "State of the Union Message to Congress," January 11, 1944, American Presidency Project, https://www.presidency.ucsb.edu/documents/state-the-union-message-congress.
30. Jacobs, "'How about Some Meat?,'" 913.
31. James Conde and Michael Greve, "Yakus and the Administrative State," *Harvard Journal of Law & Public Policy* 42, no. 3 (2019): 807–70, at 826–27.
32. Emergency Price Control Act of 1942, Pub. L. No. 77-421, 56 Stat. 23 (1942).
33. Joseph W. Aidlin, "The Constitutionality of the 1942 Price Control Act," *California Law Review* 30 (1942): 651–52.
34. Grainey, "Price Control and the Emergency Price Control Act."
35. Aidlin, "Constitutionality of the 1942 Price Control Act," 654.
36. Conde and Greve, "Yakus and the Administrative State," 827.
37. Conde and Greve, 827.
38. Lockerty v. Phillips, 319 U.S. 182 (1943).
39. Conde and Greve, "Yakus and the Administrative State," 827.
40. Yakus v. United States, 321 U.S. 414 (1944).
41. Hampton Co. v. United States, 276 U.S. 394 (1928).
42. Yakus v. United States, 321 U.S. 414.
43. Bowles v. Willingham, 321 U.S. 503 (1944).
44. Marriner Eccles, "Extension of Emergency Price Control Act of 1942," *Federal Reserve Bulletin*, April 1944, 329.
45. Bartels, "Office of Price Administration and the Legacy of the New Deal," 22.
46. Jacobs, "'How about Some Meat?,'" 933.
47. Harry Truman, "Radio Address to the American People on Wages and Prices in the Reconversion Period," October 30, 1945, American Presidency Project, https://www.presidency.ucsb.edu/documents/radio-address-the-american-people-wages-and-prices-the-reconversion-period.

48. "President Truman's Statement of Labor Policy," *New York Times,* August 16, 1945, available at http://www.ibiblio.org/pha/policy/1945/1945-08-16b.html.
49. Quoted in Francis Carlton, "The GM Strike: A New Stage in Collective Bargaining," *Antioch Review* 6, no. 3 (1946): 426–41, at 427.
50. Quoted in Carlton, 427.
51. Robert Hetzel, "The Evolution of US Monetary Policy" (Working Paper No. 18-1, Federal Reserve Bank of Richmond, Richmond, VA, 2018).
52. Jacobs, "'How about Some Meat?,'" 938.
53. Jacobs, 914.
54. Jacobs, 913–14.
55. Dwight Waldo, *The Administrative State: A Study of the Political Theory of American Public Administration* (New York: Ronald Press Co., 1948).
56. Franklin D. Roosevelt, "Message to Congress Recommending Reorganization of the Executive Branch," January 12, 1937, American Presidency Project, https://www.presidency.ucsb.edu/documents/message-congress-recommending-reorganization-the-executive-branch.
57. Roni Elias, "The Legislative History of the Administrative Procedure Act," *Fordham Environmental Law Review* 27, no. 2 (2015): 207–24.
58. Friedman and Schwartz, *Monetary History of the United States,* 596.
59. "Employment Act of 1946," Federal Reserve History, https://www.federalreservehistory.org/essays/employment-act-of-1946.
60. Sandra Kollen Ghizoni, "Creation of the Bretton Woods System," Federal Reserve History, https://www.federalreservehistory.org/essays/bretton-woods-created.
61. Hetzel, "Evolution of US Monetary Policy," 12.
62. Friedman and Schwartz, *Monetary History of the United States,* 626.
63. For these data, see "Consumer Price Index, All Items for United States," FRED, https://fred.stlouisfed.org/series/M04128USM350NNBR.
64. Quoted in Timberlake, "Tale of Another Chairman," 34.
65. Committee on Independent Regulatory Commissions, *Task Force Report on Regulatory Commissions, Appendix N* (report prepared for Commission on Organization of the Executive Branch of the Government, January 3, 1949), 109.
66. Committee on Independent Regulatory Commissions, 110.
67. Committee on Independent Regulatory Commissions, 111.
68. Committee on Independent Regulatory Commissions, 110.

Chapter Nine

1. Milton Friedman, "Should There Be an Independent Monetary Authority?," in *Search of a Monetary Constitution,* ed. Leland B. Yeager (Cambridge, MA: Harvard University Press, 1962), 219–43.
2. Quoted in Donna Miles, "Nation Marks Korean War's 60th Anniversary," National Guard, June 24, 2010, https://www.nationalguard.mil/News/Article/580701/nation-marks-korean-wars-60th-anniversary/.

3. "Paying for Korea," *The Economist*, August 26, 1950, 409, quoted in Carola Binder and Gillian Brunet, "Inflation Expectations and Consumption: Evidence from 1951," *Economic Inquiry* 60 (2022): 954–74, at 957.
4. David Ginsburg, "Price Stabilization 1950–1952: Retrospect and Prospect," *University of Pennsylvania Law Review* 100, no. 4 (1952): 514–43, at 518, 520, https://scholarship.law.upenn.edu/cgi/viewcontent.cgi?article=7992&context=penn_law_review.
5. Rockoff, *Drastic Measures*, 178.
6. Rockoff, 178.
7. Rockoff, 178.
8. "Paying for Korea," *The Economist*, August 26, 1950, 409–10.
9. James A. Durham, "Congressional Response to Administrative Regulation: The 1951 and 1952 Price Control Amendments," *Yale Law Journal* 62, no. 1 (1952): 1–53.
10. Donald L. Kemmerer, "Perspective on the Recent Actions of the Federal Reserve Authorities," *Analysts Journal* 6, no. 4 (1950): 7–9.
11. Rockoff, *Drastic Measures*, 179.
12. Rockoff, 181.
13. William Burt and William Kennedy, "Congressional Review of Price Control," *University of Pennsylvania Law Review* 101 (1952): 333–77, at 341.
14. Burt and Kennedy, 334–35.
15. Burt and Kennedy, 334–35.
16. Burt and Kennedy, 352.
17. Harry S. Truman, "Special Message to the Congress after Further Review of the Defense Production Act Amendments," August 23, 1951, American Presidency Project, https://www.presidency.ucsb.edu/documents/special-message-the-congress-after-further-review-the-defense-production-act-amendments.
18. Steve Crabtree, "The Gallup Brain: Americans and the Korean War," Gallup, February 4, 2003, https://news.gallup.com/poll/7741/gallup-brain-americans-korean-war.aspx.
19. Burt and Kennedy, "Congressional Review of Price Control," 361.
20. Herbert H. Hyman and Paul B. Sheatsley, "Political Appeal of President Eisenhower," *Public Opinion Quarterly* 17, no. 4 (1953): 443–60, at 443.
21. Rockoff, *Drastic Measures*, 185.
22. Friedman and Schwartz, *Monetary History of the United States*, 596.
23. Quoted in Timberlake, "Tale of Another Chairman," 34.
24. "Monetary, Credit and Fiscal Policies: Report of the Subcommittee of the Joint Committee on the Economic Report," Senate Doc. 129, January 1950, quoted in Timberlake, 35.
25. Friedman and Schwartz, *Monetary History of the United States*, 593–95.
26. Christina Romer and David Romer, "A Rehabilitation of Monetary Policy in the 1950's," *American Economic Review* 92, no. 2 (2002): 121–27.
27. Romer and Romer, 123.
28. Romer and Romer, 123.

29. A. W. Phillips. 1958. "The Relation between Unemployment and the Rate of Change of Money Wage Rates in the United Kingdom, 1861–1957," *Economica* 25 (100): 283–99.
30. Irving Fisher, "'I Discovered the Phillips Curve': A Statistical Relation between Unemployment and Price Changes," *Journal of Political Economy* 81, no. 2 (1973): 496–502.
31. Fisher, 498.
32. Fisher, 502.
33. Minutes of the Federal Open Market Committee (FOMC), October 4, 1955, 8, quoted in Romer and Romer, "Rehabilitation of Monetary Policy in the 1950's," 123.
34. Minutes of the FOMC, August 2, 1955, 13, quoted in Romer and Romer, "Rehabilitation of Monetary Policy in the 1950's," 122.
35. Quoted in "William McChesney Martin Jr.," Federal Reserve History, https://www.federalreservehistory.org/people/william-mcchesney-martin-jr.
36. Richard W. Gable, "The Politics and Economics of the 1957–1958 Recession," *Western Political Quarterly* 12, no. 2 (1959): 557–59, at 558–59.
37. *Hearings before the Joint Economic Committee: Pursuant to Sec. 5(a) of Public Law 304 (79th Congress)*, 86th Cong. 469 (1959), https://babel.hathitrust.org/cgi/pt?id=uc1.31822019289172&view=1up&seq=1.
38. *Hearings before the Joint Economic Committee: Pursuant to Sec. 5(a) of Public Law 304 (79th Congress)*, 86th Cong. 473 (1959), https://babel.hathitrust.org/cgi/pt?id=uc1.31822019289172&view=1up&seq=1.
39. Dwight D. Eisenhower, "Letter of Transmittal," in *Economic Report of the President* (Washington, DC: Government Printing Office: January 20, 1959), iii–vii, https://fraser.stlouisfed.org/files/docs/publications/ERP/1959/ERP_1959.pdf.
40. Eisenhower, vi.
41. Cabinet Committee on Price Stability for Economic Growth, "Interim Report to the President," *Annals of the American Academy of Political and Social Science* 326 (1959): 133–38.
42. Cabinet Committee on Price Stability for Economic Growth.
43. Cabinet Committee on Price Stability for Economic Growth.
44. Cabinet Committee on Price Stability for Economic Growth.
45. "Martin, the Money Man, Heads into a Fight: The Federal Reserve's Chairman Likes to Stay Aloof from Politics, but He Faces Election Year Tiff over Tight Money," *Business Week*, January 30, 1960.
46. "Martin, the Money Man, Heads into a Fight."
47. *Hearings before the Subcommittee on Defense Procurement of the Joint Economic Committee*, 86th Cong. 181 (February 1960).
48. *Hearings before the Subcommittee on Defense Procurement of the Joint Economic Committee*, 86th Cong. 181 (February 1960).
49. Allan Meltzer, "US Policy in the Bretton Woods Era," *Federal Reserve Bank of St. Louis* (1991): 54–85, at 58, https://files.stlouisfed.org/files/htdocs/publications/review/91/05/Bretton_May_Jun1991.pdf.

50. Meltzer, 56.
51. Meltzer, 58.
52. Meltzer, 57.
53. "Recession to Recovery, 1960–62: A Case Study in Flexible Monetary Policy," *Federal Reserve Bank of Atlanta Monthly Review* (1962): 1–6, at 4.
54. Meltzer, "US Policy in the Bretton Woods Era," 59.
55. Meltzer, 57.
56. For these data, see "Consumer Price Index for All Urban Consumers: All Items in US City Average," FRED, https://fred.stlouisfed.org/series/CPIAUCSL.
57. John F. Kennedy, "Press Conference 30," April 11, 1962, John F. Kennedy Presidential Library and Museum, https://www.jfklibrary.org/archives/other-resources/john-f-kennedy-press-conferences/news-conference-30.
58. Kennedy.
59. Quoted in David Lawder and Heather Timmons, "Analysis: Are High Prices Unpatriotic or as American as You Can Get?," Reuters, June 21, 2022, https://www.reuters.com/world/us/are-high-prices-unpatriotic-or-american-you-can-get-2022-06-21/.
60. Kent Germany, "Lyndon B. Johnson: Domestic Affairs," Miller Center, https://millercenter.org/president/lbjohnson/domestic-affairs.
61. Edward Berkowitz, "Medicare and Medicaid: The Past as Prologue," *Health Care Finance Review* 27, no. 2 (2005): 11–23.
62. Thomas B. Gore, "A Forgotten Landmark Medical Study from 1932 by the Committee on the Cost of Medical Care," *Proceedings of Baylor University Medical Center* 26, no. 2 (2013): 142–43.
63. Wright Patman, memoranda regarding responses to Patman, June 10, 1965, box 20, folder 9, series V, subseries A, Patman Hearings, 1962–1969, William McChesney Martin Jr. Papers, https://fraser.stlouisfed.org/archival/1341/item/472997, FRASER, Board of Governors of the Federal Reserve System.
64. Wright Patman, June 10, 1965.
65. "Banking: Fight over the Federal Reserve," *Time*, February 14, 1964, https://content.time.com/time/subscriber/article/0,33009,870767,00.html.
66. "Banking."
67. Quote from the home page of FOIA.gov.
68. Board of Governors of the Federal Reserve, "Preliminary Memorandum on S. 1160," 1966, https://nsarchive2.gwu.edu/NSAEBB/NSAEBB194/Document%2030.pdf.
69. Wright Patman, June 10, 1965.
70. Helen Fessenden, "1965: The Year the Fed and LBJ Clashed," *Federal Reserve Bank of Richmond Econ Focus* (2016), https://www.richmondfed.org/publications/research/econ_focus/2016/q3-4/federal_reserve.
71. Todd, *Balance of Power*.
72. Edward Nelson, *Milton Friedman and Economic Debate in the United States, 1932–1972*, vol. 1 (Chicago: University of Chicago Press, 2020).

73. Milton Friedman, *Dollars and Deficits* (Englewood Cliffs, NJ: Prentice Hall, 1968), quoted in Nelson, 68.
74. Fessenden, "Year the Fed and LBJ Clashed."
75. Romer and Romer, "Rehabilitation of Monetary Policy in the 1950's."
76. Milton Friedman, "The Role of Monetary Policy," *American Economic Review* 58, no. 1 (1968): 1–17.
77. Edmund Phelps, "Phillips Curves, Expectations of Inflation, and Optimal Unemployment over Time," *Economica* 34, no. 135 (1967): 254–81.
78. R. E. Parker, *Reflections on the Great Depression* (Cheltenham, UK: Edward Elgar Publishing, 2002), 46.
79. Michael Bordo and Hugh Rockoff, "The Influence of Irving Fisher on Milton Friedman's Monetary Economics," *Journal of the History of Economic Thought* 35, no. 2 (2013): 153–77.

Chapter Ten

1. Gerald Ford, Address to Joint Session of Congress and the Nation, August 13, 1971, American Presidency Project, https://www.presidency.ucsb.edu/documents/address-joint-session-the-congress.
2. N. Gregory Mankiw and Ricardo Reis, "Friedman's Presidential Address in the Evolution of Macroeconomic Thought," *Journal of Economic Perspectives* 32, no. 1 (2018): 81–96.
3. "Business: The Rising Risk of Recession," *Time*, December 19, 1969, https://content.time.com/time/subscriber/article/0,33009,941750-2,00.html.
4. Milton Friedman, "A New Chairman at the Fed," *Newsweek*, February 2, 1970, 68, available at the Hoover Institution Library and Archives, https://miltonfriedman.hoover.org/internal/media/dispatcher/214051/full.
5. "Business: The Rising Risk of Recession," *Time*, December 19, 1969, https://content.time.com/time/subscriber/article/0,33009,941750–2,00.html.
6. Friedman, "A New Chairman at the Fed," 68.
7. Quoted in Edward Nelson, "Friedman and the Federal Reserve Chairs in the 1970s," in *Milton Friedman: Contributions to Economics and Public Policy*, ed. J. Daniel Hammond and Robert A. Cord (Oxford: Oxford University Press, 2016), 313–33, at 319.
8. Friedman, "New Chairman at the Fed," 68.
9. Quoted in Burton Abrams, "How Richard Nixon Pressured Arthur Burns: Evidence from the Nixon Tapes," *Journal of Economic Perspectives* 20, no. 4 (2006): 177–88, at 186.
10. Nelson, "Friedman and the Federal Reserve Chairs in the 1970s."
11. Quoted in Nelson, "Friedman and the Federal Reserve Chairs in the 1970s," 327.
12. Nelson.
13. Rockoff, *Drastic Measures*, 201.
14. Jacobs, "'How about Some Meat?,'" 911.

15. Quoted in Abrams and Butkiewicz, "The Political Economy of Wage and Price Controls: Evidence from the Nixon Tapes," *Public Choice* 170 (2017): 63–78.
16. Phillip Cagan, "Controls and Monetary Policy," in *A New Look at Inflation: Economic Policy in the Early 1970s* (Washington, DC: American Enterprise Institute for Public Policy Research, 1973), 13.
17. Richard Nixon, "Address to the Nation Outlining a New Economic Policy: 'The Challenge of Peace,'" August 15, 1971, American Presidency Project, https://www.presidency.ucsb.edu/documents/address-the-nation-outlining-new-economic-policy-the-challenge-peace.
18. *Economic Report of the President Transmitted to the Congress* (Washington, DC: Government Printing Office, 1972), 69.
19. Cagan, "Controls and Monetary Policy," 15.
20. Cagan.
21. Amalgamated Meat Cutters v. Connally, 337 F. Supp. 737 (1971).
22. Burton Abrams, "How Richard Nixon Pressured Arthur Burns: Evidence from the Nixon Tapes," *Journal of Economic Perspectives* 20, no. 4 (2006): 177–88.
23. Gene Healy, "Remembering Nixon's Wage and Price Controls," August 16, 2011, Cato Institute, https://www.cato.org/commentary/remembering-nixons-wage-price-controls.
24. Philip Shabecoff, "Phase 3—Big Step toward a Free Economy," *New York Times*, January 14, 1973, https://timesmachine.nytimes.com/timesmachine/1973/01/14/issue.html.
25. Edward Cowan, "Mandatory Wage-Price Controls Ended Except in Food, Health, Building Fields," *New York Times*, January 12, 1973.
26. R. W. Apple Jr., "Nixon Freezes Prices for up to 60 Days, Then Will Establish Phase 4 Controls," *New York Times*, June 14, 1973, https://timesmachine.nytimes.com/timesmachine/1973/06/14/90446785.html.
27. Quoted in "Business and Labor Say Freeze Fails to Meet Problems," *New York Times*, June 14, 1973, https://timesmachine.nytimes.com/timesmachine/1973/06/14/90446785.html.
28. Cagan, "Controls and Monetary Policy," 2–3.
29. Milton Friedman, "Three Views of Nixonomics and Where It Leads," *Newsweek*, January 31, 1972, available at the Hoover Institution Library and Archives, https://miltonfriedman.hoover.org/internal/media/dispatcher/214088/full.
30. *How Well Are Fluctuating Exchange Rates Working? Hearings before the Joint Economic Committee, Subcommittee on International Economics*, 93rd Cong. 130 (1973).
31. Rockoff, *Drastic Measures*, 211–12.
32. Arthur Burns, "Letter on Monetary Policy," *Federal Reserve Bank of St. Louis Review*, November 1973, 15–22.
33. Milton Friedman, "Letter on Monetary Policy," *Federal Reserve Bank of St. Louis Review*, March 1974, 20–23.
34. Rockoff, *Drastic Measures*, 212.
35. For these data, see "Consumer Price Index for All Urban Consumers: All Items

in US City Average," FRED, https://fred.stlouisfed.org/series/CPIAUCSL; "Unemployment Rate," FRED, https://fred.stlouisfed.org/series/UNRATE.

36. Andrew D. Moran, "More Than a Caretaker: The Economic Policy of Gerald R. Ford," *Presidential Studies Quarterly* 41, no. 1 (2011): 39–63, at 41.
37. Gerald Ford, "Address to a Joint Session of the Congress on the Economy," October 8, 1974, American Presidency Project, https://www.presidency.ucsb.edu/documents/address-joint-session-the-congress-the-economy.
38. Ford.
39. Ford.
40. John Robert Greene, "Gerald Ford: Domestic Affairs," Miller Center, https://millercenter.org/president/ford/domestic-affairs.
41. Greene.
42. Eileen Shanahan, "Ford Raises Feed on Imported Oil; Foes Seek Freeze," *New York Times*, January 24, 1975.
43. Gerald Ford, "Address on Energy Policy," May 27, 1975, Miller Center, https://millercenter.org/the-presidency/presidential-speeches/may-27-1975-address-energy-policy.
44. Philip Shabecoff, "Ford Signs Bill on Energy That Ends Policy Impasse and Cuts Crude Oil Prices," *New York Times*, December 23, 1975.
45. Shabecoff.
46. Arthur Burns, "The Anguish of Central Banking" (Per Jacobsson Lecture, Belgrade, Yugoslavia, September 30, 1979), 15–16.
47. Burns, 15–16.
48. Burns, 12.
49. Burns, 13.
50. Burns, 15–16.
51. Paul Bullock, ed., *A Full Employment Policy for America: A Symposium at UCLA* (Los Angeles: Manpower Research Center, Institute of Industrial Relations, University of California, Los Angeles, 1973), quoted in Aurélien Goutsmedt, "How the Phillips Curve Shaped Full Employment Policy in the 1970s: The Debates on the Humphrey-Hawkins Act," *History of Political Economy* 54, no. 4 (2022): 619–53.
52. Goutsmedt, 628–29.
53. Goutsmedt, 628–29.
54. Goutsmedt, 628–29.
55. Elizabeth Becker, "The Secrets and Lies of the Vietnam War, Exposed in One Epic Document," *New York Times*, June 9, 2021.
56. Federal Open Market Committee of the Federal Reserve System v. Merrill, 443 U.S. 340 (1979).
57. Federal Open Market Committee of the Federal Reserve System v. Merrill, 443 U.S. 340.
58. Federal Open Market Committee of the Federal Reserve System v. Merrill, 443 U.S. 340.
59. Merrill v. Federal Open Market Committee, 516 F. Supp. 1028 (1981).

60. Merrill v. Federal Open Market Committee, 516 F. Supp. 1028.
61. Tim Todd, *A Corollary of Accountability: A History of FOMC Policy Communication* (Kansas City, MO: Federal Reserve Bank of Kansas City, 2016), 14; Robert J. Barro, "Rational Expectations and the Role of Monetary Policy," *Journal of Monetary Economics* 2 (1976): 1–32.
62. Reuss v. Balles, 584 F.2d 461 (1978).
63. Reuss v. Balles, 584 F.2d 461.
64. Reuss v. Balles, 584 F.2d 461.
65. Reuss v. Balles, 584 F.2d 461.
66. Riegle v. Federal Open Market Committee, 84 F.R.D. 114 (1979).
67. Riegle v. Federal Open Market Committee, 211 U.S. App. D.C. 284 (1981).
68. Riegle v. Federal Open Market Committee, 211 U.S. App. D.C. at 284.
69. Stuart Taylor Jr., "High Court Won't Hear Case on Fed," *New York Times*, June 7, 1988.
70. Jimmy Carter, "Anti-Inflation Program," October 24, 1978, *American Experience* (PBS), https://www.pbs.org/wgbh/americanexperience/features/carter-anti-inflation/.
71. Barry Bosworth, "The Carter Administration's Anti-Inflation Program," *Proceedings of the Academy of Political Science* 33, no. 3 (1979): 12–19.
72. Bosworth, 12–19.
73. Congressional Budget Office, *Inflation and Growth: The Economic Policy Dilemma* (Washington, DC: Congress of the United States, Congressional Budget Office, 1978), 34.
74. Statement of Harry S. Havens before the Subcommittee on Commerce, Consumer, and Monetary Affairs of the Committee on Government Operations, US House of Representatives, March 11, 1980, US General Accounting Office, Washington, DC, https://www.gao.gov/products/111888.
75. Bosworth, "Carter Administration's Anti-Inflation Program," 17.
76. G. William Miller, Statement before the Committee on Banking, Housing and Urban Affairs, US Senate, Board of Governors of the Federal Reserve System, April 25, 1978, https://fraser.stlouisfed.org/title/450/item/8168.
77. Carl H. Madden, "Government Controls versus Market Discipline." *Proceedings of the Academy of Political Science* 33, no. 2 (1979): 203–18.
78. Comptroller General's Report to the Chairman, General Economic Committee, "The Council on Wage and Price Stability Has Not Stressed Productivity in Its Efforts To Reduce Inflation," US General Accounting Office, Washington, DC, October 16, 1980, https://www.gao.gov/products/fgmsd-81-8.
79. Statement of Harry S. Havens.
80. Milton Friedman, "Subsidizing OPEC Oil," *Newsweek*, June 23, 1975, 75.
81. "Oil and Petroleum Products Explained: Oil Imports and Exports," US Energy Information Administration, https://www.eia.gov/energyexplained/oil-and-petroleum-products/imports-and-exports.php.
82. Joseph Yager, "The Energy Battles of 1979," in *Energy Policy in Perspective*, ed. Crauford D. Goodwin (Washington, DC: Brookings Institution, 1981), 601–36.

83. Salvatore Lazzari, *The Crude Oil Windfall Profit Tax of the 1980s: Implications for Current Energy Policy* (Washington, DC: Congressional Research Service, 2006), https://liheapch.acf.hhs.gov/pubs/oilwindfall.pdf.
84. Bill Medley, "Volcker's Announcement of Anti-Inflation Measures," Federal Reserve History, https://www.federalreservehistory.org/essays/anti-inflation-measures.
85. Art Pine and Kathy Sawyer, "Kennedy Introduces Bill on Wage-Price Controls," *Washington Post*, April 4, 1980.
86. Jon Ward, "The Humiliating Handshake and the Near-Fistfight that Broke the Democratic Party," *Politico*, January 21, 2019, https://www.politico.com/magazine/story/2019/01/21/camelots-end-kennedy-vs-carter-democratic-convention-1980-224030/.
87. Ronald Reagan, "Debate between Jimmy Carter and Ronald Reagan," October 28, 1980, Miller Center, https://millercenter.org/the-presidency/presidential-speeches/october-28–1980-debate-ronald-reagan.

Chapter Eleven

1. Paul Volcker, "The Triumph of Central Banking?" (Per Jacobsson Lecture, Washington, DC, 1990), 5.
2. Ronald Reagan, "White House Report on the Program for Economic Recovery," February 18, 1981, Ronald Reagan Presidential Library and Museum, https://www.reaganlibrary.gov/archives/speech/white-house-report-program-economic-recovery-0.
3. Lazzari, "Crude Oil Windfall Profit Tax of the 1980s."
4. Richard C. Auxier, "Reagan's Recession," Pew Research Center, December 14, 2010, https://www.pewresearch.org/2010/12/14/reagans-recession/.
5. David L. Greenberg and Ames K. Lower, "Crude Oil Decontrol by Reagan," *New York Times*, March 19, 1981, 23; Peter Behr and John M. Berry, "Reagan Decontrols Gasoline, Crude in Deregulation Debut," *Washington Post*, January 29, 1981.
6. *Federal Reserve's First Monetary Policy Report for 1981: Hearings before the Committee on Banking, Housing, and Urban Affairs*, 97th Cong. 28 (1981), https://fraser.stlouisfed.org/title/monetary-policy-oversight-671/federal-reserve-s-first-monetary-policy-report-1981-22310.
7. Quoted in Clyde H. Farnsworth, "Volcker Sees More Tightening," *New York Times*, July 22, 1981.
8. Reagan, "White House Report on the Program for Economic Recovery."
9. Michael McCarthy, "The Monetary Hawks." *Jacobin*, August 3, 2016, https://jacobin.com/2016/08/paul-volcker-ronald-reagan-fed-shock-inflation-unions/.
10. Jeff Spross, "Everyone Loves Paul Volcker: Everyone Is Wrong," *The Week*, December 4, 2018, https://theweek.com/articles/810196/everyone-loves-paul-volcker-everyone-wrong.
11. Paul Volcker, "The Education of Paul Volcker: The Austrian School vs. Keynes-

ianism," Commanding Heights (PBS), September 26, 2000, https://www.pbs.org/wgbh/commandingheights/shared/minitext/int_paulvolcker.html#6.

12. Quoted in Steven R. Weisman, "Volcker Renamed by Reagan to Run Federal Reserve," *New York Times*, June 19, 1983.
13. Committee for Monetary Reform v. Board of Governors of Federal Reserve System, 766 F.2d 538 (D.C. Cir. 1983), https://law.resource.org/pub/us/case/reporter/F2/766/766.F2d.538.84-5067.html.
14. Committee for Monetary Reform v. Board of Governors of Federal Reserve System, 766 F.2d 538 (1985).
15. "Ronald Reagan: Prouder, Stronger, Better," 1984, television advertisement, available at CNN, http://www.cnn.com/ALLPOLITICS/1996/candidates/ad.archive/
16. Robert D. Hershey Jr., "Volcker Out after 8 Years as Federal Reserve Chief; Volcker Chooses Greenspan," *New York Times*, June 3, 1987.
17. Tom Redburn, "Volcker Goes from Villain to Hero, but Will He Stay?," *Los Angeles Times*, April 5, 1987.
18. Frederic Mishkin, "International Experiences with Different Monetary Policy Regimes," *Journal of Monetary Economics* 43, no. 3 (1999): 579–605.
19. US Gold Commission, "Volume I," in *Report to the Congress of the Commission on the Role of Gold in the Domestic and International Monetary Systems* (Washington, DC: US Gold Commission, March 1982), 17, available at FRASER, https://fraser.stlouisfed.org/title/339/item/6346.
20. US Gold Commission.
21. Robert E. Lucas Jr., "Expectations and the Neutrality of Money," *Journal of Economic Theory* 4, no. 2 (1972): 103–24.
22. Robert J. Barro and David B. Gordon, "Rules, Discretion and Reputation in a Model of Monetary Policy," *Journal of Monetary Economics* 12, no. 1 (1983): 101–21, at 101.
23. Barro and Gordon, 101.
24. Binyamin Appelbaum and Robert D. Hershey Jr., "Paul A. Volcker, Fed Chairman Who Waged War on Inflation, Is Dead at 92," *New York Times*, December 9, 2019.
25. Volcker, "Triumph of Central Banking?," 14.
26. Volcker, 14.
27. Bernanke and Mishkin, "Inflation Targeting," 97.
28. Bernanke and Mishkin, 102.
29. Hershey, "Volcker Out after 8 Years as Federal Reserve Chief."
30. Directing the Federal Open Market Committee of the Federal Reserve System to Adopt and Pursue Monetary Policies Leading to, and Then Maintaining, Zero Inflation, H.R. Res. 409, 101st Cong. (1989), https://www.congress.gov/bill/101st-congress/house-joint-resolution/409/text?r=7&s=1.
31. Mack-Saxton Bill, H.R. 2360, 104th Cong. (1990).
32. The related bills are H.R. 653, 106th Cong. (1999); H.R. 2547, 108th Cong. (2003); and H.R. 498, 109th Cong. (2005).

33. James Galbraith and Henry Reuss, "Will Congress Declare War on a Windmill?," *New York Times*, June 2, 1996.
34. Galbraith and Reuss.
35. Alan Blinder and Ricardo Reis, "Understanding the Greenspan Standard" (paper presented at the Federal Reserve Bank of Kansas City symposium "The Greenspan Era: Lessons for the Future," Jackson Hole, WY, 2005), 5.
36. Blinder and Reis, 5.
37. Blinder and Reis.
38. Devin Leonard and Peter Coy, "Alan Greenspan on His Fed Legacy and the Economy," *Business Week*, August 13, 2012, 65.
39. Janet L. Yellen, "Revolution and Evolution in Central Bank Communications" (speech at the Haas School of Business, University of California, Berkeley, November 13, 2012).
40. Quoted in Steven Greenhouse, "Showdown: The Populist vs. the Fed," *New York Times*, October 12, 1993.
41. Greenhouse.
42. Todd, *Balance of Power*.
43. *The Federal Reserve Accountability Act of 1993: Hearing before the Committee on Banking, Finance, and Urban Affairs*, 103rd Cong. 2–3 (1993) (Lee Hamilton), https://fraser.stlouisfed.org/title/1154.
44. Quoted in Greenhouse, "Showdown."
45. Quoted in Greenhouse.
46. *The Federal Reserve Accountability Act of 1993: Hearing before the Committee on Banking, Finance, and Urban Affairs*, 103rd Cong. 16 (1993) (Alan Greenspan), https://fraser.stlouisfed.org/title/1154.
47. Greenspan.
48. Quoted in Todd, *Corollary of Accountability*, 6.
49. "OIP Guidance: Applying the 'Forseeable Harm' Standard under Exemption Five," *FOIA Update*, January 1, 1994, Office of Information Policy, https://www.justice.gov/oip/blog/foia-update-oip-guidance-applying-forseeable-harm-standard-under-exemption-five.
50. "Meeting of the Federal Open Market Committee" (transcript), Washington, DC, November 16, 1993, https://www.federalreserve.gov/monetarypolicy/files/FOMC19931116meeting.pdf.
51. Todd, *Corollary of Accountability*, 32.
52. "Meeting of the Federal Open Market Committee" (transcript), Washington, DC, February 3–4, 1994, 29, https://www.federalreserve.gov/monetarypolicy/files/FOMC19940204meeting.pdf.
53. "Meeting of the Federal Open Market Committee," 29, 32.
54. Federal Reserve, "Press Release," February 4, 1994, https://www.federalreserve.gov/fomc/19940204default.htm.
55. Quoted in Todd, *Corollary of Accountability*, 38.
56. Paul Krugman, "Health Economics 101," *New York Times*, November 15, 2005, sec. A.

57. Krugman.
58. S. Vincent Rajkumar, "The High Cost of Prescription Drugs: Causes and Solutions," *Blood Cancer Journal* 10, no. 71 (2020): 1–5.
59. Wendy H. Schacht and John R. Thomas, *The Hatch-Waxman Act: Legislative Changes in the 108th Congress Affecting Pharmaceutical Patents* (Washington, DC: Congressional Research Service, 2004), https://www.ipmall.info/sites/default/files/hosted_resources/crs/RL32377_040430.pdf.
60. Milt Freudenheim, "Drug Companies Feeling Pressure of Clinton's Plan to Keep Their Prices Down," *New York Times*, September 30, 1993, 22.
61. Adam Clymer, "National Health Program, President's Greatest Goal, Declared Dead in Congress," *New York Times*, September 27, 1994, 1.
62. Thomas R. Oliver, Philip R. Lee, and Helene L. Lipton, "A Political History of Medicare and Prescription Drug Coverage," *Milbank Quarterly* 82, no. 2 (2004): 283–354, at 291.
63. Oliver, Lee, and Lipton, 290.
64. Robin Toner, "Political Memo; Seems the Last Word on Medicare Wasn't," *New York Times*, March 17, 2004.
65. Martin Bodenstein, Christopher J. Erceg, and Luca Guerrieri, "Optimal Monetary Policy with Distinct Core and Headline Inflation Rates," *Journal of Monetary Economics* 55 (2008): S18–S33.
66. Lael Brainard, "What Can We Learn from the Pandemic and the War about Supply Shocks, Inflation, and Monetary Policy?" (21st BIS Annual Conference, Central Banking after the Pandemic: Challenges Ahead, Bank for International Settlements, Basel, Switzerland, 2022).
67. Marvin Goodfriend and Robert King, "The Incredible Volcker Disinflation," *Journal of Monetary Economics* 52 (2005): 981–1015.
68. Carola Binder and Christos Makridis, "Stuck in the Seventies: Gas Prices and Consumer Sentiment," *Review of Economics and Statistics* 104, no. 2 (2022): 293–305.
69. Vikas Bajaj, "Lawmakers Want Government to Hold Down Gas Prices," *New York Times*, September 6, 2005.
70. Gasoline Price Stabilization Act of 2005, H.R. 3544, 109th Cong. (2005).
71. Energy Emergency Consumer Protection Act of 2005, S. 1735, 109th Cong. (2005).
72. Gasoline Consumer Anti-Price-Gouging Protection Act, S. 94, 110th Cong. (2007).
73. Charles Goodhart and Boris Hofmann, "House Prices, Money, Credit, and the Macroeconomy," *Oxford Review of Economic Policy* 24, no. 1 (2008): 180–205.
74. John Williams, "Measuring the Effects of Monetary Policy on House Prices and the Economy," in *Expanding the Boundaries of Monetary Policy in Asia and the Pacific: Proceedings of a Conference Held on 19–21 August 2015 in Jakarta, Indonesia, and Co-Hosted by Bank Indonesia and the Bank for International Settlements*, ed. Bank for International Settlements (Jakarta: Bank for International Settlements, 2016), 7–16.

75. "After the Fall," *The Economist,* June 16, 2005.
76. Nell Henderson, "Bernanke: There's No Housing Bubble to Go Bust," *NBC News,* October 27, 2005.
77. Ben Bernanke, "Asset-Price 'Bubbles' and Monetary Policy" (remarks at the New York Chapter of the National Association for Business Economics, New York, October 15, 2002).
78. *The Nomination of Ben S. Bernanke, of New Jersey, to be a Member and Chairman of the Board of Governors of the Federal Reserve System: Hearing before the Committee on Banking, Housing, and Urban Affairs,* 109th Cong. 29 (2005) (Ben Bernanke), https://www.congress.gov/109/chrg/shrg26610/CHRG-109shrg26610.pdf.
79. For these data, see "Consumer Price Index for All Urban Consumers: All Items in US City Average," FRED, https://fred.stlouisfed.org/series/CPIAUCSL.

Chapter Twelve

1. Ben Bernanke, "Closing Remarks" (Ceremony Commemorating the Centennial of the Federal Reserve Act, Washington, DC, December 16, 2013), https://www.federalreserve.gov/newsevents/speech/bernanke20131216b.htm.
2. *Nomination of Ben S. Bernanke.*
3. Ben S. Bernanke, "A Perspective on Inflation Targeting" (presentation at the Annual Washington Policy Conference of the National Association of Business Economists, Washington, DC, March 25, 2003).
4. FOMC statement, August 12, 2003, quoted in Ben Bernanke, *21st Century Monetary Policy: The Federal Reserve from the Great Inflation to COVID-19* (New York City: W. W. Norton and Co., 2022).
5. Bernanke.
6. Marvin Goodfriend, "Inflation Targeting in the United States?," in *The Inflation-Targeting Debate,* ed. Ben S. Bernanke and Michael Woodford (Chicago: University of Chicago Press, 2004), 311–52.
7. Jeffrey Lacker, FOMC transcript, October 24–25, 2006, 129, https://www.federalreserve.gov/monetarypolicy/files/FOMC20061025meeting.pdf.
8. Lacker, 128.
9. Krishna Guha, "Fed Chief Warned on Inflation Target," *Financial Times,* February 2007.
10. Ben Bernanke, FOMC transcript, March 20–21, 2007, 111, https://www.federalreserve.gov/monetarypolicy/files/FOMC20070321meeting.pdf.
11. Richard Fisher, FOMC transcript, March 20–21, 2007, 114–15, https://www.federalreserve.gov/monetarypolicy/files/FOMC20070321meeting.pdf.
12. Cathy Minehan, FOMC transcript, March 20–21, 2007, 150–51, https://www.federalreserve.gov/monetarypolicy/files/FOMC20070321meeting.pdf.
13. Janet Yellen, FOMC transcript, March 20–21, 2007, 145, https://www.federalreserve.gov/monetarypolicy/files/FOMC20070321meeting.pdf.
14. Frederic Mishkin, FOMC transcript, March 20–21, 2007, 123, https://www.federalreserve.gov/monetarypolicy/files/FOMC20070321meeting.pdf.

15. Yellen, FOMC transcript, 146.
16. Ben Bernanke, "The Federal Reserve and the Financial Crisis." Lecture 3, George Washington University School of Business, https://www.federalreserve.gov/newsevents/files/chairman-bernanke-lecture3-20120327.pdf.
17. Ben Bernanke, "Monetary Policy and the Housing Bubble" (presentation at the annual meeting of the American Economic Association, Atlanta, January 3, 2010).
18. Ben Bernanke, "Remarks at the Conference to Honor Milton Friedman" (University of Chicago, November 8, 2002).
19. Bernanke, *21st Century Monetary Policy*.
20. Bernanke.
21. Krishna Guha, "Deflation Risk Boosts Inflation Target Case," *Financial Times*, November 4, 2008.
22. FOMC transcript, December 15–16, 2008, https://www.federalreserve.gov/monetarypolicy/files/FOMC20081216meeting.pdf.
23. FOMC statement, August 12, 2003, https://www.federalreserve.gov/boarddocs/press/monetary/2003/20030812/default.htm.
24. "Timelines of Policy Actions and Communications: Forward Guidance about the Federal Funds Rate," Board of Governors of the Federal Reserve System, https://www.federalreserve.gov/monetarypolicy/timeline-forward-guidance-about-the-federal-funds-rate.htm.
25. Willem Van Zandweghe, "The Phillips Curve and the Missing Disinflation from the Great Recession," *Federal Reserve Bank of Kansas City Economic Review* (2019): 5–31, https://www.kansascityfed.org/research/economic-review/2q19-vanzandweghe-phillips-curve-missing-disinflation-great-recession/.
26. Olivier Coibion and Yuriy Gorodnichenko, "Is the Phillips Curve Alive and Well after All? Inflation Expectations and the Missing Disinflation," *American Economic Journal: Macroeconomics* 7, no. 1 (2015): 197–232.
27. Van Zandweghe, "The Phillips Curve and the Missing Disinflation from the Great Recession."
28. Carola Binder, "Inflation Expectations and the Price at the Pump," *Journal of Macroeconomics* 58 (2018): 1–18.
29. Arthur Delaney, "Audit the Fed Effort Wins Support from an Unusual Coalition," *Huffington Post*, March 18, 2010.
30. Ben Bernanke, "'Audit the Fed' Is Not about Auditing the Fed," *Brookings*, January 11, 2016.
31. Christina D. Romer, "Dear Ben: It's Time for Your Volcker Moment," *New York Times*, October 29, 2011.
32. Romer.
33. Robert Hall and N. Gregory Mankiw, "Nominal Income Targeting," in *Monetary Policy*, ed. N. Gregory Mankiw (Chicago: University of Chicago Press, 1994), 71–94.
34. Christopher Erceg, Michael Kiley, and David López-Salido, "Alternative Monetary Policy Frameworks" (press release, October 6, 2011), https://www.federalreserve.gov/monetarypolicy/files/FOMC20111006memo02.pdf.

35. Erceg, Kiley, and López-Salido.
36. Eric Rosengren, FOMC transcript, November 1–2, 2011, 35, https://www.federalreserve.gov/monetarypolicy/files/FOMC20111102meeting.pdf.
37. Charles Plosser, FOMC transcript, November 1–2, 2011, 41, https://www.federalreserve.gov/monetarypolicy/files/FOMC20111102meeting.pdf.
38. Plosser, 41.
39. Janet Yellen, FOMC transcript, November 1–2, 2011, 81–82, https://www.federalreserve.gov/monetarypolicy/files/FOMC20111102meeting.pdf.
40. Yellen, 78.
41. Federal Open Market Committee, "Statement on Longer-Run Goals and Monetary Policy Strategy," January 24, 2012, https://www.federalreserve.gov/monetarypolicy/files/FOMC_LongerRunGoals_201201.pdf.
42. Federal Open Market Committee.
43. "Unemployed Take Their Case to Fed Officials at Jackson Hole," Reuters, August 23, 2014.
44. Alison R. Park, "Fed Chair Yellen Meets with 'Fed Up' Coalition" (press release, 2014), https://www.populardemocracy.org/news/fed-chair-yellen-meets-fed-coalition.
45. FOMC Statement, December 16, 2015, https://www.federalreserve.gov/newsevents/pressreleases/monetary20151216a.htm.
46. Dean Baker and Jared Bernstein, "Full Employment and the Path to Shared Prosperity," *Dissent Magazine,* 2014, https://www.dissentmagazine.org/article/full-employment-and-the-path-to-shared-prosperity.
47. Charles Evans, "Low Inflation and the Symmetry of the 2 Percent Target" (speech delivered before the UBS European Conference in London, November 15, 2017), https://www.chicagofed.org/publications/speeches/2017/11-15-2017-low-inflation-and-symmetry-of-two-percent-target-charles-evans-london-ubs.
48. "Fed Up: Building an Economy That Works for All of Us 2014–2016," Fed Up and the Center for Popular Democracy, August 17, 2016, https://fedupcampaign.org/wp-content/uploads/2021/05/fed-up-yearbook-FINAL.pdf.
49. Carola Binder and Christina Parajon Skinner, "Laboratories of Central Banking," *Review of Banking and Financial Law* 42, no. 1 (2023): 235–300.
50. Josh Bivens and Jordan Haedtler, "Impressive, Incomplete, and Under Threat: Janet Yellen's Legacy at the Federal Reserve" (white paper, Economic Policy Institute, Center for Popular Democracy, and Fed Up, August 3, 2017), 1–2, https://www.epi.org/publication/impressive-incomplete-and-under-threat-janet-yellens-legacy-at-the-federal-reserve/.
51. Stephanie Kelton and Paul McCulley, "The Fed Chair Should Be a 'Principled Populist,'" *New York Times,* October 30, 2017.
52. Donald Trump (@realDonaldTrump), tweet, September 11, 2019.
53. Donald Trump (@realDonaldTrump), tweet, August 23, 2019.
54. Kevin Carmichael, "In the Age of Trump, Central Banks Are Only One Populist Uprising Away from Losing Cherished Independence," *Financial Post,* Au-

gust 22, 2018, https://financialpost.com/news/economy/central-banks-wise-to-court-public-in-an-era-of-populism.

55. Carola Binder, "Federal Reserve Communication and the Media," *Journal of Media Economics* 30, no. 4 (2017): 191–214.
56. Carola Binder, "Fed Speak on Main Street: Central Bank Communication and Household Expectations," *Journal of Macroeconomics* 52 (2017): 238–51.
57. Carola Binder and Christina Skinner, "Legitimacy of the Federal Reserve," *Stanford Journal of Law, Business, and Finance* 28, no. 1 (2023): 2–40.
58. Jerome Powell, "Federal Reserve to Review Strategies, Tools, and Communication Practices It Uses to Pursue Its Mandate of Maximum Employment and Price Stability" (press release), Board of Governors of the Federal Reserve System, November 15, 2018, https://www.federalreserve.gov/newsevents/pressreleases/monetary20181115a.htm.
59. "Fed Listens: Perspectives from the Public," Federal Reserve System, June 2020, 2, https://www.federalreserve.gov/publications/files/fedlistens-report-20200612.pdf.
60. "Fed Listens," 7.
61. "Fed Listens," 6.
62. Elizabeth Warren, "Elizabeth Warren's Remarks at St. Anselm College," December 12, 2019, https://2020.elizabethwarren.com/st-anselm-speech.
63. Dylan Matthews, "The Fed's Bad Predictions Are Hurting Us," *Vox*, May 24, 2019.
64. Carola Binder, "NGDP Targeting and the Public," *Cato Journal* 40, no. 2 (2020): 321–42, https://www.cato.org/cato-journal/spring/summer-2020/ngdp-targeting-public.
65. "Government," Gallup, https://news.gallup.com/poll/27286/government.aspx.
66. "Government."
67. Binder, "NGDP Targeting and the Public."
68. L. Randall Wray, *Modern Money Theory: A Primer on Macroeconomics for Sovereign Monetary Systems* (New York: Palgrave Macmillan: 2015).
69. Yeva Nersisyan and L. Randall Wray, "How to Pay for the Green New Deal" (Working Paper No. 931, Levy Economics Institute of Bard College, Annandale-on-Hudson, NY, 2019).
70. Dylan Matthews, "Modern Monetary Theory, Explained," *Vox*, April 16, 2019, https://www.vox.com/future-perfect/2019/4/16/18251646/modern-monetary-theory-new-moment-explained.

Chapter Thirteen

1. Jerome Powell, "Transcript of Chair Powell's Press Conference," June 15, 2022, p. 22, accessed at https://www.federalreserve.gov/mediacenter/files/FOMCpresconf20220615.pdf.
2. Daniella Diaz, Geneva Sands, and Cristina Alesci, "Protective Equipment Costs Increase over 1,000% amid Competition and Surge in Demand," *CNN*, April 17,

2020, https://edition.cnn.com/2020/04/16/politics/ppe-price-costs-rising-economy-personal-protective-equipment/index.html.

3. Consumer Federation of America, "2020 Consumer Complaint Survey Report," July 26, 2021, https://consumerfed.org/reports/2020-consumer-complaint-survey-report/.
4. Patricia A. Conners, "Price Gouging and the Pandemic: State Attorneys General Enforcement Trends and Developments," *American Bar Association: The Public Lawyer*, August 10, 2022.
5. Christopher Ondeck, John Ingrassia, Kelly Landers Hawthorne, Nathaniel Miller, Nicollette Moser, and Jennifer Tarr, "State Price Gouging Laws and Price Controls: A Historical View on a Questionable Objective," *National Law Review* 10, no. 262 (2020), https://www.natlawreview.com/article/state-price-gouging-laws-and-price-controls-historical-view-questionable-objective.
6. N.Y. Gen. Bus. Law § 396-R, Current through 2023, NY Law Chapter 208, Section 396-R—Price gouging, https://casetext.com/statute/consolidated-laws-of-new-york/chapter-general-business/article-26-miscellaneous/section-396-r-price-gouging.
7. Ondeck et al., "State Price Gouging Laws and Price Controls."
8. "33 Attorneys General Warn Amazon, Facebook, eBay, Craigslist: You Aren't Exempt from Price Gouging Laws," Oregon Department of Justice, March 25, 2020, https://www.doj.state.or.us/media-home/news-media-releases/33-attorneys-general-warn-amazon-facebook-ebay-craigslist-you-arent-exempt-from-price-gouging-laws/.
9. Craig Carpenito, Daniel Kim, and Noah Childrey, "The Federal Response to Hoarding and Price Gouging During the COVID-19 Pandemic," *American Bar Association: The Public Lawyer*, August 10, 2022.
10. Carpenito, Kim, and Childrey.
11. Kobi Finestone and Ewan Kingston, "Crisis Prices: The Ethics of Market Controls during a Global Pandemic," *Business Ethics Quarterly* 32, no. 1 (2021): 12–40, at 36.
12. Finestone and Kingston.
13. Finestone and Kingston, 15.
14. Rik Chakraborti and Gavin Roberts, "Learning to Hoard: The Effects of Preexisting and Surprise Price-Gouging Regulation during the COVID-19 Pandemic," *Journal of Consumer Policy* 44, no. 4 (2021): 507–29.
15. Rik Chakraborti and Gavin Roberts, "How Price-Gouging Regulation Undermined COVID-19 Mitigation: Evidence of Unintended Consequences," *Public Choice* (2023): https://www.ncbi.nlm.nih.gov/pmc/articles/PMC10111309/#:~:text=Using%20county%2Dlevel%20daily%20data,home%2Dorder%2Dinduced%20decreases.
16. Paul Ginsburg and Steven Lieberman, "Government Regulated or Negotiated Drug Prices: Key Design Considerations," *Brookings*, August 30, 2021, https://www.brookings.edu/essay/government-regulated-or-negotiated-drug-prices-key-design-considerations/.

17. "Congressional Progressive Leaders Announce Principles on COVID-19 Drug Pricing for Next Coronavirus Response Package" (press release), US Congresswoman Jan Schakowsky, April 15, 2020, https://schakowsky.house.gov/media/press-releases/congressional-progressive-leaders-announce-principles-covid-19-drug-pricing.
18. "Letter to Members of Congress," May 7, 2020, https://www.documentcloud.org/documents/6933586-Pharma-Letter.html.
19. Jennifer Kates, Cynthia Cox, and Josh Michaud, "How Much Could COVID-19 Vaccines Cost the US after Commercialization?," KFF, March 10, 2023, https://www.kff.org/coronavirus-covid-19/issue-brief/how-much-could-covid-19-vaccines-cost-the-u-s-after-commercialization/.
20. Carola Binder, "Coronavirus Fears and Macroeconomic Expectations," *Review of Economics and Statistics* 102, no. 4 (2020): 721–30; Brent H. Meyer, Brian Prescott, and Xuguang Simon Sheng, "The Impact of the COVID-19 Pandemic on Business Expectations," *International Journal of Forecasting* 38, no. 2 (2022): 529–44.
21. Jane Ihrig, Gretchen Weinbach, and Scott Wolla, "How the Fed Has Responded to the COVID-19 Pandemic," Federal Reserve Bank of St. Louis, https://www.stlouisfed.org/open-vault/2020/august/fed-response-covid19-pandemic.
22. "Economic Impact Payments," US Department of the Treasury, https://home.treasury.gov/policy-issues/coronavirus/assistance-for-american-families-and-workers/economic-impact-payments.
23. For these data, see "Unemployment Rate," FRED, https://fred.stlouisfed.org/series/UNRATE; "Labor Force Participation Rate," FRED, https://fred.stlouisfed.org/series/CIVPART; "Personal Consumption Expenditures: Chain-Type Price Index," FRED, https://fred.stlouisfed.org/series/PCEPI.
24. Federal Open Market Committee, "Statement of Longer-Run Goals and Monetary Policy Strategy," August 27, 2020.
25. Federal Open Market Committee.
26. Jonnelle Marte and Howard Schneider, "Fed Policymakers Do Their Own Math on 'Average' Inflation," Reuters, August 28, 2020, https://www.reuters.com/article/us-usa-fed-kaplan/fed-policymakers-do-their-own-math-on-average-inflation-idUSKBN25O1VB.
27. Chris Bickerton and Carlo Invernizzi Accetti, *Technopopulism: The New Logic of Democratic Politics* (Oxford: Oxford University Press, 2021).
28. Chris Bickerton, "The Rise of the Technopopulists," *New Statesman*, October 21, 2020, https://www.newstatesman.com/world/2020/10/rise-technopopulists.
29. Christopher Bickerton and Carlo Invernizzi Accetti, "Populism and Technocracy: Opposites or Complements?," *Critical Review of International Social and Political Philosophy* 20, no. 2 (2017): 186–206.
30. Kenneth Rogoff, "How Central-Bank Independence Dies," *Project Syndicate*, May 31, 2019.
31. Carola Binder, "Technopopulism and Central Banks," in *Populism and the Future of the Fed*, ed. James Dorn (Washington, DC: Cato Institute, 2022), 51–61.
32. Jerome Powell, "New Economic Challenges and the Fed's Monetary Policy Re-

view" (presentation at Navigating the Decade Ahead: Implications for Monetary Policy, an economic policy symposium sponsored by the Federal Reserve Bank of Kansas City, Jackson Hole, WY, August 27, 2020), https://www.federalreserve.gov/newsevents/speech/powell20200827a.htm.

33. For these data, see "Unemployment Rate," FRED, https://fred.stlouisfed.org/series/UNRATE; "Personal Consumption Expenditures: Chain-Type Price Index," FRED, https://fred.stlouisfed.org/series/PCEPI.

34. Wendy Edelberg and Louise Sheiner, "The Macroeconomic Implications of Biden's $1.9 Trillion Fiscal Package," Brookings, January 28, 2021, https://www.brookings.edu/blog/up-front/2021/01/28/the-macroeconomic-implications-of-bidens-1-9-trillion-fiscal-package/.

35. *Semiannual Monetary Report to Congress: Hearing before the Committee on Banking, Housing, and Urban Affairs, Oversight on the Monetary Policy Report to Congress Pursuant to the Full Employment and Balanced Growth Act of 1978*, 117th Cong. (2021) https://www.govinfo.gov/content/pkg/CHRG-117shrg44741/html/CHRG-117shrg44741.htm.

36. *Semiannual Monetary Report to Congress.*

37. Christina Romer, "The Fiscal Policy Response to the Pandemic," *Brookings Papers on Economic Activity*, Spring 2021, 89–110.

38. For these data, see "Personal Consumption Expenditures: Chain-Type Price Index," FRED, https://fred.stlouisfed.org/series/PCEPI; "Personal Consumption Expenditures Excluding Food and Energy (Chain-Type Price Index)," FRED, https://fred.stlouisfed.org/series/PCEPILFE.

39. Scott Horsley, "Think Inflation Is Bad Now? Let's Take a Step Back to the 1970s," *NPR*, May 29, 2021, https://www.npr.org/2021/05/29/1001023637/think-inflation-is-bad-now-lets-take-a-step-back-to-the-1970s.

40. Quoted in Horsley.

41. For these data, see "5-Year, 5-Year Forward Inflation Expectation Rate," FRED, https://fred.stlouisfed.org/series/T5YIFR.

42. Regis Barnichon, Luiz E. Oliveira, and Adam H. Shapiro, "Is the American Rescue Plan Taking Us Back to the '60s?" *Federal Reserve Bank of San Francisco Economic Letter* (October 18, 2021), no. 27, https://www.frbsf.org/economic-research/publications/economic-letter/2021/october/is-american-rescue-plan-taking-us-back-to-1960s/.

43. Carola Binder, "Consumer Inflation Uncertainty Is Rising" (policy brief, Mercatus Center, 2022).

44. David Beckworth, "The Neutral Level of NGDP and the NGDP Gap: Q3 2021" (policy brief, Mercatus Center, 2021).

45. Tyler Atkinson, Evan F. Koenig, and Ezra Max, "Nominal GDP Outlook Suggests It's Time to End Monetary Accommodation," Federal Reserve Bank of Dallas, January 13, 2022, https://www.dallasfed.org/research/economics/2022/0113.

46. Jordan Williams, "Larry Summers Blasts $1.9 T Stimulus as 'Least Responsible' Economic Policy in 40 Years," *The Hill*, March 20, 2021.

47. For these data, see "Unemployment Rate," FRED, https://fred.stlouisfed.org

/series/UNRATE; "Labor Force Participation Rate," FRED, https://fred.stlouisfed.org/series/CIVPART.

48. Quoted in "Transitioning Away from 'Transitory' Inflation," *Financial Times*, December 1, 2021.
49. "At Hearing, Warren Calls Out Corporations for Abusing Their Market Power to Raise Consumer Prices and Boost Profits," Elizabeth Warren, February 17, 2022, https://www.warren.senate.gov/newsroom/press-releases/at-hearing-warren-calls-out-corporations-for-abusing-their-market-power-to-raise-consumer-prices-and-boost-profits.
50. "At Hearing, Warren Questions Federal Reserve Nominee about Market Concentration and Price Gouging Driving Inflation," Elizabeth Warren, January 13, 2022, https://www.warren.senate.gov/newsroom/press-releases/at-hearing-warren-questions-federal-reserve-nominee-about-market-concentration-and-price-gouging-driving-inflation.
51. "Fact Sheet: United States Bans Imports of Russian Oil, Liquefied Natural Gas, and Coal," White House, March 8, 2022, https://www.whitehouse.gov/briefing-room/statements-releases/2022/03/08/fact-sheet-united-states-bans-imports-of-russian-oil-liquefied-natural-gas-and-coal/.
52. "Fact Sheet: President Biden's Plan to Respond to Putin's Price Hike at the Pump," White House, March 31, 2022, https://www.whitehouse.gov/briefing-room/statements-releases/2022/03/31/fact-sheet-president-bidens-plan-to-respond-to-putins-price-hike-at-the-pump/.
53. Benjamin Harris and Catherine Wolfram, "The Price Impact of the Strategic Petroleum Reserve Release," US Department of the Treasury, July 26, 2022, https://home.treasury.gov/news/featured-stories/the-price-impact-of-the-strategic-petroleum-reserve-release.
54. Quoted in Brendan Rascius, "As Strategic Oil Reserve Is Drained to Record Low Levels, Is It Lowering Gas Prices?," *News and Observer*, September 30, 2022, https://www.newsobserver.com/news/nation-world/national/article266578691.html.
55. "President Biden's Plan to Respond to Putin's Price Hike at the Pump."
56. Quoted in Peter Baker and Clifford Krauss, "Biden Slaps Oil Companies for Profiteering at the Pump," *New York Times*, June 15, 2022.
57. David Lawder and Heather Timmons, "Analysis: Are High Prices Unpatriotic or as American as You Can Get?," Reuters, June 21, 2022, https://www.reuters.com/world/us/are-high-prices-unpatriotic-or-american-you-can-get-2022-06-21/.
58. "Biden Wants to Penalize Oil Companies with Unused Leases," Institute for Energy Research, April 7, 2022, https://www.instituteforenergyresearch.org/regulation/biden-wants-to-penalize-oil-companies-with-unused-leases/.
59. Spencer Cox, "Letter to President Joe Biden," Utah Gov. Spencer J. Cox, March 7, 2022, https://governor.utah.gov/2022/03/07/developing-american-energy/.
60. Lydia DePillis, "Is 'Greedflation' Rewriting Economics, or Do Old Rules Still Apply?" *New York Times*, June 3, 2022.

61. “Sanders Introduces Legislation to Reinstate the WWII Windfall Profit Tax to Combat Rising Inequality, Inflation, and Corporate Profiteering,” Bernie Sanders: US Senator for Vermont, March 25, 2022, https://www.sanders.senate.gov/press-releases/news-sanders-introduces-legislation-to-reinstate-the-wwii-windfall-profit-tax-to-combat-rising-inequality-inflation-and-corporate-profiteering/.
62. “Warren, Baldwin, Schakowsky, Colleagues Introduce Bicameral Legislation to Crack Down on Corporate Price Gouging,” Elizabeth Warren, May 12, 2022, https://www.warren.senate.gov/newsroom/press-releases/warren-baldwin-schakowsky-colleagues-introduce-bicameral-legislation-to-crack-down-on-corporate-price-gouging.
63. “Reps. Schrier, Porter Introduce Legislation to Stop Price Gouging at the Gas Pump,” Congresswoman Kim Schrier, May 6, 2022, https://schrier.house.gov/media/press-releases/reps-schrier-porter-introduce-legislation-stop-price-gouging-gas-pump.
64. Quoted in Christopher Anstey, “Summers Compares Price-Gouging Bill to Trump’s Bleach Injections,” *Bloomberg News*, May 13, 2022.
65. Frank Newport, “How Do Americans View Higher Inflation?” *Gallup*, June 10, 2022, https://news.gallup.com/opinion/polling-matters/393584/americans-view-higher-inflation.aspx.
66. Federal Open Market Committee, “Transcript of Chair Powell’s Press Conference,” May 4, 2022, https://www.federalreserve.gov/mediacenter/files/FOMCpresconf20220504.pdf.
67. Federal Open Market Committee.
68. Federal Open Market Committee.
69. Federal Open Market Committee.
70. Federal Open Market Committee.
71. Elizabeth Warren, “Jerome Powell’s Fed Pursues a Painful and Ineffective Inflation Cure,” *Wall Street Journal*, July 24, 2022.
72. Taylor Orth, “Most Americans Support the Climate and Energy Legislation Passed by the Senate,” YouGov, August 12, 2022, https://today.yougov.com/topics/politics/articles-reports/2022/08/12/most-support-climate-and-energy-legislation-poll.
73. Carola Binder, “Inflation Reduction Act—What’s in a Name?” *The Hill*, August 3, 2022.
74. Stephanie Kelton, “Catch Me on the Mehdi Hasan Show Later Today,” *The Lens* (blog), June 20, 2022, https://stephaniekelton.substack.com/p/catch-me-on-the-mehdi-hasan-show.
75. Kelton.
76. Jerome Powell, “Monetary Policy and Price Stability” (presentation at Reassessing Constraints on the Economy and Policy, an economic policy symposium sponsored by the Federal Reserve Bank of Kansas City, Jackson Hole, WY, August 26, 2022).

77. Sherrod Brown, "Letter to Jerome Powell," US Committee on Banking, Housing, and Urban Affairs, October 25, 2022, https://www.banking.senate.gov/imo/media/doc/fed_full_employment_letter.pdf.
78. FOMC Statement, March 22, 2023, https://www.federalreserve.gov/newsevents/pressreleases/monetary20230322a.htm.
79. Jerome Powell, "Chair Powell's Press Conference," July 26, 2023, 18–19, https://www.federalreserve.gov/mediacenter/files/FOMCpresconf20230726.pdf.

Chapter Fourteen

1. Mansfield, *Short History of OPA*, 273.
2. Paul Tucker, *Unelected Power: The Quest for Legitimacy in Central Banking and the Regulatory State* (Princeton, NJ: Princeton University Press, 2019).
3. Roosevelt, "First Inaugural Address."
4. Roosevelt.
5. "Foreign Stock Exchanges—New York," *The Economist*, May 13, 1933, quoted in Andrew Jalil and Gisela Rua, "Inflation Expectations and in Spring 1933," *Explorations in Economic History* 62 (2016): 26–50.
6. Edwin Kemmerer, "Testimony before the Senate Banking Committee," 1941, quoted in George Selgin, "The New Deal and Recovery, Part 4: FDR's Fed," *Cato at Liberty* (blog), July 6, 2020, https://www.cato.org/blog/new-deal-recovery-part-4-fdrs-fed.
7. Emergency Price Control Act of 1942, Pub. L. No. 77-421, 56 Stat. 23 (1942).
8. Volcker, "Triumph of Central Banking?," 17.
9. Matthews, "Fed's Bad Predictions Are Hurting Us."
10. Powell, "Monetary Policy and Price Stability."
11. Susan Milligan, "The Growing Fear for American Democracy," *US News and World Report*, October 12, 2022, accessed at https://www.usnews.com/news/articles/2022-10-12/the-growing-fear-for-american-democracy.
12. Robert Shiller, "Why Do People Dislike Inflation?," in *Reducing Inflation: Motivation and Strategy* (Chicago: University of Chicago Press, 1997), 13–70.
13. Stein and Siegel, "What Should the White House Do to Combat Inflation?"
14. Todd Tucker, "Price Controls: How the US Has Used Them and How They Can Help Shape Industries" (policy brief, Roosevelt Institute, New York, November 2021).
15. Rockoff, *Drastic Measures*, 246.
16. Steven Levitsky and Daniel Ziblatt, "Why Autocrats Love Emergencies: Crises—Real and Imaginary—Loosen Normal Constitutional Constraints," *New York Times*, January 12, 2019.
17. Christina Parajon Skinner, "The Monetary Executive," *George Washington Law Review* 91 (2023): 164–223.
18. *A Guide to Emergency Powers and Their Use* (New York: Brennan Center for Justice, New York University School of Law, 2019).

19. Julius Krein, "Trump Needed the 'Boneheads' More Than He Knew," *New York Times*, December 7, 2020.
20. Krein.
21. Editorial Board, "Ease Up on the Executive Actions, Joe," *New York Times*, January 27, 2021.
22. David Leonhardt, "'A Crisis Coming': The Twin Threats to American Democracy," *New York Times*, September 17, 2022.
23. John Cochrane, "Central Banks and Climate: A Case of Mission Creep," *Defining Ideas*, November 13, 2020.
24. Bickerton and Accetti, *Technopopulism*, 157.
25. Powell, "New Economic Challenges and the Fed's Monetary Policy Review."
26. "Elizabeth Warren: Fed Chair Has Failed at Both His Jobs," *Politico*, March 19, 2023, https://www.politico.com/news/2023/03/19/warren-fed-jerome-powell-failed-00087752.
27. Quoted in Christopher Rugaber, "Inflation Pressures Put Powell in Spotlight before Congress," *AP News*, March 6, 2023, https://apnews.com/article/federal-reserve-inflation-powell-interest-rates-congress-7c8bbd37c528daacbe32489a3156d111.
28. Gold Standard Act of 1984, H.R. 5986, 98th Cong. (1984).
29. Gold Standard Restoration Act, H.R. 9157, 117th Cong. (2022) ("to define the dollar as a fixed weight of gold, and for other purposes"), https://www.congress.gov/117/bills/hr9157/BILLS-117hr9157ih.pdf.
30. Alex Mooney, "Congressman Mooney Introduces the Gold Standard Restoration Act," US Congressman Alex Mooney, October 10, 2022, https://mooney.house.gov/congressman-mooney-introduces-the-gold-standard-restoration-act/.
31. Robert Murphy, "The Economics of Bitcoin," Econlib, June 3, 2013, https://www.econlib.org/library/Columns/y2013/Murphybitcoin.html.
32. Lawrence White, "Bitcoin after 10 Years," Cato at Liberty (blog), October 23, 2018, https://www.alt-m.org/2018/10/23/bitcoin-after-10-years/.
33. *Stabilization: Hearings before the Committee on Banking and Currency on H.R. 7895, a Bill to Amend Paragraph (d) of Section 14 of the Federal Reserve Act, as Amended, to Provide for the Stabilization of the Price Level for Commodities in General*, 69th Cong. 295 (1926), https://fraser.stlouisfed.org/title/stabilization-108/part-i-1271.
34. Binder, "Technopopulism and Central Banks," 51–61.
35. David Beckworth and Patrick Horan, "The Fate of FAIT: Salvaging the Fed's Framework" (working paper, Mercatus Center, 2022).

INDEX